Power Shifts and Global Governance

Power Shifts and Global Governance

Challenges from South and North

Edited by

Ashwani Kumar and Dirk Messner

ANTHEM PRESS
LONDON · NEW YORK · DELHI

d·i·e

Deutsches Institut für
Entwicklungspolitik

German Development
Institute

Federal Ministry
for Economic Cooperation
and Development

in Went

Capacity Building International
Germany

Anthem Press
An imprint of Wimbledon Publishing Company
www.anthempress.com

This edition first published in UK and USA 2011
by ANTHEM PRESS
75-76 Blackfriars Road, London SE1 8HA, UK
or PO Box 9779, London SW19 7ZG, UK
and
244 Madison Ave. #116, New York, NY 10016, USA

British Library Cataloguing in Publication Data
A catalogue record for this book is available from the British Library.

Library of Congress Cataloging in Publication Data
A catalog record for this book has been requested.

ISBN-13: 978 1 84331 834 7 (Pbk)
ISBN-10: 1 84331 834 2 (Pbk)

1 3 5 7 9 10 8 6 4 2

TABLE OF CONTENTS

LIST OF CONTRIBUTORS

Günther Taube has studied economics and development studies in Braunschweig, Hamburg and the University of East Anglia. He is a graduate of the post-graduate training programme of the German Development Institute and holds a PhD in Economics from the Free University of Berlin. He was employed for more than 10 years by the International Monetary Fund (IMF) in Washington, D.C. Since 2005 he has been Head of Department "International Regulatory Framework, Good Governance, Economic Policy" at InWEnt – Capacity Building International, Germany.

Dirk Messner is Director of the German Development Institute (DIE) in Bonn and Professor of Political Science at the University Duisburg-Essen. He is also a member of the German Advisory Council on Global Change (WBGU). Areas of specialisation include: globalization and global governance; global environmental change/climate change and impacts on international development; world economy, international competitiveness/ systemic competitiveness; development in Latin America and Asia; state and development/governance theories/network theories; development policy; China and India as drivers of global change.

Ashwani Kumar is Associate Professor at the Tata Institute of Social Sciences, Mumbai. He holds a PhD in Political Science from University of Oklahoma. He is author of "Community Warriors" (2008, Anthem Press). He is one of the Chief-Editors of LSE-Yearbook on Global Civil Society 2009 (International Sage; London). He has been a visiting fellow in the Centre for the Study of Global Governance at LSE (London). His teaching and research areas include democracy, civil society and development studies. He is also member of the Central Employment Guarantee Council (Government of India).

Thomas Fues has been with the German Development Institute (DIE), Bonn, as Senior Fellow since 2004. His main research interests are global governance, emerging powers, United Nations and international development cooperation. Recent publications include articles on G8 reform, the role of China and India in the global system, the UN development sector, human rights and global governance. In addition to his research tasks, he heads the training department at DIE.

Rogerio F. Pinto is a Brazilian national and holds a Master's degree in Political Science from the University of North Carolina and a Doctorate in Public Administration from the University of Southern California. He has been an international consultant in Public Management and Institutional Development with over 35 years of experience in international development as staff of the World Bank, the Inter-American Development Bank and the Organization of American States. Currently, he is on the faculty of the Brazilian School of Public and Business Management of the Getulio Vargas Foundation.

Jose Antonio Puppim de Oliveira is Assistant Director & Senior Research Fellow at the Institute of Advanced Studies (IAS), United Nations University (UNU) since August 2008. He has academic interests in the political economy of sustainable development. Before coming to IAS, he worked for the University College London – UCL (UK), the Getulio Vargas Foundation FGV/EBAPE (Brazil), and the University of Santiago de Compostela (Spain). He holds a PhD in Planning from the Massachusetts Institute of Technology (MIT, USA).

David Mayer-Foulkes is currently Professor of Economics at CIDE in Mexico City, and is director of the journal Economia Mexicana. He is a Mexican and studied his BA and PhD in Mathematics at Oxford and UC Berkeley. His micro and macro poverty trap models for underdevelopment explain the persistence of low levels of productivity and human development under globalization, and also the 2008 economic crisis. He has researched for PAHO, the World Bank, IADB and UNDP.

Gustavo Fondevilla is professor at the Centro de Investigación y Docencia Económicas (CIDE-Center for Research and Teaching in the Social Sciences). He is author of "Political Models of Social Integration" (München, 2002), and "Institutions, Legality and the Rule of Law" (México, 2005). His main research interests are public security, judicial reform and international development cooperation. He also heads the "Public Security and Rule of Law Studies Program" supported by the CIDE and others national and international organizations.

Elizabeth Sidiropoulos is the National Director of the South African Institute of International Affairs, a position she has held since 2005. She is also the editor-in-chief of the *South African Journal of International Affairs*.

Her research interests include South African foreign policy, the role of new powers in Africa and global governance reform.

Eduardo Vega-López is a Full-Time Professor at the Faculty of Economics (National Authonomous University of Mexico, UNAM), where he leads a post-graduate programme on Environmental and Ecological Economics and heads the Chair *Jesús Silva-Herzog Cathedra* on Environment, Sustainable Development and Climate Change. He was for more than twelve years a federal and local public servant on environmental and planning positions. In 2006, he was the Local Minister of Environment at the Mexico City Government.

Roberto Escalante-Semerena is a full time professor at the Faculty of Economics in the National Authonomous University of Mexico (UNAM). He teaches rural development and environmental economics. He has participated in many international conferences and written articles and books published by national and international publishers. At present, he researches topics related to climate change and its economic impacts. His forthcoming book on "The state of agriculture in Latin America" accounts for the economic and environmental issues of such economic sector.

Tiejun Zhang is senior researcher at Shanghai Institute for International Studies. He got his PhD degree in Peace and Development Studies from Goteborg University, Sweden. His research interests lie in the areas of China's foreign policy, East Asian regionalism, Sino-European relations and Chinese engagement with Africa. He has publications both in China and the West, including two books and a number of papers.

Rafael Duarte Villa is currently Associated Professor of political and international relations of the Department of Political Science and the Institute of International Relations of the University of Sao Paulo (USP) – Brazil. He holds a PhD in political science and has also worked as 'scholar researcher' at Columbia University in 2008. Since 2004, he has been coordinating the Center of Researches for International Relations (NUPRII) of the USP. His Areas of specialization include international security, and Latin America´s security and foreign policies.

Vijaya Katti is Professor & Chairperson (Resereach) at Indian institute of Foreign Trade (New Delhi). She has done extensive resereach and teaching on foreign trade related issues. She has been resource person on WTO in various countries including UAE, Tanzania, Indonesia, Mexio etc. She has also been a Guest Scholar at German Devleopment Institute (Bonn).

Ravi Shanker is currently working as Director of the Jaypee Business School Noida (India) and also holds the position of Professor of Marketing at Indian Institute of Foreign Trade (New Delhi). He holds a PhD in Management Sciences and his books on 'Services Marketing: The Indian Perspective' and 'Services Management', 'Foreign Trade: Concepts Policies and Practices' (Hindi) and 'Advertising and Public Relations' (Hindi) have been received with critical acclaim. He has also conducted training programmes for companies like HMT Limited, MMTC, ONGC, ABB, BPCL, VLCC, and Jaypee Hotels etc in India.

Vicente Paolo B. Yu III is currently Programme Coordinator for Global Governance for Development Programme of the South Centre, an intergovernmental thinktank for developing countries. His areas of specialization include international trade and environmental law and policy, including on climate change. He graduated with political science (with honors) and law degrees from the University of the Philippines, and obtained his Masters of Law degree (with distinction) from Georgetown University where he was a Fulbright Scholar.

Ibrahim Saleh is currently Chair of the Journalism Research and Education Section, The International Association for Media & Communication Research (IAMCR). He holds a PhD in Political Communication & National Development. He is a Liaison Officer of the Academic Council on the United Nations System (ACUNS) and co-founder of the Arab-European Media Observatory & Global Partner Organization of the UN Alliance of Civilization Media Literacy Education Clearinghouse. He has also published a number of articles and books including "Unveiling the Truth about Middle Eastern Media".

Doha Abdelhamid is currently a senior policy advisor to the Minister-President of the Central Agency for Organization and Administration in Egypt. She holds PhD in financial economics from the UK, with specialist training in development monitoring & evaluation from Canada. She is also a Global Task Force Member in the Inwent-World Bank Institute for Training Effectiveness Metrics. In January 2008, her book publication: *'Essays in International Regulatory Competition in Theory and Practice: Lessons and Experiences from the Developing and Developed Financial World'* won her the Ahram Foundation's Best Regional Scientific Contribution of the Year. She is active in civil society and academia as well.

Chengxin Chen is currently research fellow at Institute of Political Science, Chinese Academy of Social Sciences, Beijing. She specializes in democratic politics and governance. She was participant of Managing Global Governance Programme (DIE), International Young Diplomat Training Programme (BMZ), and visiting scholar of South Centre, Geneva. She co-wrote the book 'Grass-root Economy and Democratic Politics' (Social Sciences Academic Press, 2008). Recent publications include articles on International Comparison of Social Work and Review of Global Governance Study in China.

Garth le Pere is currently Executive Director of the Institute for Global Dialogue in South Africa. In 2008, Dr le Pere was appointed Extraordinary Professor of Political Science at the University of Pretoria. He holds an undergraduate degree in Political Science with highest honours from Rutgers University (New Jersey, USA) and did PhD in Political Science at Yale University (Connecticut, USA). He has recently co-authored a book, *China, Africa and South Africa: South-South co-operation in a global era* (Institute for Global Dialogue, 2007).

Mario Riestra Mario is currently advisor to the General Director of the National Copyright Institute in Mexico. He holds a degree in Political Science and International Relations from CIDE University in Mexico City. He is also a graduate of the Post-graduate course in Managing Global Governance at the German Development Institute (DIE) and spent a period as guest researcher in the Heiligendamm Support Unit at OECD in Paris, 2007 as part of a scholarship of the German Federal Agency, Inwent.

FOREWORD

Dr. Günther Taube

This publication on power shifts and global governance challenges is the output of a collaborative effort of scholars and policymakers who are part of a network that is part of a programme called Managing Global Governance (MGG) that started in 2007. At three levels – theoretical frameworks of global governance, country and regional perspectives, case studies of global governance processes or architectures – the contributions to this book seek to explore global governance issues. For example, the book includes contributions that look at the role of civil society in global governance from a theoretical perspective, analyse regional security issues in Latin America, discuss China's engagement in Africa or develop proposals for possible summit and UN reforms.

The contributors to this book come from Brazil, China, India, Mexico, South Africa and Germany. It is probably fair to say that they all share the concern that global governance processes and structures are becoming increasingly important as we all need to protect global public goods or address global challenges such as climate change, international financial market stability, peace and security, while also focussing on jointly formulated development objectives such as the Millennium Development Goals (MDGs). I believe it is also fair to say that all of those who have contributed to this book are of the view that emerging or new powers such as China, India, Brazil, Mexico, South Africa and others should play a more prominent role in global governance processes and institutions. Finally, I believe at least those of us from Germany who have worked on this book and indeed everyone on the MGG team at Capacity Building International (InWEnt) and German Development Institute (DIE) feels that we can learn a lot from perspectives from the emerging powers on global governance, and that we should make efforts at discussing German/European perspectives on global governance with those from emerging powers.

It is against this background that the MGG programme, out of which this publication has grown, started in the spring of 2006 with a first partner workshop to which we invited representatives of interested partner organizations from the five emerging powers mentioned above. At this workshop we discussed in a participatory manner the MGG programme, which then started officially in January 2007 with the first six-month MGG training course with some 20 participants from Brazil, China, India, Mexico and South Africa. The beginning of this first course in January 2007 was chosen to coincide with Germany's taking over the European Union (EU) and G8-presidency for six months. German Chancellor Merkel invited the same five countries that participated from the beginning in the MGG programme – Brazil, China, India, Mexico, South Africa – in an outreach effort to the G8-summit in June 2007, initiating the Heiligendamm Process.

The MGG programme is implemented jointly by InWEnt and DIE on behalf of the Federal Ministry of Economic Cooperation and Development (BMZ). The programme is complemented by a two-week module called International Futures by the Federal Foreign Office of Germany. The programme's pilot phase came to a close in June 2009. However, the programme will continue at least for another 5 years, as an evaluation of the pilot phase has produced very favourable results and the BMZ has subsequently decided to continue providing the financing for its continuation.

By June of 2009, the fifth six-month training course of the MGG programme drew to a close. Upon its completion, some 100 participants from emerging powers will have become part of the MGG network. Since 2008, two more countries – Egypt and Indonesia – participate in the programme. The network of partner organizations – government organizations as well as policy-oriented research bodies – has grown to over 50. In addition to the six-month training course, many activities and networking opportunities have been initiated for individual participants as well as for partner organisations.

On the research front, a good number of joint research projects have been initiated. It was against the background of this fertile and intensifying exchange that the proposal of a book project emerged from discussions within the MGG context. The book is finished now, thanks to a great collaborative effort of the 'editor group' consisting of Ashwani Kumar (Tata Institute of Social Sciences, Mumbai), Zhang Tiejun (Shanghai Institute of International Studies), Siddharth Mallavarapu (Jawaharlal Nehru University, New Delhi), Rafael Duarte Villa (University of Sao Paulo), David Mayer Foulkes (Centro de Investigación y Docencia Económicas,Mexico), Elizabeth Sidiropoulos (South African Institute of International Affairs, Johannesburg) and Dirk Messner and Thomas Fues (DIE, Bonn). Special thanks go to Ashwani Kumar of the Tata Institute of Social Sciences in Mumbai for having co-edited this book. On behalf of the 'editors group' I would like to thank all authors for their contributions to this book.

All of those involved in the preparation of the book hope that it will provide readers with a set of interesting insights and that it will stimulate more debate and dialogue on global governance issues.

Dr. Günther Taube
August 2009

Power Shifts and Global Governance

Part One:

THEORETICAL AND ANALYTICAL REFLECTIONS ON GLOBAL GOVERNANCE

Chapter 1

INTRODUCTION
GLOBAL GOVERNANCE: ISSUES,
TRENDS AND CHALLENGES

Ashwani Kumar and Dirk Messner

The origins of this book lie in the workshop of the Global Governance Research Network at the German Development Institute (DIE) in January 2007. The workshop expectedly brought together a brilliant, energetic and diverse group of senior scholars, policy makers and researchers from north and south setting forth a fruitful and productive process of introspection and reflection on emerging architectures of global governance. Encouraged by the instant consensus around some of the core ideas of the Global Governance Network, we immediately formulated a publishing project that understandably promised not only to examine 'major power shifts', but also broadened its net to include emerging powers and also 'global civil society actors' whom James Rosenau provocatively called 'sovereignty free actors' as major constituencies of the new global order (Rosenau 1990). As the world has become increasingly more globalized, more complex and also more vulnerable at this point of time, we undertake the task of comprehending and exploring political, economic, social and environmental processes of power shifts and prospects of deliberative democracy on a global scale. There is no doubt that global capitalism has come to witness one of the darkest and gloomiest periods in recent world history. Underlying this existential crisis is a deeper structural, political and moral crisis in the existing structures of global governance. Undoubtedly, the days of "casino capitalism" and "single superpower" are over as the world is keenly waiting for what Karl Polanyi would have called another 'great transformation'. (Polanyi 1957) Simple Keynesian solutions perhaps would neither sustain "liberalism" nor "capitalism" in the midst of violent social eruptions and gradual disintegration of the globalization that runs the risk of robbing individuals, groups and nations of their freedom, creativity and human potentialities. Therefore, as political theorist and civil society activist Mary Kaldor argues 'the new Keynes has to be a Neo-Schumpeterian. Neo-Schumpeterianism is both supply side and demand side; it is about matching the social and institutional framework to the techno-economic paradigm' (Kaldor2008). In other words, the inventive, innovative 'new deal' has not only to establish a deeply inclusive system of global governance, but also needs to eradicate global poverty and arrest the increasing catastrophe of environmental disasters. In short, global governance in the present century is fundamentally an audacious political act of re-imagining and re-inventing the existing structures, institutions and norms of global political, economic and ethical order.

Animated by theoretical eclecticism and methodological diversity, the book, thus, does not intend to advance any partisan approach or a new model of understanding global governance. Guided by 'practical reason', it actually attempts to begin a reflexive conversation and seeks to raise more questions than it answers; how do we confront a new world order where traditional boundaries, identities and practices have been altered beyond recognition? How do we contextualize newer forms of governance in the face of globalization? What are the consequences of the rise of new transnational powers for the emerging architecture of global governance? What kind of proposals can be formulated which ensure greater partnership between north and south? Do non-state actors or more particularly, civil society actors, matter in the governance? How do we create a new 'new deal' to address the issues of poverty, climate change and human security at the global level? Is there any realistic hope for institutionalizing cosmopolitan democracy at the global level?

Global Governance: From International Cooperation to Post-National Governance

Therefore it is important that we begin the book with an elaboration on global governance both as an idea and also as a practice. According to Nikolas Rose, governance means cutting 'experiences in certain ways, to distribute attractions and repulsions, passions, and fears across it, to bring new facets and forces, new intensities and relation into being'(Rose 1999, 26). At the core of governance lies conception of 'embedded self' and self-government in the contemporary global order.

Therefore, governance as an idea refers to processes of multiple levels of 'governing without government' in which the nation- state is reconciled with only playing a strategic, instrumental role with different layers of autonomous political authority and legitimacy. Following this generic understanding of governance, we recognise the specific historical contingencies, shifts and moments that have produced the varying and conflicting discourses on the evolving nature of global governance. For instance, contemporary global governances processes cannot be detached from the transformatory forces released by the domino effects of the dramatic collapse of the Soviet Union, the discovery of civil society, the globalization of capital and the revolutions in information technology in the 1990s. Looking at the rapidly changing political developments in the global order in recent times, we can assuredly begin arguing that unlike the traditional international system of sovereign nation-states, the emerging architecture of global governance have fervently sought to frame newer supranational laws, regulations and institutions whose authority reaches beyond conventional borders. There is no denying that nation-states continue to exist, national sovereignty still matters and governments manage to populate the foci of power in the global order, yet there is no doubt that the 'Westphalia Order' has collapsed beyond repair and 'embedded liberalism' is in danger of being replaced by the fury of global economic meltdown. The new global order is undoubtedly more plural, diffused, vocal and tumultuous. It is increasingly being organized by newer norms of interdependence and cooperation that involve myriad United Nations (UN) conventions, especially on trade, development and human rights; supranational institutions like the European Union (EU); and non-government organizations (NGOs); and also social movements at the grassroots. Liberals and radicals bitterly contest the forms and content of governance, but they generally agree that there are global problems such as global poverty, climate warming, trade disputes, financial meltdown and terrorism; diseases such as HIV/AIDS; human rights violations that cannot be solved within the framework of nation-state. In other words, many scholars have come to recognize the emergence of a 'transnational social and political space of participation' and also discover what David Held calls 'a system of overlapping authority and divided loyalties'. (Held;1995, p. 97) Challenging the practice of locating democracy within a particular nation-state, Held persuasively argues that 'in a world where transnational actors and forces cut across the boundaries of national communities in diverse ways, and where powerful states make decisions not just for their peoples but for others as well, the questions of who should be accountable to whom, and on what basis, do not easily resolve themselves. Overlapping spheres of influence, interference and interest create dilemmas at the centre of democratic thought'(Held 1998, 17–29).

In this background of a rapidly evolving complex interconnected world powered by 'new economy', cosmopolitan democratic theory has emerged as a novel way of addressing the issue of broadening popular sovereignty and democratic legitimacy beyond the nation-state. In this framework of governance, nation-states do not necessarily have to vanish, but only need to subject their regional, national and local sovereignties to a democratically negotiated cosmopolitan legal framework while retaining their freedom of self-governance at diverse levels. This resembles what Jurgen Habermas calls 'postnational constellation' (Habermas 2001). Noting the increasing appeal of cosmopolitan trends in contemporary democratic political theory, Paul Wapner writes

> Ever since the Stoics imagined a single world, organized by a set of common principles, thinkers and practitioners have worked to conceptualise and bring into reality mechanisms to coordinate the diverse activities of a complex, multifarious world. For some, this project meant establishing a world government to legislate common laws and policies. For others, it meant simply building institutions of common understanding and practices supported by sovereign entities below the level of world government. (Wapner 1997, 82)

Alongside cosmopolitans, multiculturalists, republicans and post-structuralists have also empathised the need for transnational governance and reconfiguring collective identities beyond the conventional borders (Connolly 1995; Eschle and Maiguashca 2005; Walker 1993). Therefore, global governance is indeed a 'postnational' political project that has challenged the capacity of the social sciences especially in conventional international relations (IR) theories and also sparked the imaginations of civil society activists to generate new theoretical insights and practical tools to explain contemporary transformations in the global order. With the world moving away from political realism to newer forms of collective 'communicative rationality', it has now become increasingly clear that new forms of global processes of change can no longer be understood with a single source of authority, legitimacy and agency. The world is now more plural, differentiated, democratic and also inclusive than we would have imagined a decade ago. Noting the emerging contours of global order, the Commission on Global Governance in the 1995 report 'Our Global Neighbour-hood: The Report of the Commission on Global Governance' insightfully pointed out

> Governance is the sum of the many ways individual and institutions, public and private, manage their common affairs. It is a continuing process through which conflict or diverse interests may be accommodated and cooperative action may be taken. It includes formal institutions and regimes empowered to enforce compliance, as well as informal arrangements that people and institutions either have agreed to or perceive to be in their interest... At the global level, governance has been viewed primarily as intergovernmental relationships, but it must now be understood as also involving non-governmental organizations (NGOs),

citizens' movements, multinational corporations and the global capital market. Interacting with these are global mass media of dramatically enlarged influence.

The appreciation of newer global challenges in the 1990s has dramatically changed the theoretical and analytical landscapes of IR theories promoting a vigorous debate between proponents of internationalism and protagonists of global governance. Reflecting on momentous changes in the world politics since the end of cold war, John Ruggie argues

> Simply put, postwar institutions, including the United Nations, were built for an inter-national world, but we have entered a global world. International institutions were designed to reduce external frictions between states; our challenge today is to devise more inclusive forms of *global governance* [italics in the original]. (Plattner 2007, 118)

Global Governance: Discourses and Practices

The words 'global' and 'governance' have become buzzwords in international relations, international political economy and comparative politics during the last two decades. In practice, it has come to refer many things. Reflecting on the chaotic universe of governance, Lawrence Finkelstein blurted out that 'we say governance because we don't really know what to call what is going on' (Finkelstein 1995, 3:338). In fact, it has become a fuzzy and contested concept with deceptive content. There is no doubt that the fuzziness of the concept can be attributed to its newness and also a lack of general agreement on the boundaries of the concept. Scholars and policy makers have still been struggling to identify normative, descriptive and political components of global governance. Trained in conventional IR theories, many scholars continue to work with familiar nineteenth-century notions of the nation state (Brown2000). IR experts often dwell on the emergence of a world government, but many explain it in term of continuing global dominance of US power (Meyer, Boli and Ramirez 1997). Global governance is also a contested concept because its usage varies according to conflicting political practices and choices of the analysts and policy makers. Support for global governance in reality often depends upon the structural locations of the participants in the new global order. In advanced western countries, global governance is seen as a kind of reinvention of political *laissez-faire*, the political equivalent of neo-liberalism. It has also become associated with hegemonic structures of economic globalization of the market. This view has found deep resonance in poor southern countries that resist the regressive globalizing forces and argue for consolidating the national state as the site of generating counter hegemonic forces. Advocating the need to resist the forces of 'monopoly-liberal world order', neo-Gramscians such as Robert Cox argue that 'the national context remains the only place where an historic bloc can be founded, although world-economy and world –political conditions materially influence the prospects for such an enterprise' (Cox 1999, 25:1). In other words, global governance is viewed as hegemonic effects of liberalization, privatization and the globalization of capital by many in the developing countries where vast majorities of the people still live in poverty, environment degradation and the worst forms of violence. Interestingly, despite their theoretical, ideological and rhetorical differences, neoliberals and critical theorists share their belief in what some scholars call 'methodological nationalism'. Interestingly, conventional IR theories still maintain formal separation between 'national' and 'international', 'domestic' and 'foreign' and ' insider and outsider' at a time when politics and society are being increasingly de-bounded and de-spatialized. National societies and economies continue to frame the debates on globalized economy ignoring independent influences of multinational corporations, international organizations, international non-governmental organizations and parallel submits. It is this widely held belief in the dominance of the supremacy of 'nation' as the fundamental unit of social science analysis that has complicated the nature of global governance. Arguing for a methodological shift from the nationalist perspective to cosmopolitan perspective, Ulrich Beck writes

> Methodological nationalism equates societies with nation-states societies and sees states and their governments as the cornerstones of social science analysis. It assumes that humanity is naturally divided into a limited number of nations which organise themselves internally as nation-states and set external boundaries to distinguish themselves from other nation-states. It goes even further: this outer delimitation as well as the competition between nation-states represents the most fundamental category of political organisation. Much social science assumes the coincidence of social boundaries with state boundaries, thus presupposing that social action occurs primarily. (Beck 2003, 45–6)

Most scholars, governments, think tanks and international organizations consider global governance as an 'orderly management of global affairs' or, more precisely, globalization (Held 1995). In this framework of analysis, global governance processes proceed from a global orientation and are responses largely to certain globalizing tendencies that are perceived to be neither wholly regressive nor purely progressive. To situate the argument in the context, it may be argued that globalization has created newer opportunities structures in the areas of development, trade, finance, technology, human rights, democracy etc. In contrast, globalization has also exacerbated global inequality, poverty and environmental degradation. The list of adverse effects also includes failures in resource conservation, a lack of support for the global public goods and also the neglect of international organizations in solving the global poverty. Noting the globalizing effects of capitalism, Jeffrey Sachs says 'capitalism has now spread to nearly 90% of the world's population, since nearly all parts of the world are now linked through open trade, convertible currencies, flows of foreign investment and political commitments to private ownership as the engine of economic growth' (Sachs 1997, 11–12). It is this process of economic globalization that has come under the scanner of proponents of global governance in order to increase the society's control over the predatory behaviour of markets. However, global governance is not only about economic globalization but also about vertically and horizontally interconnected non-hierarchical processes, mechanisms and rules of behaviour and decision making in the global context. Globalization or globalizing 'governance without government' has encompassed such complex processes of integration and fragmentation that almost all aspects of our lives and experiences are now being constantly impacted, regulated and supervised by multiple regimes of power. Commenting on what he calls 'overlapping communities of fate', Held writes

> The story of our increasingly global order – 'globalization' – is not a singular one. Globalization is not just economic; for it also involves growing aspirations for international law and justice. From the United Nations to the European Union, from changes to the laws of war to the entrenchment of human rights, from the emergence of international environmental regimes to the foundation of the International Criminal Court, there is also another narrative being told – a narrative which seeks to reframe human activity and entrench it in law, rights and responsibilities. (Held 2005)

Global governance has also been seen as world government or global government, or what Hedley Bull calls 'international society'. Contextualizing 'international society' in a state-centred perspective, Bull argues that international society 'exists when a group of states, conscious of certain common interests and common values, form a society in the sense that they conceive themselves to be bound by a common set of rulers in their relations with one another, and share in the working of common institutions' (Bull 1995, 13). Though political scientists have increasingly moved away from this state-centric notion of world government and now associate global governance with the global spread of democracy, many in IR theory continue to link global governance to newer norms of institutionalized behaviour of cooperation across nation-states and international governmental entities. In this sense, global governance becomes a neutral concept having no normative edges. Analytically, the term 'global governance' refers to major transformations in the nature of nation-state system, globalization, emergence of global civil society, free flows of information, qualified multilateralism etc. Inspired by neo-liberal discourses on economic globalization and supported by New Public Management theories, it has, in practice, come to mean minimal state, efficiency of the market and provision of public goods and services through market practices than public sector. In practice, it emphasizes reinvention of the welfare state by raising the issues of cost, efficiency and affectivity as well as newer ways of introducing public accountability and transparency. Though we appreciate public-private partnerships as one of the signifying elements of global governance, we consciously depart from New Public Management oriented perspectives on global governance where it has become synonymous for withdrawal of the social welfare state and the application of market principles towards solving collective problems. Ideologically, the term has become contested due to its specific association with the changing discourses in the major international organizations, especially the World Bank in the late 1980s. The term was instrumentally used by the World Bank as a condition for securing international aid and fighting the menace of debt and poverty. In other words, international organizations and donor agencies often perceive global governance as standard-operating problem-solving template arising out of consequences of inter-state diplomatic enterprises and aimed at exploring the existing modes of successful cooperation among an array of diverse actors. In Europe, the term is viewed from the perspective of 'multilateral' level of cooperation. In Europe, global governance has a specific resonance due to the successful functioning of the EU that has not only pooled a common reservoir of resources for collective action, but also rendered traditional notions of sovereignty and governance irrelevant.

At a minimum level, global governance may be thought of as the broadening, widening and deepening of formal and informal transnational processes of interconnectedness in most vital aspects of contemporary global social life. This meaning stems from a wide array of concrete and normative contexts—from existing intergovernmental-multilateral international organizations to non-state civil society actors to spontaneous forces of social movements. In fact, the complexities of global governance can be traced to a paradigmatic shift from structures of 'solid modernity' to fluid processes of what Bauman calls 'liquid modernity' in an increasingly multilateral and multicultural world (Bauman 1999). As a consequence of embracing this minimalist definition, the core of the global governance has come to refer to 'the acquisition of authoritative decision-making capacity by non-state and supra-state actors'(Fuchs 2002). These supra-state actors have been subsumed under what scholars call 'global civil society', a possible antidote to war(Kaldor 2003). We often define global governance quite instrumentally by making reference to new fault lines, cracks and divisions in the new international order that have no single authority or source of legitimacy. Often, we turn to international organizations (UN, World Bank, etc.), international NGOs (Greenpeace, Transparency International), submit meetings (World Economic Forums), parallel conferences (World Social Forum etc.), human rights regimes and climate regimes to identify structural features of global governance. Considering the conceptual history of the term 'global governance', we indeed concur with Thomas Weiss's observation that 'many academic and international practitioners employ 'governance' to connote a complex set of structures and processes, both public and private, while more popular writers tend to use it synonymously with 'government' (Weiss 2000, 5:795). Therefore, we agree with Rosenau's observation that 'there is no single organizing principle on which global governance rests, no emergent order around which communities and nations are likely to converge. Global Governance is the sum of myriad—literally millions of—control mechanisms driven by different histories, goals, structures and processes... In terms of governance, the world is too disaggregated for grand logics that postulate a measure of global coherence' (Rosenau 1995). In other words, we consider not only economic globalization but also a vast array of political and cultural globalizing forces that include existing international organizations, intergovernmental organizations, supranational entities, transnational corporations, global civil society actors, social movements, parallel submit and conferences etc. as the driving force behind global governance. It is this idea of global governance that has come to articulate a deliberate attempt in IR theories to forge a new 'episteme' after the end of what is called 'embedded-liberalism compromise'(Ruggie 1982; Harvey 2005). The collapse of 'embedded liberalism' has become more pronounced in the aftermath of current global economic meltdown. In retrospect, there is no doubt that the dominance of realism as the reigning ideology in IR has suffered a sharp decline in the recent times. And scholars in IR have been forced to revise their 'anachronistic statist rhetoric' and pay greater attention to 'global governance' as a new recipe for averting the disasters of the new global order being shaped by globalization. There is no doubt that global governance indicates both a transformation and a shift in the ontology of major 'traditional perspectives within IR' which is rooted in the Westphalia-centric anarchical world system. Global governance has not only challenged realism, but also refused to accept liberal institutionalism's artificial separation of world politics into two realms of political economy and security necessary for securing and stabilizing cooperation. More importantly, global governance has seriously questioned 'regime theories' popularized by Kenneth Waltz and Robert Keohane for their overly positivistic and rational-choice-based interpretations of cases of cooperation in global politics. The regime theorists mistakenly take global governance as forming transnational regime of cooperation resolving or alleviating collection-action problems in a specific issue-area (Holsti 1992). Noting the significance of transnational state in creating a new framework of cooperation, Beck writes

> The model of the transnational state thus conflicts with all other models of cooperation. Transnational states come together in response to globalization and thereby develop their regional sovereignty and identity beyond the national level. They are thus cooperative and individual states—individual states on the basis of cooperative states. In other words, interstate unions open up new scope for action by post-national individual states. (Beck 2000, 133)

Many western policy makers and scholars, as well as two prominent 'Asian Drivers' from India and China", trump the importance of creating seamless web of overlapping institutions, networks and regimes as a powerful force of stability and peace in the emerging global order. This 'institutionalized cooperation' is indeed one of the necessary constitutive elements of global governance, but this is not sufficient for global governance. Europe is particularly in a more advantageous and also complex situation as it has witnessed not only the continuing of NATO, but also the discovery of the EU as the new means of overcoming fears and stabilizing peace. Although die-hard realists such as John Mearscheimer and Joseph Grieco still believe that global order is largely anarchical and that institutionalized cooperation has no independent effect on the state behaviour, liberal institutionalists like Robert Keohane and Joseph Nye have forcefully supported the case of institutions as altering the absolute and relative self interests of state and helping stabilize a peaceful global order. They tout multilateralism as a 'generalized principle of conduct' in the emerging global order. Liberal institutionalism accepts the realist view that states act on the basis of self-interest, and concentrates on devising rules that facilitate cooperation among states (Jervis 1999; Mearscheimer 1995). Following the model of 'rational egoism' premised on the prescriptions of prisoner dilemma, liberals have failed to anticipate implications of global governance. Rejecting pessimism of realists and challenging liberal institutionalists' false belief in self-interest induced cooperation, proponents of global governance refuse to interpret the world as a constant competition for security and power-hard or soft. Instead of calculating its relative gains, states in the global governance framework focus more on maximizing their absolute gains and contribute to strengthening of 'cosmopolitan multilateralism'. Significantly, different institutional arrangements have extended beyond traditional economic and security issues to environment, poverty, human rights and development. Elaborating on these far reaching consequences of global governance, Rosenau argues 'that 'global governance is conceived to include systems of rule at all levels of human activity—from the family to the international organization-in which the pursuit of goals though the exercise of control has transnational repercussions'(Rosenau 1995, 1:131).

Polycentric Governance and Globalization: Challenges of Governance

In other words, global governance attaches equal importance to traditional nation-states, intergovernmental organizations, multilateral agencies, supranational actors, business forums, non-governmental organizations, civil society groups, human rights groups and research and advocacy groups who campaign on global issues like development, climate, poverty etc. In essence, global governance has come to refer to a multilateral, multivocal and multiversal perspective on world politics. In this seamless 'polycentric' conception of global politics, local, national, regional and global processes are inseparably linked. Describing polycentrism as a new form of global governance, Jan Scholte perceptively writes

> Polycentrism includes the regulation of country domains, but also treats local, regional, and global spheres as sites of governance in their own right. Thus, for example, under polycentrism policies regarding local environmental concerns, regional investment strategies, and global communications networks are not reduced to questions of 'national interest.' Instead, public policy acquires transscalar logic where local, national, regional, and global dimensions are interconnected but also distinct from one another'. Not only has polycentrism involved the growth of multiple sites of societal governance alongside states, but states themselves have tended to disaggregate into multiple relatively autonomous policy decision points. (Scholte 2008, 15:305–350)

The polycentric ways of governing may seem like a typical non-western 'bazaar', a cacophonous world with transactions in the never-ending alleys of negotiations and compromises. In this emerging polycentrism, the vital life sustaining issues are handled in complex structures of delimited political spheres at the grassroots and deliberative and decision making structures needed to support 'global commons' increasingly acquire transnational character. This border concept of global governance, indeed, raises the issues of resisting hierarchies of power and transforming the existing power relations. The plurality of actors and increasing porosity of borders in trade, monetary and financial systems has accentuated the increasing disparities within and between nations. Not surprisingly, the emerging politics of 'multilateralism from the bottom' and transnational networks linking international organizations and social movements and framing the agenda for collective decisions have challenged the conventional politics of multilateralism. And this has predictably resulted in challenging the 'multilateralism of the powerful', auditing the governance-deficit major international organizations and demanding to reform the regressive practices of global capital.

Significantly, this has coincided with major power shifts in the global politics. The spectacular rise of China and India, so-called 'Asian Drivers', and also the growing influence of Brazil, South Africa and Mexico has radicalized the demands for altering the institutions, norms and practices of global governance. More importantly, actors in global civil society have emphasized setting up new mechanisms and norms of introducing accountability and transparency in order to address the continuing 'global governance deficit' in the functioning of international organizations and agencies (Hass 2004). The rising southern countries have noticed deficit in the structures of power and resources at the global level. Most southern countries feel excluded from the collective decisions making processes, especially those relating to 'global commons'. The poor and marginalized in these countries have increasingly become more vociferous, and rebellious constituencies of emerging global civil society regularly protest against the dominance of so-called 'global elites' and the hegemony of unfettered flow of capital across borders. The 'global ideological shift' towards market-driven development has increasingly become a bone of contention between global elites and global poor. It is not hard to notice that the political and strategic mechanisms to steer the global system from the top are dated and positively slanted towards developed western powers. There seems to have developed an inexcusable inertia to support the more progressive global policies aimed at ameliorating the conditions of poor at large. Reflecting on the risks and costs of globalized market economy, the UN Development Programme's Human Development Report starkly noted that 'when the market goes too far in dominating social and political outcomes, the opportunities and rewards of globalization spread unequally and inequitably—concentrating power and wealth in a select group of people, nations, corporations' (UNDP 1999, 1). In a stunning indictment of iniquitous practices of WTO (World Trade Organization), a 'statement of International Civil Society', contended that 'the WTO system, rules and procedures are undemocratic, untransparent and nonaccountable and have operated to marginalize the majority of the world's people' (Members of International Civil Society 1999). Therefore, it does not come as a surprise that 'Millennium Development Goals' still languish in endless discussion over technicalities of jurisdictions and sectoral allocations. The shift from specialization to 'interlinings' has not taken place. Most international organizations and agencies still mirror defunct Cold War principles of organizing the world. Identifying the four major global challenges and proposals for reforms, Colin Bradford writes,

> First, the United Nations Security Council as a creation of the post-World War II alliance in 1945 is confronting a crisis of obsolescence. Not only are Germany and Japan, the second and third largest economies in the world, not represented as permanent members of the Security Council, but, with the important exception of China, there are no developing countries represented either. Second, since the WTO meetings in Seattle in 1999, there is a growing demand for changing the voting shares in the Bretton Woods Institutions (the World Bank and the International Monetary Fund) to better reflect current realities. Third, embedded in these reform issues but beyond them is the growing reality and tension concerning the unipolar nature of the military, economic, media, and political power of the United States in its conduct of foreign policy. Fourth, global challenges in the global age seem to be characterized more by interconnectedness rather than by isolation. This throws an international system based on 'specialized agencies' into a state of inadequacy as the nature of contemporary interconnected problems exceeds their expertise based on specialization. (Bradford 2005)

Global Deliberative Democracy: A Post–Liberal Project of Global Governance

Interestingly, the clamours for reforms and transformation in the prevailing forms of global governance have come to be linked with need for establishing and sustaining deliberative democracy at the global level. Challenging the Habermasian state-centric conception of democracy, James Bohman and others have come to support more plural, decentred versions of governance. The deliberative version of global governance has been premised on the promises to guarantee human flourishing in every possible arenas of social and political interactions across various cities, nations, and global institutions. This new perspective on global governance calls into questions traditional meaning of self-determination and amends the normative core of the notion of democracy by placing it across multiple levels of governance rather than at some fixed level or single source of agency. Further, focusing on inequalities of social power, deliberative global democrats advocate for institutional reforms as well as opening increasing engagements between civil societies and transnational regimes to create 'democratic public spheres' across a variety of regimes around the world. In contrast to conventional 'regimes theories' where constituents' voices are only counted and aggregated but never really heard and represented in shaping collective decisions, deliberative global governance promises to create more reflexive and participatory opportunities in the global structures of governance. Outlining emerging contours of deliberative global governance, Bohman writes,

> The greatest impetus for more democracy in the international arena lies in a vigorous civil society containing oppositional public spheres in which actors organize against the state or appeal to it when making violations of agreements public. As various international institutions emerge, they, too, can become the focus of a critical public sphere as actors in transnational civil society expand and maintain their public interaction across various political cultural and functional boundaries. (Bohman 2007, 39–40)

To conclude, global governance theoretically and normatively is embedded in the principles of participatory, deliberative and cosmopolitan democracy; it is 'deliberative' as it aims to expand and deepen processes of public reasoning at the heart of global decision-making, or if it at least aims to make global decision-making more responsive and transparent to public reasoning. Therefore, advocates of global governance are more positively inclined to apply the norms of deliberation not only to major state-centric global governance bodies, such as the UN, the WTO, the World Bank, etc., but also to audit international NGOs, civil society associations, non-governmental organisations or transnational public spheres. In this broader conception of governance, global north and south come to share a growing global consciousness, 'the sense of a common community of mankind' (Shaw 2000; Robertson 1990). Despite institutional differences in the forms of national governance or informal power differentials in foreign policies, this collective enterprise of global governance promises to identify failures in development, the persistence of chronic poverty, failed states, environmental degradation, violation of human rights, lack of progress towards democracy and the challenges posed by the forces of regressive globalization. In short, the future of global governance depends on creating, fostering and sustaining transnational public spaces for collaborating on the ways and means of realizing a new 'social contract', not just a 'new deal'! Therefore, even if we fail to reach agreements on a possible 'Another World', we can still aspire to be a moral and political community sharing common goals, projects, aspirations, skills and talents with our fellows in varying, overlapping frameworks of experiences across borders. Anticipating cosmopolitan forms of governance centuries ago Stoic philosopher Marcus Aurelius wisely exhorted 'If reason is common, so too is law; and if this is common, then we are fellow citizens. If this is so, we share in a kind of organized polity, and if this is so, the world is as if it were a city-state'(Dallmayr 2003, 3:421–422).

Design of the Book: Arguments and Narratives of the Global Governance

The chapters in the book reflect, stimulate, deliberate and introspect on some of the critical aspects of major power shifts that have been powered by the processes and mechanisms of globalization since the 1990s. Significantly, the chapters address specific issues of development and foreign policies arising out of the growing challenges of global governance. It is hoped that the book will be read, discussed and reflected upon by scholars, policy makers, researchers and students in the international relations, international political economy, global social movements, globalization studies etc. In practical terms, the book has been designed to facilitate a dialogue on the innovative ways and means of responding to major theoretical, normative and empirical challenges emanating from newer sources of global governance. Rather than limit our understanding within the known boundaries of the literature on international relations, security studies, foreign policies and globalization, we have followed the usual hermeneutic approach towards commissioning the various chapters for the book. We have taken our original mandate seriously and believe that chosen texts/chapters help provoke a diverse, innovative range of critical thinking and refection on emerging rules, norms and institutions of global governance from both northern and southern perspectives. Rather than offering a monolithic, linear understanding of global governance, the emphasis is placed on forging linkages between competing theoretical interpretations informed by regional and country perspectives. The chapters have been arranged at three overlapping levels of theoretical framework, country and regional perspectives.

The first part of the book offers global governance from a theoretical and analytical perspective that includes exploring the significance of emerging global civil society actors and networks. In his essay, Dirk Messner describes major lessons from the current global financial crisis and analyses dynamics towards a global transformation that is taking place in the first half of the twenty-first century. He argues that we are witnessing the fundamental erosion of an international order in which the Western societies were the centre and the measure of all things (the G7 is a reflection of this eroding constellation of power), the age of industrialization (based as it was on the delusion of an infinite supply of natural resources and infinite capacities of the atmosphere, the oceans and the global forests to absorb greenhouse gas emissions and other collateral wastes of our consumption patterns) and the illusion that the nation-state could, despite accelerating globalization, somehow just muddle on as it has in the course of the past 200 years. He insightfully and forcefully contends that the challenge now is to create a truly viable, sustainable globalization that accepts the global characteristics of the twenty-first century.

Realizing that the utopia of a self-regulated market has failed as much as the utopia of socialism, Messner forcefully argues for inventing an embedded global market economy that invests seriously in worldwide poverty reduction and strategies to avoid accelerated processes of social polarization. Accepting that the Western hegemony is coming to an end, he unfolds his vision for a peaceful global power transition. A global lack of social and human capital is the main driver of international instability, mistrust and violence, Messner argues. Since globally dominating business model, based on blind growth, fossil fuels and short-term investment returns has simply destroyed the world, he advocates the need for building a low carbon and resource efficient global economy to avoid dangerous changes in the Earth system. Echoing a distinctive European perspective, Messner concludes quite persuasively that existing global interdependencies require a radically new notion of international cooperation that is simultaneously cosmopolitan and vernacular.

Revolving around a fusion of Kantian and Foucauldian perspectives, the chapter by Ashwani Kumar provides an overview of global civil society and its emerging cosmopolitan character. Situated in normative and theoretical arguments, the chapter explores the case of global civil society as a new paradigm of global governance and also a possible emancipatory 'cosmopolitan political project' to the emerging challenges of democracy, justice and inclusive governance at the global level. Though global civil society is often perceived as a multilayered, contested, decentred space of associationalism, he considers it as an epic and irreversible 'double movement' of people seeking to transform hegemonic structures of global governance, protect human rights, minimize violence and increase the sphere of democratic life across the borderless world. He suggests that global civil society not only 'feeds on and reacts to globalization', it also remains relatively autonomous in its character and aspirations. Interestingly, though noting the limits of the global civil society, he defends the case of global civil society both as an open confrontational space for 'headline-grabbing protests, demonstrations, and rebellions', and also lesser-visible yet powerful forms of 'everyday struggles of resistance' by subordinate groups around the world. Continuing the theoretical reflection on 'Tragedy of the Commons' as one of the fundamental challenges of global governance, Pinto and Pummim in their chapter on 'Institutional and Policy Implications of International Public Goods: The Case of Global Commons' examine the International Public Goods (IPGs) engendered by the 'Vertical Global Programs' (VGPs). The chapter particularly explores the extent to which countries participating in VGPs are required to cede portions of their 'sovereignty' when entering into these arrangements and how they adapt to this contingency. By exploring the right mix of IPGs and National Public Goods (NPGs) and the attendant institutional arrangements, this chapter may be useful in guiding state reform efforts against the backdrop of the increased relevance of the provision of IPGs through VGPs as a means to address the challenge of the global commons. Specifically, the chapter seeks to identify a few elements to factor into national state reform, given the irreversible trend towards globalization and ensuing integration on a global or regional scale. It argues that, while the nation-state, as we know it, may be receding, it can be strengthened through proper interfacing with institutions of global governance. These inquiries should also generate a framework to assess global and national incentives underpinning their respective policies and provide insights into implications for the design of VGPs by international institutions.

In a significant exploration of the theoretical and empirical gaps in the debate on globalization, David Meyer's chapter 'Economic Challenges for Global Governance' examines the historical consequences of globalization from below and rekindles the classic debates on the nature of underdevelopment. Incorporating findings from a theory of globalization that focuses on the interaction between technological change, international trade and foreign direct investment (FDI), the author explains the simultaneous historical emergence of development and underdevelopment, and their persistence in the context of globalization. To explain this increasing economic polarization, the author argues to move beyond theories based on competitive markets and diminishing returns that predict equalization in growth rates and productivity under free trade and investment. This chapter outlines how trade, FDI, technological change, institutions and the demographic transition interact, intersect and impact development and under-development in the context of globalization. Both trade and FDI can generate asymmetric incentives for innovation in advanced countries and therefore generating multiple steady states in economic growth. Concluding that the present wave of globalization emerged from a weakening of domestic governments and a strengthening of *laissez-faire*, Meyer quite presciently argues that market economies have always needed sufficiently strong institutions to control them. For a global market economy to work, effective global governance is needed to create sufficiently strong global institutions to ensure the provision of economic development for all. This is the economic challenge for global governance.

Analysing theoretically global governance within the context of multilateralism, Gustavo Fondevila in his chapter 'The Rule of Law in Multilateral Institutions and International AID for Development: Judicial Reform in the Global Order' examines the prospects of international cooperation in terms of the reform of state, focusing on judicial reform in particular. An understanding of the global governance structure is being sought out of an analysis of the development and evolution of international aid backing judicial reforms. The author argues that an attempt to integrate the world systems into a common understanding and administration of justice and to integrate the developing countries within a process of judicial globalization has to reorient the countries in their local and cultural contexts with a perspective of inclusion of the communities which have been hitherto ignored by the dominant legal systems. International cooperation has to re-invent itself to the needs of varied groups, but with an overall movement towards transparency in the system and with certain shared beliefs that help in the formation of the global economy. For the purpose of the same, the author seeks to outline certain general, concrete and desirable criterion that would be necessary for a nation to partake in the global process. Having undertaken an analysis of the theoretical underpinnings and the contours to which an international collaboration would seek to take, Fondevila also explores the empirical terrain of how such a judicial reform has been undertaken across Latin America, Eastern Europe and Africa, thus laying forward the further agendas the collaboration needs to concentrate upon.

The arguments and narratives in the second part of the book revolve around country-specific analyses around foreign policy and development. The chapters approach global governance from the perspectives of 'power shifts' that not only involve exploring increasing complexities in foreign policies, but also challenges of sustainable development. The chapters link experiences of countries in the north and south to major discourses of global governance. Elizabeth Sidiropoulos's chapter 'Global Power Shifts and South Africa's Southern Agenda: Caught between African Solidarity and Regional Leadership' revolves around 'power shifts' that have challenged the dominance of international political economy by 'transatlantic west'. Noticing monumental shifts in the structures of global political economy, she persuasively and brilliantly argues that the global power shifts experienced in the world in the first decade of the twenty-first century provide a unique opportunity for South Africa to pursue more effectively one of its key foreign policy objectives, viz. reforming the institutions of global governance, which continue to mirror outdated power configurations. Supporting the case of strategic multilateralism, the author argues for developing strong alliances with like-minded countries of the developing south, such as Brazil, India and China. She concludes on a cautionary note that South Africa's close alignment with big emerging powers may conflict with some of the core commitments of South Africa's foreign policy, producing contradictory policy outcomes. This contradiction in foreign policy is unlikely to be resolved in the medium term, and may also become more difficult to manage as the balance of power shifts more dramatically to the so-called 'Asian Drivers'.

Eduardo Vega and Roberto Escalante in their chapter on 'Mexico as an Emerging Power in the Present World Scenario' address an interesting paradox of Mexico becoming integrated into the global economy without any national development strategy. They argue that since 1982, the Mexican economy has increasingly abandoned its international low profile to develop into a more active player in the open markets, but it has not always produced successful results. Amidst periodic bouts of political crises and economic cycle of boom and bust, Mexico since 1982 has undertaken massive programs of economic liberalization and established different stabilization and macroeconomic adjustment programs. This has not unsurprisingly led to creating two Mexicos: rich metropolitan areas and poor, marginalized peripheries. Highlighting the regressive aspects of economic globalization, they argue that Mexico is better placed than Brazil, South Africa, India and China in terms of gross and net national income per capita, but is located at the bottom of the Organization for Economic Cooperation and Development (OECD) country in terms of social inequity measured. Suggesting an ambitious and long-term national development strategy for Mexico's successful participation in the emerging structures of global governance, the authors accord urgency to reconstructing the welfare state.

Tiejun Zhang's chapter 'Trilateral Relations among Africa, China and Europe: A Chinese Perspective' attempts to analyse the dualities and thus also the complexity of China, relevant to the trilateral relations. Secondly, the chapter describes the static and dynamic features of the trilateral relations. Thirdly, Zhang discusses the ideological background of the Chinese and European approaches to Africa. Fourthly, he focuses on the Chinese engagement, with particular reference on the motivations and attractiveness of Chinese engagement with Africa. Fifthly, the chapter makes a contrast between the Chinese and European approaches to Africa, in the dichotomy of good governance vs. effective governance. Concluding the chapter, the author argues that though on the surface the Chinese and European approaches to Africa show the contradiction between each other, they in fact can be complementary to a certain extent, and more coordination and cooperation are needed in this area. This is indeed vital for the stability in the order of global governance!

Continuing in the mode of country specific analysis of foreign policy and its consequences for governance, Rafael Duarte Villa's chapter 'South America and US Relations: Implications for Regional Security' seeks to unravel the layers and layers of American policies towards South America, especially towards the illegal drug industry which has found its deep roots in Latin America. Borrowing from the concept of 'new wars', a term coined by Mary Kaldor, it seeks to locate varied responses to the issue of drug trafficking, a response that builds around a certain understanding of the policy that legitimizes military and other economic operations under the name of security. An analysis of two specific policies with their focus on v the anti-Andean drug strategy is an attempt to understand the shifting nature of the discourse on security itself where even crises of a social and political nature are transformed as 'existential threats' to be easily carved and incorporated into the security agenda. The differentiation of the nature of the problem and its departure from its roots calls for a differentiated form of action which departs away from the larger claims of democracy itself and alters the response towards the same. The chapter locates the shift in trajectory towards a response to drug trafficking from originally a problem at the source to the connection of it with larger terror movements of transnational nature, especially in the wake of 9/11.

Shifting focus from specific foreign policy issue to political economy aspects of governance, Eduardo Vega Lopez's chapter 'Mexico as an Emerging Power in the Present World Scenario: Global Economy without National Development Strategy?' seeks to capture the development of the Mexico over the past 25 years. The years from 1982–94 have seen the movement from financial crises to economic liberalization and have also been characterised as the lost decade for the country. While the period from 1995–2007 has seen stabilisation in the economy, it has come at the expense of insufficient growth which has resulted in greater inequity in the society and has been characterised by the simultaneous growth of two Mexicos – shining and suffering Mexico. Describing this phenomenon as 'national equizophrenia', the author explores the paradoxical effects of emerging political economy in Mexico. Some of the malaises that beset Mexico's movement towards attaining development are social inequality, public insecurity and juridical weakness. Without a movement towards greater economic growth, better standards of welfare, increased opportunities for the unemployed youth and better health and education system the economy will keep on languishing at the bottom of the OECD country, the author insightfully argues.

The two chapters from India insightfully undertake the task of analysing fascinating aspects of emerging experience of global governance from theoretically newer perspectives. Exploring the theme of 'regional integration' as one of the critical elements of emerging architecture of global governance, Vijaya Katti in her chapter 'The Future Development in Global Governance – Multilateralism and Regionalization process: India's Role' seeks to examine India's role in the regional economic integration and also in the development cooperation in the context of Africa. Globalization has meant an increasing integration of the economies world over, but its other face has also left a lot to be desired in the sense of increasing inequalities and also leaving a large section of the population out of its benefits. The rise of some of the developing countries in the world economic scene has almost meant the craving for an increasing space within the global political order and this meant a movement towards a deeper integration where Regional Trade Agreements (RTAs) and Preferential Trade Agreements (PTAs) have been the order of the day. The author argues that India being an important and strategic player in the global market needs to be understood in the same context and its movement towards an increasing regional integration need to be analysed. She also notes that India has increasingly emerged as a key player in providing development assistance to developing countries especially in Africa. In the changing dynamics of regional integration and cooperation, India promises to offer a more constructive and collaborative role than has normally been noted in the conventional literature on 'regionalism and development cooperation'. The paper is divided in two sections. Section one covers India's role in regional integration and section two covers Indian development cooperation aspect.

Ravi Shanker's chapter 'Managing Social Issues for Sustainable Development: the Indian Experiences' is methodologically and theoretically quite innovative as he attempts to re-invent the whole idea of social marketing from the perspective of inclusive development. Leaning subtly to the insights of global governance, he forcefully argues that the success of any social development programme requires an overall integrative and wholesome strategy of intervention ranging from the problem definition to its final implementation and evaluation. Given the changing nature of developmental state in India, the importance of social marketing has acquired urgency for the policy makers and also the civil society actors. Although the market has emerged as an important player, social planning continues to play a critical role in the development. Building a case for social marketing in the Indian context through examples, Shanker argues that programmes where a proper planning was undertaken the schemes were tailored towards the socio-cultural situations and where all the levers where put in place were a success. This could be observed in the Population Service International's (PSI) success of working within the red light areas in Mumbai for the control of the AIDS epidemic or in the case of the immunization programme. However, in cases like family planning where an overall integrative approach was not undertaken and where intervention was undertaken with quite an 'arbitrary' approach, the successes have been far and few. The lesson from this chapter – that governance also requires a social marketing framework for its success – is quite revealing.

The third and concluding part of the book deals with case studies in global governance. The shifting global economic and political order has meant increasing inequalities across the globe, especially between the developed and the developing countries. These inequalities can also be traced due to the inequities in the political structures in the global organizations that have governed global trade practices and policies. A movement towards greater democratization of these organizations requires a sustained struggle by the global south through formations of strategic alliances, increased participation and calling for greater stakes in the decision making process in these organisations. Vicente Paolo, through his paper 'Unity in Diversity: South Coalitions as Governance Adaptation Vehicles in Global Trade Governance', has brilliantly outlined some of these struggles and coalitions which have attempted to realign the global trade structures. These alliances have been built around shared interests and common understanding with specific countries undertaking different roles in different contexts from leadership to organization and even keeping the pack together from the forays of the developed world. The chapter sees that while at the level of the WTO these alliances seemed to have weathered the storm, when it comes to the UN Conference on Trade and Development (UNCTAD) this seems to be a dwindling alliance, especially during the crisis of the 80s, but there has been renewed vigour and effort which is now being seen in the same. Alliances are an important step towards reforming the global governance structures and what the author likes to call the 'intellectual liberation' of the global south. In a moving analysis of the so-called 'dangerous zone' in global politics, Ibrahim Saleh challenges some of the orthodoxies on the role of media in shaping the global opinion on questions of war and peace in the Middle East. In the chapter on 'In the Foggy Middle Eastern: Just Wars Remain the Name of the Game', Saleh, through an empirical and theoretical analysis, seeks to unravel the layers and layers of muddy visibility or 'fog' that have encircled the media in the Middle East which has fed into the hands of the government as well as the Islamic Right. Theoretically drawing from the Just War theory, news framing and Global Opinion theory, the chapter tries to locate the media through empirical analysis of various media devices in Egypt, meandering across news discourses of Nile TV, TV International and government controlled free to air channels as well as the coverage of the cartoon controversy in two Egyptian dailies, finally entering into the realm of coverage of the 'Just Wars'. The media discourses have been a domain of manipulation across the spectrum from the liberals to the conservatives, who have feasted on the lack of voice in the civil society and whose edifice rests on the split in the social fabric that somewhere hangs between the tradition and modernity of systems hanging on to the romantic idealized past. The uncritical nature of the media and a loss of self reflection on their part has meant it to be manoeuvred by varied interest, thus transforming the sphere into a battleground of 'warring narratives and interpretation' which has resulted in a 'media fatigue' in the region. Monitoring and evaluation plays an important role in the realization of the development aspirations of any country and especially if the country is languishing at the bottom of the development parameter. The case for an effective Monitoring and Evaluation (M&E) strategy for the Arab countries has been made by Doha Abdelhamid in her insightfully written chapter 'ECD in the Arab Region: How M&E is 'Perceived' and 'Applied'?'. Lack of development is as much an outcome of the governance structures as that of the evaluation structures that exist in a set up. The movement towards the betterment of human lives by human development has to orient itself through a partnership among the state and civil society structures and with global partners to develop monitoring and evaluation structures, but for the success of the same the demand has to be intrinsic to the system rather than the outcome of a donor driven strategy. The paper meanders through the governance structures of the Arab states with an understanding of the development needs of the system and seeks to offer possible areas of interventions and collaborative strategies for different stakeholders within the system for the development of the region.

The UN is the most important arena and actor in global environmental governance. However, international environmental problems have not only been reduced, but also multiplied beyond our control in the recent times. Against this background, Chengxin Chen seeks to examine and evaluate the role of the UN Environment Program (UNEP) in shaping the nature of global governance. Building on the assumptions of the UNEP as a key institution of global environmental governance and on the need for developing countries to promote the process of development as well as environmental protection, the chapter 'UNEP Institutional Reform With Its Impact On Developing Countries' seeks to understand the need for institutional reforms in the UNEP and its impact on developing countries. It also seeks to understand the political implications of such a reform for these countries and how better these countries could utilize these processes and also strengthen it at the same time. For the purpose of the same research, the author undertakes a multiple methodology design combining interviews along with documentary research and a study of institutional reform models. The chapter meanders through an analysis of the need for such reforms by unravelling the debates that have led to the process and also certain obstacles that have stalled the progress of these reforms in the developing countries. A holistic analysis of UNEP structures and its capacity to deal with the issues of the developing countries thus leads the author to suggest certain policy recommendations and arrangements for global environmental governance in a harmonious world order.

Garth Le Pere and others in their chapter 'The Heiligendamm Process and Emerging powers: More of the Same or a Genuine Global Governance Innovation?' examines the implications of the Heiligendamm Process (HP) for the system of global governance and asks some critical questions: Will the 'structured dialogue' lead to a more inclusive summit arrangement and strengthen the position of emerging countries in the international order? Will the G-5 be able to coordinate their positions and extract concessions not only from industrialized countries that benefit themselves, but also the developing world in general? Or will the HP, on the contrary and in the end, exacerbate north-south antagonism since it could prove incapable of delivering tangible outcomes? For the purpose of the same the chapter first outlines the background and structure of the HP. Secondly, the paper pays special attention to the role of emerging/middle powers in the global system. Since the G-5 is a 'newcomer' in the summit architecture, the third section will examine the underlying interest structures of the G-5 countries and analyse their potential for consensus-building. Authors conclude with the possible contributions that the HP could make in promoting a more cooperative world order and one that better serves the interests of the developing world. The paper thus sees the HP as a legitimate attempt to broaden the institutional basis for informal policy dialogue among traditional and emerging powers in the context of the highly contested terrain of global governance. However, the process carries certain risks for all parties involved. The intentions of the G-8 seem, at this stage, highly ambiguous, contradictory and vague. We cannot ascertain yet whether industrialized countries are genuinely interested in inclusive summit architecture or, more cynically perhaps, if they rather see the HP as a window-dressing exercise meant to subtly preserve their global eminence. The G-5 appears similarly undecided on what to make of the process, particularly if it fails to deliver tangible progress for the developing world. Continued G-5 interaction with the G-8 will only make sense if this leads to substantive policy shifts by industrialized countries in key global issue areas.

Conclusion: Acknowledgements

The book is an exercise in developing an eclectic theoretical framework rooted in the growing diversity of actors, ideas and norms in the emerging architecture of global governance. Perhaps this has happened partly by choice and partly by default. The book is not a typical or usual academic exercise, but reflects more of an outcome of a fruitful, joyful and productive network of scholars and researchers linking north and south, governments and civil society actors, researchers and policy makers. One of the major goals of this publishing project is to recognize the significance of extending the boundaries of 'institutionalized cooperation' and exploring the possibility of setting up a new epistemic community at the global level. In fact, the book is an acknowledgment of a collective spirit of cooperation and understanding beyond borders. We are deeply indebted to everyone who offered advice and incise comments on the draft chapters presented in the follow-up workshop at DIE in Bonn in April 2008. Colleagues and friends in the 'Global Governance Research Network' have been extremely supportive and have always responded to our efforts to cut through the blind spots in this venture. Special thanks must go to the contributors who have so generously and vigorously supported this project. A special word of praise must go to Dr. Thomas Fues (DIE) who has been the moving spirit behind this collective project. We must say that it is his rare dedication that has made this book possible. We are also indebted to the generous intellectual and financial support from InWent (Capacity Development International, Germany) for this project. Undoubtedly, this work would not have possible without the support of German Development Institute (DIE). In many ways, this book symbolizes DIE's commitment to promote international cooperation beyond borders. Many thanks to Tej Sood, CEO of Anthem Press, for not only agreeing to publish the book, but also for taking interest in the timely production of the book in the midst of global economic meltdown.

References

Albert, M. and Kopp–Malek T. 2002. 'The Pragmatism of Global and European Governance: Emerging Forms of the Political 'Beyond Westphalia'', *Millennium: Journal of International Studies* (31)3.

Archibugi, D. 2008. *The Global Commonwealth of Nations: Towards Cosmopolitan Democracy*. Princeton: University of Princeton Press.

Bauman, Z. 2000. *Liquid Modernity*. Cambridge, UK: Polity Press.

Beck, U. 2000. *Globalization*. Cambridge, UK: Polity Press.

_____.2003. 'The Analysis of Global Inequality: From National to Cosmopolitan Perspective' in M. Kaldor, H. Anheier and M. Glasius (eds), *Global Civil Society*.

Bohman, J. 2007. *Democracy Across Borders: From Dêmos to Dêmoi*. Cambridge, Mass.: MIT Press.

Bradford, C. 2005. 'Global Governance for the 21st Century', The Brookings Institution Paper. Online: http://www.brookings.edu/views/papers/20051024bradford.pdf (accessed 15 December 2008).

Brown, C. 2000. 'Cosmopolitanism, World Citizenship, and Global Civil Society', *Critical Review of International Social and Political Philosophy* 3(1).

Bull, H. 1995. *The Anarchical Society: A Study of Order in World Politics (2nd edition)*. New York: Macmillan.

Commission on Global Governance. 1995. *Our Global Neighbour-hood: The Report of the Commission on Global Governance*. Oxford: Oxford University Press.

Connolly, W. E. 1995. *The Ethos of Pluralization*. Minneapolis: University of Minneapolis Press.

Cox, R. W. 1999. 'Civil Society at the Turn of the Millennium: Prospects for an Alternative World Order', *Review of International Studies* 25(1).

Dallmayr, F. 2003. 'Cosmopolitanism: Moral and Political', *Political Theory* 31(3).

Eschle, C. and Maiguashca, B. (eds). 2005. *Critical Theories, International Relations and 'The Anti-Globalization movement': The Politics of Global Resistance*. London: Routledge.

Falk, R. 1995. *On Humane Governance: Toward a New Global Politics*. Pennsylvania: Pennsylvania University Press.

Finkelstein, L. S. 1995. 'What Is Global Governance?', *Global Governance* 1(3).

Fuchs, D. A. 2002. 'Globalization and Global Governance: Discourses on Political Order at the Turn of the Century' in D. Fuchs and F. Kratochwil (eds), *Transformative Change and Global Order: Reflections on Theory and Practice*, Münster: LIT Verlag.

Grande, E. and Risse, T. 2000. 'Bridging the Gap. Konzeptionelle Anforderungen an die Politik wissenschaftliche Analyse von Globalisierungsprozessen', *Zeitschrift für Internationale Beziehungen*, 7(2).

Gruber, L. 2000. *Ruling the World: Power Politics and the Rise of Supranational Institutions*. Princeton: Princeton University Press.

Habermas, J. 2001. *The Postnational Constellation*, Cambridge, UK: Polity Press.

Hall, R. B. and Biersteker, T. J. (eds). 2002 *The Emergence of Private Authority in Global Governance*. Cambridge, UK: Cambridge University Press.

Harvey, D. 2005. *A Brief History of Neoliberalism*. Oxford: Oxford University Press.

Hasenclever, A., Mayer, P. and Rittberger, V. 1997. *Theories of International Regimes*. Cambridge, UK: Cambridge University Press.

Hass, P. 2004. 'Addressing the Global Governance Deficit', *Global Environmental Politics* 4(4).

Hirst, P. and Thompson, G. 1996. *Globalization in Question*. London: Blackwell.

Holsti, K. J. 1992. 'Governance without Government: Polyarchy in Nineteenth Century European International Politics' in J. Rosenau and E. Czempiel (eds), *Governance without Government: Order and Change in World*, Cambridge, Cambridge University Press.

Held, D. 1995. *Democracy and the Global Order: From the Modern State to Cosmopolitan Governance*. Cambridge, UK: Polity Press.

———.1998. 'Democracy and Globalization' in D. Archibugi, D. Held and M. Köhler (eds), *Reimagining Political Community: Studies in Cosmopolitan Democracy*, Stanford: Stanford University Press. Online: http://www.zmk.uni-freiburg.de/ss2000/texts/held.htm (accessed 14 December 2008).

———.2005. 'Globalization, International Law and Human Rights', Public Lecture on 20 September 2005 at Human Rights Centre, University of Connecticut. Online:http://www.lse.ac.uk/Depts/global/Publications/PublicLectures/PL_Globali zationInternationalLawandHumanRights.pdf (accessed 9 December 2008).

Held, D., McGrew, A., Glodbatt, D. and Perrato, J. 1999. *Global Transformations. Politics, Economics and Culture*. Stanford: Stanford University Press.

Jervis, R. 1999. 'Realism, Neoliberalism and Cooperation: Understanding the Debate', *International Security* 24(1).

Kaldor, M. 2003. 'The Idea of Global Civil Society', *International Affairs* 79(3).

———.2008. 'Crisis as prelude to a new Golden Age', *Open Democracy*. Online: http://www.opendemocracy.net/article/crisis-as-prelude-to-a-new-golden-age (accessed 14 January 2009).

Linklater, A.1998. *The Transformation of Political Community: Ethical Foundations of the Post-Westphalian Era*. Cambridge, UK: Polity Press.

Lipschutz, R. D. 1996. *Global Civil Society and Global Environmental Governance: The Politics of Nature from Place to Planet*. Albany: SUNY Press.

Mearscheimer, J. 1995. 'The False Promise of International Institutions', *International Security* 19(3).

Members of International Civil Society. 1999. *Statement from Members of International Civil Society Opposing a Millennium Round*, UK: Friends of the Earth.

Murphy, C. N. 2000. 'Global Governance: Poorly Done and Poorly Understood', *International Affairs* 76.

O'Brien, R., Goetz, A. M., Scholte, J. A. and Williams, M. 2000. *Contesting Global Governance: Multilateral Economic Institutions and Global Social Movement*s Cambridge, UK: Cambridge University Press.

Robertson, R.1990. *Globalisation: Social and Cultural Theory*. London: Sage.

Rose, N. 1999. *Powers of Freedom: Reframing Political Thought*. Cambridge, UK: Cambridge University Press.

Rosenau, J. N. 1995. 'Governance in the Twenty-first Century', *Global Governance* 1(1).

———.1992. 'Governance Order, and Change in World Politics' in J. N.

Rosenau (ed.), *Governance without Government*, Washington: George Washington University.

Ruggie, J. G. 1982. 'International Regimes, Transactions, and Change: Embedded Liberalism in the Postwar Economic Order', *International Organization* 36(2).

———.2000. 'J Douglas Gibson Lecture, Queen's University, ON, Canada' in Marc Plattner, *Democracy Without Borders: Global Challenges to Liberal Democracy*, Maryland: Rowman & Littlefield.

———.2001. 'Global Governance Net: The Global Compact as Learning Network', *Global Governance* 7(4).

Sachs, J. 1997. 'New Members Please Apply', *Time*.

Scholte, J. A. 2008. 'Reconstructing Contemporary Democracy', *Indiana Journal of Global Legal Studies* 15(1).

Shaw, M. 2000. *Theory of the Global State: Global Reality as an Unfinished Revolution*. Cambridge, UK: Cambridge University Press.

Stoker, G. 1998. 'Governance Theory: Five Propositions', *International Social Science Journal* 155.

United Nations Development Program. 1999. *Human Development Report*, New York: Oxford University Press.

Walker, R. B. J. 1993. *Inside/Outside: International Relations as Political Theory*. Cambridge, UK: Cambridge University Press.

Wapner, P. 1997. 'Governance in Global Civil Society' in Oran R.Young (ed.), *Global Governance: Drawing Insights from Environmental Experiences*, Cambridge: MIT Press.

Weiss, T. G. 2000. 'Governance, Good Governance and Global Governance: Conceptual and Actual Challenges', *Third World Quarterly* 21(5).

Young, O. R. 1999. *Governance in World Affairs*. Ithaca, New York: Cornell University Press.

Chapter 2

FOUR LESSONS FROM THE PRESENT GLOBAL FINANCIAL CRISIS FOR THE 21ST CENTURY: AN ESSAY ON GLOBAL TRANSFORMATION FROM A EUROPEAN PERSPECTIVE

Dirk Messner

All ages come to an end. The Ice Age was succeeded by the Bronze Age, the Renaissance was followed by the Reformation, great powers have succeeded one another, Rome, Great Britain, the US(Senge et al. 2008, 7). Nothing's here to stay. With the present financial crisis, another age is drawing to a close – but not, as many globalization critics may think with glee, the age of globalization. What we now see going down is an international order in which the Western societies are the center and the measure of all things (the G7 is a reflection of this eroding constellation of power), the age of industrialization (based as it was on the delusion of an infinite supply of natural resources and infinite capacities of the atmosphere, the oceans and the global forests to absorb greenhouse gas emissions and other collateral wastes of our consumption patterns), and the illusion that the nation-state could, despite accelerating globalization, somehow just muddle on as it has in the course of the past 200 years. The concern now is to create a truly viable, sustainable globalization that accepts the global challenges of the twenty-first century.

The present global financial debacle is opening up a window of opportunity to place these central challenges involved in building the world order of the 21st century squarely at the top of the agendas of world politics and of the global economy instead of merely talking on and on about them, as they have been talked about at the conferences of the World Economic

Forum, the World Social Summit of Non Governmental Organisations (NGO), or the German Bundestag's Commission of Inquiry on 'Globalization of the World Economy' (1998–2002) (Enquete Kommission Globalisierung der Weltwirtschaft 2003) – in order then to return to business as usual in the 'real world' of politics and economics.

What we need is a change of perspective. We need to adapt our institutions, policies, and business strategies to the new realities of a globalized world that we have been discussing for more than a decade without drawing the necessary political and economic conclusions. As Albert Einstein once noted succinctly, 'We can't solve problems by using the same kind of thinking we used when we created them.' There are four key lessons that we can learn from the financial crisis. They are not, per se, revolutionary, but the point that needs to be made is that they have until now not served as the basis of the strategic decisions made in business and politics. They are likely to be shared by many national and global decision-makers, indeed it is not seldom that we have heard these very same decision-makers utter them, though rarely in their main statements, more often over a second beer, among friends and colleagues or in unofficial speeches ... without political or economic impacts. The reason is simple: if these lessons were taken seriously they would contribute in key ways to setting the stage for a far reaching global transformation, that were, up to the present crisis, decried as unrealistic, naive and politically unrealizable. The key elements of this global transformation are:

- inventing an embedded global market economy, realizing that the utopia of a self-regulated market has failed as much as the utopia of socialism did only 20 years ago;
- organizing a peaceful global power transition, accepting that the Western hegemony is coming to an end;
- investing seriously in worldwide poverty reduction and strategies to avoid accelerated processes of social polarization, understanding that a global lack of social and human capital is the main driver of international instability, mistrust and violence;
- building a low carbon and resource efficient global economy to avoid dangerous changes in the Earth system, accepting that there is no polite way to say that the globally dominating business model, based on blind growth, fossil fuels and short-term investment returns is simply destroying the world.

In other words, the financial crisis is opening up a window of opportunity to bring about changes that would have no prospects of success in 'normal times'.

Four Lessons on the Road to Sustainable Globalization

The first lesson to be learned from the financial crisis is that the 'Milton Friedman Mode' has come to an end, the notion that the principles of self-interest and the market are sufficient to organize national economies and the world economy, indeed even societies and the emerging world society. In November 2008, in *Wirtschaftswoche* and the *Financial Times*, US economist Jagdish Bhagwati pointed out that the collapse of the dream of absolute self-regulation has set free, in the global financial markets, a huge potential for destructive creativity – reversing the Schumpeterian idea of the 'creative destruction' caused by technological innovation. The 'Milton Friedman Mode' is closely linked with the TINA concept propagated since the Reagan-Thatcher era: 'There Is No Alternative' to the unleashed market economy. The concern now is to embed the global economy in a new institutional framework – a Bretton Woods II – and all of a sudden the iron TINA makes place for a supple AUN: 'Alternatives Urgently Needed'. Institutional innovations are what is called for. The first international conference on the reorganization of the world's financial markets was held in November 2008 in Washington DC. The countries attending included not only the G7/8 but also important emerging countries like China, India, Brazil, South Africa and Saudi Arabia. The Washington conference will be followed by a series of high level meetings in 2009. What a new dynamic! Just some months ago no one would have thought possible a debate of this kind on the future of the world economic order. What is at stake now is nothing less than a sustainable regulatory course for the global economy, one that does justice to the diversity of market economies around the globe, now that the Wall Street model has, in the course of only some weeks at the end of 2008, self-destructed before our very eyes. It will be more than interesting to observe in 2009 what new ideas Europe, China, India, Brazil, South Africa and not at least the new US-administration have in mind for the debate on our common global future.

The second lesson implies a need to take leave of the idea that 'globalization is Westernization' (Kupchan 2002). China is already what the US has always claimed to be, an indispensable actor of world politics and the world economy: The world's third-largest economy, China now holds the world biggest currency reserves, amounting to US$ 1.8 trillion, and is developing a high level of innovative dynamism (Kaplinsky/Messner 2008). If India continues on the economic success path it embarked on a number of years ago, the two Asian giants will, in the coming two decades, profoundly alter the structures of the global economy. What we are witnessing is a set of tectonic power shifts. The winners of globalization are Asian. In addition, countries like Brazil, South Africa, and some Arab countries are on the rise (Khanna 2008). The G7/8 as the all-powerful governance center of the world economy is a thing of the past. The first discernible feature of the new multipolar order is a latent leadership crisis. The Obama administration will have to start out by cleaning up the collateral damage of the financial crisis and the impacts of the loss of US-soft power during the Bush administration, Europe is the most interesting laboratorium for regional cooperation and integration, but still lacks the global clout. The OECD world as a whole is going to have to learn to accept 'yesterday's have-nots' as genuine partners, and while China is powerful, it has yet to find a new global role for itself for the 21st century.

Power is in the midst of a process of global redistribution, and the emerging new regulatory pattern for the global economy is not yet discernible. All of the parties involved will have to show a good measure of sensibility, to build new trust, and in the wake of the Wall street disaster listening to and learning from one another is more important than ever. John Mearsheimer, a US political scientist and policy advisor, recently caused somewhat of a furor when he published a text entitled 'The rise of China will not be peaceful', arguing that a conflict between the US and China is unavoidable (Mearsheimer 2006). This statement is obviously exaggerated, even dangerous, because it could result in a self fulfilling prophecy. But many other authors argue that the rise of new global powers and the decline of old super powers have always been critical, often conflictive moments in history (Kennedy 1989, Kupchan et al. 2001, Humphrey/Messner 2008). It is absolutely clear, that there is no automatism towards a peaceful power transition. Political initiatives are needed to manage the ongoing global power shift. Against this background the conferences on the future of the financial markets offer an opportunity to create global commonalities and responsibilities and to reduce conflict potential. At the same time, the debate on the world economic order is ushering in a transition from the age of the classic nation-state, with the declarations of independence and claims to national sovereignty that have gone hand in hand with it to a globalized twenty-first century. The new body of rules governing the world economy must be based on something like a 'charter of global interdependencies'. Global governance is on its way to becoming a key concept of international politics. Old and new powers need to learn that there is no viable way back to classical power politics and hegemonic concepts of global leadership: the nineteenth and twentieth century thinking of global politics is coming to an end.

The third lesson we need to learn is that an ever more closely networked world economy is simply not compatible with a situation in which two billion people are forced to live on less than two dollars a day and social polarization in and between societies continues to accelerate. That is a dead-end road. And this is not only a normative or humanitarian statement. From a sustainable globalization perspective, the main messages is: There will be no way to put an end to state failure, violence, international terrorism unless 'globalization with a human face' becomes a lived reality. This simple truth must not be allowed to be drowned out by the clamor of the global financial crisis and the gloom of the coming recession. In the future we are going to have to get our priorities right. The fact that US$ 3 trillion have been mobilized for the war in Iraq, that only Europe at the end of 2008, in a mere week's time, has spanned a €2 trillion safety net for its banking system, while months and years are frittered away in negotiations with the developing countries on a support fund to finance the adaptation of vulnerable countries to climate change – and this in an age in which one third of mankind is forced to live on what, for western people, amounts to a half pack of cigarettes – this cannot be the final point of the process of human civilization. Now that the illusion is over that financial capital can be multiplied infinitely, and with returns of over 25 per cent, the time has come to invest in the social capital of world society. And 'peanuts' will not suffice to build a stable, secure and legitimate new world order.

What can developing countries expect in coming months and years, as a result of the global financial crisis and the emerging global recession (Maxwell and Messner 2008)? We know what global economic turbulences will mean for poor countries because we have been here before. Beginning thirty years ago the oil price shock of the late 1970s, combined with successive debt crises, pushed many developing countries, especially in Africa, into Balance of Payments and fiscal problems which left them running for help to the International Monetary Fund and the World Bank. A long period of so-called 'structural adjustment' followed. Slowly, and often controversially, macro-economic balances were re-established. But in the meantime growth was often negative, investment collapsed, poverty rocketed and malnutrition spread like a disease. It is not for nothing that the 1980s are known as the lost decade of African and Latin American development. By its close Africa had fallen even further behind the rest of the world.

The impacts of the recent crisis are already on the way in the developing world. Their exports will fall, in both price and volume, affecting also service exports like tourism. Remittances will shrink. Foreign Direct Investment is likely to fall. Aid is very unlikely to rise as promised. Another lost decade is on the cards. In a globally interconnected world, that is not only bad news for the poor, but also for the international system as a whole.

The fourth lesson is that unmitigated climate change threatens to radically alter the Earth system. The climate crisis is in essence an energy, food, and security crisis, one that will pose far greater challenges for our industrial growth capitalism than the deep recent crisis of the financial system. Never before in the history of modern mankind have global temperatures risen as rapidly as they are set to do in the present century if climate policy fails to achieve results. Climate change could trigger tipping points in the Earth's system (Lenton et al. 2008): The

Amazon rainforest could fall victim to desiccation, the monsoon systems in Asia could collapse, 40 per cent of the world species could vanish. Drought, water scarcity, extreme weather events and rises in sea levels could overstrain the adaptive capacities of many societies in the second half of the century. These climate impacts will be exacerbated by a number of other scarcity problems, leading the implicit assumption on which the age of industrialism was based–infinite availability of natural resources – ad absurdum: peak oil, peak soil, peak water. All this we know from the reports issued in 2007 by the UN Development Programme and the Intergovernmental Panel on Climate Change (IPCC). In a report published in 2008, the German Advisory Council on Global Change (WBGU 2008a) underlines that climate change constitutes an international security risk. The UK economist Nicolas Stern, who sees climate change as the greatest market failure in the history of mankind, has calculated the immense costs of climate change (Stern 2006). They would far exceed the costs caused by the present financial crisis, to say nothing of the fact that the effects of climate change would be irreversible – for example, beginning at a certain point, it will prove impossible to stop the melting of the polar ice caps, and the impacts will haunt us for thousands of years to come. Mankind seems to be doing its level best to ruin the Earth system as a whole. Virtually no one disagrees with this statement – not in Berlin, not in London, Beijing, New Delhi, nor in Washington, not even in the headquarters of most business corporations.

The process of global change needed to meet this challenge facing mankind is huge in scope and the pressure to act is growing by the day. A global climate regime must be in place by the end of 2009. In order to avoid dangerous climate change, from 2015 on, global emissions must start to decline throughout the world. By 2050 the OECD countries must reduce their greenhouse gas emissions by 80 per cent. China will have to contribute by gradually reducing its per capita emissions, even though several hundred million people in China continue to live close to or below the poverty line. And the bad news is that the world is still far away from being on track! On the contrary, global warming is even accelerating: greenhouse gas emissions are growing much faster in the current decade than during the 1980–90s, the carbon intensity of the global economy is increasing and the efficiency of CO^2 sinks on land and oceans in absorbing anthropogenic emissions is declining. 'All of these changes characterize a carbon cycle that is generating stronger-than-expected and sooner-than-expected climate forcing'.(Canadell et al. 2007) Avoiding dangerous global warming is a task of huge dimensions. And even though this is all common sense we still have to look far and wide for actors prepared to embark on courses even close to adequate to the dimensions of the challenge. What we see at work here is a repression easily as virulent as what we saw in the years in which the present financial crisis was brewing. People, political systems, and business enterprises seem to find it troublesome to think ahead, or indeed to act on the basis of a long-term perspective. However, what is at stake is perfectly clear: transition from the fossil to the non-fossil world economy-a truly millennial task in the wake of 200 years of natural-resource-driven growth. The necessity of building a world energy system based very largely on renewable resources will prove to be one of the major challenges of the decades to come. That this 'third industrial revolution', of which John Schellnhuber of the Potsdam Institute for Climate Impact Research has been speaking for years, is likely to come about on the basis of corporate pledges and self-regulation of the market – that is something that today not even an Alan Greenspan would assert.

Taking these four lessons together, we see clearly that we are faced with a radical, far reaching global transformation. Problems that have been discussed, and just as quickly repressed, for some two decades now may in this way be brought into clearer focus. The question that needs to be answered is what direction efforts to set the stage for this transformation will take – above and beyond the need to stabilize and reorganize the world's financial markets.

Some Relevant Steps into the Right Direction

Five steps mark the path to a reshaping of the global order. And I see a special role for Europe – as the largest trading partner of the developing countries, the largest provider of development aid, the key protagonist on climate change and a region with dense cultural and political networks across all developing regions. As the global development agenda moves rapidly from a national preoccupation to one which requires cross-country collaboration, Europe might be well-placed to bring together its economic, political and also military assets.

First, successful management of the current economic global crisis requires a clear-sighted focus on the welfare of the poorest. In the 1980s, UNICEF in particular pioneered the idea of 'adjustment with a human face'. Thirty years later we need to focus on the safety nets, welfare programmes, long-term investment in health and education and employment prospects of the poorest. UK Prime Minister Gordon Brown has recognised this in the UK. The EU should now play a far more visible role in the multilateral development agencies and it should take the lead by presenting in 2009 a development policy action plan designed to respond to the impacts of the financial crisis in the developing world. For an immediate crisis response it is important that multi and bilateral donors provide quick-disbursing funds and play a countercyclical role by providing credit in areas from which private banks have retreated. Globally, we need to 'manage recession with a human face' (Maxwell/Messner 2009).

In practice this means a double guarantee: to individuals that their welfare will be protected by means of social security programmes and to countries that help will be provided with the costs of social protection, so that budget deficits and inflation do not spiral out of control. The World Food Programme (WFP) plays a vital role to stabilize social safety nets. Therefore the WFP should be fully funded on a long-term rather than on an ad hoc basis. The world showed that it could mobilise on these fronts to tackle the 2008 crisis of rising food prices. It must do so again to tackle next year's crisis of failing livelihoods. It follows that aid flows must be not just sustained but increased. Rich countries made ambitious promises at the Gleneagles Summit of the G8 in 2005, and have repeated them many times since, most recently at the EU Council in June 2008, the Hokkaido G8 in July and the Doha Financing for Development Conference in November 2008. But actual delivery is currently 30 per cent below the target for 2010.

Meanwhile, the talk is of cutting aid, not increasing it. Italy, for example, has proposed cuts of up to 56 per cent in its latest budget. The UK so far is holding firm and Germany is working hard towards its target. Quite right. It would be a bad start for the project of building 'a social market economy on a global scale' of which German Chancellor Merkel has spoken if the bailout of the global banking system were to entail budget cuts affecting the poorest 20 per cent of mankind. Those intent on preventing the emergence of further anti-Western resentments should have no trouble understanding the logic of aid.

Beyond this kind of 'managing recession with a human face programme' global development cooperation should focus soon on a key long-term issue: investments in agriculture need to be increased in many developing countries. At the global horizon the problem of competing land use and soil scarcity is emerging, food security might be at stake: the world population increases to around 9 billion in 2050, global food production must be raised by 50 per cent during the next two – three decades, bioenergy will gain importance and land-intensive food consumption patterns become ever more widespread – not least as a result of dynamic economic development in Asia. Against this background, global land-use management will become a key future task if land-related conflicts are to be avoided (WBGU 2008b). The EU should place this challenge on the global development agenda.

Second, the search for a new globalization must not become the march to anti-globalization. Markets have stumbled, not failed. They need to be managed, not mauled. For a generation, trade has grown at twice the rate of economies overall and this has contributed to poverty reduction on a scale not seen since the Industrial Revolution. But at the same time, income inequality has risen too fast and has sometimes reduced the size of benefits to the poor, so better and more progressive tax regimes are needed around the world. Investment in better regulation and better national and global public goods are also needed to reverse recession, and create the possibility of further, shared growth.

Trade liberalization would be of value, but we are realistic about the scope for a successful Doha Development deal, at least in 2009. As others have observed, however, there may be other routes to trade facilitation, not least investment in infrastructure in the poorest countries, to reduce costs. In Uganda, for example, according to Tony Blair's Africa Commission, poor roads are equivalent to an 80 per cent tariff on textile exports.

Regarding the global financial sector a new global institutional framework is needed. It must be based on the ideas of transparency, reliable risk management, long-term thinking and investment instead of high risk and short-term speculation and control mechanisms to cope with the complexity of financial products and processes. Beyond this highly relevant global governance issues public development institutions, particularly from current account surplus countries with excess savings (Germany, but also Japan and China) should increase their capital and co-finance emergency-lending to stabilize safety nets and long-term investments in developing countries. OECD countries should understand that, given the interdependencies between global markets, increases in investments in emerging markets and developing countries are as beneficial to themselves as the envisaged domestic fiscal stimuli on which they are currently concentrated. After recycling global surpluses for the consumption in the US and instead of buying toxic assets, there should be a process of long term investments in clean energy and sustainable agriculture in developing countries with large investment gaps and therefore high returns (Wolff 2008).

Third, the climate summit set for Copenhagen in late 2009 must not end in failure. The looming recession has led some in the business community and some governments to question the EU's climate targets. Instead, Europe must retain its pioneering role in climate policy, with concrete proposals for what Achim Steiner at the UN Environment Programme called a Green New Deal. The forces in support of the status quo are considerable. But everyone knows that we have to rebuild our economies anyway. Our short term oriented financial sectors collapsed and maintaining our fossil based growth models would result in dangerous climate change within the next generation. Long term, strategic thinking and decision making is required. That's why the financial crisis is a chance to define now future oriented incentive structures and rules towards a global low carbon economy. We need to fight the impacts of the financial crisis, the recession and climate change simultaneously with significant low carbon investments, innovation initiatives, and eco-efficiency oriented business models. Most of the anti-crisis investment programmes of European governments, formulated at the end of 2008, are disappointing against this background, because they do not link the considerable public investments and growth policies with a clear and long term perspective to build bridges into a non-fossil era.

A key priority must be the creation of an international carbon market: carbon taxes, a cap-and-trade system, a renewable energy mandate – or some combination of all of these. Unambiguous commitments, like those proposed in the UK's new Climate Change Bill, would create the incentives for transformative behavior by businesses and for 'green innovators' across the globe. Given that the new US administration is thinking exactly into this direction, a future oriented carbon market could emerge as an interesting arena for a renewed transatlantic partnership and for a global alliance to avoid dangerous climate change.

Large-scale public and private investments in renewable energy need to be part of the New Deal. The German Advisory Council on Global Change (WBGU) has proposed setting up an internationally visible European-Chinese-Indian Research Institute for Efficient Energy Systems dedicated to jointly training the engineers needed to get on with the task of building a non-fossil global energy system (see www.wgbu.de). A climate and energy flagship project of this kind with the two central new powers of the twenty-first century, open for other actors to join, would serve to underline that the next wave of innovation in the world economy must be based on low-carbon technologies. At the same time, and mindful of the need for a global balance of interests, rich countries should launch an initiative designed to provide significant contributions to reducing the energy poverty presently affecting 2.3 billion people throughout the world (WBGU 2008b, 305).

As another cornerstone of a low carbon transformation strategy the EU should also launch a significant programme designed to develop climate-compatible cities. Over 50 per cent of mankind lives in cities, and the figure is rising. Cities are responsible for 75 per cent of global energy consumption and 80 per cent of energy-related greenhouse gas emissions. By 2020 it would be important for 200 European cities to be able to demonstrate how greenhouse gases can be effectively reduced by 80 per cent by the year 2050. An initiative of this kind would be a major generator of jobs and green innovation. There are already some models. In the south of Shanghai, an eco-city called Dongtan is being built for a population of 80,000; in Abu Dhabi (United Arab Emirates) the renowned British architect Norman Foster plans to build a sustainable city. Until now, nothing comparable exists in Europe or the US.

Let us think positively for a moment. We might see an interesting domino effect during 2009–10. Imagine the EU moving into the low carbon direction, improving its future oriented competitive advantages. And imagine the new US President Obama, translating into political and economic practice what his climate policy advisors has been telling him and the US audience during the election campaign in 2008, again and again: fighting climate change via innovation is like investing into the next green Silicon Valley. If this dynamic would accelerate we would obviously see a rethinking of economic strategies in Beijing too. This story is about leadership, vision, and realism – accepting simply the limits of the Earth System.

Fourth, the need for global collective action is an inescapable conclusion of recent events. Efforts towards effective global governance initiatives and processes should be pushed forward. Coordinated action has been essential to prevent financial contagion. As even the former President Bush and Alan Greenspan have recognized, new initiatives will be needed to buttress the security of financial markets, with new regulatory regimes.

It is important to make sure that developing countries are fully engaged in these discussions. Resentment was already evident about who is or who is not on the invitation list for Washington in November 2008. It cannot be right for all except the richest members of the world community to be presented with a done deal imposed without consent. At the same time, and as the President of the World Bank, Robert Zoellick, has recently observed, there is no time to argue the fine points of who might or might not have a Security Council seat or membership of the G-20. A flexible, network solution is needed, open and participatory, but focused on decision-making. A middle way is needed between the closed shop of the UN Security Council and what has come to look like the talking shop of the World Trade Organisation (WTO).

The EU may have models to offer. The model of Qualified Majority Voting reflects many painful compromises in EU Councils, but does offer a way of taking different interests into account (Maxwell and Messner 2008). Could this be applied in the Economic and Social Council (ECOSOC), or even in the General Assembly? Alternatively, is it time to revisit the idea of an Economic Security Council, taking into account the enormous challenges that global poverty, resource scarcity and climate change imply? Could the EU ask people like Kofi Annan, Wangari Maathai, Klaus Töpfer and Rajendra Pachauri to formulate the three or four most pressing institutional reforms of the United Nations, based on all the existing reports on more effective and legitimate multilateral governance, and could Europe mobilize the political power to make real progress in this field? Now, as many decision makers understand, that global problems need global solutions and effective global organizations. And beyond intergovernmental multilateralism it seems obvious that flexible global governance networks might prove quite effective. If Europe looks around for partners in the climate arena, the new US President might be an ally (hopefully), it would make sense to try to make NEPAD a strong climate partner, but there are other important actors with significant power resources too: the World Business Council for Sustainable Development, the C-40 Cities, a group of the world's largest cities to tackle climate change, the multitude of 'climate and development oriented NGOs' in Europe and worldwide, the World Economic Forum's Global Agenda Councils, with several hundred opinion leaders, or management gurus like Peter Senge (Senge et al. 2008) and Thomas Friedman (Friedman 2008). Global Governance is not only about states. Flexible global governance networks could create political momentum.

Fifth, we need to recognize that all these reform initiatives are not at all purely technocratic. Mental maps have to change. The narrow shareholder concept as a role model for the global economy and the power politics idea as a blueprint to organize global politics should be substituted by a set of ideas, compatible with the challenges of the twenty-first century:

- investing in the regeneration of social and natural capital as the foundations of all real wealth,
- accelerating social innovations, adaptation, and learning by nurturing cultural diversity (Senge 2008, 353),
- increasing economic efficiency by revolutionizing resource and energy efficiency,
- balancing interests and competition of and between states, economies and individual actors with global governance initiatives characterized by norms like fairness, cooperation, mutual trust and recognition – not in a naïve sense, but understanding that global interdependencies require a new level of international cooperation,
- recognizing that, as the Indian cultural historian Homi Bhabha said, dialogue on an equal footing in a globally interconnected world is possible only if we succeed in comprehending our own national and regional interests and identities as radically incomplete,
- learning that climate change places as on a much large stage in time, because human activities are threatening the Earth's system longer-term climate process itself.

My suggestion is that Europe should move forward this outlined global development agenda. Europe's unity, built over the past generation, sprang from the pain of two wars. We face new sources of pain and enormous new global challenges during the coming years. 2009 is an important year for Europe, with elections to the European Parliament in June and a new Commission taking office in November. The survival or otherwise of the Lisbon Treaty will also be decided. Everyone knows that European partnership is difficult, often even stressful. But the 'Building Europe – Strategy' of the last two decades, aimed at integrating the former socialist economies of Eastern Europe into the European Union is no longer enough. Europe needs to define rapidly its role as a responsible global actor. Globalization is at a crossroad – Europe needs to act, not alone, acting with others. Delivering Bretton Woods II – and contributing to build a sustainable globalization.

References

Canadell, J. et al. 2007. 'Contributions to accelerating atmospheric CO^2 growth from economic activity, carbon intensity, and efficiency of natural sinks', *PNAS*, November 20, No. 47, 18866–18870 (www.pnas.org).

Enquete Kommission des Deutschen Bundestages Globalisierung der Weltwirtschaft. 2003. *Globalisierung der Weltwirtschaft.* Herausforderungen und Antworten, Berlin: Deutscher Bundestag.

Gu, J., Humphrey, J. and Messner, D. 2008. 'Global Governance and developing countries: The implications of the rise of China', *World Development* (36)2.

IPCC. 2007. *Climate Change 2007.* Synthesis Report, www.ipcc.ch

Kaplinsky, R. and Messner, D. 2008. 'Introduction: The Impacts of the Asian Drivers on the Developing World', *World Development* (36)2.

Kennedy, P. 1989. *The Rise and the Fall of Big Powers.* New York: Vintage Books.

Khanna, P. 2008. *The Second World. Empires and Influence in the New Global Order.* New York: Random House.

Kupchan, C. et al. 2001. *Power in transition: The Peaceful Change of International Order,* Tokyo/ New York: United Nations University Press.

Kupchan, C. 2002. 'The End of the West', *The Atlantic Monthly* (4).

Lenton et al. 2008. 'Tipping Elements in the Earth's Climate System', *PNAS* (6). (www.pnas.org)

Maywell, S. and Messner, D. 2008. 'A New Global Order. Bretton Woods II and San Francisco II', *Open Democracy* (11). Online: www.opendemocracy.net

Mearsheimer, J. 2006. 'China's Unpeaceful Rise', *Current History* (105).

Senge, P. et al. 2008. *The Necessary Revolution: How individuals and organizations are working together to create a sustainable world.* New York/ London: Doubleday.

Stern, N. 2006. *The Economics of Climate Change.* London: HM Treasury.

UNDP. 2008. *Human Development Report 2007/2008: Fighting Climate Change.* New York: Palgrave Macmillan.

WBGU (German Advisory Council on Global Change). 2008a.: *Climate Change as a Security Risk.* London: Earthscan.

————.2008b. *Zukunftsfähige Bioenergie und nachhaltige Landnutzung.* Berlin: Springer Verlag.

Winters, A. and Yusuf, S. 2007. *Dancing with Giants. China, India, and the Global Economy.* Washington: World Bank.

Chapter 3

GLOBAL CIVIL SOCIETY: EMERGENT FORMS OF COSMOPOLITAN DEMOCRACY AND JUSTICE

Ashwani Kumar

Introduction

In this chapter, I argue for the global civil society as normatively and theoretically a new paradigm of global governance and also a possible emancipatory 'cosmopolitan political project' to the emerging challenges of democracy, justice and inclusive governance at the global level. Though global civil society is often perceived as a multilayered, contested and decentred space of associtionalism, I consider it an epic and irreversible 'double movement' of people seeking to transform hegemonic structures of global governance, protect human rights, minimize violence and increase the sphere of democratic life across the borderless world. And I suggest that this argument can be further explored, expanded and defended by offering at least four reasons.

First, I argue that globalization, benign or regressive, has created unique 'political opportunity structures and processes' rendering state-centric conventional theories of international relations and global governance completely irrelevant. Fuelled by the twin processes of associational and informational revolutions in the 1980s, global civil society has slowly and sturdily emerged as 'a supranational sphere of social and political participation' for a vast majority of people who have had not opportunity in the past to be heard in the hegemonic structures of international organizations. It is clear from the scope, reach and velocity of globalization that sovereignty of the modern nation-state has exhausted its imaginative power to continually secure the consent and allegiance of the population living under its shadow. Though it remains differentiated from the state and market, it is not neutral to power relations constituted, informed and transformed by state and market. In other words, global civil society not only 'feeds on and reacts to globalization', it also remains relatively autonomous in its character and aspirations (Anheier, Glasius et al. 2001).

Second, given its mind-boggling diversity of actors, range of issues and strategies, global civil society has inverted the traditional boundaries between the state (political power) and the civil society in almost all parts of the world. Building on traditions of anti-colonial struggles against imperialism, legacies of the socialist internationalism, humanitarian interventions and inspired by Central European and Latin American struggles against the dictatorial regimes in the 1980s, the global civil society has transgressed the nation-bound concept of civil society, overturned the 'imagined nationalism' and also rejected 'methodological nationalism'. In reality, it owes its existence to 'multiplicity of points of resistance' located spatially yet deterritorialized enough to embrace the entire globe. In this sense, global civil society 'resembles a bazaar' of democratic protest anchored in the ever growing multiplying encounters among nations, races, classes, languages, regions, religious, etc across the globe. Given its potential and penchant to organize protest at multiple points simultaneously without any fixed centre, global civil society has challenged newer forms of 'mobile, slippery, shifty, evasive and fugitive power' structures of what Bauman calls 'liquid modernity' (Bauman 2000).

Third, global civil society has interestingly become at once an open confrontational space for 'headline-grabbing protests, demonstrations, and rebellions', and lesser-visible yet powerful forms of 'everyday struggles of resistance' by subordinate groups around the world (Scott 1990). At times, global civil society mobilizes, organizes and guides groups and individuals in a definitive strategic to achieve concrete victories over their adversaries. Often, global civil society ends up only 'inflaming certain points of the body, certain movements in life and certain types of behaviour' in the multivocal global struggles against existing network of power relations (Foucault 1980). In short, each resistance of the global civil society is a special type of resistance linked into a loose, mobile, transparent transnational network of social movements and grassroots civil society groups. Even where global civil society fails to register concrete gains, its 'peripheral' effects continue to energize future struggles against social exclusion of multiple kinds and forms. In short, global civil society represents no permanent headquarters of resistance where all the power of the counterpublics is concentrated and locked into zero-sum struggles with predatory practices of regressive globalization. In contrast, it is produced from 'one moment to the next moment' of struggle, dissent and protest against the evils effects of 'turbo capitalism' and also 'protection-failures' of the modern welfare state system (Keane 2001; Jones 1999).

Fourth, though global civil society has come to be seen by many as a genuine and novel expression of 'transnational networks' of social movements and global resistance, it still remains sufficiently 'fuzzy', meaningfully problematic and deeply contested. Raising the issues of representation, voice, integrity, autonomy and agency, critics of global civil society often forcefully and perhaps legitimately argue that 'for like national civil societies, global civil society is also dominated by a handful of agents, and like national civil societies not all actors find either access to or voice in this sphere'(Chandhoke 2005). In other words, global civil society has been seen by many as a thinly disguised form of continued dominance of urban, industrialized, technologically superior liberal democratic Western societies over the poor and impoverished southern societies in which majorities of the disadvantaged and marginalized people of the world live (Shaw 1999). Despite these accusations and charges, global civil society has often successfully mobilized global public opinion against the 'economic orthodoxies of neoliberalism and the '"inverted" totalitarianism' and environmental decay across borders.

I will develop my argument and defend the reasons outlined above in a theoretical, analytical and descriptive way. First, I will sketch the historical origins and conflicting meanings of the notion of global civil society. Then I will attempt to theorize on the reality and limitations of global civil society. In the final section, I propose to elaborate on the charges of the critics of global civil society and also make an attempt to defend it as a cosmopolitan project.

Conceptual Framework: What is Global Civil Society?

A few decades age, the term 'global civil society' would not only have only been problematic, but also seen as 'imaginary' at best and an oxymoron at the worst. Not because the term was never heard in some muted or hybrid sense in discourses on the international relations, international political economy, security studies, development and democracy, but also because attempts to unravel what Immanuel Kant called 'universal civil society' (*einer allgemin das Recht verwaltenden burgerlichen Gesellschaft*) often tended to confine rapidly increasing and proliferating waves of social struggles for 'transnational democratizing projects' within the physical, political and chronological borders of nation-state (Rupert 2000). The idea that civil society (*societas civils*) is nation bound and associationalism is a privilege of rich Western democratic nations had ultimately been given a dramatic burial by the fury of globalizing forces released by the collapse of Soviet Union, the rediscovery of 'civil society' and the revolution in information and communication technology (ICT) in the 1980s. This led to emergence of multiple global public spheres as 'global networks', 'scapes', or 'f lows' (Castells 1996; Appadurai 1990; Urry 2000). In other words, discourses on global civil society have been shaped by globalization, especially 'globalization-from-below'. In fact, identifying global civil society as a new kind of 'social activism' arising out of globalization, Richard Falk writes,

> Global civil society refers to the field of action and thought occupied by individual and collective initiatives of a voluntary, non-profit character both within states and transnationally. These initiatives proceed from a global orientation and are responses, in part at least, to certain globalizing tendencies that are perceived to be partially or totally adverse...The historic role of globalization-from-below is to challenge and transform the negative features of globalization-from-above, both by providing alternative ideological and political space to that currently occupied by market-oriented and statist outlooks and by offering resistances to the excesses and distortions that can be properly attributed to globalization in its current phase. (Falk 1998, 26:99–110)

Indeed, global civil society has been defined instrumentally and structurally by a constituency of non-governmental organizations (NGOs) and grassroots civil society organizations as a means and ways of 'forging private troubles into public issues' into an increasingly globalized world to counter balance the neoliberal institutions of global governance (Bauman 1999). This so-called 'army of termites eating away the wooden structure of a house inch by inch' derives its multiple meanings from mobile and organic quality of historical contexts, political struggles and moral courage (Cheru 1997). The puzzling diversity of actors and porosity of boundaries of global civil society has led scholars and observers to cast it as an ambiguous, amorphous, romantic, and contested concept in social science literature and policy circles. Surprisingly, despite its newness and concomitant fuzziness civil society scholars and activists have not been deterred from generating lively, provocative and proactive social science literature on the concept of global civil society (Scholte 2000; Baker 2002; Kaldor 2003; Keane 2003; Taylor 2004; Germain and Kenny 2005; Bartelson 2006). Interestingly, the notion of global civil society is so fuzzy and puzzling that it has also been described and explored variously as 'global citizen action', 'global village', 'global civilization', 'global/transnational social movements', 'transnational advocacy networks', 'a new multilateralism', etc.(Keck and Sikkink 1998; McLuhan 1989; Falk 1990; Edwards and Gaventa 2001; Cohen and Rai 2000; Khagram, Riker et.al. 2002). Several edited volumes have been produced to document, explore and analyse various dimensions of global civil society (Willetts 1996; Florini 2000; Scholte and Schnabel,2002; Clark 2003). The London School of Economics' prestigious annul publication *LSE Yearbook on Global Civil Society* has emerged as the major guide on the changing contours of global civil society since 2001

(Anheier, Glasius et al. 2001). More importantly, the editors and authors of the LSE Yearbook have strongly resisted the dominant knowledge claims of the reigning ideology of 'methodological nationalism' and insisted on replacing it by what they called 'methodological cosmopolitanism'. In the very first edition, they argue thattransnational civil society requires a 'transdisciplinary social science' (Anheier, Glasius et.al. 2001). Explaining the growing need for a paradigmatic shift in the social sciences, Ulrich Beck provocatively writes,

> in order to analyze the dynamics of global civil society...we need a methodological shift from the dominant national perspective to a cosmopolitan perspective....Methodological nationalism equates societies with nation-state societies and sees states and their governments as the corner stone of social science analysis... As long as the national perspective reins both in political action and a social science analysis, poverty and wealth will continue to be localized in the national, not the global context.(Beck 2003, 45–6).

In short, the emergence of global civil society is deeply informed by the emergence of an epistemic community looking for alternative epistemological and ontological ideas, discourses and practices of global governance.

Theorizing and Analysing Global Civil Society

Historically speaking, global civil society has appeared as the 'sphere of cross-border relations and collective activities outside the international reach of states and markets' (Pianta 2001, 171). Of course, realists in international relations theory and purists in political sociology on the state-society relations happily dismiss the notion as an oxymoron, arguing that civil society can only exist and flourish within the confines of nation-state system. Though liberals, communitarians, radicals, conservatives, globalizers and anti-globalizers vehemently and vociferously disagree on the nature of 'global' and 'civil society', it has increasingly become an axiomatic truth that the so-called 'protean', 'promiscuous', 'unfamiliar neologism of the 1990s' – global civil society – today matters in realizing the dreams of just global order. Reflecting on global civil society as the unfolding march of cosmopolitan democracy, Mary Kaldor joyfully writes

> Global Civil Society ... is about 'civilizing' or democratising globalization, about the process through which groups, movements and individuals can demand a global rule of law, global justice and global empowerment. (Kaldor 2003, 12)

It is instructive to note that the Hegelian holy trinity of family, civil society and state in traditional political theory does not envisage the possibility of an autonomous sphere of political action at the global level. In contrast to the linear and bounded Hegelian conception of civil society in which human beings are mere bearers of interests or commodity, we often find a multivocal unbounded associational space in which human beings are active agents of change at the global level. In practical terms, this actually means that global civil society is an intentionally organized, politically constituted and relatively spontaneous space of freedom to mobilize defiant, restive, non-coercive and non-hierarchical 'counterpublics' at various transit points across borders. The Focauldian 'points, knots or focuses of resistance' in global civil society are spread over at varying densities, ambitions and capacities in a seamless web of social movements, international NGOs, grassroots civil societies, advocacy groups, charity organizations, business forums etc. Identifying global qualities of civil society, Jan Scholte argues,

> [global civil society] encompasses civil activity that (a) addresses transworld issues; (b) involves transborder commutation; (c) has a global organization; (d) works on premise of supranational solidarity. Often these four attributes go hand in hand, but civil associations can also have a global character in one or several of these four respects. For example, localized groups those campaigns on a supraterritorial problem like climate change could be considered part of global civil society even though the associating lacks a transborder organization and indeed might only rarely communicate with civil groups elsewhere in the world. Conversely, global civil networks might mobilize in respect of a local development like the 1994 genocide in Rawanda. (Scholte 1999)

Thus global civil society is understandably quite messy as it includes both southern grassroots civil society groups who make use of transnational networks or who address their demands to intergovernmental/ multilateral agencies to ameliorate their conditions, publicize their campaigns for social justice and human rights as well as Northern-based NGOs, think tanks, charity organizations, human rights groups, labour unions, peasant associations, business forums, research and advocacy groups who campaign about global issues like development, climate, poverty, interstate conflicts etc.

In short, global civil society links and organizes vertically and horizontally both 'spectacles of resistance' at the global level and 'everyday struggles' at the grassroots around the world. Though it was originally influenced by the classic distinctions between state and market, public and private sphere and civil and political in the domestic sphere of politics, global civil society has gradually emerged as the most genuine and novel expression of uniting rapidly proliferating 'transnational networks' of social movements with the mindboggling array of grassroots civil society organizations in various parts of the world. It has increasingly come to stand for a new political agency of those struggling for democratic rights and social justice amidst the pressures of globalization. Secondly, the various associational networks and forums have also come to be known for innovating and practicing new entrepreneurial skills in influencing and changing the policy-making environment at the local, regional and international level. Within this context of transnational social movements, global civil society has played an increasing role in radicalizing global governance policies, especially in regard to the needs for global democracy, human rights, social justice and environmental sustainability. Dramatically arising out of the cataclysmic political events in the 1980s described variously as 'anti-politics', 'parallel polis', 'living in truth', 'power of the powerless', 'revolt against totalitarian regimes', 'third wave of democracy' etc., global civil society has now become the sufficiently autonomous associational space for global resistance against the iniquitous global order. Reflecting on the historical experience of the birth of global civil society, John Keane writes

[global civil society] was "born at the three overlapping streams of concern among publically minded intellectuals at the end of the 1980s; the revival of the old language of civil society, especially in central–eastern Europe, after the military crushing of the Prague Spring in 1968; the new awareness, stimulated by the peace and ecological movements, of ourselves as members of a fragile and potentially self-destructive world system; and the widespread perception that the implosion of soviet type communist systems implied a new global order. (Keane 2001, 23)

In this new emancipatory project of global order, the world no longer resembles/ looks like anarchic fearful Hobessian order but increasingly appears as a desirable, possible, palpable, intimate sphere of ordinary people resisting the hegemonic institutions, norms and rules of global governance dominated by customary international governmental organizations. Despite political, ideological and cultural differences among the various stake-holders of the civil society, the core of the global civil society is constituted by voluntary associations outside the realms of the state and the market. (Habermas 1992a, 453; Keane 1988a, 14). Theoretically, the emergence of global civil society has followed a different historical route; it has not only redefined the traditional boundaries between the state and civil society, but also bypassed the traditional hierarchies of nation-state system. Though inspired by a Gramscian conceptualization of civil society as historically contingent 'non-state and non-economic space of social interaction', global civil society has refused to be part of state (political society) in its limited sense of administrative, governmental and coercive apparatus. In other words, global civil society forums and networks do not attempt to stand as protective shields behind the rapidly crumbling structures of nation-states. Therefore, the apparently contradictory and discordant ensemble of the global civil society forums and networks is actually the reflection of formation of a new 'historic bloc' in which the nation-state has exhausted its potential to rule over people. The reflective, dialogical and deliberative character of global civil society and its potential to reinvigorate democratic process in the emerging structures of global governance have been grounded in the deliberate efforts to discover, promote and protect newer participatory public spaces at the global level. Philosophically speaking, global civil society is an attempt to release us from the bondage of what philosopher Habermas calls 'philosophy of subject'. Seen from this perspective, global civil society is materially and discursively a new order of 'communicative rationality'. Defining the nature of this rationality, Habermas writes,

> The communicative rationality recalls older ideas of logos, inasmuch as it brings along with it the connotations of a non- coercively unifying, consensus building force of a discourse in which the participants overcome their at first subjectively based views in favour of a rationally motivated agreement. (Habermas 1987)

Inspired by Habermasian ideas of freely and publicly argued rational discourse, the World Social Forum, a major constituent forum of global civil society, identifies itself as 'an open meeting place for reflective thinking, democratic debate of ideas, free exchange of experiences, interlinking for effective action, by groups, and movements of civil society that are opposed to neo-liberalism and domination of the world by capital and any form of imperialism, and are committed to building a society centred on the human person'. Seen from this non-institutional social movement perspective, global civil society is a seamless web of citizen-centric solidaristic (it is innovative use—keep it) and volunteristic activities for justice at the global level. It is true that 'civil society', understood by Tocqueville as the autonomous 'associational life', significantly enhances the capability of democracy to counteract authoritarian powers of the state, but only a 'school of virtue' or mere 'civility' is not enough to check and alter the power imbalances in society, local or global. In fact, prominent East European dissidents such as Havel, Weffort etc., discovered Tocquvellian associational space to express their disillusionment not only with state power, but also with mass politics. They succeeded in overthrowing the authoritarian state, but failed in mobilizing people against the lingering layers of inequity in the society. In contrast, global civil society values autonomy of the associational space but also resists 'uncivil' structures of inequality and social exclusion. In other words, global civil society is neither a romanticized Lockean contract between governed and governor nor a simple uncomplicated abstract Hegelian 'system of needs'. Writing on emancipatory potential of civil society, Robert Cox argues,

> Civil Society is not just an assemblage of actors, i.e. autonomous social groups. It is also the realm of contesting ideas in which the intersubjectivity meaning upon which people's sense of 'reality' are based can become transformed and new concepts of the natural society can emerge. (Cox 1999)

Global civil society thus quite significantly affords a novel opportunity to revisit and also re-kindle the debate on civil society from newer perspectives, locations and experiences. Following Montesquieu-Tocquvellian and also learning from continuing Hegelian-Marxian traditions of state-civil society theory, most scholars and civil society activists today recognize that 'civil society is inherently a political project' that essentially means resisting dominant structures of power, enhancing the hold of popular sovereignty in decision making, creating conditions for universal rule of law and also, more importantly, re-conceptualizing rights of poor and disadvantaged people in the global structures of power. Therefore, resistance has become one of the defining markers of global civil society. In this conceptualisation of civil society, governance moves beyond formal statist-bureaucratic structures and acquires a people-centred robust framework of 'rights-based development' that simultaneously affirms the associative obligations of various stakeholders in the global civil society (Alexander 1998). In this sense, global civil society leans back on to the classical Greek notion of the 'good society' at the global level. Although critics often complain about the 'outright bizarre' and undemocratic nature of various forms of global civil society associationalism, the enthusiasts look at the global civil society as the sphere of Kantian 'perpetual peace' that does not include nations, groups and individuals advocating and supporting violence (Carothers 2000; Scholte 2003). So in a thicker democratic version of global civil society, secretive, fundamentalist and violent groups such as Al Qaeda and Shining Path do not become part of global 'good' civil society. In short, global civil society challenges widely popular yet flawed neo-Tocquvellian idea that all forms of engagement or association are inherently democratic and progressive.

Therefore, global civil society as 'an area of political action that goes beyond the nation-state' legitimately and provocatively transcends boundaries of traditional sovereignty and citizenship in a rapidly changing world that has slowly and surely moving towards embracing 'cosmopolitan democracy' rather than traditional liberal democracy (Archibugi and Held 1995). The realist, state-centric paradigms of international relations and, more particularly, international political economy have been seriously undermined by the emergence of the global civil society. The increasing globalization of transnational social movements, NGOs and grassroots civil society activists in the 1990s has made older theories of balance of power or balance of terror irrelevant. Right from the start, global civil society has begun its historical and conceptual journey by rejecting the largely mythical hegemonic thesis in international relations that anarchy governs the world. It has also disputed and challenged the accepted wisdom among scholars of international relations that democratization of IR would be a natural outcome of 'territorially-bound domestic regimes'. Contrary to realist and liberal institutionalists' prescriptions of global order, global civil society scholars and activists argue that cooperation between nations and beyond can be sustained only when people are bought to the centre of imagination of global governance as participating, debating and mobilizing each other against the injustices of the global capitalist order and reinstituting the rights of marginalized groups, communities and individuals. Though global civil society apparently shares the popular liberal institutionalist agenda of creating conditions for cooperation and peace through multilateralism and transnational regimes of human rights, it rejects the core claims of both realism and liberal institutionalism in international relations. The fundamental neo-realist premises such as such as 'rational egoism', 'perpetual anarchy', 'self-help system' etc. have no place in the global civil society. Seen from a post-realist, post-nationalist social imaginary, global civil society has become an alternative to the 'anarchical structure, inequality and exclusions of the state system' (Pasha and Blaney 1998, 418). It is significant to note that global civil society has burst onto the global scene by mobilizing people not only against 'totalitarian excesses', but also against the iniquitous nature of hegemonic global institutions of development and cooperation such as the World Trade Organization (WTO), World Bank and International Monetary Fund (IMF) etc. In this sense, global civil society has emerged as a fundamental challenge to dominant theories of International relations and International political economy. Kaldor, writing normatively about the essentially progressive character of the notion of global civil society, says that 'global civil society is also about the meaning of human equality in an increasingly unjust world' (Kaldor 2003).

Global Civil Society and its Emerging Architecture

The emerging architecture of global civil society has been largely shaped by the revolutionary transformations in the technological infrastructure of information systems, telecommunications and transportation lines. In other words, global civil society is embedded in the 'Information Age' that has radically altered traditional boundaries of space and time. Global civil society includes older charities, humanitarian groups, foundations, international NGOs, social movement networks, grassroots civil society groups, advocacy groups etc. International Red Cross, Greenpeace, World Wildlife Fund, Oxfam, World Vision, Ford Foundation, Christian Aid, CARE and Amnesty International are some of the most visible faces of the global civil society. They also ironically represent professionalised, bureaucratized and also corporatized aspects of global civil society. Over time, newer faces of a more radicalized and democratized global civil society have emerged. The Seattle battle comprising around 50,000 people in over 500 protest groups in December 1999 led not only to the collapse of the Seattle trade meeting, but also exposed the predatory and iniquitous actions of international financial institutions in regard to poor developing societies in the south. The inaugural meeting of the World Social Forum at Porto Alegre in January 2001 has provided an enduring institutional associational space for the activists of the global civil society to challenge the existing framework of global governance. Global Social Forum, with its local and regional forums around the world, has also slowly emerged as a 'global justice movement'. The exploitation of cheap labour in poorer countries was dramatically highlighted by Jonah Peretti's globally circulated email correspondence with Nike in February 2001. This showed how global civil society democratized 'cyberspace', hitherto a bastion of global elites. Global civil society has also acquired more prominence as a result of successfully mobilizing the transnationally available policy networks. Transnational networks are usually characterised by their advocacy and outreach functions through transnational campaigns, initiatives and movements by highlighting the politics of resistance. Examples of successful campaigns include the campaign for the establishment of the International Criminal Court (ICC) in 1995. This has deeply impacted the existing framework of human rights. The Jubilee campaign on Third World Debt (1996), which induced the creditor governments and the IMF to take the first steps toward debt relief of the highly indebted poor countries, is often credited with raising the issue of global social equity. Global civil society has made some significant intervention in the areas of development policies at the global level. For instance, Global Call to Action Against Poverty (GCAP) has often been hailed as the largest ever anti-poverty alliance, forging making an alliance of about 150 million people in 72 countries. One of the highlights of this campaign was sending 30 million text messages (SMS) to G8 leaders, which made some progress possible, especially on the issue of debt at the 2005 G8 Submit in Gleneagles (Holland 2005). The international campaign to ban landmines (1992), which managed to secure support in the intergovernmental conference in Ottawa where the Mine Ban Treaty was signed (1997), is often hailed as one of the lasting effects of growing international associationalism to minimize violence. Beyond campaigns, however, transnational networks also carry out alternative practices—such as fair trade—that are largely separated from the spheres of global politics and the global economy. The Global Transparency Initiative (GTI) has negotiated with the Asian Development Bank (ADB) to adopt a new Public Communications Policy for greater disclosure and transparency. The global civil society networks have revolutionized cyberspace activism to the extent that even remote grassroots civil society organizations have been able to contribute to making of global public opinion. For instance, Narmada Bachao Andolan (NBA) from India, beginning as a grassroots movement against the construction of a big dam in 1988, eventually got linked up with international NGOs, advocacy groups and forums that pressurized the World Bank to withdraw its financial support to the dam. Some NGOs do not directly become part of transnational network, yet they organize globally–oriented groups at the grassroots. For instance, South India Federation of Fishermen Societies provides livelihood support to smaller fish workers in eight districts of southern parts of India. The World Conference Against Racism, Racial Discrimination, Xenophobia and Related Intolerance (WCAR) in 2001 in Durban not only illustrated the growing struggle against the lingering 'global apartheid' in the institutions of global governance, but also globalized the social struggles against the caste untouchability (Indian Usage)—hitherto warped hidden in the geographical boundaries of India.

Global civil society has not only made some significant social interventions, but also put new ideas and issues onto the agenda of new architectures of global governance. For instance, climate change has been forcefully argued by international NGOs and global networks as 'global public goods', forcing developed nation-states and United Nations (UN) agencies to accept climate change as a global challenge rather than a narrow country-specific issue. Global civil society is not only limited to resistance, but also involved in capacity-building and training programmes for grassroots activists in various parts of the world. For instance, Asia-Pacific Resource and Research Centre for Women (ARROW), established in 1993 in Kuala Lumpur, Malaysia, works to promote and protect women's health rights, especially in the areas of sexuality and reproductive health, by research and training for grassroots workers. With members spread in almost 100 countries, the World Alliance of Citizen Participation (CIVICUS) helps local civil society organisations to build their capacity and achieve their goals. Based on requests from members, CIVICUS has produced several toolkits to enable organisations to improve their capacity in a number of areas. Global civil society forums and associations have also been strengthened and sustained by information technology revolution. Committed to alternate modes of articulation and dissemination of critical debates especially from the perspectives of human rights and democracy, Open Democracy News Analysis has slowly emerged as a major forum for global civil society activists and scholars. Therefore, global civil society not only agitates in the realm of a high modernity induced spectacle of protest, but also energises and articulates low-intensity, less-visible, unheard voices of everyday forms of resistance against the growing tyranny of 'liquid modernity' at the grassroots around the world. Protests and dissents centring on local livelihood resources, religion oppression, gender discrimination, sexual orientation etc. have mostly taken the form 'hidden transcripts' against hegemonic discourses and practices around the world. For instance, so-called 'petty acts of resistance' such as veils of Muslin women, turbans of Sikhs, organic foods, tattoos, whistle blowers, street theatre, pop music, silly rumours, gossips etc. often surreptitiously contest the dominant social and cultural practices of global political economy. The public expression of 'hidden transcripts' has been facilitated by a peculiar combination of older techniques of resistance and newer, diffused forms of social protest. Petition writing, poster making, bumper stickers, black badges, gossips, cyber chat rooms, social networking sites, blogs, occasionally spam mails etc. have slowly emerged 'networks of micro resistance against networks of micro-power' (Foucault 1980). Rather than demonstrating on single issues or agitating in an open and direct manner, activists have successfully used the techniques of 'naming and shaming' in resisting the disciplinary and normalizing practices of global power relations. In this sense, global civil society has become the site where increasingly 'counterhegemoic consciousness is elaborated' even if it is not readily realized (Scott 1990). The evolving infrastructure of the politics of protest, reform and change invariably refers to the increasing legitimacy of the 'ideas of equity, participation and public fairness' in the new architecture of global governance (Heffner 1999). In short, though the 'infrastructure of global civil society includes a vast array of NGOs, voluntary associations, non-profit groups, charities, interest associations...Diaspora networks, dot.causes and social forums' global civil society has increasingly come to refer to political mobilization of global associational forums and grassroots civil society actions from the perspectives of social movement in a truly transnational context.

Dynamics and Limits of Global Civil Society

As a 'movement of movements' or 'network of networks', global civil society networks and forums have not been spared from the biases, prejudices and contradictions of dominant power relations. The ideological and political conflicts among supporters, reformers, rejectionists and fundamentalists in regard to globalization have marred the smooth functioning of the global civil society. The gradual assimilation and co-option of NGOs, especially by the World Bank, IMF and ABD have raised issues of integrity, accountability and representation for global civil society (Clark, 2003). Many critics believe that existing parts of global civil society are primary dominated and controlled by the powerful Western powers attempting to penetrate non-western and especially developing societies to further their ideological, political and economic agendas (Keane 2001). Critics argue that most of the big and influential global civil society actors are Eurocentric. Many of them are strategically located in the advanced western countries; they have better access to political, economic and media resources, skills and opportunities. *LSE Yearbook on Global Civil Society* has noted that most of the international NGOs were located in the industrialized parts of the north and their numbers grew manifold from 1,300 to 47,000 (Anheier, Glasius et al 2003). Although data on the proliferation of civil society groups indicate that global civil society is becoming thicker, it has not escaped from charges of practicing exclusionary politics. Voicing serious concerns about the issue of dominance and representation in the sphere of civil society, Neera Chandhoke wryly writes,

> Not every group possesses the necessary vocabulary, the powerful rhetoric, the rich and evocative imaginaries, and the fine honed conceptual tools that are capable of drawing resonances in the public sphere of civil societies. Nor can every social movement or political group, for rather mundane reasons of logistics and funds, be present in global civil society or even in their own civil society to put forward its own perspective on the vital problems that affect human kind deeply. Like national civil societies global civil society can prove to be exclusive and exclusionary, empowering for some and disempowering for many, accessible to some and inaccessible to many. In short, the prospect of direct democracy in which all groups participate to hammer out a new political order is at best a distant dream for national civil society. And the hope that global civil society will provide the space for direct democracy in which every group can represent its own interests is frankly a chimera. (Chandhoke 2005, 360)

Many NGOs and civil society groups have increasingly been co-opted in the policy making process of dominant trade and financial institutions. In fact,

World Bank's so-called NGO Working Group on the World Bank is often accused of subverting the agenda of civil society and furthering neoliberal economic agenda. As a result of the growing cooption of civil society, global civil society's resistance against the neoliberal driven agenda of global capitalism has weakened in the recent past. As most international NGOs comprise professionals, experts and activists mainly from the middle class and urban backgrounds, they often do not voice concerns of the disadvantaged and also restrict access to others, especially those from poorer countries. There also exists an increasing divorce between the everyday experiences of ordinary people and the organized global groups in the arena of civil society. Many civil society organizations and forums suffer from lack of internal democracy, transparency and accountability. Critics genuinely worry that global civil society may eventually become 'the world's largest unregulated industry' (Mecan-Markar 2005). Pointing out some of the undemocratic features of civil society organization Jan Scholte writes

> Some civic associations offer their members no opportunity for participation beyond the payment of subscriptions. No less than a government department or a business corporation, a civic organisation can be run with top-down managerial authoritarianism. In addition, policy making in global civic associations can be quite opaque to outsiders: in terms of who takes decisions, by what means, from among which options, and with what justifications. Civic groups can be further deficient in respect of transparency when they do not publish financial statements or even a declaration of objectives, let alone full-scale reports of their activities. Moreover, the leadership of many civic organisations is self-selected, raising troubling questions of accountability and potential conflicts of interest. In short, civil society operations are no more intrinsically democratic than programmes in the public or the private sector.
>
> (Scholte, 1999)

However, it would be erroneous to think that only international NGOs and northern advocacy groups comprise global civil society. Individuals, grassroots civil society groups, human rights forums, loose coalitions of social movements and various policy networks are also the constitutive elements of global civil society. Some of the most effective global civil society forums have less open and non-hierarchical structures of participation and representation. Through submit meetings and conferences, the range of protests against the nexus of markets-governments in degrading the environment, abusing the livelihood resources of poor and violating human rights has grown outside Europe and North America. Thus, most criticisms and charges ignore the mobile, melange and evolving nature of the civil society and appear far-fetched in some cases. Significantly, these criticisms ignore Gramsci's insights about the complexities of waging 'war of position' amidst the regressive forces of globalization and violence. In other words, global civil society is struggling to make the transition from treating its constituents as 'subjects' to treating them as equal and sovereign 'global citizens'. Reflecting on the nature of representation and participation in a genuine public sphere, Benhabib writes,

> each participant must have an equal chance to initiate, and to continue communication; each must have an equal chance to make assertions, recommendations, and explanations; all must have equal chances to express their wishes, desires and feelings; and finally, within dialogue, speakers must be free to thematize those power relations that in ordinary contexts would constrain the wholly free articulation of opinions and positions. (Benhabib 1992, 89).

Organizations such as One World Trust have recently suggested making existing undemocratic pyramidal structures of accountability more transparent and open to those on whose behalf the NGOs claim to speak. Action Aid International has started implementing downward accountability at all levels of policy making and implementation. Recently, attempts have been made by global civil society activists and social movement networks to seek new partners, allies and supports in the global south to remove the lingering 'patterns of inequality that mark the globalised world more generally' (Scholte 2002). Moving the event from the previous venue of Porto Alegre in Brazil, the Mumbai meeting of World Social Forum in 2004 took global civil society to many people from across Asia. Thousands of people took part from throughout India – grassroots civil society groups, trade unions, women's groups, gay groups, socialist groups, anti-war groups, anti-capitalist groups and groups of the oppressed such as the dalits (untouchables) – who were very visible at the forum. In retrospect, many activists pointed out that this was the real beginning of making 'another world is possible'. – (world social forum's famous slogan) This does not mean global civil society has not suffered reverses, disappointments and failures. In fact, civil society-induced global associationalism has failed to stop cases of ethnic conflicts, riots, border conflicts and terror around the world. More specifically, the disastrous failure of global civil society has been noticed in the case of the US's unilateral military intervention in Iraq in 2003. Paradoxically, the war on Iraq took place at the time when almost 11 million people had participated in anti-war protest in 800 cities around the world (Anheier, Glasius et al., 2003).

Thus, it is significant that any conceptualization of global civil society must first raise marginalized groups and socially excluded classes, groups and individuals to a position of 'collective equality' at the global level before civil society begins the process of what Habermas calls 'rational communication' between free and equal citizens. Rather than just noting the 'neutral', 'polymorphous' and fixed character of global civil society, it would be worthwhile if we treat global civil society as an open-ended process whereby inegalitarian structures of power, discrimination and exclusion, especially in the arena of global politics, are interrogated, criticized, challenged and ultimately reversed. Therefore, there is a distinct possibility that questions asked about how global civil society will affect modes of governance may differ according to specific trajectories of politics, policy regimes, social-cultural circumstances and path-dependency forces in complex forms of local and global contexts. Therefore, global civil society offers us newer opportunities to do a creative 'social audit' of various conflicting and contradictory forms of global governance from the perspectives of oppressed people, communities and groups. In other words, identifying, measuring and evaluating lingering debilitating forms of social exclusion must figure prominently in efforts to remove 'graded inequality' in international power systems that include corporatized international NGOs and bureaucratized global civil society forums. Seen from this perspective, the very idea of global civil society leads us to ask searching and probing questions. For instance, how can international NGOs create conditions for distributive justice? Can global civil society give poor people a voice in the decision making process? And more importantly, how do we intend to hold non-state actors accountable and responsive towards the poor and disadvantaged?

Towards Cosmopolitan Democracy (*jus cosmopoliticum*)

In the end, global civil society may mean many things, but its normative core remains rooted in the political project of cosmopolitan ideas of democracy, justice and peace. Civil society is no longer identified with global capitalism, but increasingly with participating, resisting sovereign citizenry across borders. At the subjective level, it refers to the beginning elaboration and consolidation of a rebel's consciousness at the global level. At the pragmatic level, it is actually a relatively autonomous site of contestation, diversity and solidarity – a site of 'one', 'no' and 'yeses' (Klein 2002). Though it has not yet succeeded in reversing the regressive paths of globalization, it represents a 'historic bloc' in reforming, altering and transforming norms, rules and institutions of hegemonic global governance systems. More significantly, global civil society has increasingly emerged as an antidote to war, offering real opportunities for human emancipation at the global level (Kaldor 2004). It is often suggested that global civil society is a utopian project, as it often falls short on practical details of alternative ways of transforming the existing framework of the global governance. But, as we have noted in the preceding discussion, global civil society's rejection of a univocal choice between competing ideological and political polarities is quite 'strategic, activist and inspirational'. Beyond the cacophony of demands for redistribution of global resources and equity, global civil society promises us a shared destiny with all its ambivalences, peculiarities and obligations. Slowly, the loosely organized 'movement of movements' has become a multifaceted, overlapping ring of communities with democratic strivings, federalist contours, egalitarian outlooks and subalternist leanings. Incidentally, the emergence of global civil society has also coincided with a slow yet paradigmatic shift in the global consciousness towards embracing cosmopolitan values and reducing inequality, as well as a preference for democratic forms of governance and cultural diversity. The idea that civil society is integral to the emergent architecture of global governance has increasingly reduced the political and policy differences among liberals, republicans, realists and cosmopolitans, forcing them to think of a new 'global social contract'. We agree that the future is not pre-determined, yet we can conclude by saying that global civil society marks the beginning of creative, critical and also conflicting dialogues over normative, substantive and procedural aspects of emerging forms of cosmopolitan democracy where, as Immanuel Kant evocatively and loudly pointed out, 'right violated anywhere could be felt everywhere'. Such efforts seem eminently worthy of admiration, respect and reflection, allowing us to bid a decent 'farewell to the end of history'!

Acknowledgments

This work would not have been possible without my involvement as one of the chief-editors with the *LSE Yearbook on Global Civil Society 2009* and intellectual support from the works of my colleagues especially Mary Kaldor, Jan Aart Scholte, Haken Seckinelgin, Glasius, Marlies, Fiona Holland, and Sabine Selchow at LSE. I also thank the Centre for the study of Global Governance at LSE and Tata Institute of Social Sciences (Mumbai) for facilitating my Visiting Fellowship at LSE in 2008–9.

References

Alexander, J. C. (ed.). 1998. *Real Civil Societies: Dilemmas of Institutionalization*. London: Sage.
Anheier, H., Glasius, M. and Kaldor, M. (eds). 2001. *Global Civil Society 2010/2*. London: Sage Publications.
Anheier, H. and Themudo, N. 2002. *Organisational Forms of Global Civil Society: Implications of Going Global*. Oxford: Oxford University Press.

Appadurai, A.1990. 'Disjuncture and Difference in the Global Cultural Economy', *Public Culture* 2(2).

Archibugi, D. and Held, D. (eds). 1995. *Cosmopolitan Democracy: An Agenda for a New World Order*. Cambridge, UK: Polity Press.

Baker, G. 2002. 'Problems in the Theorisation of Global Civil Society', *Political Studies* 50(5).

Bartelson, J. 2006. 'Making Sense of Global Civil Society', *European Journal of International Relations* 12(3).

Bauman, Z. 1999. *In Search of Politics*. Cambridge, UK: Polity Press.

————.2000. *Liquid Modernity*. Cambridge, UK: Polity Press.

Beck, U. 2003. 'The Analysis of Global Inequality: From National to Cosmopolitan Perspective', in H. Anheier, M. Glasius and M. Kaldor (eds), *Global Civil Society 2003*, Oxford: Oxford University Press.

Benhabib, S. 1992. 'Models of Public *Space: Hannah Arendt, the Liberal Tradition and Juger Habermas*', in C. Calhoun (ed.), *Habermas and the Public Sphere*, Cambridge, Mass: The MIT Press.

Carothers, T. 1999–2000. 'Thinking again: Civil Society', *Foreign Policy* Winter.

Castells, M. 1996. *The Rise of the Network Society The Information Age: Economy, Society and Culture Volume 1*. Oxford: Blackwell.

Chandhoke, N. 2005. 'How Global is Global Civil Society?', *Journal of World–Systems Research* 1(2).

Cheru, F. 1997. 'The Silent Revolution and Weapons of the Weak: Transformation and Innovation From Below', in S. Gill and J. H. Mittleman (eds), *Innovation and Transformation in International Studies*, Cambridge, UK: Cambridge University Press.

Clark, J. D. (ed.). 2003. *Globalizing Civic Engagement: Civil Society and Transnational Action*. London: Earthscan.

Cohen, R. and Rai, S. M. (eds). 2000. Global *Social Movements*. London: Athlone.

Cox, R. W. 1999. 'Civil Society at the Turn of the Millennium: Prospects for an Alternative World Order', Review of International Studies, 25(1).

Dryzek, J. 1990. *Discursive Democracy: Politics, Policy and Political Science*. Cambridge: Cambridge University Press.

Edwards, M. 2002. *Herding Cats? Civil Society and Global Governance*. London: Institute for Public Policy Research.

Edwards, M. and Gaventa, J. (eds). 2001. *Global Citizen Action*. Boulder, CO: Rienner.

Falk, R. 1998. 'Global Civil Society: Perspectives, Initiatives, Movements', *Oxford Development Studies* 26(1).

Florini, A. M. (ed.). 2000. *The Third Force: The Rise of Transnational Civil Society*. Tokyo/Washington, DC: Japan Centre for International Exchange and Carnegie Endowment for International Peace.

Foucault, M. 1980. *Power/Knowledge: Selected Interviews and Other Writings 1972–1977*. New York: Pantheon.

Germain, R. and Kerry, M. (eds). 2005. *The Idea of Global Civil Society*. London: Routledge.

Habermas, J. 1987. *Philosophical Discourse of Modernity*. Cambridge, UK: Polity Press.

Held, D. 1995. *Democracy and Global Order*. Cambridge, UK: Polity Press.

Holland, F. 2005. 'Mainstreaming Africa', in H. Anheier, M. Glasius and M. Kaldor (eds), *Global Civil Society2005/6*, London: Sage Publications.

Jones, C. 1999. *Global Justice: Defending Cosmopolitanism*. Oxford: Oxford University Press.

Kaldor, M. 2003. *Global Civil Society: An Answer to War*. Cambridge, UK: Polity Press.

————.2003. 'The Idea of Global Civil Society', *International Affairs* 79(3).

Keane, J. 2001. 'Global Civil Society?', in H. Anheier, M. Glasius and M. Kaldor (eds)., *Global Civil Society 2001*, Oxford: Oxford University Press.

———.2003. *Global Civil Society?*. Cambridge, UK: Cambridge University Press.

Keck, M. E. and Sikkink, K. 1998. *Activists Beyond Borders: Advocacy Networks in International Politics*. Ithaca: Cornell University Press.

Khagram, S., Riker, J. V. and Sikkink, K. (eds). 2002. *Restructuring World Politics: Transnational Social Movements, Networks, and Norms*. Minneapolis: University of Minnesota Press.

Klein, N. 2002. 'Farewell to the End of History: Organization and Vision in Anti-Corporate Movements', *Socialist Registrar* 1–13.

McLuhan, M. 1989. *The Global Village: Transformations in World Life and Media in the 21st Century*. New York: Oxford University Press.

Rupert, M. 2000. *Ideologies of Globalization: Contending Visions of New World Order*. London: Routledge.

Scholte, J. A. 1999. *Global Civil Society: Changing the World?*. Working Paper No. 31/99. Centre for the Study of Globalisation and Regionalisation (CSGR), University of Warwick. Online: http;//www2.warwick.ac.uk/fac/soc/csgr/research/workingpaeprs/1999/wp3199.pdf (accessed 30 November 2008).

Scholte, J. A. and Schnabel, A.(eds). 2002. *Civil Society and Global Finance*. London: Routledge.

Scott, J. C. 1990. *Domination and the Arts of Resistance: Hidden Transcripts*. New Heaven: Yale University Press.

Shaw, M. 1999 'Civil Society', in L. Kurtz (ed.), *Encyclopaedia of Violence, Peace and Armed Conflict*, San Diego: Academic Press.

Taylor, R. 2004. *Creating a Better World: Interpreting Global Civil Society*. Bloomfield, CT: Kumarian.

Urry, J. 2000. *Sociology Beyond Societies: Mobilities for the Twenty-First Century*. London: Routledge.

Willetts, P. (ed.). 1996. *Conscience of the World: The Influence of the Non-Governmental on the UN System*. Washington, D.C: Brookings Institution.

Chapter 4

INSTITUTIONAL AND POLICY IMPLICATIONS OF INTERNATIONAL PUBLIC GOODS: THE CASE OF GLOBAL COMMONS[1]

Rogerio F. Pinto and Jose Antonio Puppim de Oliveira

Introduction

We could be facing today, at the global level, the phenomenon that Garret Hardin identified in 1968 at the local level, which he called the 'Tragedy of the Commons' (Hardin 1968). In the twenty first century, nation-states are behaving in ways similar to Hardin's herdsmen when they over used and/or abused pastures on which their livelihood depended. Predatory practices for short term gains to individual national or local interests, if unchecked, may entail long term losses to the global community, including those that used the resources for short term gain. Given the externalities of globalization,[2] this contemporary phenomenon is part of the problem, but can also be part of its solution by means of global governance mechanisms to balance short-term individual gains with long-term global sustainability. The challenge of protecting the global commons – a type of common pool resource, like the ozone layer – calls for reaching beyond the boundaries of the nation state and local interests to seek collective solutions at the global level and to share in the promises that globalization holds. Collective needs and interests in a global world transcend national boundaries and require mechanisms for global governance creating demand for a range of International Public Goods (IPGs). A 2007 World Bank Report on global public goods states 'protection of the environmental commons through collective action at the global, regional and country levels will be a key challenge for the twenty first century. Supply of this

Global Public Good (GPG) has become so critical that it can no longer be kept separate from national or regional development strategies'.

The response of the international community to this global dilemma and its cross-border imperatives is reflected in the current trend towards Vertical Global Programs (VGPs),[3] which provide support for global benefits that transcend interests of individual countries, complementing the traditional focus on country-by-country international assistance (Kaul and Conceição 2006; World Bank 2007).[4] When intended to provide IPGs to sustain global commons, those programs present a particular challenge as, in their pursuit of global interests, they may clash with the provision of National Public Goods (NPGs),[5] creating critical alignment problems between the collective policies driving global initiatives and national institutions, policy premises and implementation mechanisms. The congruence of interests, priorities, stakeholders and time horizons of the global community with those of the host country where VGPs are implemented cannot be assumed to obtain in many cases, and usually translates into misalignments. This chapter examines the IPGs engendered by the VGPs, contrasts them with NPGs, and the underlying imperatives guiding both national and international policy and governance mechanisms. It particularly explores the extent to which countries participating in VGPs are required to cede portions of their 'sovereignty' when entering into these arrangements and how they adapt to this contingency. By exploring the right mix of IPGs and NPGs and the attendant institutional arrangements, this chapter may be useful in guiding state reform efforts against the backdrop of the increased relevance of the provision of IPGs through VGPs as a means to address the challenge of the global commons. Specifically, the chapter seeks to identify a few elements to factor into national state reform, given the irreversible trend towards globalization and ensuing integration on a global or regional scale. It argues that, while the nation-state, as we know it, may be receding, it can be strengthened through proper interfacing with institutions of global governance. These inquiries should also generate a framework to assess global and national incentives underpinning their respective policies and provide insights into implications for the design of VGPs by international institutions. The first section of the chapter reviews the essentials of public goods theory, defines IPGs and NPGs, and discusses the dynamics of their interaction and its implications for national policy making.

The second section defines the global commons as common pool assets[6] of global scope and reviews pertinent IPGs and the governance requirements to sustain them. It also defines categories of IPGs, and discusses the inherent conflict between, on the one hand, IPGs and those NPGs tied to the expediency of national development policy, especially of emerging countries such as Brazil, and on the other, those IPGs tied to the sustainability of global commons, mostly by virtue of VGPs.

The third section illustrates the underlying arguments of the chapter by reviewing the impact of environmental VGPs on Brazilian (a) policy making, (b) institutional arrangements to host such programs and (c) different types of implementation mechanisms of national policy with impact on the global commons. The fourth section discusses the rationale for a balance of NPGs and IPGs of VGPs and the role of international organizations.

The fifth and final section explores the institutional options available to emerging countries to reconcile national development goals with sustainability of the global commons, supported by proper governance of VGPs and how they can be incorporated into state reforms.

National and International Public Goods (NPGs and IPGs): Implications for National Policy

In short, public goods theory offers a typology based on economic properties of goods, such as 'excludability' and 'subtractability' (or rivalry) (Olson 2000).[7] A pure public good in general is neither excludable nor subtractable nor non-rivalrous. Exclusion from consumption of public goods is costly and impracticable, as several individuals can consume it at a time and consumption by one does not reduce availability to others. While control or influence over pure public goods by citizens is affected through vote and voice, over private goods it is carried out through price exchange and exit. Externalities and economies of scale are also important determinants of the public nature of a good. Among public goods, there are those that ensure a level of governance required by the functioning of the market as well as of government so that public and private goods can be produced efficiently and effectively. These are known as government goods and they can be either national or international. Policy, legal and regulatory frameworks are examples of national government goods (Piccioto 1995). Those produced by international conventions and protocols are international government goods. IPGs produced by VGPs are examples of such goods.

Technological advances – mostly in information and communications – have brought about a myriad of private goods whose multinational sourcing and marketing render them essentially international, hence subject to international regulation as both production and consumption cut across national boundaries. Because of their private nature, competitiveness among producers of these private goods facilitates mechanisms of choice and exit as a means of value satisfaction by consumers.

IPGs, in turn, are the product of established international organizations or international collaborative protocols such as in trade, health, security, drug trafficking and other areas of global interest. Citizens of all the signatory countries on an individual or collective basis consume these goods or services. Global civil society is also a significant contributor to IPGs. For example, the World Social Forum, the International Criminal Court (ICC), the Debt Relief Initiative – benefiting highly indebted countries- and the Mine Ban Treaty of 1997, among others, are all products of the activism of global civil society that have no roots in any particular country. Unlike the IPGs engendered by governmental international agencies, hence bound by the power and governance structures that underpin them, the former are the product of more genuine global collective action. Given their increased importance in a globalized world, the provision and regulation of IPGs can no longer be left to individual countries or the limitations of bilateralism, inherent in traditional diplomacy. The International Task Force on Global Public Goods relates IPGs to 'issues (i) deemed to be important to the international community including both developed and developing countries; (ii) typically cannot or will not, be adequately addressed by individual countries or entities acting alone, and in such cases (iii) are best addressed collectively on a multilateral basis' (World Bank 2007).

Unlike NPGs, which are amenable to citizen pressure through collective action by way of vote or voice, IPGs by and large are beyond the reach of regular citizenry, as a means to influence their provision. In those cases where NPGs from countries with regional or global influence – mostly in the developed world – have spill over effects on other countries, they effectively become international. For example, monetary policy set by the US Federal Reserve Board has far reaching implications for both international and national financial markets, yet it is a US government good. The same applies *inter-alia* to regulation, monitoring and enforcement of laws on immigration, illicit drug use and traffic, air traffic safety, public health and drug safety, money laundering, sanitary and agricultural policies of the developed countries. Arguably most of these can carry far greater implications for citizens of countries within the sphere of influence of the US than either national or international public goods, rendering them quasi-international public goods (Q-IPGs).

Immigration patterns from developing countries are other examples of the remarkable consequences of the spill over effect of NPGs from developed countries. Citizens of countries where public goods such as security, health, education or economic policy framework, to name a few, do not measure up to their expectations, have a strong incentive to migrate to nation-states where the standards for these public goods are higher. This is clearly a form of exit from a set of public goods, symptomatic of the breakdown of voice and vote mechanisms within certain nation-states, mostly of developing countries. While it can be argued that primarily labor markets and the level of economic activity of targeted countries drive immigration patterns, the attractiveness of higher wages and working conditions are largely determined by labor and social policies, both NPGs.[8]

As the size of immigration and refugee flows from unstable developing to developed countries increase, the host states find themselves in a position of having to generate public goods for an ever-increasing population of non-citizens, as is the case of the US and European Union (EU) countries. This raises issues of citizenship ambiguities and mixed civic orientations with policy implications for both the host and countries of immigrant origin concerned. Pressures on policy raise issues of institutional scope and state reform, depending on whether the country of origin wishes to discourage and jointly regulate or encourage exit immigration.[9] This will, in turn, have far reaching implications for the mix of NPGs and IPGs that a given country may wish to provide and those that are provided by assorted international sources, as part of its development strategy.

Given the greater adaptability and capacity to reform of the developed host country – as in the case of the US in the post 9/11 era – policy changes are swifter and more effective than those in the country of immigration origin. Immigration patterns, therefore, become driven primarily by the policies of host countries and by the level of neglect or capacity for NPGs by the country of immigration origin. Choice of state, under these circumstances, devalues citizenship and civic loyalty of emigration countries, further eroding the integrity and resilience of their nation state, an added argument for state reforms sensitive to the dynamics of international public goods (Falk 1998). The Q-IPGs generated by developed countries and the predicament caused by immigration flows point to the *under supply* by multilateral mechanisms of much demanded IPGs. This gap has called for developed countries to step in and fill the void on a bilateral basis, mostly in the pursuit of their national interest, causing externalities with far reaching effects on the broader global community.[10] Arguably, this was the alleged rationale for the US to invade Iraq in view of the UN Security Council's inability to make the Iraq regime comply with its multiple resolutions.

Global Common Pool Resources and Development Policy

A Global Common constitutes a natural endowment of global value which may span the entire planet as the ozone layer, for example, or may be located within national jurisdictions but with spill-over properties with global externalities (positive or negative), such as pastures, fisheries, aquifers and forests. In public goods theory, global commons constitute a common pool resource (Ostrom 1990) rather than a pure public good, which is the product of collective human action, not the case of a natural endowment. A global common represents a finite stock of a natural resource, while a pure public good represents a flow of services. While common pool goods are generally regarded as excludable and 'non-rivalrous', excludability and subtractability are not entirely applicable to them. For example, the use or abuse of common pool resources such as pastures, fisheries and underground water reduces the use/quality of the commons by others, which would render them both excludable and rivalrous.[11] Greenhouse emissions as a result of abusing a global common are unique as they cause adverse climate change that affects all on a global scale. The global value of these commons is rooted in properties such as being tied to long-term global human survival or sustained livelihood of segments of the planet's population that cut across national boundaries.

Global commons often provide the natural resource foundation on which local businesses and populations derive their livelihood. In the case of forests, for example, they constitute a natural source of raw materials for companies operating in agro-industrial, cattle-raising, logging and assorted harvesting which drive them to practices which may be inconsistent with the sustainability of these commons. In the case of developing countries, with aggressive growth policies pursued through national government goods (a type of NPG), the short-term interests of these stakeholders usually take priority over those of the wider global community, as they have a stronger voice in local and even national politics. While these interests may favor their protection only against immediate adverse effects of local scope, the global interests generally converge, *inter-alia* on the preservation of water and air quality, biodiversity and protection against climate change.

Developing countries face the multiple challenges of having to improve their NPGs, as their provision depends directly on government action and are needed in the short-term for political and economic reasons (e.g., sustaining economic activity and generating political dividends). These countries are less concerned about complying with international conventions to protect global commons which may lie within their borders, as the provision of IPGs does not depend directly on one government and do not deliver economic or political results in the short-term. Developing countries may, however, be persuaded by international organizations managing and/or monitoring conventions and protocols concerned with these commons to promote their sustainability. Compliance with these conventions may also be supported by VGPs intended to facilitate it, if qualifying countries solicit such assistance, which is not always the case. Short- and long-term development priorities and general welfare of citizens of developing countries call for a combination of NPGs and IPGs. As discussed above, the preservation of the global commons has to compete with other pressing challenges that need international cooperation such as trade regulation, public health, drug safety, product safety, immigration, peace keeping, refugee management and general security, among others, which interestingly enough are also provided by Q-IPGs.[12]

Given the uniqueness of global commons, their controversial nature and their critical value to humanity, a useful distinction can be made between: (a) those IPGs directed to their protection and (b) those directed to the global challenges listed above.[13] The latter (b) are readily identifiable, measurable, both in their origin and their consequences. Their regulatory mechanisms are well established and accepted worldwide, commanding a high level of international consensus. Moreover, because of their nature, (b) can be controlled by countries individually without the cooperation of other countries (even though cooperative actions among countries could be more effective and efficient). IPGs to protect global commons (a), however, are still tentative in nature and the object of some international contention such as in the case of global warming and the trials and tribulations of the Kyoto Treaty. These circumstances render these IPGs and their VGPs vulnerable to national resistance when they clash with NPGs directed to national development.

Furthermore, the provision of NPGs and IPGs can be in conflict with each other and among them. The first type of conflict is that between the NPGs of two countries. An example of the NPG-NPG conflict is provided by US policy proposed by trade and environmental protection authorities to place tariff barriers on imports of shrimp from Brazil that were harvested in a way that unintentionally put at risk an endangered type of tropical water turtle (known as the 'shrimp turtle'). The protection of this species was enforced by virtue of US policy in the name of preservation of animal biodiversity, a form of global common, but clearly not in the short-term interest of Brazilian 'shrimpers', a vocal and resourceful interest group that Brazilian authorities had to heed to. In this case, institutions and policies were in place to protect the interest of the shrimp exporters, regardless of the specifications contained in US policy and in the International Convention on Biodiversity. A second type of conflict is between a NPG and an IPG, such as the case of policies and programs to protect tropical forests, discussed below. This conflict provides an illustration of what Wolfgang Reinecke calls internal and external sovereignty, reflecting Max Weber's assertion that internal sovereignty is the capacity of a state to formulate and execute public policy (Maggi and Messner 2002) Finally, policies for different IPGs can oppose each other. For example, the Montreal Protocol led to the emergence of HFCs (Hydro-fluorocarbon) as substitutes for CFCs (Chloro-fluorocarbon), which were regarded as the main villains in the destruction of a global common (the ozone layer), but HFCs are heavy polluters in terms of global warming.[14]

However, there are opportunities to coordinate the provision of NPGs and IPGs. For example, Brazil's bio-fuels development program is an example of its unique approach to climate control by reducing carbon emissions from the use of fossil fuel, mostly from automotive applications. It is also a case where the global and national interests can be served in respect to Greenhouse Gas Emissions (GGE), as it represents a very promising new economic frontier in Brazil with considerable impact on automotive fossil fuel consumption globally.[15]

NPGs are usually the target of most state reforms focused on policy and institutions, as they respond to the needs of national constituencies and bear on development efforts. To the extent that IPGs interfere or complement NPGs, state and policy reformers also target them. However, the issues of national policies, institutions and their alignment with those of VGPs delivering IPGs to sustain global commons are still not high priority on state reform agendas. For this reason, international networks, NGOs and multilateral development agencies such as those that gathered around the Paris High Level Forum on Aid Effectiveness[16] are proactive in bringing about these types of reforms, a clear case of international collective action to protect the global commons. The rationale for the VGPs is that, left exclusively to national policy, the degradation and demise of these global commons would be certain and commensurate with the speed and rate of developmental growth around the world.

The principles that apply to local commons tied to local economic activity do not necessarily apply to global commons (Puppim de Oliveira, 2009). Scales, scope of stakeholders, organization, political influence and power, costs and benefits, time horizons and externalities, are different. There are isolated cases where local communities have indeed engaged in clean development, based on tradition of protecting and preserving local commons, without much external support. This is the case of some traditional indigenous communities in the Brazilian Amazon and elsewhere, which preserve forest biodiversity on the grounds of ancestral practices. Communities can also build and successfully manage commons (water), such as through irrigation systems in Nepal (Ostrom 1990).

The merit of VGPs rests on the IPGs that they deliver. The question that follows is: What are these IPGs, and what is their value added? As they are usually tied to international conventions and protocols, they perform a critical function of assisting and funding compliance by signatory countries. This function also includes translating the principles contained in conventions into operational rules, standards and criteria, and performance monitoring by beneficiaries. Because the effort of sustaining global commons involves projects of high technical and scientific content, these IPGs also contribute to the development and dissemination of scientific knowledge and technology to carry out the projects for prevention and correction of practices that compromise the commons. The metrics and measurement of deterioration or mitigation rates are important features of the IPGs provided by VGPs. Moreover, the pull effect of VGPs is considerable not only in terms of increased awareness of the global commons risks, but also in terms of the emergence of institutional arrangements and capacity to implement projects at the local level.

The Case of Brazil

Participation in VGPs In regards to VGPs, Brazil has made modest strides to reconcile its development quest and compliance with most international protocols protecting global commons. In effect, although exact figures are not available, it appears that Brazil spends only some 5–25 per cent of its own resources and relies substantially on the financial assistance from VGPs to carry out its own projects to protect global commons (Diewald and Pinto 2006). The most conclusive evidence of this modest performance is in respect to GGEs, tied to economic activity in the Amazon rain forest, where the pressures from local stakeholders and large agro-industry and cattle ranchers bear down on government with considerable success. This has led to the government's inability to bring deforestation under control, despite the fact that deterioration of the Amazon biome translates into a loss of environmental services that have *national* negative externalities in the form of degradation of soils, water quality and supply, floods, quality of air and local climate destabilization. Paradoxically, in Brazil there still is less public outcry and concerted opposition to the loss of these environmental services to national resources than to the negative externalities on a global level.

Brazil participates in all VGPs linked to conventions that it has signed. The motivation to do so is not only its intention to comply with its respective obligations, but also the incentive provided by the funding it gets from them. As discussed below, the United Nations Framework Convention on Climate Change (UNFCCC) may be an exception to this. Brazil has been at odds with certain provisions of the Kyoto Protocol, a treaty to mitigate and adapt to GGEs causing climate change. Brazil's contention regards mostly GGEs and carbon exchange under the Clean Development Mechanism (CDM), despite being one of the leaders in the promotion and application of this mechanism. Brazil is responsible for some 3 per cent of the world's GGEs, mostly from forest burning and clearing. GGEs by the Amazon forest account for 2.5 per cent of the 3 per cent share of Brazil's GGE (Diewald and Pinto 2006).[17] There is clearly tension and outright conflict between the interests of segments of Brazilian society and the national as well as international environment protection advocates. VGPs regarding the environment are caught in this tension, as the issues surrounding the environment are far more controversial than those of the global HIV/AIDS, Tuberculosis and Malaria (GFATM) VGP, for example, where there is a far greater level of consensus around its goals and modus operandi.

Brazil is one of the largest clients of the Global Environment Facility (GEF),[18] a financial mechanism to channel funds for the implementation of the UNFCCC, the Convention on Biological Diversity (CBD) and the UN Convention to Combat Desertification (UNCCD).[19] Access to GEF funding is through so-called intermediary agencies such as the World Bank, UN Development Program (UNDP) and International Fund for Agricultural Development (IFAD). The problematic rules of engagement among these agencies and GEF have contributed to faltering collaboration and even competition among them.

GEF's interface with Brazilian authorities is through the Ministry of Foreign Relations (MRE) as it is the diplomatic and political entry point for any VGPs. The 'technical' focal point is the Secretariat for International Affairs (SEAIN) of the Ministry of Planning, which in effect has no technical expertise in environmental matters and has a reactive rather than proactive coordination role. SEAIN serves as the secretariat to the Work Group on Project Assessment (GTAP) consisting of representatives of the MRE, the Ministry of Science and Technology and the Ministry of Planning, which reviews projects submitted by government agencies as well as by offering VGPs. The Ministry of the Environment (MMA) was conspicuously absent from the GTAP until 2007 (Diewald and Pinto 2006).

The institutional interface of the Montreal Protocol (MP) and its funding mechanism, in turn is quite different. The policy making and host entity for the Montreal Protocol Fund (MPF) is the Directorate for Environmental Quality and Human Settlements of the MMA, and the Brazilian Environmental Agency (IBAMA)[20] carries out the monitoring and on site enforcement of the rules and standards of the MP. The Carbon Credits Program under the CDM is managed mostly within the private sector under the guidance and oversight of the National Commission on Climate Change and the Ministry of Science and Technology.[21]

As a member of the GEF council, Brazil has had reservations with regards to its governance mostly due to a perception that GEF's autonomy fails to yield to the circumstances and policies of its member countries. This dispute is in part due to Brazil's perception of GEF as the lead enforcer of the Kyoto protocol provision requiring developing countries to adapt to climate change requirements as opposed to staying within the mitigation limits applied to

Group I countries (which have no target commitment). The World Bank as GEF's lead executing arm is also object of the same criticism.

Regarding the Kyoto Protocol, Brazil advocates against the limitation or reduction of current levels of GGE (mitigation) for developing countries and argues that the onus of such reduction should rest on the developed countries (those of Annex I of the protocol/UNFCCC). It also does not support carbon credits under the CDM for forest conservation from clear felling to allow the destruction of rain forests through a market mechanism that exchanges aid for deforestation.

The problematic commitment of Brazil to the Kyoto Protocol is no match to the national pressures to keep the Amazon rainforest as the base for various types of economic activity, which contribute significantly to Brazil's 3 per cent world share of GGEs. This explains in part the low priority of climate change related activities in Brazil's national budget, despite its capture of substantial funds through GEF and being a large player in the carbon credit program (CDM).

Desertification of semi-arid areas of the northeast of Brazil has a much greater short-term impact in terms of degradation of soil and water sources than the local externalities of deforestation, so in principle it should favor the VGP tied to the UN Convention to Combat Desertification (UNCCD) over any VGP tied to the funding of GEF, CDM, or IBRD Carbon funds, which is not the case. Paradoxically, Brazil has worked to bring about the UNCCD and takes the lead to get it implemented, yet has been under-funded by its VGPs to support its efforts to combat desertification, and relies mostly on its own funding.[22]

The Brazilian Tropical Forests

This natural endowment has global value due to its biodiversity and impact on global climate. However, forest protection for medium and long-term global interest may go against short-term interests of forest dwellers, businesses and national authorities. Timber extraction and alternative uses of land are critical for this economic frontier of Brazil. National energy policy requires the flooding of large areas for construction of hydropower plants, as in the case of the dam in the Madeira River in the Brazilian Amazon. The national government claims that it is a national priority, but environmentalists and international groups disagree and oppose it.

The issue of inclusion of the Amazon forest in negotiations between Brazil and the international community concerned with climate change provides an illustration of contrasting views on IPGs and NPGs. These contrasting views are held, by two opposing groups. First, those who argue for the removal of the forest from any international negotiations regarding its role in global warming. This group, moved by nationalistic and sovereignty motives, consists of government officials of such agencies as the Ministries of External Affairs, of Science and Technology, of Mines and Energy and certain segments of the military who feel that the forest dilemma should be dealt with entirely through NPGs. They want to bring to the table only reforestation projects and planted forests. The second group, mostly represented by officials from the MMA, NGOs both local and international is prepared to negotiate around deforestation as this inclusion may provide access to significant resources from IPGs tied to VGPs targeting the CDM. This position is intended to reconcile environmental protection with sustainable development, so it can be seen as being consistent with reconciling IPGs and NPGs. The table below summarizes the pro and con arguments for the inclusion of the Amazon forest in negotiations relating to global warming. The different opinions between these two groups were evident just before the recent Bali meeting in 2007 as well as before the sixth Conference of the Parties (COPs-6) of the Convention on Climate Change in The Hague in 2000.

Protection of the biodiversity contained in the Amazon rainforest presents a different dilemma than that of climate change, as the positive externalities of this endowment plays out differently on a global scale. Destruction of this biome deprives researchers and pharmaceutical enterprises (both national as well as international) of the biological resource base that it holds and ensuing conversion into drugs that can be brought to market for substantial benefit to all humanity, albeit at considerable profit to the risk taking pharmaceutical corporations. Extinction of endangered animal species is also of concern to environmental groups such as the World Wildlife Fund (WWF), among others, who are dedicated to the preservation of species endemic to the rain forest. The predominance of global versus national interests in regards to the preservation of biodiversity may explain why Brazil derives some 70–80 per cent of its expenditures in biodiversity protection projects from VGPs tied to the CBD, despite being at odds with some of its provisions.

The environmental dilemma of the rain forests of the Amazon and the Mata Atlantica in Brazil has led to a unique protocol of international cooperation, known as the PPG-7. The Amazon forest is of global interest because it is the largest rainforest in the world and contains one of the largest repositories of plant and animal biodiversity. Furthermore, its destruction has the potential of generating high levels of carbon dioxide emissions.

A group of donor countries that congregate as the G-7 decided, with the government of Brazil during the UN Conference on Environment and Development (UNCED) of 1992 in Rio de Janeiro, to provide a framework and funding for a program to protect and preserve the rainforests of Brazil including the Amazon and the Mata Atlantica forest. PPG7 does not fit fully within the VGP model, as it: (a) focuses only on one country; (b) the responsibility for

Table 4.1. Seven Arguments about the Inclusion of Native Forests in the Negotiations of Climate Change in Post-Kyoto[23]

Arguments of those who are against the inclusion of the native forests	Arguments of those who favor the inclusion of the native forests
1. Defending the inclusion of forest conservation is to defend the interests of the developed countries, especially the USA. They want to reduce their emissions by planting and including the forests . The forests in developed countries are growing. Instead, in Brazil, they are being reduced by uncontrolled deforestation.	Native forests are the main strategic element to participate in the carbon market by attracting CDM projects to our country, since our energy matrix is very clean (basically hydropower).
2. The preservation of the Forest is an obligation of countries according to of their legislation. They should not be rewarded for that.	The Forest Preservation Law is not enforced in our country. The rate of deforestation is over tens of thousands square kilometers a year. The CDM could help to attract resources for forest preservation.
3. Keeping the native forests does not combat the Greenhouse Effect, since they do not remove greenhouse gases already in the atmosphere.	The burning of native forests for deforestation is the main source of greenhouse gas emissions in our country (5/6 of the emissions).
4. Only projects of (a) reforestation and clean energy combat greenhouse effect, since they remove carbon from the atmosphere or avoid more emissions.	The large part of the market of CDMs would continue to stay with China and India, if native forests are not included, because their energy matrices are based mostly on fossil fuels. Also, reforestation and clean energy do not have the same potential for job creation and income generation as forest management.
5. The inclusion of native forests would discourage rich countries to reduce their emissions as they would simply exchange their surplus emissions for cheap credits based on forest management in poor developing countries.	The access to CDMs should be regulated to avoid rich countries buying excessive credits from native forests without reducing their emissions.
6. There are many uncertainties, especially in the short term, about enforcing the Forest Preservation Law over time. So including forests can be to our disadvantage, if we are not successful in stopping deforestation	Similar uncertainties exist in the projects of (a) reforestation and clean energy.
7. The inclusion of forest will multiply the offer of carbon credits in the market. This may lead to the collapse of prices, making the life easy for rich countries.	The purchase of carbon credits based on forest preservation should be limited, or even different from those based on clean energy projects of reforestation.

executing the program rests with the host country although the World Bank, at the behest of the donors, performs a key oversight and management/fiduciary function and (c) is not driven by any international convention regulating GEE or protection of biodiversity, such as UNFCCC or CBD.

Despite Brazil's full support of PPG-7 and having full responsibility for the management of this program, intended to protect a global common, the clashes with national development policy and the ensuing institutional tensions and conflicts have been numerous throughout the life of the program.[24] These clashes revolve around Brazil's own approach to protecting the forest, not necessarily with its global externalities in mind, but the national ones especially those that bear on the economic opportunities that the forest holds for local populations and national agro-industrial, cattle raising and logging interests.

The federal nature of the Brazilian state further aggravated the implementation of the PPG-7. The Brazilian Constitution, in its articles 21, 22, 23, 24, 25, 29 and 30, distributes responsibilities among units of the federation (states and municipalities). The principle driving this distribution is that of the 'predominance of interest', that is of cooperative federalism, allowing the co-existence of responsibilities of the Union (not the case of forests), common responsibilities (administrative) and concurrent (legislation) for the implementation of activities of general interest. In the case of concurrent legislation, the Federal Government establishes general norms and the States of the Federation and the Federal District customize them through complementary legislation on the basis of regional circumstances. Municipalities may legislate on matters of local interest, when necessary. Contrary to environmental legislation in general, on matters pertaining to the use and management of forests, the constitutional bias is towards centralization. Only the union can legislate on forests and the states may only issue legislation to cover gaps of federal laws. For these constitutional reasons, the states have a rather passive legislative role when it comes to forestry matters. Exception to this has been the case of the states of Minas Gerais, São Paulo and Paraná, which fall outside the jurisdiction of the Amazon forest. These limitations have had a major impact on the attempts to decentralize to the state level the implementation of programs such as the PPG-7.

The institutional theory of 'polycentricity' developed by Andersson and Ostrum provides conceptual clarity on the relationships among multiple authorities with overlapping jurisdictions, as in the case of legal basis for managerial oversight of tropical forests. It emphasizes multi-level dynamics transcending the romanticized dynamics of the local sphere and the autonomy of local communities to govern their local commons (Andersson and Ostrum 2008; Pinto 2004). PPG-7 provides a type of IPG in the form of scientific and technological knowledge, along with funding, advice, advocacy and mobilization of community and NGOs. It also assists in harmonization with the rather resourceful and diversified Brazilian scientific and socio-environmental networks concerned with the rain forest. The scope and complexity of this IPG represents a substantial management challenge. This gives cause to alignment problems not only due to stakeholders' economic interests, but also their own views on the global externalities of the rain forest. These views are further inflamed by powerful nationalistic sentiments of some such stakeholders around this national endowment, which is reflected in the commonly uttered expression '*a Amazonia é nossa*', meaning 'the Amazon is ours'.

Furthermore, the multiplicity of donors and the very complex funding system of PPG-7, which allows donors to dictate where and how their contributions are spent and through which executing agency within Brazil, further accentuates the alignment problems seen in the case of two VGPs and the PPG-7. The case of Brazil is unique in many respects in terms of its response to the climate change and biodiversity challenge and the lessons from its experience should not be generalized. The determining factors of this experience are, *inter alia*, the nature of the endowment in question, the developmental circumstances of the country and certainly the political dynamics behind the national development agenda.

Taking the dimension of ownership by Brazil of the VGPs in question, it is clear from the cases discussed above that there is no overt policy or institutional focal point systematically supporting them, despite the commitment to the convention that engenders them. The ownership that exists is fragmented, agency-specific and, taken as a whole, has not amounted to any trend towards concerted national ownership of the global commons cause. This applies especially to implementation efforts at the sub-national level. It is not surprising that with 27 federal government units and over 5,500 municipalities, in addition to the constitutional constraints listed above, implementation of VGPs has not trickled down.

In regards to national awareness and significance of the global environmental challenges, it is considerable at the higher echelons of government and within Brazilian technical and scientific communities, especially its numerous research centers and universities. This has not translated into either high priority for counterpart funding or visibility for the climate change challenge. Among the many other reasons for this are the sheer size of the country, the turmoil caused by its enormous social gap and the poverty it entails. The funds involved in VGPs benefiting Brazil pale in comparison to the funds required by the broader government effort to deal with its social challenges.

The oversight and accountability features of these VGPs in Brazil are also problematic. Institutional oversight varies and little is known about its relative performance, as it does not yet represent a topic of great interest for public management researchers. In general it has been accepted that, where oversight rests with the technical secretariat of the VGP outside Brazil, attention to harmonization and alignment is greater. Accountability of GVPs is consistent with the low priority and performance of this key institutional feature within Brazilian bureaucracy. Furthermore, to the extent that accountability hinges on the availability of targets and indicators to measure their achievement, when they are not developed, accountability becomes either based on input measurements, guess work or is simply not practiced.

Balancing NPGs and IPGs of VGPs: The Role of International Organizations

There are cases of developing countries where, through clean development practices such as sustainably-managed logging or use of renewable energy sources, local communities and businesses use these resources in an environmentally responsible manner, without much assistance from the VGPs.[25] Others, because of their development vibrancy, are recalcitrant predators of the environment and become targets of such VGPs. The dilemma of developing countries then is to balance their own growth oriented NPGs, with assorted IPGs tied to different international issues that bear on their development and the IPGs tied to VGPs concerned with global commons. The challenges posed by this dilemma require substantial creativity in terms of governance, policy and institutional arrangements, which relate to state reform. The role of international organizations in regards to these responses is crucial.

The preferred modality of IPGs by multilateral arrangements such as the International Financial Institutions (IFIs) and even the bilateral agencies takes the form of international financial and technical aid. Given that countries, in principle, have no incentive to borrow in order to fund IPGs, financial assistance, including adaptation initiatives at the national level, is mostly in the form of grants.[26] In a sense this aid is intended to strengthen national states and their capacity to increase the quality and quantity of their public goods, thus promoting the fixation of their nationals within the country and reducing the demands for non-aid IPGs, mostly those that relate to poverty reduction. While there are IPGs that seek to maximize the interest of global players such as arbitration mechanisms for trade or international finance,[27] there are many which seek to promote the development and welfare of the disadvantaged segments of world populations such as those catering to the achievement of the MDGs (Millennium Development Goals). The output of most IFIs comes under the latter category.

National governments on their own or through bilateral mechanisms are falling short of meeting this increasing welfare demand. Multilateralism, on the other hand, is striving to reinvent its role in global governance and is caught up in the tension between the plight of the have-nots around the world and the governance pressures from global economic and financial activity centered on the vibrancy in the developed part of the world and increasingly that of a select group of emerging countries such as Brazil, Russia, India and China (known as the BRICs).[28] The set of IPGs required to address poverty, and those intended to address the issues posed by global commons as well as economic and financial order engendered by globalism, are fundamentally different in their nature, purpose and targets. They are, however, intertwined with NPGs, as shown in the debate around debt forgiveness for the highly indebted poor countries (HIPC), requiring that debt proceeds be channeled to poverty reduction.

In addition to direct financial and technical assistance, international organizations produce international government goods (IGGs) in the form of governance, such as governance in areas of trade, international monetary stability, peacekeeping and human rights, among others. International NGOs, in turn, supplement them with a range of goods known as international civil goods (ICGs) that are playing an increasingly important yet unregulated role in international development by bridging the gap of IPGs and NPGs of many developing countries. It was estimated that in 2000 some 5,000 such NGOs exist that in turn support over 20,000 national NGOs around the world (Ferroni 2000).

There is now compelling evidence that the most critical global challenge today is climate change, due to the tangible effects of the increase in GGEs (Stern 2006; Gore 2006).[29] It has also become evident that the poor around the world are most likely to be the first victims of the ravages of climate change due to its consequences in terms of weather related catastrophes, flooding, diseases and drops in agriculture productivity. Their lack of resources to invest in adaptation infrastructure, such as building levies, dams or relocating population, makes them particularly vulnerable. No one doubts that organized collective efforts on a global scale are in order for both mitigation and adaptation to climate change.

International organizations, such as the various specialized agencies of the UN system and the World Bank, are now seeking greater integration between their country-based assistance and the production and delivery of IPGs, especially those tied to VGPs. As they achieve this integration, they will become well placed to help client countries reach an optimum mix of IPGs and NPGs. Moreover, these organizations are also capable of developing global strategies supporting VGPs, sensitive to individual national development strategies, their domain for many years of country-based assistance.

The ability of IFIs such as the World Bank and the International Monetary Fund (IMF) to mobilize resources on a global scale and magnitude, from both donors and international financial markets, render them instrumental to the financial viability of VGPs (IDA 2007).[30] Moreover, their convening and persuasion powers, as well as their credibility as honest brokers, can bring disparate national interest to the table and hone the consensus required to ensure the political viability of these VGPs, rendering them compatible with the provision of NPGs. More importantly, most international organizations can bring to bear the trust they have earned from their clients to help in reconciling the differences that may emerge between national and global interests supporting the VGPs. Compensation mechanisms to cover the cost of mitigation or adaptation to climate change, such as the provision of funding, may also be brought to bear, as in the case of the carbon markets, where the World Bank is a key player.

While the issue of mitigation versus adaptation remains contentious among the larger GGE offenders, the industrialized countries and the emerging developing countries, the comparative advantage of international organizations is in assisting the national efforts of the latter to reduce emissions and adapt to the consequences of climate change. This advantage is because adaptation to climate change has a far-reaching scope as it affects agricultural production, flood control infrastructure, water conservation, prevention and control of pandemic diseases, among many others, which cover a vast portion of the development assistance provided by these organizations. More recently, the efforts of these organizations to gear up for assistance in relief and humanitarian work and provide quick response to disasters also adds to their comparative advantage. The split of VGP resources between adaptation and mitigation is by implication also controversial and has generated some tension between the secretariats of these VGPs and the client countries. Brazil has been the focus of some of this tension.

Despite the clear comparative advantage of IFIs such as the World Bank to lead, manage and oversee VGPs, their role and performance are not without weaknesses. An independent evaluation in 2004 by the World Bank's Operations Evaluation Department (OED) of 26 Global Programs with World Bank involvement in assorted capacities highlights their impact on reducing poverty and on assisting developing countries in dealing with sustainable economic growth. This is especially the case if the Bank is the implementing agency (World Bank 2004). This independent evaluation points out several such weaknesses along with its strengths. Noteworthy among these are: (a) the World Bank's comparative advantage and its performance at the global versus the national level despite its main role of horizontal assistance at the national level, suggesting a disconnect between the two; (b) inadequate participation of client countries or even the Bank's operational regions concerned with VGPs, suggesting that the voice of shareholders (donors to the funds supporting the VGPs) yield greater influence than that of the other stakeholders concerned; (c) weaknesses in governance relate to the issue of balancing legitimacy and accountability for results with efficiency in achieving them. When responsibility for these rests mostly within the same international organization, it creates the potential for real or perceived conflict of interest; (d) IPGs do not represent additional ODA funding; with the exception of those funded by the private sector such as the Gates Foundation; (e) lacking independent oversight of VGPs and (f) the Bank deploys its comparative advantage more at the global level than at the country level, reflected in budgetary and staffing shortfalls for bank support of VGPs, and especially capacity building in the recipient countries. The report also highlights the Bank's shortfall in exploiting economies of scale and scope in the areas of monitoring and evaluation, knowledge creation and dissemination, capacity building, technical assistance and donor coordination. This includes the development of indicators to measure donor's performance in managing such programs.

Knowledge, both scientific and technological, is a critical ingredient of the VGPs. Because of their funding capabilities, international organizations have been able to procure and disseminate it to a considerable degree. Moreover, because the assistance and lending of the IFIs rely on substantial development research work, some of it on a comparative basis, they are well placed as a source of knowledge to bear on VGPs.[31] The race to develop knowledge relevant to the global challenge has led international organizations to invest in their staff and to procure specialized consulting work in a range of scientific fronts to nurture the scientific underpinning of VGPs. On the institutional requirements to achieve an optimum fit between the organization of VGPs and host institutions, less of an effort has been made and there is need for further research and practical work by the international organizations.[32]

Global Commons VGPs and State Reform: Governance and Institutional Options

Climate change VGPs are driven by the compelling crisis of the global commons and the willingness of many governments to comply with their obligations under the assorted international conventions and protocols linked to global environmental protection and to induce other governments to do the same. International policy considerations and the trend towards greater consistency with certain national policies are also driving forces. In the context of multiple threats to environmental global commons, the challenge for VGPs is to develop *ad hoc* rules of engagement and governance congruent with suitable institutional arrangements within host countries. As seen in the case of Brazil, these provisions and arrangements, still tentative, are far from perfect and reflect the novelty of such an institutional challenge. The literature on this topic is scant, refers mostly to health VGPs and stresses evaluation rather than institutional design and modeling (World Bank 2006; World Bank OED/IEG 2004; World Bank GPP 2006; Kaul 2006; Caines 2004; McKinsey & Co 2004).

The Brazilian case also showed that these arrangements are anything but uniform, as they vary with (a) the nature of the IPG being delivered, (b) the point of entry and engagement and (c) the constituencies and stakeholders concerned. Lack of sensitivity to these features has played an important role in the level of performance of these governance arrangements. It became apparent from the Brazil experience that, notwithstanding the agreement with the terms of the convention underpinning a given VGP, its operational rules give cause to varying performance of its implementation at country level. Furthermore, the incongruence between the international (of VGPs) and national policies plays a decisive role in the outcome of these VGPs. The multiple points of institutional entry and engagement do not necessarily share the same assumptions on the causes and remedies to the risks afflicting global commons. More importantly, they have differing notions of the international and national interests at stake. These discrepancies trickle down to the operational level of engagement, rendering implementation equally problematic and resistant to any coordination efforts either horizontally between sectors or vertically among levels of government. Finally, a policy focal point on matters relating to the global commons and how to align them to national policy is still non-existent. As seen in the case of Brazil, three key governmental entry points compete to play such a role.

Unlike NPGs, most implementation policies related to IPGs are not amenable to influence through national citizen voice, especially in countries where there are pressing domestic needs and no strong civil society movements to insert those issues in the public agenda. Yet they have an enormous impact on their lives across national boundaries, as seen in the case of the PPG7 and IPGs associated with it. Ironically, because of their international collective character, they fall beyond the reach of the citizenry that makes up the participating nations. This democratic gap has been replaced by tumultuous and disruptive voice mechanisms through the conduit of international activist NGOs, which have targeted the leading IFIs and the WTO and are likely to target others. In Brazil, the demonstrations orchestrated by national and international NGOs are the equivalent.

The overriding implication for state reform of globalization and the increasing importance of IPGs is the degree of openness relative to self-reliance driving such reforms. In his discussion of shared sovereignty among nation-states in light of the erosion of national sovereignty, Dirk Messner puts this dilemma in the following way: 'the architecture of global governance will therefore become a key factor to enable nation- states to reinvent their sovereignty and internal and external influence, legitimacy and identity' (Maggio and Messner 2002). By assessing and recognizing the increasing demand for public goods that go unmet nationally, and the extent to which IPGs and Q-IPGs are helping bridge such gaps between demand and supply, reforming countries are taking an important initial step towards realistic state reform, which can balance global and national/local interests. Moreover, openness prevails when governments of reforming nation-states recognize and accept standards for quality of public services across a range of developed countries, using them as benchmarks and factoring them into their national reform efforts. This acceptance has been accentuated as a result of participation in VGPs where certain reforms at the national level are becoming necessary, but not emphasized by the secretariats of the VGPs. By accepting international standards, nation-states are inviting competition, exchanges and modernization.[33]

International organizations are suitable conduits for openness and IFIs provide funding and technical assistance for such reforms. To a large extent assistance is based on exchanges of reform experiences and models, contributing to openness of state reform.[34] The projects that support such financing become IPGs intended to support state reforms, which in turn improve the quality of NPGs. To the extent that the latter goal is achieved, the quality of the national state rises, increasing citizen attachment to the country and decreasing undue immigration pressures and further demand for IPGs, provided that economic activity is sustained and employment generated. Moreover, this added capacity translates into greater ability to fully comply with obligations under international conventions in the environment area.

Despite the recent mistrust of multilateral agencies, they continue to have a considerable comparative advantage to meet the rising demand for IPGs (Will 2007). They manage a wealth of information and analytical work on the state of development throughout the world, which is widely disseminated. On the basis of this information and the high quality of their staff, they manage concessional funding to developing countries with some effectiveness. This is possible due to reliable mechanisms to bear the transactional risks and contract enforcement requirements associated with such flows.[35]

Many developing countries have tied their state reform efforts to external financing from IFIs and have accepted the policy conditionality that comes with it, a rule usually associated with such IPGs. This conditionality is usually tied to the adoption of market friendly policies and liberalization of trade, which follows a pattern of openness and elimination of assorted barriers (The Washington Consensus). Such reforms have generally pursued the improvement of NPGs and have been oblivious to other IPGs, as these have traditionally been services falling outside the realm of national public institutions, a perception that is likely to change.

The dilemma raised by this situation is that, for citizens from a developing nation-state, certain IPGs may be far more important than NPGs provided by their own government. In the case of VGPs tied to climate change, this importance translates into either opportunities or constraints to their welfare within the context of development as discussed above in the case of Brazil. Examples abound in the less developed parts of Latin America, for example where health, education, environment protection and, in some cases, security are ensured by assorted forms of international public or private institutional arrangements, IFIs included. State reforms intent on increasing the quantity and quality of services to its citizens, especially those that target poverty, cannot overlook this reality. While it is crucial for reforming states to harness the considerable flows of financial and technical assistance for state reform, the choice of the right mix of IPGs and NPGs is central for setting reform goals. Acceptance of the required openness in a globalized world is still difficult for countries caught up in the internal tensions of nationalism and protection of sovereignty.

While some governments of developing countries by default work with or through such international public or private institutional arrangements, these are yet to become an organic part of government and have not been systematically mainstreamed into national state reform programs or strategies. This is especially the case of IPGs tied to VGPs in the environment area. Likewise, the myriad of IPGs that are effectively consumed by citizens of nation states who rely on them, usually are not filtered through any national state policy function. Moreover, mechanisms for coordination of international assistance both financial and otherwise are notoriously weak in most developing countries, as shown in the case of Brazil.

Openness to global exposure is no substitute for self-reliance and determination in dealing with state problems inherent in the local political and administrative culture, amenable primarily to local solutions or reform measures. Among these problems, weak governance and capture by corruption stand out as particularly critical. The influence of IPGs[36] may be limited in such cases, as they pose essentially a domestic challenge and a test to the local political will to face up to it. In the environmental protection area, the incidence of corrupt practices in the case of Brazil is illustrated by the repeated scandals involving IBAMA and tied to bribes associated with illegal logging in the Amazon forest.[37]

In addition to the harnessing of international assistance and setting the right mix of IPGs and NPGs, reforming states should pay greater attention to how national governments participate and interact with multilateral organizations. The challenge here goes beyond achieving greater concessions by such bodies, as currently clamored by minority shareholders. It is instead to bring to the deliberation table of these bodies the full weight of citizenry voice of the countries represented. This can only be achieved through legitimate representation, the true test of national sovereignty. Democracy at the international level requires that representation of the member nations be democratically rooted. Joseph Stiglitz puts this challenge well when he states,

> get the balance right between state and the market, between collective action at the local, national and global levels and between government and non-governmental actors. With globalization, countries and peoples of the world are more closely integrated, therefore we need more collective action at the international level, and we cannot escape issues of democracy and social justice in the global arena.' (Stiglitz 2003)

A plausible point of departure to pursue this path would be to ensure that selection of representatives to international bodies supporting IPGs in general is subjected to equally rigorous and transparent processes for appointment to public office. While governors to such bodies, especially the IFIs are *ex-officio* positions held by ministers of state, representatives to their respective executive boards are usually subject to discretionary appointment by governments. Given the public interest at stake both domestically and internationally in the deliberating processes of these bodies, those representing a given country should be held accountable to the public as any other public office holder. Accordingly, their performance in voting and intervening in such bodies should be held up to public scrutiny.

In addition to subjecting such appointments to congressional vetting or ratification, a practice usually accorded to ambassadorial appointments, these appointees should be given the means to interface closely with domestic policy makers so as to participate actively in the choice of desirable mixes of IPGs and NPGs. For this function to be feasible, state reform efforts should strive to establish suitable focal points at the highest level of government for oversight of the 'complementarity' among IPGs and NPGs.

Along the same lines, much greater transparency and public disclosure at the national level should be required for policies, programs and the performance of international organizations. This responsibility should fall jointly with national representatives and those national entities entrusted with liaising with international organizations. This is a practice welcomed by these organizations that are likely to want to cooperate as called for by their own policies on disclosure of information. In this regard, it is noteworthy that the annual meeting of the Breton Woods IFIs in Prague in 2000, a proposal was tabled in order to post on the Internet the proceedings of such meetings, thus making them accessible on a global scale, now standard practice.

On another level, state reforms that are sensitive to public advocacy of civic groups such as domestic NGOs should facilitate access to and dissemination of standards and practices promoted by international organizations, especially in addition to such areas as labor practices, health and education, as well as in the more controversial areas such as environmental protection, anti-corruption and human rights. Through their representatives in such organizations, the governments of reforming states should build bridges with both domestic providers of goods and civic groups that represent citizen users of such goods and services. Exposure to international standards by national consumers of public goods and best public practices would serve as a means to induce better performance by public agencies of reforming states.

To the extent that international organizations are represented by member states through an open and transparent process and that their deliberations are truly participatory and democratic, their outcomes will be accepted with greater legitimacy by national citizens of its member countries. Achieving legitimacy of the outcome of such agencies is equally important as achieving the development effectiveness of the IPGs of such organizations.

In view of the growing importance of IPGs and the organizations that produce them, countries engaged in reforming their states would gain from greater consistency of conceptual and technical orientation among the staff of such organizations and their counterparts engaged in issues of state reform. This is particularly applicable to those countries whose state reform programs rely substantially on internationally funded VGPs. These VGPs should further emphasize support to host countries to resolve the institutional dilemmas behind their policies surrounding both national and global commons. Solutions to these dilemmas would involve consideration of options such as regulation of property rights of such commons and their privatization or restricted access by way of government controls and maintenance requirements. These institutional solutions require the manipulation of incentives and the establishment of rules and enforcement mechanisms. Only after their resolution is explored, should VGPs assist with issues of managerial alignment.

In regards to the proposed institutional approach, the following features of the global commons should be kept in mind: (a) the order of magnitude of the causes and consequences of the global commons challenge, and the scaling up of the institutional solutions devised for local common; (b) the cultural and institutional diversity entailed by the multiplicity of national, regional and local jurisdictions involved; (c) the interdependence among global commons and the limitations caused by the compartmentalized approach hitherto adopted; (d) the pace of change and the world-wide dissemination that globalized means of communication and information bring to the commons dilemma and (e) the need for global consensus around solutions proposed for the dilemma.

Several principles have emerged from the Brazil case and topics discussed above, which can guide the search for institutional and governance models for VGPs in their interface with host countries and serve as inputs into strategies of state reform:

1. Given the implications of VGPs to national policy and interests, a political prerequisite for any VGP is that national stakeholders and relevant constituencies participate in: (a) policy discussions, exchanges and negotiations leading to the engagement of a VGP; (b) the design of the respective institutional architecture and organizational arrangements; (c) providing some input into the selection of appointees to represent the host government in the VGPs deliberating bodies, and (d) the monitoring and evaluation of the VGPs performance as a basis for accountability to both government and the stakeholders.

2. Combining the high level of scientific and technological content of VGPs with a measure of social, economic and institutional awareness and sensitivity to the consequences of VGPs to local communities and their interests. This will require a broader range of expertise to be brought to the design and implementation of such programs.

3. National implementation arrangements for VGPs should be enhanced both vertically to sub-national levels of government and horizontally to different sector government agencies. This implementation strategy ensures a tighter fit between the sustainability of the global commons and local/national development goals. It also places the responsibility for environmental protection and enforcement of the VGPs standards with those most responsible for putting the environment at risk.

4. The fiscal principles of internalization of costs by those that benefit from activities that endanger the commons and compensating those that incur costs of preventing such endangerment. In other words, the creation of taxes and tax credits for productive operations that affect the commons. This would mirror the carbon tax being considered by several countries.

5. Seek the appropriate mix of NPGs and IPGs, designing institutional arrangements consistent with the mix, and factoring the results into the design of state reform strategies.

6. The designation of VGP host country representatives to the boards and councils of international organizations should be made with the same rigor as any public official. They should liaise with the pertinent national policy making and implementation agencies concerned with the IPG in question, as well as with the focal point concerned with IPGs. They should report regularly to their liaison agency and should be held accountable to the pertinent constituencies.

7. Increased attention should be paid to the study of the institutional and managerial implications of VGPs especially their own design and interface with host countries, with particular attention to institutional and policy alignment, in addition to managerial arrangements.

8. In the case of host countries with federal state organization, special attention must be paid to the respective constitutional responsibilities of the union, the states and local governments. Electoral calendars must also be factored in, lest the programs become victims of lack of continuity due to political successions.

9. The multiplicity of managerial rules and standards as applied by different sources of donor funding as well as the host governments wreak havoc in implementation, and their harmonization must be confronted head on.

10. Special attention must be paid to building social capital in support of those VGPs concerned with the reconciliation between protection of the commons and sustainable development ensuring the livelihood of local populations. To achieve this, the participation of civil society organizations must be assured.

References

Andersson, K. and Ostrum, E. 2008. 'Analyzing Decentralized Resources Regimes from a "polycentric" Perspective', *Policy Science* 41.

Caines, K. 2004. 'Assessing the Impact of Vertical Health Programs', UK Department for International Development.

Damiani, O. 2001. 'Organic Agriculture in Mexico: Case studies of small farmer associations in Chiapas and the Yucatan Peninsula', Rome: International Fund for Agricultural Development.

Diewald, C. and Pinto, R. 2006. 'Brazil Country Survey on Alignment of Global Programs with Country Planning and Operational Frameworks', a background report for a study by the Global Programs and Partnerships Group.

Hardin, G. 1968. 'The Tragedy of the Commons', *Science* 162.

International Development Association. 2007. 'The Role of IDA in the Global Aid Architecture: Supporting the Country-based Development Model', background paper, Resource Mobilization Department (FRM).

———.2007. 'Aid Architecture: An Overview of the Main Trends in Official Development Assistance Flows', background paper, Resource Mobilization Department (FRM).

Kaul, I. And Conceição, P. 2006. *The New Public Finance: Responding to Global Challenges*. New York: Oxford University Press.

Kaul, I. 2006. 'Managing National-International Alignment of Global Programs: Tools for assessing the Risk of Vertical –Linkage Problems', draft paper, UNDP Office of Development Studies.

Krasner, S. 2001. 'Sovereignty: Think Again', *Foreign Policy*, January/February.

Maggi, C. and Messner, D. (eds). 2002. *Gobernanza Global: Una mirada desde América Latina. El rol de la región frente a la globalización y a los nuevos desafíos de la política global*. Caracas: Fundación Desarrollo y Paz/Nueva Sociedad.

McKinsey & Company. 2004, 'Global Health Partnerships: Assessing Country Consequences', Bill and Melinda Gates Foundation.

Olson, M and Kahkonem, S, (editors) *2000 A no- so- Dismal Science: A Broader View of Economies and Society, Oxford University Press, USA.*

Ostrom, E. 1990. *Governing the Commons: The Evolution of Institutions for Collective Action.* Cambridge, UK: Cambridge University Press.

Ostrom, E., Burger, J., Field, C., Norgaard, R. and Policansky, D. 1999. 'Revisiting the Commons: Local Lessons, Global Challenges', *Science* 284.

Piccioto, R. 2000. 'Putting Institutional Economics to Work', World Bank unpublished paper.

Pinto, R. 2000. 'International Public Goods and Reform of the State: The Receding Nation State', Paper presented at a seminar on *Hemispheric Integration: Political, Economic and Social Dimensions, Brasilia,* 6–8 December.

_____.2004. 'Service Delivery in Francophone West Africa: The Challenge of Balancing Deconcentration and Decentralisation', in *Public Administration and Development* (24).

Pinto, R and Puppim de Oliveira, Jose A. (2008). Implementation Challenges in Protecting the Global Environmental Commons: The Case of Climate Change Policies in Brazil. *Public Administration and Development,* 28(5), 340–350.

Puppim de Oliveira, Jose A. (2009). The implementation of climate change related policies at the subnational level: An analysis of three countries. *Habitat International* (ISSN: 0197-3975, Elsevier), 33(3), 253–259.

_____.2002a. 'Implementing Environmental Policies in Developing Countries Through Decentralization: The case of Protected Areas in Bahia, Brazil', in *World Development* 30(10).

_____.2002b. 'The Policy making process for creating competitive assets for the use of biomass energy: The Brazilian Alcohol Program', *Renewable and Sustainable Energy Reviews* 6(1–2).

Shakow, A. 2006. 'Global Fund – World HIV/AIDS Programs: Comparative Advantage Study', Global Fund to Fight Malaria AIDS and Tuberculosis and World Bank.

Will, G. 2007. *The Washington Post,* May 2.

World Bank. 2006. 'Health Financing Revisited: A Practitioners Guide', World Bank report.

_____.2006. 'Appraising Global Partnerships–A Methodology for Improved Selectivity', Global Programs and Partnerships Group.

_____.2007. 'Global Public Goods: A Framework for the Role of the World Bank', a background report to the Development Committee, Global Programs and Partnerships Group.

World Bank Operations Evaluation Department, OED/IEG. 2004. 'Addressing the Challenge of Globalization: An Independent Evaluation of the World Bank's Approach to Global Programs', Washington, D.C.

Chapter 5

ECONOMIC CHALLENGES FOR GLOBAL GOVERNANCE

David Mayer-Foulkes

Introduction

The acceleration of globalization in the 1980s began with the revival of classical liberal economics, as Keynesian policies reached their demise. Faced with the stagflation crisis of the 1970s and the first oil crisis, Ronald Reagan and Margaret Thatcher restarted economic growth by freeing trade and investment. They cut income taxes, especially for the wealthy, deregulated and privatized the economy, reduced the power of trade unions, weakened the welfare state and lifted barriers to trade and investment at home and abroad, therefore raising incentives for investment. Many underdeveloped countries faced similar crises at the time, especially those following import substitution models[1], and fell into debt through rising interest rates and oil prices. Essentially the same macroeconomic and growth policies were applied in underdeveloped countries, following what became known as the Washington Consensus (Williamson 1990).[2] In addition, when the Berlin Wall fell in 1989, the end of the Cold War created a global market economy. As free trade and investment treaties proliferated, globalization accelerated. In particular, foreign direct investment (FDI) increased worldwide at an average rate of almost 28 per cent a year from 1983 to 1998.[3] Thus, freer markets and a reduced government role in both developed and underdeveloped countries released a fresh wave of globalization. The new schools of economic thought produced theories implying that free trade and FDI would lead to the equalization of growth rates and production levels across countries. However, these predictions were realized unevenly, with many underdeveloped countries obtaining poor results. As the new theory of economic growth developed, inquiry into the long-term persistence of income inequality between and within countries underlined the importance of dynamics in population, technology and institutions.

The purpose of this chapter is to synthesize some of the findings regarding long-term economic growth, incorporating findings from a theory of globalization (Mayer-Foulkes 2007b) that focuses on the interaction between technological change, international trade and FDI. The theory explains the simultaneous historical emergence of development and underdevelopment, and their persistence in the context of globalization. In fact, most of the history of modern economic growth occurred in the context of globalization. The 'First Great Era of Globalization' lasted from about 1820–1914. The 'Great Divergence' of incomes (Pritchett 1997) began in this very context and continues to this day (Maddison 2001; Mayer-Foulkes 2006). Our theory shows that much of the multifaceted nature of economic growth – including episodes of miracle growth – can be understood in terms of multiple steady states describing virtuous and vicious cycles in economic growth. Multiple steady states are distinct equilibria with possibly distinct equilibrium rates of growth that represent different types of trajectories of economic growth. I use these various types of steady states or equilibria to describe development and underdevelopment. The theory's links with the literature also show that globalization has important interactions with both population and institutional dynamics, each of which plays a central role in a contemporary line of research on economic growth.

The main finding in Mayer-Foulkes (2007b) is that trade and FDI tend to favour the concentration of innovation in advanced and larger countries and to inhibit it in smaller and more backward countries, whose trajectories of economic growth can therefore lag permanently in levels or in growth rates. This tendency also compounds institutional and demographic differences, thus contributing to the polarized economic performance. For globalization to pull countries out of underdevelopment effectively, it is necessary to counteract these asymmetric incentives to innovation. This has been achieved by the East Asian tigers and more recently China through the combination of export promotion and technology adoption, obtaining high rates of economic growth. However, the success of these policies depends on country size, institutional strength and geopolitical circumstances. Their implementation for smaller and more backward countries, often competing with each other for FDI, requires design and application at a global level with the support of the global institutions that regulate trade and FDI. Such global development policies can be beneficial for all because innovation is not a zero sum game. While trade and FDI raise the world growth rate, it is maximal when all countries are developed.[4]

In the absence of such global development policies, poor outcomes represented by the continuance of lower steady states can persist under globalization. Whole groups of countries may lag permanently in income levels or in growth rates. What this means is that a highly polarized world can subsist indefinitely. At lower steady states, demographic transition towards lower birth rates and institutional development tend to be slower. Under these conditions, economic integration under globalization tends to subdivide production according to factoral specialization (cheap labour and resources versus technology, physical capital and human capital), rather than sectoral specialization as occurs between core countries. Altogether, a politically unstable panorama tends to emerge, one that can generate conflict and challenge the viability of globalization.

Innovation is driven by incentives derived from market power. For this and other reasons, such as the presence of fixed costs in trade, transnational corporations (TNCs) play a central role in globalization. While aggregate world exports reached US $7 trillion dollars in 1998, aggregate sales of foreign affiliates of TNCs reached US $11 trillion dollars.[5] TNCs conduct two-thirds of world trade and half of this is intra-firm trade. TNCs carry out one-fourth of global production, two-thirds of which takes place in the host countries. By contrast, they carry out nearly all of their research and development (R&D) in their countries of origin or in developed nations.

The prominent role played by TNCs in globalization has raised their importance as well as their impact, especially on technology transfer, inequality, labour conditions and the ecology. Thus, implementing global development policies requires the capacity to regulate the role of TNCs on a global scale.

It is interesting to recall that the policies that strengthened markets and weakened government in the 1980s also raised inequality in the US. During this period, the income share of the top US percentile, no doubt related to TNCs, doubled from about 2.5 per cent to about 5 per cent (Piketty and Saez 2003). The corresponding shift in political power has led to a decline of the public role in research, education and health. Democracy in the US is at a relative low, as measured by the responsiveness of public policy to urgent needs such as green energy research. So also is the independence of the press, as has been apparent in the discussion of issues related to the Iraq war.

Conversely, when insertion into globalization economically empowers large segments of the population in underdeveloped countries, this is conducive to the type of institutional development that promotes economic growth. Such institutions include not only functioning markets, but also democratic institutions with sufficient power to promote adequate investments in human capital and public goods. As a rule, however, the presence of TNCs does not automatically contribute to such benefits; these are a function of host countries' regulation and negotiation. It follows that policies for global development imposing limits on economic concentration and adequate controls on large corporations would be favourable for maintaining and developing democratic institutions in both developed and underdeveloped countries.

To summarize, this chapter outlines how trade, FDI, technological change, institutions and the demographic transition interact. It explains development and under-development in the context of globalization. Both trade and FDI can generate asymmetric incentives for innovation concentrating innovation in advanced countries and therefore generating multiple steady states in economic growth. This means that economic polarization can persist under globalization. Nevertheless, an adequate orchestration of the forces of globalization ensuring that technological change accrues equally across countries can break the cycle of inequality and generate economic development everywhere. Such policies, based on export promotion, technological adoption, human capital formation and infrastructure investment, are not only economically favourable to all, tending to raise the world growth rate, but are also favourable to accelerating the demographic transition, strengthening democratic institutions and promoting a more harmonious global economic integration. These are the economic challenges of global governance.

While the current wave of globalization arose as the result of freeing markets and reducing the role of government, now that a global economy has emerged global institutional development must rise to the challenge. How strong do these institutions have to be? The answer is straightforward. They have to be stronger than the markets they seek to regulate (as is the case in developed countries), so that they can exercise the necessary control over the world economy by channelling the forces of globalization.

In what follows, I will first outline the stylized facts of the history of economic growth and the main mechanisms of long-term growth discussed in the literature. I will make a comparative summary of the historical and current importance of trade and FDI. Then I outline the impact that trade and FDI have on innovation incentives. This explains how globalization can generate economic advantages for leading countries, independently of other country differences such as institutional or demographic characteristics. I argue that forces in the areas of technological change, human capital formation, institutional development and the demographic transition complement each other in giving rise to development and underdevelopment as distinct steady states. I then discuss current global development policy in the light of these findings. Finally, the conclusion follows.

Salient Facts in the History of Globalization and Economic Development

Modern economic growth begins with the Industrial Revolution in the second half of the eighteenth century. When Great Britain took off, it became the leading military and industrial power. It prided itself as the *Workshop of the World*, trading industrial goods for raw materials, and established a *Pax Britannica* lasting through the nineteenth century and up to 1914.

Deindustrialization

Deindustrialization was one of the main economic impacts suffered by the periphery as a consequence of its trade with the core between 1750–1913.[6] For example, while India had been a major textile exporter in the early eighteenth century, by the middle of the nineteenth century it had lost all of its export market and much of its domestic market. While India produced about 25 per cent of world industrial output in 1750, this figure had fallen to only 2 per cent by 1900 (Clingingsmith and Williamson 2005). Figure 5.1 illustrates the process of deindustrialization of the underdeveloped world, whose proportion of manufacturing production declined dramatically.

The Great Divergence

The Great Divergence in per capita income between the poorest and the richest countries characterized economic growth in the nineteenth and twentieth centuries. Pritchett (1997) estimates that the proportional gap in per capita incomes between the richest and poorest countries grew by a factor of five from 1870 to 1998. Similarly, according to Maddison (2001), the proportional gap increased from 3 to 19 between 1820 and 1998. The Great Divergence

Figure 5.1. Deindustrialization. Manufacturing Production 1750–1938.

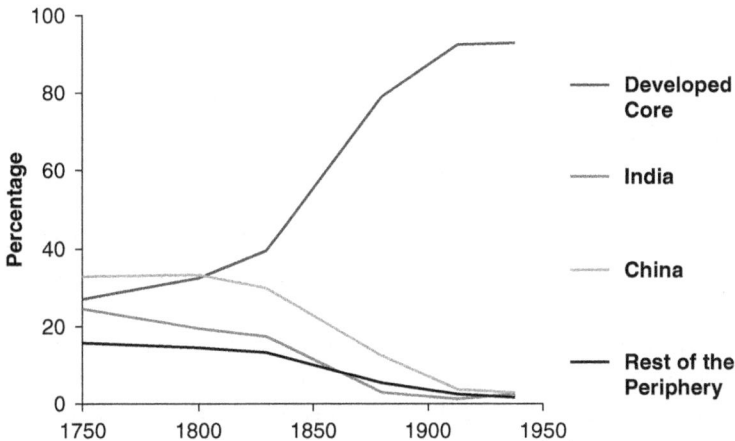

Source: Williamson (2004), Table 1.

Figure 5.2. The Great Divergence.

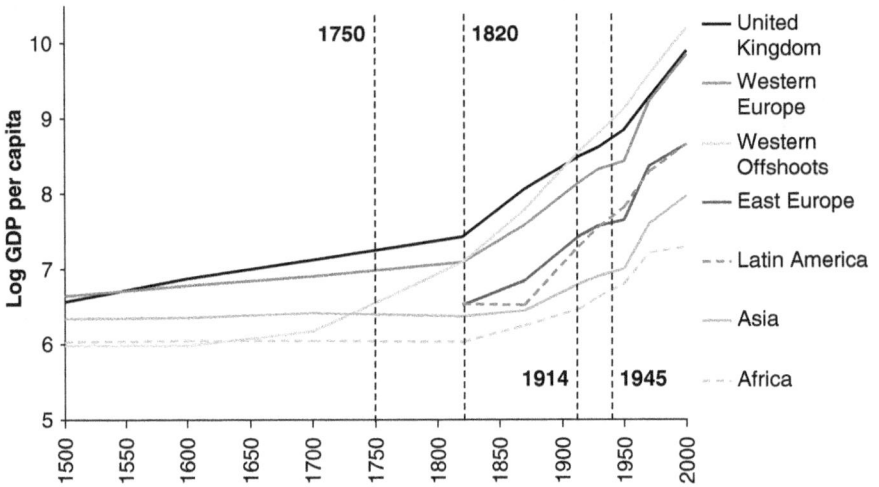

Source: Maddison (2001).

originated during the First Great Era of Globalization and it continues to this day. The proportional gap between the per capita income of the richest and poorest groups of countries increased by a factor of 1.75 from 1950 to 1998 (Maddison 2001), and between the richest and poorest convergence groups reported in Mayer-Foulkes (2006) by a factor of 2.6 from 1960 to 1995 (see the discussion on Figure 5.5 below). Figure 5.2 shows the Great Divergence by graphing the per capita income of different regions of the world.

The Role of Productivity

Capital accumulation was traditionally considered to be the main engine of economic growth. Later theories complemented this with human capital. Nevertheless, increasing evidence shows that income differences between countries are mainly due to productivity differences (Knight, Loayza and Villanueva 1993; Islam, 1995; Caselli, Esquivel and Lefort 1996; Klenow and Rodriguez-Clare 1997; Hall and Jones 1999; Easterly and Levine 2002; Martin and Mitra 2001; Parente and Prescott 1999). A way of stating the economic importance of productivity is to emphasize that it is technology (rather than capital) that seeks labour while also providing the incentives for capital accumulation. Technological convergence is now considered an engine for convergence between countries, as illustrated for the Organisation for Economic Co-operation and Development (OECD) by Dollar and Wolff (1993).

Concentration of Innovation

Throughout the history of modern economic growth the concentration of innovation has been very high. Table 5.1 gives an approximate idea of this, showing that the majority of noteworthy inventions from the seventeenth century to the present were conducted in the UK and the US.

A closer look at more recent innovation is provided by patent data. Figure 5.3 shows, on the one hand, that two or three countries hold most foreign patents in the US, and on the other that attaining development is related to holding patents.

***Table 5.1.* Inventions by Country of Origin (per cent)**

	17th C	18th C	19th C	1990–1949	1950–1999	Average
U.S.	0.0	17.4	32.1	51.5	67.3	33.6
U.K.	55.6	52.2	37.0	20.6	16.4	36.3
Germany	11.1	4.3	9.9	11.8	0.0	7.4
Russia	0.0	0.0	1.2	0.0	9.1	2.1
France	18.5	17.4	12.3	4.4	0.0	10.5
Total (%)	85.2	91.3	92.6	88.2	92.7	90.0

Source: Web page by Kryss Katsiavriades and Talaat Qureshi.[7]

Figure 5.3. Percentage of Foreign U.S. Patents.

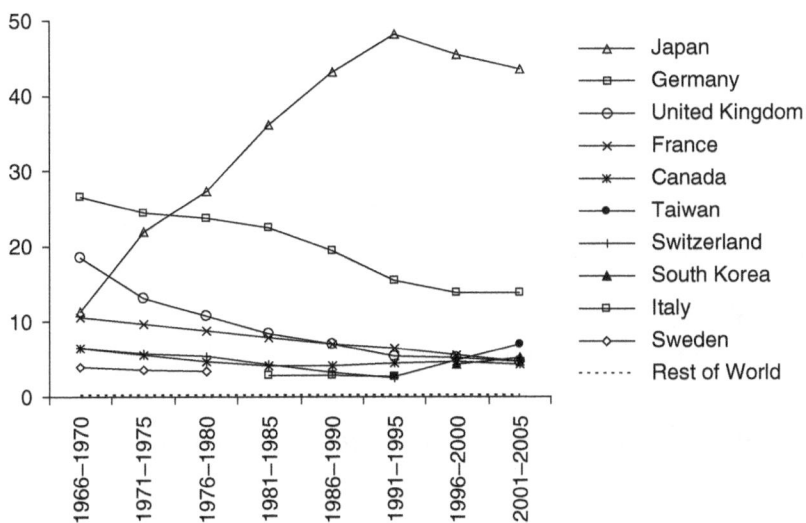

Data Source: US Patent Office.

Figure 5.4. Patents Held in US Versus GDP.

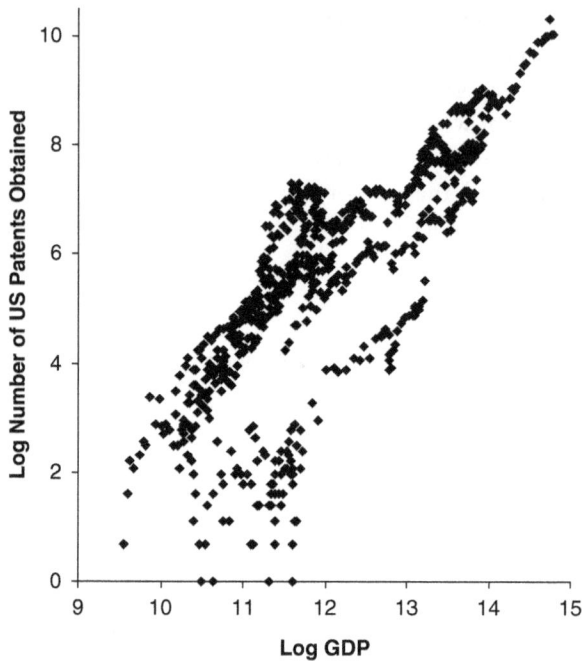

Data Source: US Patent Office.

Figure 5.4 shows a scatter plot of the logarithm of the number of US patents held by a foreign country against the logarithm of its GDP, the data ranging over the years 1963 to 2006. The highly significant slope is 1.42, showing that, at least ex-post, innovation is an increasing function of GDP.

Patent application data is also available from the World Intellectual Property Organization. During the period 2003–6, five countries accounted for 75 per cent of the applications: the US (33.5 per cent), Japan (17.8 per cent), Germany (11.6 per cent), Korea (4.5 per cent), France (4.1 per cent) and the UK (3.6 per cent).

The theoretical model outlined below suggests an explanation for innovation concentration and its relation with trade and FDI.

The Role of Trade and Foreign Investment in Economic Growth

Trade has played an important role since the early days of modern economic growth. It is one of the crucial aspects analysed by Maddison (2001) in his depiction of the economic ascent of Western Europe from the year 1000 AD to the present, passing through Venice, Portugal, The Netherlands and Great Britain. Cotton exports (the leading sector in the Industrial Revolution) in late eighteenth- and early nineteenth-century England grew from 6 per cent of total British exports in 1784–6 to a high of 48.5 per cent in 1834–6 (Chapman 1999). The growth of this sector, and the incentives to increase its productivity, were directly linked to low-priced imports of raw materials from India at this initial juncture of the Great Divergence (Broadberry and Gupta 2005). Trade played an important role in the development of institutions before 1750. The Dutch West India Company, for instance, was founded in 1602 together with the Amsterdam Stock Exchange. It was the first company to issue shares. In 1609, the Bank of Amsterdam introduced debt with interest. The consolidation of England as a country (1529–1660) was also connected with its naval and commercial development. In 1632 the monopoly law was introduced and in 1694 the Bank of England was established.[8]

Propelled by manufacture based on the steam engine, Great Britain embraced free trade in order to obtain raw materials and to sell its industrial products. Thus, the First Great Era of Globalization emerged, lasting from approximately 1820 until 1914. Free trade turned out to be a more efficient policy for enrichment than colonialism (Beaudreau 2004; Semmel 1970), and this was the motivation behind gunboat diplomacy. Large- scale FDI was prevalent by the end of the nineteenth century.[9] Investments in colonized and dependent countries were an extraordinary source of revenue, thanks to the extremely low price of labour and raw materials. In his book, *Imperialism, the Highest Stage of Capitalism* (1916), Lenin criticized the vast amounts of capital invested abroad at rates of return that were much higher than those of the countries of origin. In 1914, British assets in other countries reached sums of between 124 and 180 per cent of its GDP. Of the total British investment between 1865 and 1914, approximately the same amount went to the underdeveloped countries of Africa, Asia and Latin America (29.6 per cent), as to the United Kingdom (31.8 per cent) (Ferguson 2003). Svedberg (1978) estimates that of the 19 billion dollars of accumulated investment in developing countries during 1913–14, between 44 and 60 per cent was direct foreign investment.

The process of globalization was interrupted from 1914–1945 because of the two World Wars and the Great Depression, and also due to changes in hegemony. During the post-war period, a second stage of globalization emerged, this time led by the United States. By 1960, the United States owned nearly half of the world's direct foreign investment. Between 1950 and 1970, direct American investment in European manufacture rose almost fifteen-fold, while between 1970 and 1993 direct investment – both American investment abroad and foreign investment in the US – grew fivefold (Graham 1995). Today, foreign investment is possibly a more powerful force for globalization than trade.

All modern 'free trade' agreements are treaties on free trade *as well as* on investment, thus allowing globalization to proceed at full strength. FDI has grown enormously since the eighties.[10] Outward flow increased worldwide by an average of almost 28 per cent annually from 1983 to 1998. This is three times the growth of world exports. Even so, FDI has not reached the relative levels that characterized the first period of globalization. The amount of American FDI in 2001 was around 13.6 per cent of the GIP,[11] far below the corresponding British amount in 1914.

The following numbers give an approximate idea of the relative importance of trade and FDI today. As mentioned above, aggregate world exports reached US $7 trillion dollars in 1998, while aggregate sales of foreign affiliates of TNCs reached US $11 trillion dollars. Two-thirds of world trade are connected with TNCs. Internal trade for these companies amounts to one-half of this. TNCs carry out one-fourth of global production, one-third of which takes place in countries of origin. Approximately 26.3 per cent of United States' FDI in 2000 and of global FDI in 1998[12] flowed to the underdeveloped world, where about 21.2 per cent of world income was generated in 1997.[13] By contrast, TNCs carry out nearly all of their R&D in their countries of origin or in developed nations.

When analysing the asymmetric impact of trade and FDI innovation incentives, our discussion goes beyond much of the theoretical analysis of the impact of trade on innovation and economic growth. Most theories, whether of economic growth or trade, imply that free trade and FDI will equalize the growth rates and levels of productivity of different countries (Helpman 1993; Eaton, Gutierrez and Kortum, 1998; Eaton and Kortum 2001, 2003, 2004). However, Rodriguez and Rodrik (1999) find little evidence that policies of trade openness are significantly linked to economic growth. In his research on international technology diffusion, Keller (2004) finds that international diffusion is neither inevitable nor automatic; rather, it requires investment inside the country. In fact, as already pointed out, the Great Divergence – whose main dimension is productivity, and which continues today – happened in the context of globalization itself.

Miracle Growth

Another distinctive characteristic of the history of economic growth, especially in the twentieth century, is miracle growth, which means a relatively long period – up to several decades – of an accelerated growth of at least 5 per cent annually. The majority of countries that attained industrialization and development went through a phase of miraculous growth. Such are the cases of Denmark, Sweden, Italy, Japan, South Korea, Taiwan, Hong Kong, Singapore, Ireland

and Germany in the nineteenth century; Western Germany after World War II; Cyprus, Iceland, Spain, Malta, Portugal, Israel; and currently China and India. Some countries experienced periods of miraculous growth without fully reaching development, as in the case of Argentina, India, Nigeria, Brazil and Mexico in the sixties and seventies. Pipitone (1995) conducts a series of case studies of this phenomenon from a historical perspective. In Wan's (2004) comparative economic case studies of the Asian Tigers' growth experiences, the reference convergence trajectories include at least two decades of growth higher than 5 per cent, viewed explicitly as a transition to a higher stationary state.

All of these experiences strongly suggest that miracle economic growth represents the transitional path between two steady states: underdevelopment and development. The policies applied by these countries, i.e. technology transfer and export promotion, directly indicate the nature of the barriers they overcame.

Persistence of Middle Income Levels

Underdevelopment is a diverse phenomenon. The theory outlined below predicts the existence of two types of lower steady states. The lowest type, *divergence in growth rates*, represents lagging economies with lower growth rates than the leading economies, accounting for long-term divergence and for contemporary semi-stagnant economies, as in the case of Sub-Saharan Africa. Any policy that improves the innovation rate, either directly or indirectly, will have growth effects. The second type, *divergence in levels*, represents middle steady state economies that maintain a fixed relative lag in relation to leading countries, with policy improvements yielding effects in levels. These represent a not sufficiently well recognized stylized fact: the persistence of middle income levels. For example, the average per-capita income of 19 Latin American countries relative to the US actually decreased between 1960 and 1999 from 0.25 to 0.20. The relative level 0.20 represents a lag of around 80 years behind the US, assuming what would seem an unattainable catch up rate of 2 per cent per year above the US growth rate. The importance of this middle-income persistence tends to be neglected. It is believed that since these countries grew at an average rate of 1.5 per cent instead of 2.1 per cent, it must be just a matter of fine-tuning to get at least parallel growth, which is deemed to be a sufficient objective. The point is, however, that if a trap is maintaining the level difference, or the divergence, unlocking it would lead to miracle growth and enormous welfare gains. Ignoring it, on the contrary, may doom proposed economic policies.

These mid-level trajectories have a long history with quite different rates of divergence. According to Maddison's (2001) data, between 1820 and 2000, income per capita multiplied by 3.6 and 5.7 times in India and China, 8.6 and 9.5 in Brazil and Mexico and 22.3 in the U.S.

The Demographic Transition

After the Industrial Revolution, advanced countries experienced a period of high population growth followed by a decline in birth rates that stabilized the population. This process is known as the demographic transition. Before this transition, it is thought that a Malthusian equilibrium was obtained, with incomes at subsistence levels and population levels dictated by current technologies. The achievement of high per capita income levels depended on reduced birth rates, the result of a preference for fewer educated rather than many uneducated children (Galor and Weil 2000). However, lagging countries experienced delayed and more explosive demographic transition (Chesnais 1992; Lee 2003; Doepke 2006). This is because, due to the impact of trade with advanced countries, lagging countries tend to escape the subsistence restriction with lower incentives for choosing quantity over quality (Galor and Mountford 2006, 2008). The theory we outline explains how globalization contributes to this, by generating asymmetric incentives for innovation that favour advanced countries.

The Role of Institutions

In a series of papers, a strong case is made for the role of institutions in economic growth (Acemoglu, Simon and Robinson 2000, 2004, 2005; Acemoglu and Robinson 2006; Rodrik 2005). First, European Atlantic trade is found to have had an impact on institutional formation in Europe. Second, in the colonies, the type of colonial intention (e.g. extraction of resources versus adoptive home) is found to have had a permanent impact on institutional formation. Third, a theory is developed thanks to which the distribution of *de facto* power, itself influenced by the income distribution, can sustain or lead to changes in *de jure* regimes favouring democracy.

The importance of the extension of property rights, a basic market institution, to wide segments of the population as an antecedent of the Industrial Revolution, as well as the impact of trade, is also documented in Richardson and Bogart (2008).

Engerman and Sokoloff (1994a, b) suggest that the types of natural resources found in Latin America may have resulted in specialization in activities with a low demand for human capital, leading to the formation of deficient institutions less conducive to the formation of such capital. Such deficient institutions also influence the shape of tax institutions (Sokoloff and

Zolt 2006). In effect, an unequal distribution of income leads to institutions that are less democratic, do not protect property rights, and tend to defend ruling elites.

Convergence

Last, but not least, convergence must be mentioned as one of the salient facts of economic growth. An important body of literature finds that, although there is no absolute convergence (which is hardly surprising, in the face of the Great Divergence), there is conditional convergence. This means that each economy has a tendency to converge to an equilibrium *growth trajectory* that depends on its characteristics and initial conditions. This conclusion corroborates the predictions of models with diminishing returns to the accumulation of physical capital, human capital and/or technology. However, when multiple steady states exist, either in growth rates or in levels, conditional convergence occurs *within* and is consistent with divergence *between* steady states.

In the presence of multiple steady states, true convergence occurs when an economy so modifies its dynamics that it transitions from a lower to a higher steady state. This is what Wan (2004) argues occurred in East Asian countries, as they experienced miracle growth. By combining income and life expectancy data, Mayer-Foulkes (2006) gives econometric evidence for the existence of low, middle and high steady states, with some groups of countries remaining in these steady states and others transitioning between them (Figure 5.5).

In Figure 5.5, Group 1 represents developed countries with high per capita income and life expectancy. It consists mostly of Western European and North American countries. Group 2 represents a set of countries transitioning from underdevelopment to development, attaining high levels of income and consolidating high levels of health. It consists mainly of East Asian countries. Group 3 represents underdeveloped countries with middle income levels and relatively high life expectancy. It consists of most Latin American and Caribbean as well as Middle Eastern and North African countries, plus Turkey. Group 4 represents a set of underdeveloped countries with both income and life expectancy transitioning upwards towards middle levels. It comprises most South Asian countries including India, and the top third of Sub-Saharan countries. Group 5 consists of the bottom two thirds of Sub-Saharan countries, with low income and health levels. This study confirms that the Great Divergence continued into the twentieth century, and also gives strong evidence for the existence of multiple steady states in economic growth and human development.

Figure 5.5. Income and Life Expectancy Growth Trajectories for Five Country Groups (corridors represent mean and three standard deviations for each group).

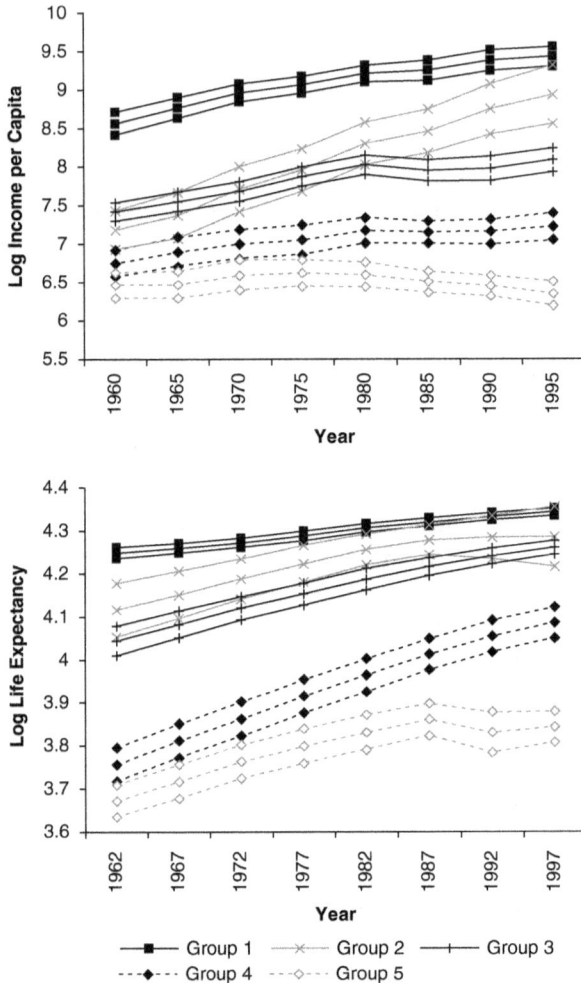

Source: Mayer-Foulkes (2006).

Summary

To summarize, when modern economic growth emerged with the Industrial Revolution, it did so in the context of trade. A process of deindustrialization occurred in lagging countries. Economies specialized either in industry or in the production of raw materials and worldwide commodity market integration took place (Findlay and O'Rourke 2001; O'Rourke and Williamson 1999). As the advanced countries consolidated their economies,

Figure 5.6. Diagramatic Rendering of Long-Term History of Economic Growth as Emergence of Multiple Steady States.

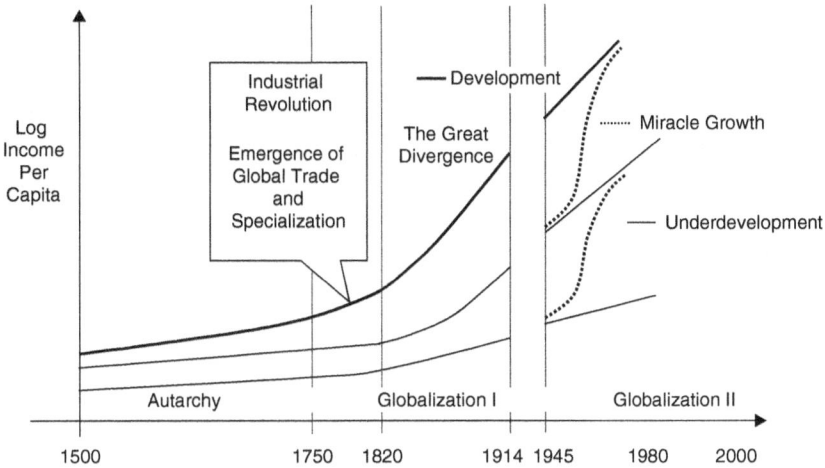

foreign direct investment also emerged, taking a role at least as important as trade, and strengthening asymmetric incentives for innovation, as will be explained below. During this time, income per capita rose much faster in the developed than in the underdeveloped world, and invention and innovation concentrated in the most advanced countries. These countries experienced a demographic transition, while in lagging countries this transition was delayed and more explosive, due, at least partly, to the differential impact of trade. Even before the Industrial Revolution, trade had an impact in institutional formation in Europe, specifically on the formation of market and democratic institutions. In lagging countries, lower incentives for human capital slowed institutional formation, which depends on more equal income distributions leading to a more democratic distribution of de facto power.

This summary of the long-term history of economic growth, including the simultaneous emergence of development and underdevelopment, is rendered diagrammatically in Figure 5.6. The Industrial Revolution in Great Britain (with approximate dates 1750–1820) ended global autarchy and engendered globalization and the Great Divergence. Modern economic growth took place in the developed world, while the rest of the world entered underdevelopment, experiencing divergence in levels and in growth rates. Development and underdevelopment are understood, according to our theory, as distinct types of trajectories of economic growth, converging to different equilibria. When countries caught up, they overcame barriers holding them to lower equilibria and experienced miracle economic growth.

Discussions about the interactions between technology, population and institutions are common in the literature. What is different and specific to the current argument is that 1) development and underdevelopment represent distinct steady states in economic growth trajectories, and 2) trade and FDI contribute to their formation by generating asymmetric incentives to innovation. This explains why, after European countries had accumulated an initial technological and institutional advantage – partially gained through trade during the period 1500–1750, when the Industrial Revolution took off simultaneously with global trade – a polarized economic specialization characterized by technological differentiation (industry versus raw materials) emerged after 1820. Development and underdevelopment emerged simultaneously.

Trade, FDI and Innovation Incentives

Let us take a look at how trade and FDI can generate asymmetric incentives to innovation that favour advanced countries, thus contributing to the existence of multiple stationary states in economic growth.

Schumpeterian Theory of Technological Change

The Schumpeterian (Schumpeter 1934) conception of economic growth has for its basis intentional innovation that seeks technical improvements with the aim of increasing returns. It is accompanied by the *creative destruction* of competitors. When modelling this process, a clear distinction is made between knowledge for production, that is, technology, and the use of human capital for both production and research (Aghion and Howitt 1992, 1998). These models describe the basic dynamics of technological change conceptualizing it as a force that produced incentives for capital accumulation. Howitt's (2000) multi-country model shows that the diffusion of production knowledge can constitute an engine for growth and convergence. The diffusion of ideas amounts to an *advantage of backwardness* through access to advanced technologies developed by other countries (Gerschenkron 1952).

In its beginnings, the endogenous theory of technological change concentrated on R&D,[14] so its relevance was circumscribed to developed countries. However, using a broad conception of innovation, the theory has gained acceptance as a description of technological change in general. It can thus be used to address problems that generate divergence and underdevelopment. For example, if human capital thresholds are involved in going beyond implementation to achieve R&D, multiple steady states can result that can explain long-term divergence (Howitt and Mayer-Foulkes 2005). Financial development can determine technological absorption rates and also explain long-term divergence (Aghion, Howitt and Mayer-Foulkes 2005). Essentially, a *disadvantage of backwardness* results when resources for technological change are proportional to current technological levels. If initial conditions are too low, countries will not converge to the higher steady state, but instead will converge to a lower steady state, which maintains a permanent technological lag in levels or in growth rates.

Trade and Innovation

I begin from the proposition that trade assigns production across countries according to comparative advantages pertaining either to the production of specific goods or to factor prices such as labour and capital. From this starting point, I outline why this assignment of production leads also to an assignment of innovation across countries. I then further discuss the impact of FDI. This discussion is formalized in Mayer-Foulkes (2007a, b).

Let us take as reference a very simple case. Consider a subdivision of the world economy in two regions, Region 1 and Region 2, trading domestically produced goods. Suppose that there is a continuum of sectors of production, and that each region has a specific, common technological level across all these sectors. Suppose that Region 1 is more advanced than Region 2. Suppose also that there is a gradient of comparative advantage across these sectors, so that some are relatively easier to produce in Region 1, while others are relatively easier to produce in Region 2. Suppose that all production is performed for the world market, and suppose, for simplicity, that consumer preferences imply an equal level of expenditure across all sectors. Finally, suppose that there are constant returns to scale in production.[15] Under trade, an equilibrium will result in which one set of sectors is produced in Region 1, while the remaining sectors are produced in Region 2. Such an equilibrium is indicated in the bottom panel of Figure 5.7, *Trade between unequal regions*. The base of each rectangle indicates the set of sectors produced in each region, while the height of each rectangle indicates the amount of production in each sector. This will be higher than under autarchy, because production is specialized according to comparative advantage. The area of each rectangle indicates the GDP of each region, and the total world product is the sum of the areas of both rectangles. In each region the consumption of the goods produced by each sector is proportional to the areas of the rectangles. Each region will produce in the sectors in which production is most economical given its resource mix (including the relative abundance of labour versus capital). Supposing that capital accumulates in proportion to technological levels (which determine its productivity), the main determinants of economy size will be the technological level and population size of each region. Note

Figure 5.7. Assignment of Production and Innovation by Trade and FDI (see text).

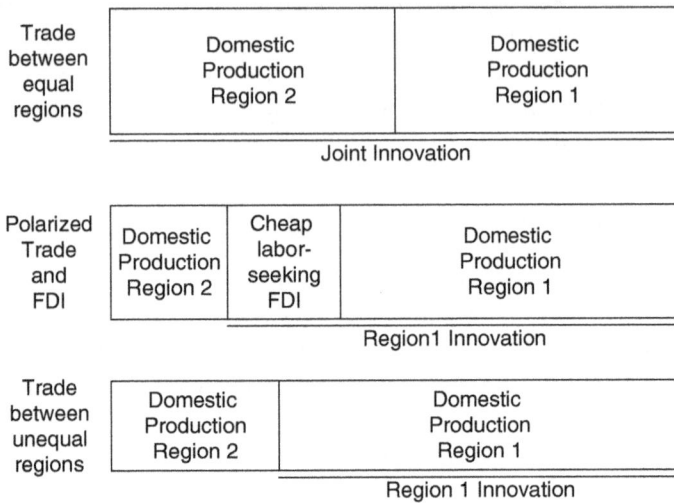

Trade between equal regions	Domestic Production Region 2	Domestic Production Region 1

Joint Innovation

Polarized Trade and FDI	Domestic Production Region 2	Cheap labor-seeking FDI	Domestic Production Region 1

Region1 Innovation

Trade between unequal regions	Domestic Production Region 2	Domestic Production Region 1

Region 1 Innovation

that in Region 2, having a lower technological level, more labour will be assigned to production in each sector. Finally, price equalization of goods in both regions will imply that wages are proportional to the productivity of labour, which, as mentioned, is given by the technological level. Sectoral profits, on the other hand, will tend to be proportional to aggregate production and therefore equal across sectors in both regions.

An important conclusion is that, other things being equal, the number of sectors produced in each region (the rectangle base) is proportional to its aggregate income, which depends on its technological level and population size. Now, observe that any innovations in production in each sector must be implemented in the region producing it. Hence, other things being equal, each region will implement a number of innovations proportional to its aggregate income. As a result, trade concentrates innovation in larger and more advanced countries.

We now extend this simple framework to include FDI. Specifically, suppose that in some sectors it is possible to use the technology of Region 1 to produce in Region 2, where labour is cheaper. Thus, we consider labor-seeking FDI. Resource-seeking and market-seeking FDI can be thought of similarly. Thus, in a given subset of sectors, investment by foreign firms from Region 1 is feasible in Region 2. The reverse does not make sense, because Region 2 can only take less advanced technologies to Region 1. The feasibility of FDI may depend on a variety of country-specific and exogenous factors, including geographical factors, the possibility of transport, of setting up production facilities, of using the advanced technology, and so on. In the middle panel of Figure 5.7, *Polarized Trade and FDI*, the middle rectangle represents those sectors for which FDI is feasible. These employ labour from Region 2 and produce with technologies from Region 1. Since this labour is more productive, aggregate world production is higher, so the demand for goods from all sectors is higher. For this reason the rectangles in the middle panel are higher than those in the lower panel. GDP of Region 1 is now the sum of its own rectangle plus the profit component of the FDI rectangle, while GDP of Region 2 is now the sum of its own rectangle plus the labour component of the FDI rectangle. In an extreme case, all production in Region 2 will be carried out by FDI; no domestic sectors will exist. This would model a banana republic.

Note that in the presence of FDI, Region 1 will implement innovations in a higher, and Region 2 in a lower number of sectors than under free trade. Region 1 investors, owning better technologies, can threaten local innovators with setting a price below their production cost. Therefore, they face no competition in production or innovation. Thus, domestic innovation is crowded out in the sectors occupied by FDI. On the other hand, such investors can pay lower local wages and, thus, obtain extraordinary profits. As a result, higher incentives for innovation operate for Region 1 in these sectors, and FDI contributes to concentrating innovation in more advanced countries.

In our analysis of innovation we make some standard assumptions about cross-country technological change. First, as stated above, we assume that each country or region has a specific technological level. Note that when countries are highly integrated, as in the case of the European Union, the discussion may only apply to the union as a whole in relation to other countries. Next, we assume that technological change is costly, and that the cost of a proportional change is proportional to the technological level. This implies that dedicating a constant proportion of income to technological change will result in a constant rate of growth. The incentives for investing in technological change derive from the market power yielded by new knowledge. The simplest assumption is that each sector is a world monopoly, although it is enough that some degree of world market power be present. In our analysis, each FDI sector is a world monopoly run by a TNC. Finally, we assume that there is an *advantage to backwardness*, in the sense defined by Gerschenkron (1952); that is, the presence of technologies from more advanced countries makes technological change cheaper in less advanced countries.

We concluded above that trade and FDI assign both production and innovation, and that they concentrate innovation in larger and more advanced countries. Now we make our main assumption: the more sectors a country innovates in, the easier it is to innovate in each sector. In this respect, I say that there are *sectoral innovation externalities*. Several mechanisms may cause these externalities. We will mention three here. The first is that new ideas may be useful in more than one sector, and therefore will be more productive in countries innovating in more sectors. The second is that general knowledge, formed through diffusion from all sectors, is needed for innovating in any sector, and is more easily formed when more innovation sectors are present in the same country. A third mechanism is that, in order to sustain innovation, it is necessary to support a scientific infrastructure at a fixed cost (proportional to any given technological level) to be shared by all production sectors.

Since trade and FDI concentrate innovation in larger and more advanced countries, it follows that, in the presence of sectoral innovation externalities, they will make technological change easier in those same countries, creating a *disadvantage of backwardness*. This disadvantage constitutes an economic force for divergence between countries.

The existence of such a mechanism is supported by the stylized facts pertaining to the concentration of innovation mentioned above, including the higher than 1 slope reported for log patents held by foreign countries in the US, and their log GDP (see Figure 5.4).

The possibility that FDI can crowd out innovation is illustrated in Table 5.2 for world automobile production and consumption. Automobiles represent a fairly mature product with a not-particularly-impressive rate of innovation. Many middle income countries are quite capable of engineering and producing a line of automobiles. However, doing so while facing the competition of established and advanced producers may be impossible. What does Table 5.2 show? Those countries in Europe and North America that developed the automobile continue to produce and trade it, both with each other and with other countries. By contrast, the new producers – mainly Japan and Korea – do not import automobiles. These countries developed their capabilities in automobile production by promoting their exports and performing a full import substitution, eliminating competition from FDI in automobiles. On the other hand, Latin American countries that supposedly 'substituted for imports' by allowing FDI in automobiles did not develop their own industries. East Asian development policy harnessed exports to ensure its own technological development.[16]

While FDI can crowd out innovation, on the positive side its presence may produce technological externalities favourable to growth. However, such externalities have been found to depend on local absorptive capacity (Xu 2000; Görg and Greenaway 2004). Examining a series of variables from the US Department of Commerce Bureau of Economic Analysis, Mayer-Foulkes and Nunnenkamp (2007) find that, overall, US FDI has positive effects for economic growth in developed countries and a negative effect for underdeveloped countries (see Figure 5.8).

Table 5.2. **Consolidated World Motor Vehicle Production by Nationality of Origin and Consumption, 1998 (Thousand Units)**

| | Consumers | | | | | | | |
| | Developed | | | | | LDC's | | |
Origin	NAFTA Union	European Union	Japan Korea	South Asia, Pacific	Other Europe and Turkey	Other America	South	Total
Developed								
American	9508	3846	0	0	350	52	611	14367
European	3636	11881	0	0	520	1077	1240	18354
Japanese	2851	811	10049	0	1251	88	39	15089
South Korea	0	0	0	1954	28	150	0	2132
LDC's								
Pacific	0	0	0	0	756	0	0	756
Other Europe	0	0	0	0	0	792	0	792
South America	–	–	–	–	–	–	–	–
Total	207935	214994	130637	25402	37765	28067	24570	

Producers

Source: ILO (2000).

Figure 5.8. Estimated Impact of US FDI on Relative Growth Rates According to the Relative Per Capita Income of the Host Country.[17]

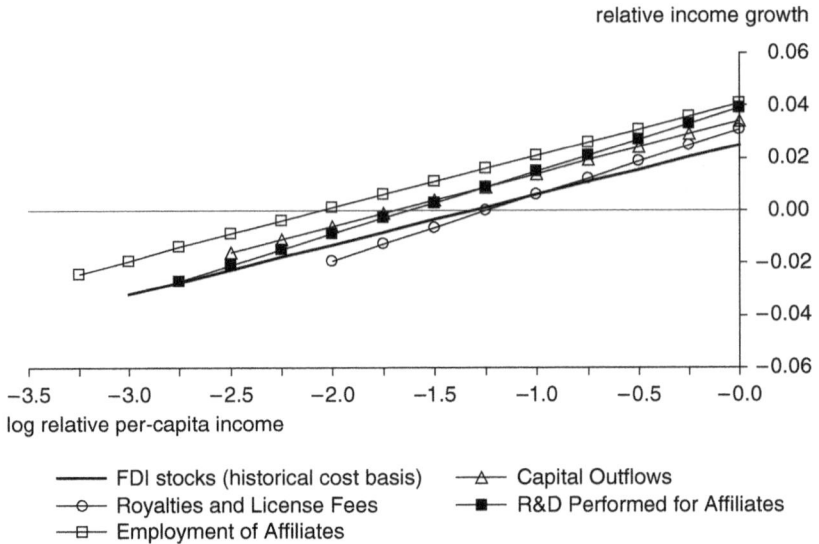

Source: Mayer-Foulkes and Nunnenkamp (2007).

To summarize, trade focuses innovation in advanced countries and creates asymmetric incentives to innovation if there are positive externalities to innovation between sectors. FDI creates asymmetric incentives to innovation favouring advanced countries that could be counterbalanced by the presence of strong enough technological externalities for the host countries. If the asymmetric innovation incentives are strong enough, multiple steady states may emerge, with divergence in levels or growth rates.

How does trade impact the world growth rate? The answer to this depends on the growth rate of the leading technological level. Consider first the lower panel in Figure 5.7. The presence of comparative advantage raises market size and therefore the incentives and resources available for innovation. On the other hand, a reduction in the number of sectors under innovation by leading countries may reduce the positive externalities between sectors.

What is the impact of FDI on the world growth rate? The answer is given by the middle panel of Figure 5.7. The market for each sector is now larger so there are higher incentives and resources for innovation than under just trade. Finally, what would happen if Region 2 were brought to full development? The answer is in the higher panel in Figure 5.7, *Trade between equal regions*. Market size and world aggregate product would increase even more, again increasing the incentives and resources for innovation. On the other hand, externalities between sectors would be reduced in Region 1 and increased in Region 2. However, if the two regions integrate into a single knowledge block, then the externalities would be highest, leading to an optimal rate of economic growth. Trade between equal regions is qualitatively different from trade between unequal regions because specialization between countries follows a sectoral rather than factoral structure. Comparative advantages are no longer based on the cost of labour. Both trade and FDI would not seek cheap labour but instead reflect specialization in different sectors.

Finally, suppose that a leading country is open and innovates in most sectors. For a backward country, how does autarchy compare with openness? According to the model, other things being equal, the answer depends on the size of its production relative to the leading country. If it is closed, incentives for innovation will be limited by its market size. Thus, closed economies can at most converge to a steady state lagging in levels. If it is open, however, it will only converge towards the leading economy if it is large enough. Otherwise, it may diverge in growth rates if, by opening to trade, its innovation becomes limited to a very few sectors.

Discussion

While globalization has accelerated in the last three decades, the history of modern economic growth has been a global history since its origins. This history has been characterized by deep polarization between countries. Technological change, institutional development, the demographic transition and human capital formation all concentrated in developed countries and lagged behind in underdeveloped ones.

To explain this polarization it is necessary to go beyond theories based on competitive markets and diminishing returns, which predict equalization in growth rates and productivity under free trade and investment. Innovation, the engine of economic growth, is driven by incentives derived from market power. It is a travesty that free trade and investment are defended on the principles of perfect competition, when in fact market power is very evidently present in globalization, and has been strengthened by it. Much of international economic exchange is in the hands of huge corporations for which economic models based on perfect competition do not apply. By ignoring this fact, free market policies, in effect, support corporate interests, whether by design or not (Stiglitz 2002). Conversely, from this point of view, development policy compensating for asymmetric innovation incentives has a component of competition policy.

The data show that FDI may be the main component of globalization, playing a larger role than trade. Moreover, we have shown that FDI generates asymmetric incentives to innovation. A series of studies show that it is questionable to automatically expect a positive impact from FDI. By contrast, in the presence of regulation and negotiation, mutual benefits are certainly possible, as is shown in the case of China. We have also shown that, in assigning production, trade assigns innovation and, therefore, concentrates it in the most advanced countries. Thus, both trade and FDI – that is, globalization – have a strong impact on the distribution of innovation, and this can generate multiple steady states and make technological differences persistent.

Low incentives for technological change compound the other dimensions of the polarization observed between developed and underdeveloped countries. By generating a low demand for human capital in underdeveloped countries, low innovation incentives prolong the demographic transition and retard institutional development. Combined, these elements make the existence of multiple steady states possible. This implies that the economic growth that market forces can deliver is constrained. The concentration of knowledge in advanced countries and low institutional development in lagging countries keep the incentives for technological change and human capital accumulation low in lagging countries, and makes inequality persist.

It is fair to say that current global development policies consist of letting markets guide free trade and investment.[18] Such market policies can only be defended under the assumption that there is essentially a single steady state for all economies. If it is true, however, that the presence of multiple steady states characterizes the global economy, such market policies are not sufficient to produce development.

To illustrate what the presence of multiple steady states may imply, I compare Mexico's and Chile's growth from 1960 to 1999 (Figure 5.9). From 1960 to 1982, Mexico used an import substitution strategy and grew at an average rate of 3.9 per cent. After this, came a series of crises lasting until 1994. Since then, following the current globalization policies, Mexico has grown somewhat weakly. Chile, on the other hand, experienced a collapse after Pinochet overthrew Allende in 1973, and only recuperated growth when it followed the Chicago liberalization policies that Reagan and Thatcher also espoused, growing at an average rate of 4.9 per cent between 1984 and 1998. At this point, it almost exactly caught up with Mexico. Its income growth under liberalization was quite comparable to Mexico's under the import substitution industrialization strategy. Both countries seem to converge to approximately similar long-term growth trajectories.

What is common to both countries' economic policies is that they did not follow export promotion. Mexico pursued import substitution until this strategy reached the limits afforded by its domestic economy. Chile liberalized trade and investment, taking a neutral stance on exports. Finding itself so far below its potential economic equilibrium, these policies were enough to make it converge

Figure 5.9. Income per capita for Mexico and Chile, 1960–1999.

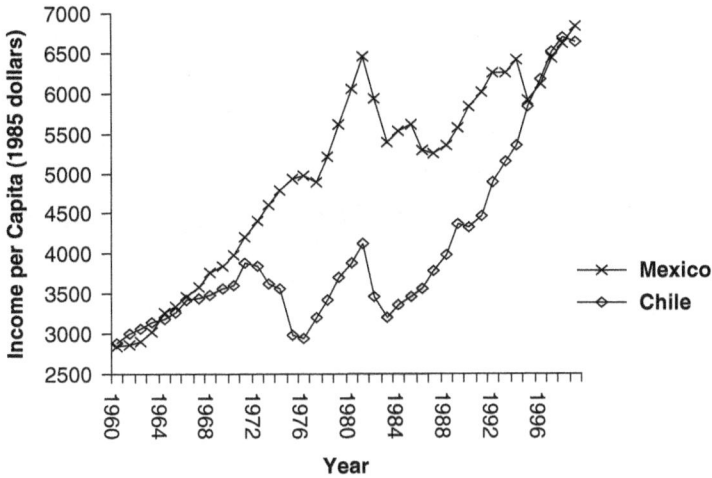

Source: World Bank Development Indicators (2001).

to its steady state – which appears to be very close to Mexico's. In a recent paper on Chile, Maloney and Rodriguez-Clare (2007) find evidence for innovation shortfalls as compared to the OECD. This finding supports the theory outlined above on asymmetric innovation incentives under trade and FDI, which explains the observed innovation gap, impeding convergence to full development.

Understanding underdevelopment as a steady state also explains the long-term ineffectiveness of foreign aid in producing development. What is needed is export promotion and technology adoption, not just trade (or aid). This will be of mutual benefit, just as the development of the East Asian countries and China has been beneficial to the US and Europe – in spite of the competition.

An alternative to export promotion would be policies effectively bridging knowledge gaps between advanced and backward countries. In addition to the Millenium Development Goals, a concerted effort for development should include Technological Development Goals aimed at reducing the huge productivity gaps that exist between countries. Indeed, workers in the field ensuring the availability of primary education for all are already asking, 'how will we now increase productivity'?

Promoting development for all is equivalent to promoting a globalization characterized by equality rather than polarization. Such a globalization will tend to reduce the wage competition between the populations of developed and underdeveloped countries, which has put pressures on the lower and middle classes of advanced countries that might, in themselves, become the source of a globalization backlash. In Obama's campaign in the US, these pressures have resulted in a call to subsidize corporations not to export their business to import cheap labour, and to reduce corporate power in setting the Washington agenda. By operating outside the reach of national laws, TNCs tend not to shoulder their full burden of responsibility. The time may have arrived to channel extraordinary profits from globalization[19] to fund global governance, global development (reducing poverty and compensating for asymmetric innovation incentives), and the provision of global public goods (such as a healthy global ecology). This would promote equal, rather than polarized globalization.

Conclusions

Throughout this chapter I have made a case for understanding development and underdevelopment as multiple steady states in economic growth that can coexist within the context of globalization. Such an understanding can explain the joint origin of development and underdevelopment, which took the form of the deindustrialization of the periphery under the impact of trade with the core, generating the Great Divergence. It is also consistent with the phenomenon of miracle growth (the usual way in which countries join the developed club) and with the persistence of middle income levels, because several types of steady states may exist, diverging in levels and in growth rates. I have highlighted the role of technological change as the main motor of economic growth, and an important variable of polarization between countries, showing, specifically in relation to trade and foreign investment, that there are dynamics in the economic sphere that generate polarization through the presence of asymmetric innovation incentives. These elements of polarization are complementary with those that other authors have pointed out regarding the interaction of trade and human capital with the demographic transition and the formation of institutions conducive to growth.

If it is the case that development and underdevelopment represent distinct steady states of economic growth, then it is imperative to design development policies accordingly. On the other hand, current development policies based on the invisible hand rely on the existence of a single steady state as an article of faith.

Policies liberalizing free trade and investment must not be confused with policies promoting exports and the transfer of knowledge. The first allow for the persistence of inequality, while the second were successful in the development of East Asia. Both trade and FDI have tremendous potential as instruments for the transfer of technology, but their impact on underdeveloped countries is usually successful only when aided by policy. Their implementation, especially in the case of smaller and more backward countries, requires global coordination.

The theory explains how the world growth rate is maximized when all countries are developed. This shows that policies pulling countries out of underdevelopment by promoting their exports, technology transfer and the diffusion of knowledge are of mutual benefit. This accords with experience in that every country's development has strengthened well-being throughout. It is remarkable that these development policies are consistent with promoting human capital formation, market and democratic institutional development, and the demographic transition everywhere, as well as with reducing the conflict that is generated by the persistence of low wages in underdeveloped countries and the division of production according to a technological polarization. Last, but not least, increased access to knowledge and resources should be helpful in constructing an ecologically sustainable development.

Although the present wave of globalization emerged from a weakening of domestic governments and a strengthening of *laissez faire*, successful globalization will require effective global governance. Market economies have always needed sufficiently strong institutions to control them. For a global market economy to work, the same is needed: sufficiently strong global institutions to ensure the provision of economic development for all. This is the economic challenge for global governance.

References

Acemoglu, D., Johnson, S., and Robinson, J. A. 2000. 'The Colonial Origins of Comparative Development: An Empirical Investigation', *NBER Working Papers 7771*, National Bureau of Economic Research.

Aghion, P. and Howitt, P. 1992. 'A Model of Growth through Creative Destruction', *Econometrica* 60.

Anderson, S., Cavanagh, J. and Lee, T. 2000. *Field Guide to the Global Economy*, New York: The New Press.

Beaudreau, B. C. 2004. *World Trade*. New York: iUniverse, Inc.

Broadberry, S. and Gupta, B. 2005. 'Cotton Textiles and the Great Divergence: Lancashire, India and Shifting Comparative Advantage, 1600–1850', Mimeo, Department of Economics, University of Warwick.

Caselli, F., Esquivel, G. and Lefort, F. 1996. 'Reopening the Convergence Debate: A New Look at Cross-Country Growth Empirics', *Journal of Economic Growth* 1.

Chapman, S. 1999. 'Introduction', in Chapman, Stanley, ed, *The Cotton Industry: Its Growth and Impact, 1600–1935*, Bristol: Thoemmes Press.

Chesnais, J. C. 1992. *The Demographic Transition: Stages, Patterns, and Economic Implications*. Oxford: Clarendon Press.

Clingingsmith, D. and Williamson, J. G. 2005. 'Mughal Decline, Climate Change, and Britain's Industrial Ascent: An Integrated Perspective on India's 18th and 19th Century Deindustrialization', *NBER Working Paper Series 11730*, National Bureau of Economic Research.

Doepke, M. 2006. 'Growth Takeoffs', forthcoming in S. N. Durlauf and L. E. Blume, (eds), *The New Palgrave Dictionary of Economics*, 2nd edition, London: Palgrave MacMillan.

Dollar, D. and Wolff, E. 1993. *Competitiveness, Convergence, and International Specialization*. Cambridge, Mass: MIT Press.

Easterly, W. and Levine, R. 2002. 'Tropics, Germs and Crops: How Endowments Influence Economic Development', *NBER Working Paper Series 9106*, National Bureau of Economic Research.

Eaton, J., Gutierrez, E. and Kortum, S. 1988. 'European Technology Policy', *Economic Policy* 27.

Engerman, S. L. and Sokoloff, K. L. 1994a. 'Factor Endowments: Institutions, and Differential Paths of Growth Among New World Economies: A View from Economic Historians of the United States', *NBER Historical Working Paper Series 0066*, National Bureau of Economic Research.

———. 1994b. 'Colonialism, Inequality, and Long-run Paths of Development', *NBER Working Paper Series 11057*, National Bureau of Economic Research.

Ferguson, N. 2003. 'British Imperialism Revisited: The Costs and Benefits of "Anglobalization"', Online: http://www.originofnations.org/British_Empire/british_empire_and_globalization.htm (accessed ??).

Findlay, R. and O'Rourke, K. H. 2001. 'Commodity Market Integration, 1500–2000', *NBER Working Papers 8579*, National Bureau of Economic Research.

Galor, O. and Weil, D. N. 2000. 'Population, Technology, and Growth: From Malthusian Stagnation to the Demographic Transition and Beyond', *American Economic Review* 90(4).

Galor, O. and Mountford, A. 2006. 'Trade and the Great Divergence: The Family Connection', American *Economic Review* 96.

———. 2008. 'Trading Population for Productivity: Theory and Evidence', Mimeo.

Gerschenkron, A. 1952. 'Economic Backwardness in Historical Perspective', in B. F. Hoselitz, Bert F (ed.), *The Progress of Underdeveloped Areas*, Chicago: University of Chicago Press.

González, R. D., Galvarriato, A. G. and Williamson, J. G. 2006. 'Globalization, De-Industrialization and Mexican Exceptionalism 1750–1879', *NBER Working Paper Series 12316*, National Bureau of Economic Research.

Görg, H. and Greenaway, D. 2004. 'Much Ado About Nothing? Do Domestic Firms Really Benefit from Foreign Direct Investment?', *World Bank Research Observer* 19(2).

Graham, E. M. 1995. 'Foreign Direct Investment in the World Economy', International Monetary Fund, Research Department, WP/95/59., Washington, D. C.

Hall, R. E. and Jones, C. I. 1999. 'Why Do Some Countries Produce So Much More Output Per Worker Than Others?', *Quarterly Journal of Economics* 114.

Helpman, E. 1993. 'Innovation, Imitation, and Intellectual Property Rights', *Econometrica* 60.

Howitt, P. 1998. *Endogenous Growth Theory*. Cambridge, Mass.: MIT Press.

———.2000. 'Endogenous Growth and Cross-Country Income Differences', *American Economic Review* 90.

Howitt, P., and Mayer-Foulkes, D. 2005. 'The Effect of Financial Development on Convergence: Theory and Evidence', *Quarterly Journal of Economics* 120(1).

———.2005. 'R&D, Implementation and Stagnation: A Schumpeterian Theory of Convergence Clubs', *Journal of Money, Credit and Banking* 37(1).

International Labour Organization. 2000. 'The Social and Labour Impact of Globalization in the Manufacture of Transport Equipment', Report for discussion at the Tripartite Meeting on the Social and Labour Impact of Globalization in the Manufacture of Transport Equipment, International Labour Office, Geneva, 8–12 May.

Islam, N. 1995. 'Growth Empirics: A Panel Data Approach', *Quarterly Journal of Economics* 110.

Johnson, S. and Robinson, J. A. 2004. 'Institutions as the Fundamental Cause of Long-Run Growth', *NBER Working Papers* 10481, National Bureau of Economic Research.

_____.2005. 'The Rise of Europe: Atlantic Trade, Institutional Change, and Economic Growth', *American Economic Review* 95(3).

Keller, W. 2004., 'International Technology Diffusion', *Journal of Economic Literature* 42(3).

Klenow, P. J. and Rodríguez-Clare, A. 1997. 'The Neoclassical Revival in Growth Economics: Has it Gone too Far?', in B. Bernanke and J. Rotemberg (eds), *NBER Macroeconomics Annual 1997*, Cambridge, Mass: MIT Press.

Knight, M., Loayza, N. and Villanueva, D. 1993. 'Testing the Neoclassical Theory of Economic Growth: A Panel Data Approach', *IMF Staff Papers* 40.

Kortum, S. 2001. 'Technology, Trade, and Growth: A Unified Framework', *European Economic Review Papers and Proceedings* 45.

_____.2003. 'A Rising Tide Raises all Ships: Trade and Diffusion as Conduits of Growth', in L. Paganetto and E. S. Phelps (eds), *Finance, Research, Education, and Growth*, London: Palgrave MacMillian.

_____.2004. 'Innovation, Diffusion, and Trade', Mimeo.

Lee, R. 2003. 'The Demographic Transition: Three Centuries of Fundamental Change', *Journal of Economic Perspectives* 17(4).

Maddison, A. 2001. *The World Economy: A Millennial Perspective*. Paris: Development Centre Studies, OECD.

Maloney, W. and Rodriguez-Clare, A, 2007. 'Innovation Shortfalls', *Review of Development Economics* 11(4).

Martin, H. and Mitra, D. 2001. 'Productivity Growth and Convergence in Agriculture versus Manufacturing', *Economic Development and Cultural Change* 49(2).

Mayer-Foulkes, D. 2006. 'Global Divergence', in G. Severov (ed.), *International Finance and Monetary Policy*, New York: Nova Science Publishers.

_____.2007a. 'Globalization and the Human Development Trap', forthcoming in *UNU-WIDER* Book on the Impact of Globalization on the Poor. Online: http://www. wider.unu.edu/publications/working-papers/research-papers/2007/en_GB/rp2007-64/ (Needs accessed date).

_____.2007b. 'The Impact of Free Trade and FDI: Banana Republic or Miracle Growth?', Mimeo.

Mayer-Foulkes, D. and Nunnenkamp, P. 2007. 'Do Multinational Enterprises Contribute to Convergence or Divergence? A Disaggregated Analysis of US FDI', revised and resubmited for a special section in *Review of Development Economics*.

O'Rourke, K. H. and Williamson, J. G. 1999. 'The Heckscher-Ohlin Model Between 1400 and 2000: When It Explained Factor Price Convergence, When It Did Not, and Why', *NBER Working Papers 7411*, National Bureau of Economic Research,

Parente, S. L. and Prescott, E. C. 1994. 'Technology Adoption and Growth', *Journal of Political Economy* 102.

_____.1999. 'Monopoly Rights: A Barrier to Riches', *American Economic Review* 89.

Piketty, T. and Saez, E. 2003. 'Income Inequality in the United States', *Quarterly Journal of Economics* 118.

Pipitone, U. 1995. *La salida del atraso: Un estudio histórico comparativo*. México: Centro de Investigación y Docencia Económicas: Fondo de Cultura Económica.

Pritchett, L. 1997. 'Divergence, Big Time', *Journal of Economic Perspectivas* 11(3).

Richardson, G. and Bogart, D. 2008. 'Institutional Adaptability and Economic Development: The Property Rights Revolution in Britain, 1700 to 1830', *NBER Working Papers 13757*, National Bureau of Economic Research.

Robinson, J. A. 2006. 'Persistence of Power, Elites and Institutions', *NBER Working Papers* 12108, National Bureau of Economic Research.

Rodríguez, F. and Rodrik, D. 1999. 'Trade Policy and Economic Growth: A Skeptic's Guide to Cross-National Evidence', *NBER Working Paper No. 7081*.

Rodrik, D. 2005. 'Growth Strategies', in P. Aghion, P and S. Durlauf (eds), *Handbook of Economic Growth*, North-Holland.

Schumpeter, J. A. 1934. *The Theory of Economic Development*, 1912, trans. Redvers Opie. Cambridge, Mass.: Harvard University Press.

Semmel, B. 1970. *The Rise of Free Trade Imperialism*. Cambridge, UK: Cambridge University Press, Cambridge.

Sokoloff, K. L. and Zolt, E. M. 2006. 'Inequality and Taxation: Evidence from the Americas on How Inequality May Influence Tax Institutions', *Tax Law Review* 59(2).

Stiglitz, J. 2002. *Globalization and Its Discontents*. New York: W W Norton.

Svedberg, P. 1978. 'The Portfolio-Direct Investment Composition of Private Foreign Investment in 1914, Revisited', *Economic Journal* 88(352).

UNCTAD. 1999. World Investment Report 1999. New York: United Nations.

Wan Jr., H. Y. 2004. *Economic Development in a Globalized Environment: East Asian Evidences*. The Netherlands: Kluwer Academic Publishers.

Williamson, J. 1990. 'What Washington Means by Policy Reform' in J. Williamson (ed.), *Latin American Adjustment: How Much Has Happened?*, Washington, D. C.: Institute for International Economics.

Williamson, J. G. 2004. 'De-Industrialization and Underdevelopment: A Comparative Assessment Around the Periphery 1750–1939', Mimeo.

————.2005. 'Globalization, De-industrialization and Underdevelopment in the Third World Before the Modern Era', Figuerola Lecture, Carlos III University, Madrid, 6 October 2005.

Xu, B. 2000. 'Multinational Enterprises, Technology Diffusion, and Host Country Productivity Growth', *Journal of Development Economics* 62(2).

Chapter 6

THE RULE OF LAW IN MULTILATERAL INSTITUTIONS AND INTERNATIONAL AID FOR DEVELOPMENT: JUDICIAL REFORM IN THE GLOBAL ORDER

Gustavo Fondevila

Introduction

Over the last few years, the concept of global governance, invoked as a useful tool to analyse certain institutional practices of governments, has acquired a preeminent level of popularity in the academic community as well as within the discourse of international cooperation. In the field of international cooperation, the term has also been recognized as an operative expression for analyzing the reform of the state. One of the main aspects of the term global governance is that it has established state management as characterized by an comprehensive approach, covering different elements of the management of the state, from private public service concessions (such as transportation) to the administration of justice. The main objective of this paper is to analyse global governance within the scope of multilateralism and international cooperation in terms of the reform of state, focusing on judicial reform in particular. It is our contention to establish that concrete analysis of the development and evolution of international aid backing judicial reform in different countries is a good means to represent certain aspects and develop general conclusions about global governance.

The origins of international aid that focuses on improving the law and judiciaries stems from the end of the Second World War. Two main aspects supported this phenomenon: (a) the increasing and constant interest in protecting human rights and (b) the creation of the international justice courts.[1] Following this period, the end of the Cold War[2] and the bipolarity represented by the two opposing economic-national models gave another meaning to international aid for improving judiciaries. Basically, the liberal model of rule of law was imposed as a fundamental ideal for the universal state and regulating legal interactions in any given society. Thus, justice[3] was transformed into the fundamental normative principle of the policy and the most essential value for legal-political institutions. Finally, democratic legal bases were seen as the most important model of government to achieve political justice.

At this time, improvements to the law and the administration of justice were considered an indirect means for fighting poverty.[4] On the one hand, rule of law institutions have been considered essential to development as individual entities and, in consequence, to improving and establishing democratic societies in which social stability is guaranteed. On the other, legal certainty creates a peaceful, safe context for economic transactions and improves the possibilities and capacities of self-development among the lower social classes. At the same time, creating a universal rule of law is seen as an important criterion for the future of global security.

Currently, promoting rule of law and legal certainty are common criteria for international cooperation. They constitute a starting point for promoting global governance in Western societies. There seems to be two strands in the interpretation of this idea: (a) to promote the existence and development of proper legal institutions for liberal rule of law and legal certainty since they are the main criteria used to evaluate the legal context of countries elected as international aid partners/recipients; and (b) to support those initiatives requested by civil society that focus on the oversight of legal institutions and to promote the ratification of several international agreements on human rights, as well as ensuring their success in countries that receive aid.

Theoretical principles of both strands are based on a comprehensive and extensive notion of rule of law that is associated with the development of democracy. The idea of multilateral agencies centers on the possibility of achieving global governance through the creation and improvement of similar institutions in different countries with common conceptions of specific issues.

The Concept of the Rule of Law in light of International Cooperation

Promoting law and justice within the context of international cooperation is based on the idea that the origins of the rule of law are closely linked to the development of a democratic political system. This idea of the rule of law is built around the following elements:

- Attention paid to human rights,
- The existence of a government's monopoly of the use of force,
- Checks and balances between public powers (over transparent due process of law),
- Legitimacy of the administration's legal principles,
- Independent and transparent administration of justice,
- Legal equality between citizens and citizenries.[5]

There is an acute difference between American and European models of international cooperation. Normally, the first is based on a concept of rule of law linked to a free market economy, while the second is based on the idea of a social-economic market. In other words, the latter is built around a social concept of the rule of law. In the European model, within the obligation of guaranteeing legal enforcement to protect individual freedom and individuals before other legal persons (even the state itself), we find the responsibility to create material conditions for improving social equality. Law and justice, then, are fundamental for this process (as in the case of social security and the labor market, for instance).

This specific understanding of the rule of law is joined by a particular legal tradition (European-Continental). In the continental legal (civil law) system, the main source of law is the positive law created by legislatures (in general terms), while in common law tradition, the main source is the typified custom expressed in individual judicial cases and decisions. This means that:

- Courts are the principal source of law.
- In most cases, judicial decisions are subject to judicial review.
- Courts ground their decisions on previous judicial decisions reached by other tribunals.
- Courts are not imposed upon or subordinated by the general administration of the state (*stare decisis*)

The common law tradition necessarily requires strong, long-term judicial institutions and sometimes this condition excludes it from being an option for developing countries. Currently, most of these countries do not have strong institutions, not even judicial ones. These countries usually prefer civil law tradition because it requires other kinds of institutions that are basically regulated by written and public norms. Generally, socialist states (such as

China or Vietnam) have also oriented their judicial reforms around European legal tradition. Nevertheless, it is possible to find elements of common law tradition in several countries that were British colonies in the nineteenth and twentieth centuries (such as South Africa, Kenya, Zambia and India).

Promoting Justice (The *Status Quaestionis*)

Targets

Different countries have achieved an acceptable level of institutional organization to comply with the model required by democratic rule of law. At the same time, however, these institutions are experiencing different problems in important areas such as transparency, efficiency and accessibility. As a result, international aid has centered its efforts on improving deficient models of rule of law which share the following characteristics, particularly with regard to their judiciaries:

- Delay and absence of transparency. These problems weaken legal certainty, the capacity for reinforcing rights and the autonomy of the judiciary.
- The co-existence of modern codifications and 'uses and practices' generates an amorphous rule of law that in some cases reduces legal certainty and affects particular social groups. For instance, in some developing countries, customary law prohibits women from owning private property.
- Usually, certain social groups (also called vulnerable groups) do not have access to formal justice. This can occur when people do not know their rights or because they lack the necessary funds. Sometimes, the reasons behind this are simpler: some places are too far from centers where courts usually operate.
- The absence of legal certainty generates certain risks for economic activity. By this, we mean those that affect its function and increase costs. In these cases, legal conditions inherent to each locality exert a negative influence on the growth of foreign investments.

International cooperation usually concentrates on long-term and complex processes of judicial reform in which the partners/receivers are politically involved.[6] This constitutes the level of sustainability for reforming laws and judiciaries. The fight against poverty is still the principal target, but this model cannot be understood without a comprehensive and far-reaching model of social justice, environmental protection, economic capacity, administrative management, as well as political endorsement of democracy, the rule of law and the pacific resolution of social conflicts.[7]

Conscientious governments normally comply with rules of democracy and develop strong legal institutions by improving the rule of law and legal certainty. These elements are required for development under the following situations:

- Rule of law and legal certainty are the basis for individual self-determination and development. The structures of rule of law are essential for democratic societies: political and social participation and inclusion require the enforcement of human rights and equality for every social group. These conditions are also fundamental for social stability. Efficient courts of consequence improve social stability and prevent economic, social and political problems from emerging.
- At the same time, rule of law and legal certainty are general conditions for economic and social development. By officially acknowledging and enforcing property rights, states fulfill the minimum criteria for developing capital and the economic order required by the market. In this sense, judicial systems with difficulties that affect legal certainty tend to increase the risks for capital investments. Legal transparency, certainty, efficacy and efficiency are the ideal contexts for generating economic activities, investments and salaried jobs. Efforts made to achieve approved international legal standards take place under the auspices of international agreements that protect and reinforce human rights. As a result, international cooperation, in terms of law and justice, contributes to improving and maintaining global security. In this sense, international cooperation operates in two different fields: (a) collaborating to improve local legal institutions, a process sustained by attaining the international standards designed for measuring the quality of the administration of justice; and (b) promoting the incorporation of developing countries into the process of judicial globalization. This means that these countries accept the jurisdiction of international conflict-solving mechanisms.

Legal Fields

There are some strategic and common fields where international cooperation centers on reforming and improving the legal systems of developing countries:

- Ratification and recognition of international human rights conventions (for instance, to support the ratification of international agreements and to fulfill the corresponding obligations for ratification).[8]
- Legal and social equality between men and women and the protection of social minorities (for instance, to abolish legal discrimination against women and to overcome socio-cultural and economic obstacles).

- To create a congruous legal context to develop a free market economy[9] (for instance, property rights, an anti-monopoly mechanism to oversee such instances and market, labor and union guarantees).
- Penal and enforcement processes
- Constitutional and administrative law
- Public law should also be included in this general category. This is defined as activities that focus on improving democratic rights (for instance, the rights of the media, political participation, electoral laws and their regulation).

These initiatives and reforms of judicial and legal institutions normally influence the following fields:

- Improvements in conflict solving and institutional management. Setting up efficient structures for the rule of law plays a vital role in political conflict solving, as well as in creating and improving socio-political stability.
- The fight against corruption. Corruption in the legal system and in the administration of justice diminishes social trust in public institutions and in the rule of law. Law is inefficient when its establishment, administration and accessibility are not effective instruments against corruption. This is true whenever institutions are not trustworthy.
- Institutional decentralization and communitarian development. Establishing a formal and transparent system for taxes, public finances and economic and occupational order, as well as a system to protect the environment and natural resources that lead to improvements in agrarian reforms (as an important way to strengthen rural development), plays an important role in decentralizing the state and reducing the gap between the citizenry and the institutional environment. This is also a way to advance social and institutional autonomy.
- The promotion of gender equality. Over recent years, gender equality has been one of the issues to which international cooperation has paid most attention.[10] It is vital to establish specific policies and projects that improve women's conditions. An extensive catalogue has been developed on this issue. The main strategies are: the creation and enforcement of new rights addressing gender equality to improve women's access to justice and inform them of their rights and the ways to implement them (for instance, the existence of legal processes against discrimination). In countries where such strategies have been implemented, public offices have also been also created to address gender issues. In countries where these initiatives have not been carried out, attention and initiatives for improving gender equality are backed and developed by civil society (often by non-governmental

organizations), but the capacity of these organizations is, obviously, less powerful than that of public institutions.

Basic Requirements

General

- *Political will for State Reforms:* One of the most relevant conditions to guarantee the level of success a judicial reform might have is the degree of agreement and obligation the State takes upon itself with the project, as well as its capacity for using public resources. When reform does not receive official support, support should be found in civil society, not only to develop the programs needed, but also to initiate and extend public discussion.
- *Political Openness of the Legal System:* Almost every legal system has an organized judiciary with its own resources, autonomy and administrative management. Commonly, judiciaries are the institutions that show the most reluctance to incorporate the necessary legal changes because they reduce institutional opacity.[11] One of the central issues for international cooperation is the political will to reform the legal system. This means having sufficient capacity and power to change the administration of the judiciary.[12]
- At the same time, the sponsor country should have sufficient legal openness to try not only to 'transfer' its legal system to aid recipients, but also to supervise and give concrete and adequate "know how" to advance reform. Given the cultural and political specificities of each country, it should also have the same degree of flexibility to promote and develop new institutions that would help improve the local legal system and its relationship with the citizenry.[13]

Concrete

- These involve specific initiatives that have an impact on different legal fields at the same time:

1. *Law in Books:* Specific and relevant knowledge to draft legislative initiatives and promote the creation of law in countries that receive international aid (for instance: seminars, workshops, etc.).
2. *Law in Action and Mobilization of Law:* To develop new jurisdictions and legal fields in terms of capacity, specialization and counsel to improve judicial, social and individual capacity in reforming the legal system and its practices.
3. *Law Enforcement:* Special counsel on administrative and technical management to enforce the law.

– *Access to Justice*: To eradicate obstacles that hinder the equal right of access to justice and to facilitate social use and access to justice by extending the capacity of the same legal system to safeguard rights and solve social conflicts. Finally, to create specific and free institutions that defend and enforce the rights of specific social groups.

– *Institutional Evaluation and Customary Law*: In many developing countries, legal pluralism is one of the main issues for the local legal system. Official legal systems coexist with traditional –customary or religious- norms that are sometimes more acceptable and useful to society than official norms are. Within this coexistence, it is possible to find a wide gap between modern law and the reality of the traditional systems of regulation. Common problems associated with this gap arise from the contradictions (a) between norms regulating private, collective and traditional property and (b) between legal norms protecting human rights and customary rules that often do not respect human rights. It is also possible to find cases in which the existence and use of customary legal systems directly improve the legal positions and situations of specific social groups. Normally, the political strategy of international cooperation has tried to integrate (or at least acknowledge) the existence of modern and customary legal systems. This strategy is only adequate in cases in which customary law does not go against international instruments designed to protect human rights or against local constitutional values.[14]

– *To Promote Women's Rights*: Customary law normally expresses a specific sense of gender inequality. Legal disadvantages directly influence women's patrimonial and property rights. This situation is clearly seen in legal fields like access to private property, land exploitation, etc. Regarding the issue, possibilities for innovation include:

1. Analyzing official legal norms from a participative perspective since in most cases customary law is not codified.
2. Structuring a congruent and modern plural legal system within the context of collective judicial reform, perhaps in collaboration with traditional authorities.
3. Improving the legal status of women in customary law.
4. Introducing traditional elements into the legislative body under strict criteria and standards of equality in legal fields such as family law or heritage law.

– *To Promote the Ombudsman*:[15] This term refers to an institution that finds, clarifies, measures and indicates certain actions the state does that do not observe human rights or have generated unjust targets or consequences.

One example of this would be corruption. This institution also works towards developing strategies to fight structural injustices. The aim in promoting this institution is to improve each citizen's legal certainty regardless of their class and cultural, social or economic background. In countries in which the institution already exists, the policy designed tends to improve its authority before official institutions and to satisfy people's legal needs. Its main strategies are:

1. To promote acknowledgment and the creation of the ombudsman in the state and society (to identify and design the institution's main issues, to propose political strategies, to develop strong dynamics of cooperation in civil society and to support the establishment of different mechanisms to ensure civic security in the case of state arbitrariness and ensure the institution's independence and autonomy).
2. To consolidate an internal system to coordinate and organize the institution.
3. To socially promote institutional skills designed to carry out these strategies.

Multilateral Figures and International Cooperation for Improving Justice

In general terms, international cooperation follows two different strategies: (a) to develop programs and projects within the framework of bilateral cooperation – normally without direct economic support – and (b) by influencing multilateral organizations that financially support the project. The plural structure[16] of this system of international cooperation is made up of both official and non-official local organizations.

In the official system, international cooperation regarding law and justice has worked in two main fields: (a) judiciary reform by designing an extensive set of strategies that improve institutional figures' know how and (b) the advancement of human rights.

Both political and civil organizations have worked toward legal counsel and lobbying for the creation of new laws and their implementation. Much of this work has also focused on access to justice mainly within the context of official democratization programs. In this process, the main fields for cooperation are labor law, labor union law within the context of constitutional law, as well as human, civic rights and administrative law and last, but not least, significant work in lobbying for and designing judicial reforms and legal counsel for vulnerable groups. Religious organizations have worked to promote different strategies that enhance legal awareness in the population at large, as well as access to justice and the radical transformation from law in books into law in action. In some cases, civic organizations have worked with other organizations and judicial training institutions.

The multilateral organizations involved in legal and judicial reform are: the World Bank, the European Union (EU), the United Nations Development Programme (UNDP) and regional development banks (Inter-American, Asian, etc.). These organizations usually work together on the same project or on similar issues. Normally, this work is sustained by means of economic and technical assistance. In the recent years, issues such as law and justice have attained an important role for the international cooperation of multilateral organisms. This process has been influenced by European standards, but principally by Germany's.

In its 2002 World Development Report, the World Bank acknowledged that an efficient judicial system plays a central role in economic development and established that the efficiency of the legal system is a fundamental target for reform in development countries, in which most of the aid is usually concentrated. While in the 90s World Bank aid focused on improving market and financial laws, a new paradigm has made the World Bank participate in other legal fields and in developing different strategies ranging from strengthening the autonomy of the judiciary to fighting corruption and improving the access to justice for all. On average, the 35 current World Bank projects on law and justice have received 380 million dollars. However, support for other issues is actually higher.

The EU backed cooperation for development called the 'Institutional Development of Responsible Governments and the Rule of Law' represents one of the six main points of international assistance. This issue in particular has been well supported, especially within the context of the European Initiative for Democracy and Human Rights (EIDHR). At this point, the EU provides technical assistance to decision makers and policy designers of legal systems, in terms of constitutional reform and national codes, as well as help in developing new judicial institutions. At the same time, European assistance tends to design and support some informative strategies to enforce and acknowledge human rights (for instance, European assistance has worked toward abolishing capital punishments).

In the field of bilateral assistance, the most important organism is the United States Agency for International Development (USAID). Nevertheless, there are other international institutions around the world such as Japan International Cooperation Agency (JICA) in Asia, Nachfolgestaaten der Sowjetunion (GUS/NUS) in the former Soviet Union and assistance from Germany, Spain and France in Latin America. However, it is also important to note that German assistance has demonstrated recent and particular interest in the Latin American environment, diversifying its assistance from economic to technical support. This paradigmatic change has also had an impact on other geographical and technical fields: economic law in Asia, communitarian and political conflicts in Africa and the rule of law in Latin American countries.

Cooperation between different international organisms can also be built around the exchange of information and experience. Sometimes shared assistance tends to improve the design and implementation of specific projects.[17] In this area, coordination of the supporters is important because open, plural competition in reforming courts and the legal system might affect developing countries' institutional environment. One important forum for coordinating and designing international standards for cooperation is the Organisation for Economic Co-operation and Development (OECD) Development Assistance Committee. In the paper entitled *Orientations on Participatory Development and Good Governance – DAC,* the states involved establish international bases of cooperation to reform legal and judicial fields. The main target of its informal website (*govnet*) presents international cooperation for improving global governance in OECD member countries. This network also includes legal issues.

Regional Activities[18]

In Latin America and Africa (particularly in the southern part), environmental issues such as law and justice are analyzed within the context of democracy, civil society and public administration. In Eastern Europe and Asia, issues of economic regulation are involved in economic development and reform toward a free market economy. Some other positive strategies, such as the promotion of human rights, are supported by models of independent local cooperation.

Latin America

Latin American countries receiving international aid normally design and implement legal reforms in the area of criminal law and its processes. In most Latin American countries, the criminal process is in writing and inquisitorial. In these kinds of legal processes, judges go through the different procedural stages such as investigation and accusation and they also emit the judicial decision. As a result, it has been established that in most Latin American countries, criminal processes do not respect the most elemental standards and principles of checks and balances (an institutional figure concentrates on different procedural stages that are designed, in principle, to ensure transparency and certainty of the legal decision).[19] This situation presents one of the most important issues for judicial reform in Latin American countries. The general target of these legal reforms is to separate the different stages that constitute the criminal process, from investigating to emitting judicial decisions. Their purpose is also to introduce other legal principles, such as oral processes and the transparency of judicial and procedural activities, into the proceedings. Within the context of reformulating the criminal system, international cooperation gives extensive and illustrative technical advice on reorganizing courts and public prosecutors' capacities as well as police activities and obligations. Plus, it also improves the technical skills of the institutional figures.[20]

Within civil society, international cooperation focuses on promoting processes of constitutional and judicial reforms, as well as developing mechanisms to improve institutional accountability.[21] These issues are also reflected in the endorsement of the ombudsman. Most developing countries present constitutional texts with values and principles corresponding to the rule of law. However, the gap between law in books and law in action (and its socio-political context) does not necessarily reflect the constitutional text.

Africa

International cooperation has focused on economic, market, criminal and administrative regulation, as well as in improving gender equality. In this geographical zone, legal pluralism has been established as a public issue, particularly in the Sub-Sahara region where customary law has had more acceptance than the modern, official and rational legal system. However, customary law often discriminates women's role in society. In short, customary regulation usually does not recognize any rights for this social group.

A second issue surrounding international cooperation and African societies has to do with the criminal process and law enforcement. Of course, it is important to promote the rule of law as part of this issue and as an interesting alternative for institutionalizing social conflicts.[22]

Although the issues described are commonly and largely supported by international cooperation, we also present a short list of other minor issues:

- To support effective and efficient access to justice (for instance, by promoting legislative commissions that support the implementation of proposed legal reforms).
- To promote the 'legal' awareness throughout the entire society (for instance, in the media, on the radio, on the Internet, etc.).
- To improve judicial autonomy through the collective participation of constitutional courts and academia.

Eastern Europe and Asia

In Eastern Europe and Asia, international cooperation has centered on promoting a comprehensive strategy to develop a free-market economy (in the case of Europe, the plan aims at improving free-market economy from a social perspective) by advancing economic rights and the legal institutions needed for this kind of economy. At the same time, international cooperation work has been designed as a comprehensive framework for technical assistance that will assist in drafting legislative initiatives and improving judicial efficiency and autonomy. It was also designed to improve these principles in other institutions conceived to enforce legal decisions. Finally, international cooperation has also been occupied in designing different strategies to disseminate legal knowledge throughout society. For instance, this strategy has been expressed through different media such as TV, the radio and newspapers.

In either case, in Eastern Europe and Asia,[23] the constant growth of efforts made to promote changes in other legal fields like administrative regulation, human rights advocacy, development of affirmative action to protect vulnerable social groups and guarantee gender equality has been obvious and noteworthy.

Global Governance and its Requirements in Terms of Justice

In the future, the tendency seems to focus on associating the promotion of law and justice as an integral part of promoting global governance. It is possible that judicial reforms are directly associated with the promotion of democracy, civil society and public administration, as well as with the development of economic reforms to establish a free-market economy.

In specific terms, cooperation will focus on pushing for legal changes in politically sensible fields. For instance, in Eastern Europe the situation of individual rights before the state looks like an alternative, while in Africa it appears that rethinking the role of rule of law institutions for solving social conflicts might be necessary.

In the future, international cooperation concerning law and justice should concentrate on the following agenda:

• Within the context of working out a legal program, initiatives promoted to sponsor judicial reforms should be joined by other general strategies that promote the democratization of international aid recipients/partners. It is necessary to increase the capacity for improving judicial review. It is equally necessary to increase the capacity of civil society and independent media.
• In countries that have received aid for justice reforms, sustaining continuity and maintenance is essential. The legal framework that corresponds to

modern rule of law institutions has been achieved in many regions must now be used and should promote the extension of its consequences. It needs to intensify internal reforms in the system. This would entail reducing the judiciary's discretion and raising awareness in terms of judicial decisions like budget management, among other initiatives, or reforms, as well as improving access to justice for certain social sectors. At this point, it is necessary to identify the needs of different regions. In Latin America, there is a long delay in drafting administrative law while in Eastern Europe and Asia, the problem deals with economic factors and the civil rights of individuals against the State (for example, the implementation of human rights).

- One very important issue deals with building justice systems in post-conflict scenarios. The resolution of social and ethnical conflicts represents a challenge to legal institutions. At the same time, rule of law institutions provide an important foundation for the construction or reconstruction of a democratic system and peaceful social order.

The agenda, including the justice reforms, should be as follows:

- There should be support for legal institutions that excludes the social ombudsman. These institutions are essential to generating society's greater acceptance of the justice reforms and seeing these reforms as part of the democratization process of state institutions and of society itself. Any measure that seeks to enhance the independence of the judiciary must be accompanied by an anti-corruption program.
- There should be support for local training and legal counsel systems aimed at improving and enhancing the powers of law for the creation as well as its implementation and use in recipient countries so that it can reduce these institutions' long-term dependency on external expertise.
- New methodologies should be implemented to lower the level of legal pluralism in certain legal systems by means of integrating traditional law with modern law state.
- There should be a program to promote access to justice for vulnerable social groups as well as to encourage the spread of modern law state (as opposed to customary law) so that these legal standards are applied in every sector of society. Here it is important to develop new initiatives in the process of legal representation and to draft new rights for legal protection.
- Democratic and civilian control of public safety (police and other security agencies) should be promoted.
- Information technology and communication (e-governance) should be introduced into the administration of justice. This may open new venues

for increased transparency, effectiveness and efficiency of the delivery and administration of justice.

Particular attention to the failure of certain policies of cooperation should take into account the following precautions:

- Not to generate excessive expectations regarding reforms. This may cause skepticism or mistrust when the reforms are gradual and slow.
- Not to indiscriminately burden institutional judicial services. Sometimes, legal reforms give rise to claims that the service itself does not meet the conditions to respond efficiently to their needs.
- Not to centralize reforms by changing the figures of the central legal system. The origins and consequences of the reform should embrace the entire judicial field, including those middle and lower sectors of the judiciary.

References

Agüero, F. and Stark, J. (eds). 1998. *Fault Lines of Democracy in Post-Transition Latin America*. Miami: North-South Center Press.

Burgos, G. 2005. *Reforma judicial en América Latina*. Onlince: http://www.ilsa.org.co/boletines/justicia/bb.htm (accessed 20 April 2005).

Carothers, T. 1999. *The Many Agendas of the Rule of Law Reform in Latin America*. London: University of London.

Carpizo, J. 2000. 'Otra reforma constitucional: la subordinación del Consejo de la Judicatura Federal', *Cuestiones Constitucionales* 2.

Domingo, P. and Sieder, R. (eds). 2001. *Rule of Law in Latin America: The International Promotion of Judicial Reform*. London: Institute of Latin American Studies.

Faundez, J. 19997. *Good Government and Law. Legal and Institutional Reform in Developing Countries*, London/New York: MacMillan Press, St. Martin's Press Inc.

Galindo, P. 2003. *Estudios, calificaciones de riesgo, y encuestas de percepción pública sobre los sistemas de justicia*. Santiago: Cejaméricas.

Garth, B., *What Makes a Successful Legal and Judicial System: Rethinking the Processes and the Criteria for Success*. Online: http://www.iigov.org/resenas/p=4_0093

The German Federal Ministry for Economic Cooperation and Development. 2000. *Empowerment von Frauen in der entwicklungspolitischen Praxis. Die 40 Mio-Dollar-Zusage von Peking für Projekt der Rechts- und sozialpolitischen Beratung.*: BMZ-Spezial.

The German Federal Ministry for Economic Cooperation and Development. 2002. *Recht und Justiz in der deutschen Entwicklungszusammenarbeit*. Online: http://www.bmz.de/de/service/infothek/fach/spezial/spezial047/spezial047_90.pdf (accessed 8 August 2007).

Goldberg, R. 2002. 'La banca extranjera en México', *El Financiero*.

Karns, M. P. and Mingst, K. A. 2004. *International Organizations: The Politics and Processes of Global Governance*. Boulder, CO: Lynne Rienner Publishers.

Méndez, J., O'Donnell, G. and Pinheiro, P. S. 1999. *The (Un)Rule of Law & the Underprivileged in Latin America*, Notre Dame, Indiana: University of Notre Dame Press.

Rosenau, J. 1999. 'Toward an Ontology for Global Governance', in M.Hewson and
T. J. Sinclair (eds), *Approaches to Global Governance Theory.* Albany, NY: State University of
New York.

Rowat, M., Malik, W. and Dakolias, M. 1995. *Judicial Reform in Latin America and the
Caribbean. Proceedings of a World Bank Conference*, World Bank Technical Paper Number
280, Washington, D.C.

United Nations. 2000. *Millenium Declaration.* Online: a/Res/55/2, http://daccessdds.un.
org/doc/UNDOC/GEN/N00/559/54/PDF/N0055954.pdf?OpenElement
(accessed 13 Sept. 2000).

Upham, F. 2002. *Mythmaking in the Rule of Law Orthodoxy.* Washington, D. C.:Carnegie
Endowment of International Peace.

Part Two:

POWER SHIFTS, REGIONAL EXPERIENCES AND GLOBAL CHALLENGES

Chapter 7

GLOBAL POWER SHIFTS AND SOUTH AFRICA'S SOUTHERN AGENDA: CAUGHT BETWEEN AFRICAN SOLIDARITY AND REGIONAL LEADERSHIP

Elizabeth Sidiropoulos[1]

Introduction

The central argument of this paper is that the global power shifts experienced in the world in the first decade of the twenty-first century provide a unique opportunity for South Africa to pursue more effectively one of its key foreign policy objectives, viz. reforming the institutions of global governance, which project outdated power configurations. It is doing this by developing strong alliances with like-minded countries of the developing south, such as India, Brazil and China. However, its close alignment with big emerging powers sometimes clashes with its commitment that Africa is at the centre of its foreign policy agenda. This contradiction in its foreign policy is unlikely to be resolved in the medium term, and may also become more difficult to manage as the balance of power shifts more dramatically to the new Asian Drivers.

South Africa has sought to emphasize that it is part of Africa and that it places its interests at the top of its foreign policy agenda. However, as the largest and most developed economy on the world's poorest continent, South Africa's interests, global perspective and objectives are often very different from those of many other African countries. While the country shirks the title of regional hegemon because of its apartheid past, its actions (political or economic) are often perceived in this light by others in Africa. Thus South Africa is both a part of, and yet apart from, the continent.

Notwithstanding this dichotomy, its global role and influence emanate in no small measure from its economic and political importance in Africa. Thus, acceptance within Africa of South Africa's regional and global role, although not sufficient, is a necessary condition for it to be the voice of Africa within southern alliances and indeed in global forums. This condition translates sometimes into adopting positions reflecting African solidarity (which can be the lowest common denominator), rather than leadership on difficult issues, both regionally and globally.

Navigating this will become more difficult for South Africa as China and India particularly (the Asian Drivers) press into Africa, seeking access to natural resources as they position themselves geopolitically to exercise more economic and political power globally. It has 'spheres of influence' and very specific national interests to pursue, though it is coy about admitting this. While the country regards its relationship with both emerging powers as strategic, South Africa's own spheres of influence will undoubtedly be affected (and potentially erode) by their growing presence. On the other hand, where African states see China and India's engagement as problematic, South Africa's close relations with these two may affect its relationship with other African states, and even confirm that South Africa continues to set itself apart from the rest. Although the geopolitical canvas still has to take its final form, these possibilities are likely to have a significant impact on how South Africa executes its global governance reform agenda and the choices it makes about Southern alliance formations.

South Africa's return to the international stage in 1994 took place at a phenomenal juncture in global politics: the end of the Cold War and the ideological divide between east and west, and the start, not of the dominance of a sole superpower (although it seemed like it at the time), but rather the seeds of a multipolar world, which was gradually shifting its centre from the Atlantic to the Pacific. By the close of the first decade of the twenty-first century, a clearer picture of this shift is emerging. The world has entered the post, post-Cold War period. The future of a liberal international order is uncertain. The honeymoon of South Africa's peaceful transition and its re-entry into the global community, regarded as a manifestation of the emergence of this order, has also begun to fade. South Africa is becoming a 'normal' country. The new government in South Africa, which took office in May 2009, although still the African National Congress, is the first post, post-apartheid administration. Against the backdrop of this changed world, South Africa will have to mediate between its need for acceptance in Africa, and the strategic imperatives of behaving as an emerging middle power.

South Africa's Foreign Policy Drivers Since 1994

It is widely accepted that since 1994, South Africa has been punching above its weight in the international arena. South Africa has been able to do so because of its keenness to engage at every level after many years of isolation, as well as the acceptance and encouragement of such a role by many players in the international community. As Jack Spence (2004) points out, the basis of this engagement has been the country's reputation, derived from its negotiated and peaceful transition from apartheid.

Two streams of engagement crucial to this discussion can be discerned in South Africa's foreign policy. The first is the African agenda, which includes conflict resolution, support for post-conflict reconstruction and economic development – all of which contribute to a central aim of the post- 1994 government – to give Africa a greater voice and impact in global institutions. A peaceful, secure and stable Africa is essential for this to be sustainable and effective. Furthermore, from a more self-interested perspective, South Africa believes that its own economic well-being is dependent on greater peace and stability on the continent that allows economic development to take place. However, South Africa also believes that the continent's travails are partly the result of a skewed global economic and political system, which makes it very difficult for poor countries to move out of their cycles of poverty and global economic marginalization.

The second is South-South Cooperation, which in the early twenty-first century has been given greater impetus and meaning because of the growing economic strength of a number of southern countries – some of which are aspiring great powers, others regional powers. South Africa regards South-South Cooperation as a vital ingredient in its objective of working to reform the global governance architecture and the skewed nature of global politics. Two other themes supported by South-South Cooperation are the strengthening of self-help initiatives among developing countries through increasing intra-south trade and investment, co-operation in science and technology and capacity building based on similar circumstances and experiences; and support for projects of the New Partnership for Africa's Development (NEPAD), especially where southern partners have unique contributions to make (Government Communication and Information System 2004).

Both of the streams highlighted above are essential elements of South Africa's multilateral agenda. Multilateralism is extremely important for the country. While some politicians may argue that multilateralism is the refuge of the weak, (especially in a world dominated by a lone superpower), South Africa's commitment has been evident in many forums where it has worked hard to forge global governance regimes. Examples include its leading role in the adoption of the Ottawa Treaty on landmines and the Nuclear Non-Proliferation Treaty. South African policy makers believe that a rules-based international system is necessary to curb the excesses of superpowers and to protect weaker states from arbitrary exercise of power and force; thus the need to reform global governance structures so that there are fairer, and reflect changing power configurations and the concerns of developing states (for example, effective global solving of socio-economic issues and the acknowledgement that fighting poverty and underdevelopment are as important human rights issues (if not more) as civic and political rights.

It is clear from the above that South Africa's global governance agenda is closely linked to its African agenda (peace, stability, poverty eradication) and to its Global South agenda of deepening South-South Cooperation at all levels. South Africa's *modus operandi* has been to develop coalitions with other states to advocate these issues. Many of these coalitions are within the south; but South Africa has also sought cooperation on global issues with northern countries. For example, it has worked together with Sweden on the Four-Nations Initiative on governance and management reform of the UN.[2] The other members were Chile and Thailand. Its role as a potential bridge-builder between north and south has also been evident in global debates about the haves and the have-nots of the international political economy, given that the country is the only one in Africa with both a developed and a developing economy; and on nuclear non-proliferation, where at the 1995 conference on the extension of the NPT, South Africa sought to act as a bridge between the views of the US and the Non-Aligned Movement (Barber 2004).

South Africa's approach has not been to seek the abolition of the existing system, but rather to 'make the rules of global governance more fair and transparent' (Gumede 2005). Identifying common goals and potential alliances between the north and the south has been an important part of that strategy.

However, a growing shift is discernible over the last few years away from emphasis on South Africa's role as a bridge builder to one that is overtly about the Global South and asserting its agenda on the international stage. This has also evolved into a more confrontational engagement at times, although it would be naïve to believe that South Africa's global engagement is one-dimensional.

A Southern Agenda for Global Governance Reform

Prior to 1994, South Africa was clearly associated with the developed world. The democratic government made a conscious decision when it came to power in 1994 to identify with the developing world and the Global South. The decision was to a large extent a reflection of the sentiment and association, harking back to the Bandung conference of 1955, with the anti-colonialist, anti-imperialist agenda articulated by countries of the south at this time.

At the 2006 Summit conference of the Non-Aligned Movement (NAM) while South Africa held the chair of the Group of 77 and China, President Thabo Mbeki remarked:

> [...] the central task facing all of us is to strengthen South-South cooperation, especially with regard to maintaining the relevance of the organisations and groupings of the South. *These various organisations, armed with specific mandates and occupying different political, economic and cultural spaces, are important in our all-round struggles against poverty, underdevelopment, unfair trade and political and socio-economic exclusion and marginalisation.* (emphasis added) Undoubtedly, this South-South Cooperation is an important means through which to empower ourselves, to help each other access modern technologies and move our nations away from underdevelopment into development. (Mbeki 2006)

Thus South-South Cooperation and South Africa's agenda in this regard is primarily about addressing global inequalities and the related global architecture. The geopolitical shifts in power make such an agenda not only more realizable, but also a necessity recognised also by many northern countries.

However, while at the broadest level, South Africa's southern agenda reflects the desire by all developing states for the removal of global economic and political apartheid, the countries which are grouped as the South have vastly differing levels of economic development, needs for assistance, quality and standards of governance and different economic and political systems. Beyond the generalities of a southern group, these states are highly heterogeneous and one-size-fits all agenda is neither feasible nor a reality. Sometimes the interests of countries of the south are in direct competition with those of other countries of the south. Suspicion of and opposition to the north are often not sufficient to find common offensive positions on issues of importance to the south. The South African government highlighted this in its ten-year review of government, published in 2004,

> South Africa and partner countries still face the challenge of unifying the South behind a common agenda for the reform of international organisations and improving in a meaningful way South-South co-operation. (GCIS 2004)

South Africa has treaded a difficult path in attempting to mitigate the differences and moving towards consensus and unity on issues of common concern. Recognizing that consensus on moving forward on reforms is more attainable via smaller groupings with key players, South Africa has used forums such as the India-Brazil-South Africa Forum and the G5 to give substance to South-South Cooperation and advocacy of global governance reforms.

Giving voice to its southern agenda has sometimes highlighted the contradictions between its African and Southern engagement; on other occasions there has been an alignment of interests.

I will briefly discuss three areas: first, reform of the Bretton Woods Institutions, where South Africa's position has largely reflected African concerns; second, the World Trade Organization (WTO) Doha negotiations, where South Africa aligned with big developing countries; and third, the reform of the UN and the Security Council.

Bretton Woods Reforms

South Africa has played a very active role on the issue of IMF reform, and is viewed by other countries as an honest broker in the process. At the time that South African assumed the chair of the G20 Finance in 2007, many hoped that it would be able to broker an agreement on quota and governance reform, because the country stands to lose from any new formula or ad hoc quota increase that is currently being discussed (Phillips 2007).

Within the Bretton Woods Institutions, South Africa has sought to emphasize its African identity. When South Africa was readmitted into the IMF it was invited by the Swiss group to become a member. This group comprises a very small number of countries[3] and membership of it would have allowed South Africa to hold the managing director seat more frequently than in the Africa group. However, the government believed that accepting that invitation so soon after South Africa returned to the African fold would reinforce perceptions in the rest of the continent that the country was not African enough.

The government's core objectives with respect to reform of the Bretton Woods Institutions are the following:[4]

- Reform of the process whereby the heads and senior management of the two institutions are selected, moving from the current approach whereby the US and Europe nominate leaders of the Bank and Fund respectively, to a merit- based approach in which developing countries have a say; and a process which is more transparent.
- Increasing the voice and representation of developing countries in decisions taken at the two institutions. However, it is not clear whether this extends to the G24 position of increasing the voice of all developing countries or simply those of 'systemically significant' developing countries.[5]

- Putting both institutions' funding bases onto a longer-term, sustainable track in light of the fact that their erstwhile principle clients in the middle-income countries group no longer access both institutions' lending facilities.
- Addressing the needs of low-income countries by broadening support strategies beyond macroeconomic adjustment to microeconomic reform, and being more sensitive to local particularities i.e., avoiding a 'one-size fits all' approach.
- Improving the effectiveness of the Fund's surveillance of the global economy.
- Supporting the Multilateral Debt Relief Initiative, through monitoring its implementation and ensuring it does not fall off the agenda. Related to this is the need to develop domestic revenue sources independent of unpredictable aid flows. This is captured in the 'fiscal space for development' agenda.
- Harnessing the World Bank's resources and expertise to build supply-side capacities in African countries, notably through provision of trade-supporting infrastructure; similarly, harnessing both the Fund and Bank's resources to build African capacities to govern their own economies.

It is clear that on most of the above points South Africa's positions focus on a particular African agenda that is not linked to a narrow self-interested approach.

WTO and the Doha Negotiations

Although the Doha Development Round may after all have produced more noise than outcome, it acted as a catalyst for a significant development in southern coalition politics, viz. the coalescing around a common position on agriculture by key developing states in Cancun in 2003. Major developing states, including South Africa, insisted no agreement on any other issues was possible at the Cancun Ministerial without concessions from the north on agricultural subsidies.

The coalition that emerged out of Cancun became known as the G-20 on agriculture and included South Africa, India and Brazil among others. The Non-Agricultural Market Access (NAMA)-11 was formed during the Hong Kong Ministerial in 2005 demanding the elimination of tariff peaks, tariffs and tariff escalation in developed countries to advance industrial development in developing countries. Both groupings' proposals in the two core market access areas of the negotiations are considered by many to represent the middle ground. The G20 is nominally led by Brazil and India, representing two ends of the G-20's spectrum of interests, while South Africa leads the NAMA-11.[6]

South Africa's involvement in these formations does not emanate from a broad African agenda of interests, as the specific focus of these two coalitions is very much the advocacy of specific interests of big developing economies. Although South Africa has no protectionist agricultural policies, on the macro level it believes that northern agricultural reforms lie at the heart of efforts to create a fairer multilateral trading environment.

In the WTO, South Africa is also a member of the Africa group. However, its relations with the Africa group have been fraught at times. Mostly this revolves around the fact that South Africa is a major investor on the continent, and hence has an array of offensive interests in keeping with its middle power status. Yet the Africa group's overall orientation is largely defensive, in line with the fact that most of its members are least-developed countries (LDCs). These countries wish to maintain preferential access into northern markets by retarding agriculture market access liberalization; defend what is left of their industrial tariff protection (a goal shared by South Africa); and resist services liberalization and further regulatory reform. Hence South Africa finds itself caught between a foreign policy logic built around notions of African solidarity and market access imperatives pushing in the direction of supporting its companies in their penetration of the continent.[7]

UN Reforms

South Africa has been an active advocate of UN reform and was nominated by former Secretary General of the UN Kofi Annan to serve on the task team that advised him on UN reform. South Africa's position on UN Security Council reform has followed the Africa line, in deference to African solidarity, although it initially favoured the compromise position adopted by the G-4 (India, Brazil, Germany and Japan), i.e., new permanent seats without a veto.

The Ezulwini Consensus of the African Union calls for two permanent seats for Africa with veto rights, if the veto right is to continue to exist, as well as five non-permanent seats. These representatives from Africa would be selected by the African Union. South Africa is in favour of reforming the UN beyond just the Security Council. South Africa has revelled in the lead it has allowed itself to take of the G77 and China in spearheading UN reform. These reforms are varied, and include improving the procurement system of the UN, better human resource management and the creation of the UN Ethics Office to highlight and guard against instances of corruption within a UN system that has been tainted by, amongst others, the Oil for Food Scandal as well as sexual violence perpetuated by UN peacekeepers in the Democratic Republic of the Congo.

South Africa also supported the creation of the Peace Building Commission and the Human Rights Council, and seeks the revitalization and strengthening of the General Assembly, which it sees as a way of reducing the power of the Security Council. In addition, South Africa is in favour of the reform of the secretariat and the strengthening of the UN Economic and Social Council (ECOSOC) (Mabhongo 2005). This is in line with the importance South Africa ascribes to socio-economic rights, not only civic and political rights, which many Western countries emphasize.

During its tenure on the UN Security Council in 2007–08, South Africa initiated discussions at the Council on how to institutionalise the links between the UN and regional organisations especially in conflict resolution.

Its point of departure is that the UN should provide financial assistance to delegate some of its political and developmental tasks to regional organizations that share the same goals and interests as the UN. South Africa believed such a development was essential for the effective attainment of peace and security in Africa.

The reform of the UN system is the strongest theme of South Africa's foreign policy, and it is consistent with its efforts to 're-establish norms and principles of multilateralism within the UN Security Council' (Le Pere, Pressens, et. al 2008). South Africa has been critical of the disproportionate power of the P-5, which has been perceived as undermining the multilateral nature of the UN. South Africa has acted as a de facto spokesperson of both NAM and the G77+ China group in its efforts to increase and strengthen multilateral engagement within the Security Council (Le Pere, Pressens, et. al 2008).

Caught Between Two Worlds: African Solidarity or Regional Leadership

The above discussion has attempted to highlight some of the challenges facing South Africa in its execution of its ambitious global governance agenda where its coalitions with big emerging states potentially offer the most effective advocacy instrument, but which simultaneously may deepen suspicion on the continent about South Africa's motives. On the other hand, resorting to more pragmatism and less leadership – what sometimes manifests itself as African solidarity, may constrain the effective execution of its regional and global aspirations. Such contradictions are not unique to South Africa.

South Africa has been described as an emerging middle power (Schoeman 2003). This term is a combination of the term 'middle power' and 'emerging power'. Traditional middle powers are countries such as New Zealand or Canada that operate in the global arena rather than the regional and use multilateral avenues to implement their global vision. An emerging power is regional and shoulders responsibility for stability and order in its neighbourhood (Habib and Selinyane 2004). An emerging power is a leader, a hegemon:

> Hegemons not only aspire to leadership, and are not only endowed with military, economic and other resources: they have a political and socio-economic vision for their transnational environments, and a political willingness to implement it. (Habib and Selinyane 2004)

In many of its foreign policy undertakings, South Africa has exhibited these qualities. However, as Habib and Selinyane demonstrate South Africa has also shown the 'tendency to be persuaded by pragmatic factors to act as only one among the many in regional engagement'.

Because of the legacy of apartheid South Africa's bully tactics in Southern Africa, the new democratic government since 1994 has been at pains to demonstrate its break with the past. Although its economic dominance inevitably invites concerns about economic hegemony, the government has been extremely sensitive to the moniker. In the economic domain especially, South Africa has not always been altruistic in its engagement with its neighbours in the Southern African Development Community and the Southern African Customs Union. However, it is an oft-held perception that hegemony is only about self-interest of the hegemon. This is of course not true. A hegemon not only has a vision for its environment, but also underwrites the order that may be created politically and economically. South Africa has carried out such functions, but on the political plane has tried to emphasise developing consensus within the sub-region or the continent. Especially on issues such as Sudan and Zimbabwe, it will not break ranks with the majority view.

Leadership and living up fully to the definition of an emerging middle power, in helping to shape global debates and outcomes is crucial if South Africa is to realize its key foreign policy objectives. Such an approach may create potential disagreements between South Africa and other African states, as it may with key southern partners such as China and India. However, these are the inevitable consequences of assuming leadership. As a young democracy, South Africa is still sensitive to criticism about its role and identity. To mature fully into the role that it should be playing, both regionally and globally, South Africa will have to develop more confidence in its complex identity and its guiding principles, which should be a peaceful and democratic Africa, and a fairer global system.

Unlike other big developing countries, such as Brazil, India and China, South Africa often emphasizes that its positions are not only shaped by its own particular interests, but also by those of the continent at large. South Africa has thus taken upon itself a much larger responsibility than other big developing countries where the concerns of their regions are largely secondary to their foreign policy positions. Adopting such an approach adds more legitimacy to South African perspectives in global forums. But it is a double-edged sword because its flipside requires South Africa to continually seek affirmation of its role from the continent.

With regard to South Africa's close relationships with major southern powers, there are also a number of potential pitfalls. Strategic partnerships with big developing countries are important for South Africa because they diversify economic and political relationships, position South Africa well at a time when global politics are in flux and new powers are emerging, provide a platform for joint action on global governance reform and create opportunities for cooperation between Africa states and these countries on some of the major developmental projects.

However, it is also the case that South Africa exerts economic influence on many African countries, especially in its neighbourhood. This influence is driven largely by the country's corporate and parastatal investments in numerous African countries. In addition, South Africa has begun its own development cooperation programme focusing on the continent. Coupled with its conflict resolution initiatives, these have helped to carve South African 'spheres of influence' on the continent. China's courting of African states, which has been followed by India and possibly Russia, will no doubt begin to challenge South Africa's economic dominance and its political influence. As this accelerates it may strain South Africa's relationships with such countries and may result in a more assertive political engagement by South Africa in key African countries.

South Africa should not refrain from using the strengths it has to advance the agenda of the south, its own agenda and the global agenda. Unlike other big emerging powers it is not perceived as a threat because its size means it cannot aspire to be the global great power that China or India may become. In the African context, South Africa has displayed both the willingness and the capacity to play a stabilising role. Its own relative stability provides security for this project in the way that Nigeria's ongoing conflict does not.

Thus, reticence amounts to false modesty and undermines the openings that are being created by the geopolitical shifts to transform the existing system. Nor is it in anyone's interests that South Africa should not fulfil its regional and global role to the greatest possible extent. For South Africa to fully play the role it should in the process of reforming the global governance architecture, it will need to overcome its need to overcompensate for its complex African identity. It will also need to consider building strategic partnerships with a number of key African states, much as it is doing with other Southern states. South Africa cannot escape its relative size on the continent. As the world transitions to a multipolar system where some of the great powers will be developing countries, regional powers need to minimise the emphasis on solidarity if that means adopting the lowest common denominator as a plan of action.

References

Barber, J. 2004. *Mandela's World*. Oxford: James Currey.

Government Communication and Information System (GCIS). 2004. The Presidency, *Ten-year review*.

Gumede, W. M. 2005. *Thabo Mbeki and the Battle for the Soul of the ANC*. Cape Town: Zebra.

Habib, A. and Selinyane, N. 2004. 'South Africa's Foreign Policy and a Realistic Vision of an African Century' in *Apartheid Past, Renaissance Future*. Johannesburg: South Africa Institute of International Affairs.

Le Pere, G., Pressens, M., Ruiters, M. and Zondi, S. 2008. 'South Africa's Participation In The System Of Global Governance', Draft Review prepared for the Presidency's Fifteen Year Review, Institute for Global Dialogue.

Mabhongo, X. 2005. 'Statement by Mr. Xolisa Mabhongo, Charge D' Affaires at the Informal Meeting to Consider the Draft Outcome Document for the High-Level Plenary Meeting of the General Assembly to be held in September 2005', Online: http://www.southafricanewyork.net/pmun/view_speech.php?speech=4096320 (accessed 22 June 2005).

Mbeki, T. 2006. Address by the Chairperson of the Group of 77 and China, President Thabo Mbeki at the XIV Summit Conference of the Non-Aligned Movement (NAM), Havana, Cuba 14 September 2006.

Phillips, L. 2007. 'Closing the Deal: IMF reform in 2007', ODI Briefing Paper 26.

Schoeman, M. 2003. 'South Africa as an emerging middle power' in J. Daniel, A. Habib and R. Southall (eds), *State of the Nation: South Africa 2003–2004*. Cape Town: HSRC Press.

Spence, J. 2004. 'South Africa's Foreign Policy: Vision and Reality', in E. Sidiropoulos (ed.), *Apartheid Past, Renaissance Future: South Africa's Foreign Policy 1994–2004*. Johannesburg: South Africa Institute of International Affairs.

Chapter 8

MEXICO AS AN EMERGING POWER IN THE PRESENT WORLD SCENARIO: GLOBAL ECONOMY WITHOUT NATIONAL DEVELOPMENT STRATEGY?[1]

Roberto Escalante-Semerena and Eduardo Vega-López

Introduction

From a long-term perspective, the Mexican economy has achieved important and structural changes since 1982. From that year to date, the Mexican economy has deeply modified its macroeconomic priorities to manage economic policy instruments, the correlation between its economic determinants to growth and its external linkages to face the emerging regional and global markets. From then to now, the Mexican economy has increasingly abandoned its international low profile to develop into a more active player in the open markets; however, it must be said, not always with successful results.

In 1994, in the middle of a deep political crisis and just a few months before a new economic recession, Mexico had reached at least three significant goals related to its external sector: i) to modify the composition of its exports; ii) to start with Canada and the US the North American Free Trade Agreement (NAFTA), signed in 1992; and, iii) to join, as a formal member, the Organization for the Economic Cooperation and Development (OECD).

Following a severe social and political turmoil, 1994 ended with the sadly known 'December error' and recession ensued. The Mexican economy suffered its deepest recession with higher inflation in 1995: the annual percent change of the GDP was -6.2 and the annual per cent change of the consumer prices at the end of the year reached 52 points. The increasing correlation of the economic and manufacturing cycles between Mexico and the US, the control of inflation in lower figures, the informal or non-registered economy and the rise of emigration of Mexican citizens to the US were the most relevant economic trends registered from 1996 to 2007.

With the argument to strengthening the national growth capacity and be competitive in global and open markets, the Mexican federal government has promoted a series of structural reforms on three economic strategic public policies: fiscal, energy and labour. As expected, a heated debate had also manifestations of political conflict around these issues and the net progress is still hard to measure and the results are quite polemic.

The insufficient economic growth of the recent years, the importance of the remittances from abroad, the unfolding of new branches of NAFTA, the new opportunities and challenges derived from the global warming scenarios and the commitments linked to the Kyoto Protocol are amongst the main issues addressed by the Mexican economy and society as a whole. Even though Mexico has considerable potential to play a more active role in a global context, there are constraints that stem from persistent problems such as social inequality, public insecurity and juridical weakness.

In view of the above there are concerns related to the lack of strong social and economical progress at the national level. It is possible to argue on the role that Mexico could play as an emerging power in the global economy in the next years. Is this possible without a national and successful development strategy?

From Financial Crisis to Economic Liberalization (1982–1994)

1982 represented a transcendent turning point for the Mexican economy and society. That year, economic growth was folded as a national priority and replaced by strong financial constraints. The new priorities were to pay the external debt, to reduce the hyperinflation and to reduce the public unbalanced ratio of GDP. To do that, the currency value was adjusted, imports were cut and the investment and expenses of the federal government dramatically came down.

The remains of the eighties registered low or negative annual per cent change of economic activity, annual inflation rates near to or upper than 100 per cent and severe reductions of GDP per capita. In fact, the GDP per capita registered in 1981 was recovered until 1992. For this reason that period is known in Mexico, and in other Latin American countries with similar experiences, as the 'lost decade'.

During those years, following the current recommendations from the International Monetary Fund (IMF) and the World Bank, the federal government accelerated and consolidated the Mexican economic privatization and liberalization.

Table 8.1. **Mexico 1981–1995: Economic Growth and Inflation**

	GDP, Constant Prices, Annual % Change	GDP per capita, US $	Inflation, Annual % Change, Consumer Prices, End of Period
1981	8,5	3,817	28,7
1982	–0,5	2,708	98,8
1983	–3,5	2,160	80,8
1984	3,4	2,493	59,2
1985	2,2	2,591	63,7
1986	–3,1	1,758	105,7
1987	1,7	1,890	159,2
1988	1,2	2,286	51,7
1989	4,2	2,730	19,7
1990	5,1	3,156	29,9
1991	4,2	3,709	18,8
1992	3,6	4,210	11,9
1993	2,0	4,585	8,0
1994	4,4	4,699	7,1
1995	–6,2	3,140	52,0

Source: International Monetary Fund, World Economic Outlook Database, October 2007.

In that context, the problems related to social inequity and poverty became serious issues of internal political governance. In 1990, Mexico had more than 83 million inhabitants, the 30 per cent poorest of that population received around 8 per cent of national income, while the 10 per cent richest earned around 38 per cent.

In 1994, Mexico experienced extreme and paradoxical events: on one hand, the beginning of NAFTA and its OECD membership and, on the other hand, the presidential elections in the context of the Zapatista radical movement, economic uncertainties, generalized speculative behaviour and political murders. That year ended with impressive financial transfers to abroad and with internal conflicts in the Mexican society as a whole. The new presidential period started registering the deepest recession with higher inflation. In 1995, the GDP per capita was nearly the same than five years before and lower than 14 years before.

Permanent Stabilization and Insufficient Growth (1995–2007)

During the previous period, Mexico established different stabilization and macroeconomic adjustment programs. As a mid- and long-term structural

Graph 8.1. Liberalisation: Trade to GDP Ratios (*Difference between 2006 and 1993 ratios in percentage points*).

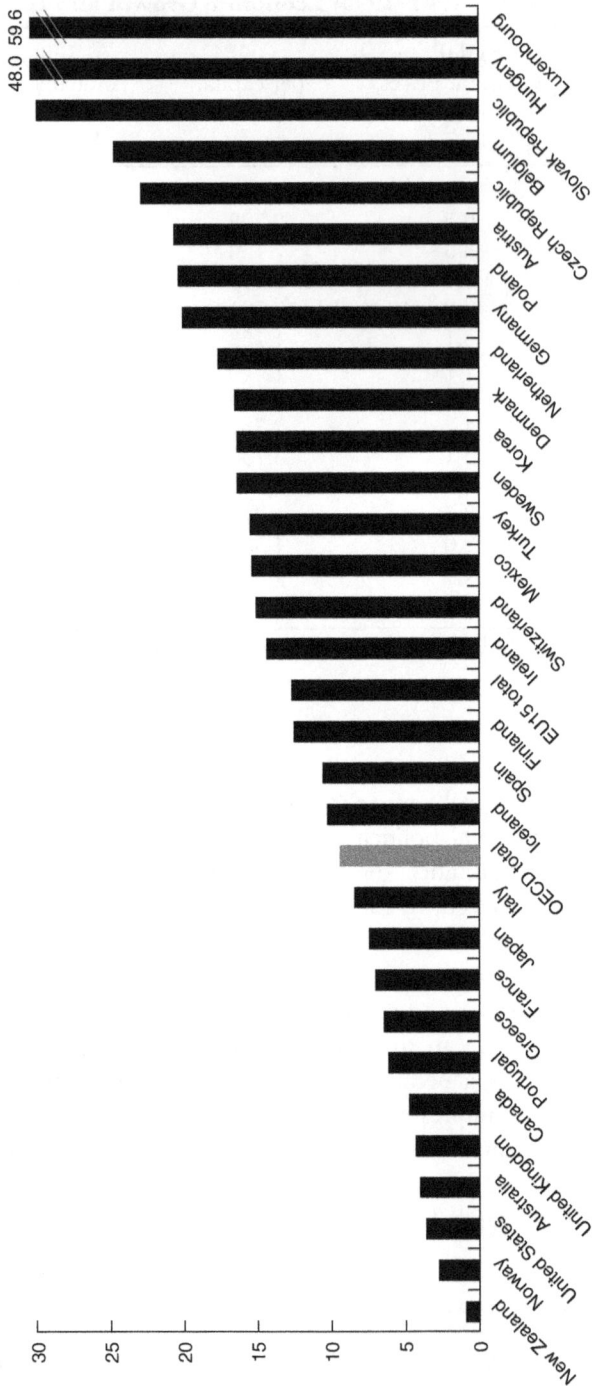

Fuente: OECD Factbook 2008, April 2008.

***Table 8.2.* Mexico 1990: National Income Distribution**

Population, %	National Income, %
30	8
20	11
20	16
20	27
10	38

Source: National Institute of Statistics, Geography and Information, INEGI Database.

process, the privatization and liberalization of the Mexican economy continued controlling inflation in low figures and increasingly linking the macroeconomic cycles of Mexico and the US. This situation is evident in the bolded and italised figures of the Table 8.3.

Since 2001, Mexico has achieved low profile inflation, but also has registered an insufficient and unbalanced economic growth. During 2001–03, while agricultural activities grew, manufacturing production and the industrial sector as a whole descended. The opposite performance occurred in 2005. These inconvenient sectoral decouplings unfortunately also exist in the regional linkages inside Mexico. Hence, we have a 'national ezquizophrenia': there is a Mexico where modernity, dynamic processes, global economy and competitiveness are strong components of a genuine national reality; but this reality coexists with the 'other Mexico' where its important characteristics are poverty, deep social inequalities, compulsive emigration, traditional productive methods, regional marginality, etc.

For example, the institutional and economic capacities installed in the most important metropolitan zones linked to cities like Mexico, Monterrey, Guadalajara, Puebla, Toluca, Querétaro or Cancún are impressive. More impressive are the economic and social contrasts amongst these metropolitan zones and other rural and urban regions of the country where the economic potentiality and social forecasts are quite depressed.

Now Mexico has around 108 millions inhabitants and each year around one million of them reach the age of 18 years old. Thus, federal and local institutions and the national economy should offer an average of a million new jobs for a million new citizens yearly. The annual per cent change of GDP in recent years (see Table 8.3) has been insufficient to attend this labour demand, and in the following years could be worse regarding the expected trends on less economic growth. In addition, the gross fixed investment as a proportion of GDP, less than 20 per cent in recent years, will persist in a low profile.

Table 8.3. **Mexico and USA: Decoupling and Coupling Macroeconomics Trends**

	Mexican GDP, Constant Prices, Annual % Change	Mexican Inflation, Annual % Change, Consumer Prices, End of Period	USA GDP, Constant Prices, Annual % Change	USA Inflation, Annual % Change, Consumer Prices, End of Period
1982	–0,5	98,8	–1,9	3,8
1983	–3,5	80,8	4,5	3,8
1984	3,4	59,2	7,2	4,0
1985	2,2	63,7	4,1	3,8
1986	–3,1	105,7	3,5	1,2
1987	1,7	159,2	3,4	4,3
1988	1,2	51,7	4,1	4,4
1989	**4,2**	19,7	**3,5**	4,6
1990	5,1	29,9	1,9	6,3
1991	4,2	18,8	–0,2	3,0
1992	**3,6**	11,9	**3,3**	3,0
1993	**2,0**	*8,0*	**2,7**	*2,8*
1994	**4,4**	*7,1*	**4,0**	*2,6*
1995	–6,2	52,0	2,5	2,5
1996	5,2	27,7	3,7	3,4
1997	6,8	15,7	4,5	1,7
1998	**5,0**	18,6	**4,2**	1,6
1999	**3,8**	12,3	**4,4**	2,7
2000	**6,6**	*9,0*	**3,7**	*3,4*
2001	**0,0**	*4,4*	**0,8**	*1,6*
2002	**0,8**	*5,7*	**1,6**	*2,5*
2003	**1,4**	*4,0*	**2,5**	*1,9*
2004	**4,2**	*5,2*	**3,6**	*3,3*
2005	**2,8**	*3,3*	**3,1**	*3,4*
2006	**4,8**	*4,1*	**2,9**	*2,5*
2007	**2,9**	*3,6*	**1,9**	*3,3*
2008*	**1,9**	*3,6*	**1,0**	*2,2*

Source: International Monetary Fund, World Economic Outlook Database, October 2007.
* Re-estimated figures.

Additionally in recent years, without proper political manners and without success, the Mexican federal government has tried to set up 'structural reforms' in some important public issues: fiscal policy, energy and labour market regulation. These three issues, at least, are the key institutional changes required in Mexico to expect more dynamic growth, more social opportunities to labour re-qualification, more capacities to compete in the global economy and in a long-term perspective and more possibility to lead regional processes in some economic branches, technological innovations, political initiatives and/or some global environmental commitments.

Graph 8.2. Population Growth Rates (*Average annual growth in percentage, 1993–2006 or latest available period*).

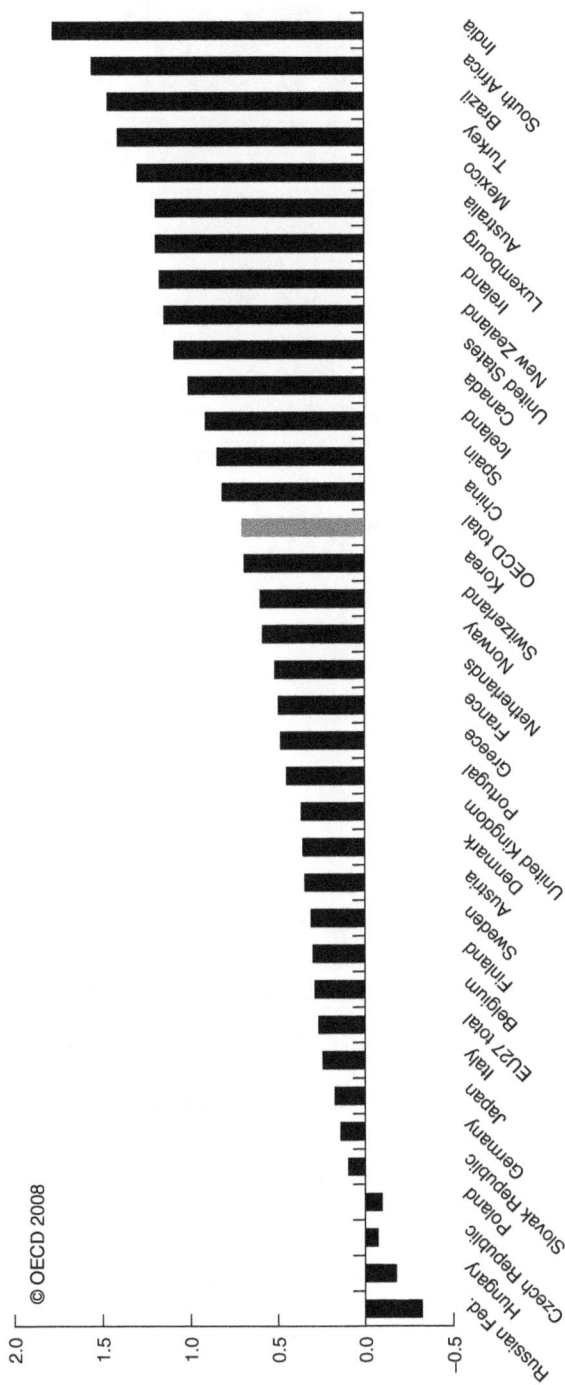

© OECD 2008

Fuente: OECD Factbook 2008, April 2008.

Graph 8.3. Gross Fixed Capital Formation (*As a percentage of GDP*).

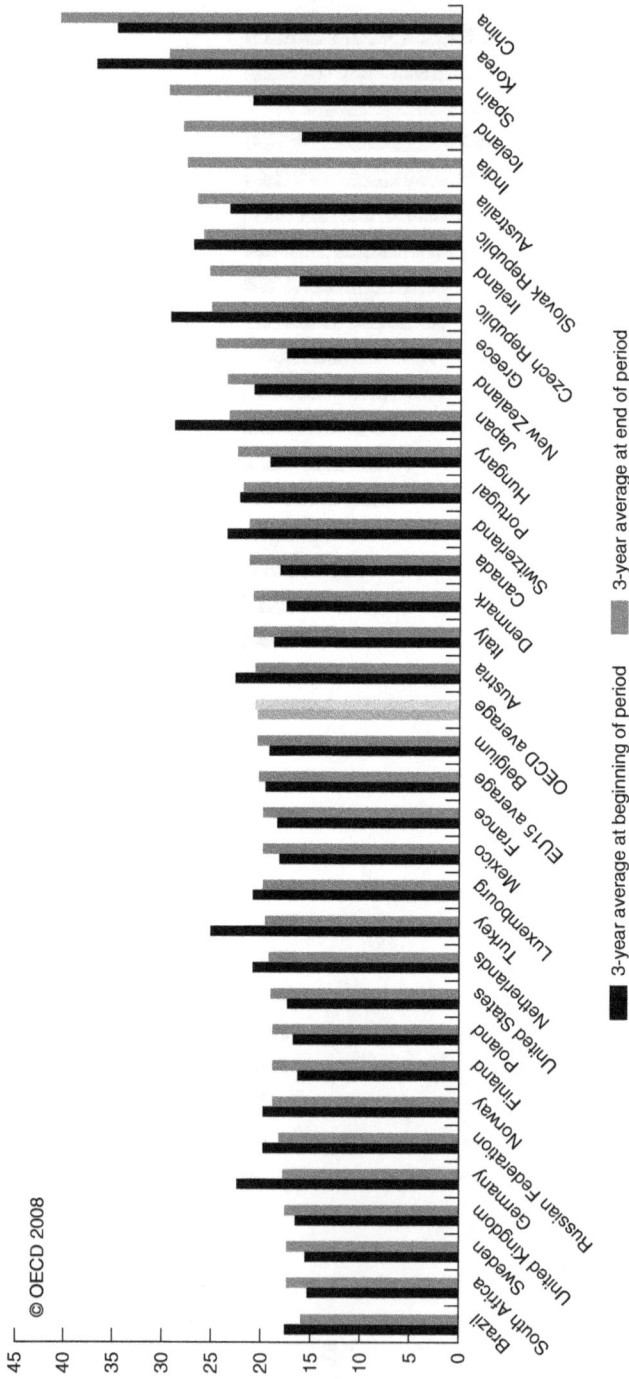

© OECD 2008

■ 3-year average at beginning of period   ▨ 3-year average at end of period

Fuente: OECD Factbook 2008, April 2008.

Final Remarks: Mexico as an Emerging Power in the Global Economy?

In terms of gross and net national income per capita, Mexico is better than Brazil, South Africa, India and China, but is located in the pre-last place in the OECD countries figures. In fact, Mexico is the last OECD country listed in terms of social inequity measured by Gini coefficients (see Graphs 8.4 and 5). The worst is that the social inequity in Mexico, it seems, is not being solved in a persistent and structural manner.

Social inequity represents a serious Mexican problem in terms of nutrition (the less difficult aspect to solve), income (not easy to solve without economic growth) and opportunities to develop personal and professional capacities and to get better standards of welfare (the most difficult issue to achieve).Hence, social inequity must face it with economic growth, but also with explicit social policies to ameliorate education, health, information and labour capacities.

Sadly, Mexico is the last in OECD countries in terms of performance on reading, science skills and mathematics (see Graph 8.6). So, the problem to develop a productive population and a competitive economy is one of the main targets that Mexico has urgently to define and achieve.

Information and labour capacity cannot continue absent in the Mexican public policies link to the formal sector of the economy. Mexico needs an ambitious and long-term national development strategy and not only disarticulated and short-term initiatives.

If Mexico wants to play the role of an emerging power in the global arena, it has to promote economic growth, institutional opportunities to get welfare and better quality standards of life for its population. Mexico must have a national strategy to compete and to get development as sustainable development.

Graph 8.4. Gross and Net National Income per capita (*US dollars, current prices and PPPs, 2006 or latest available year*).

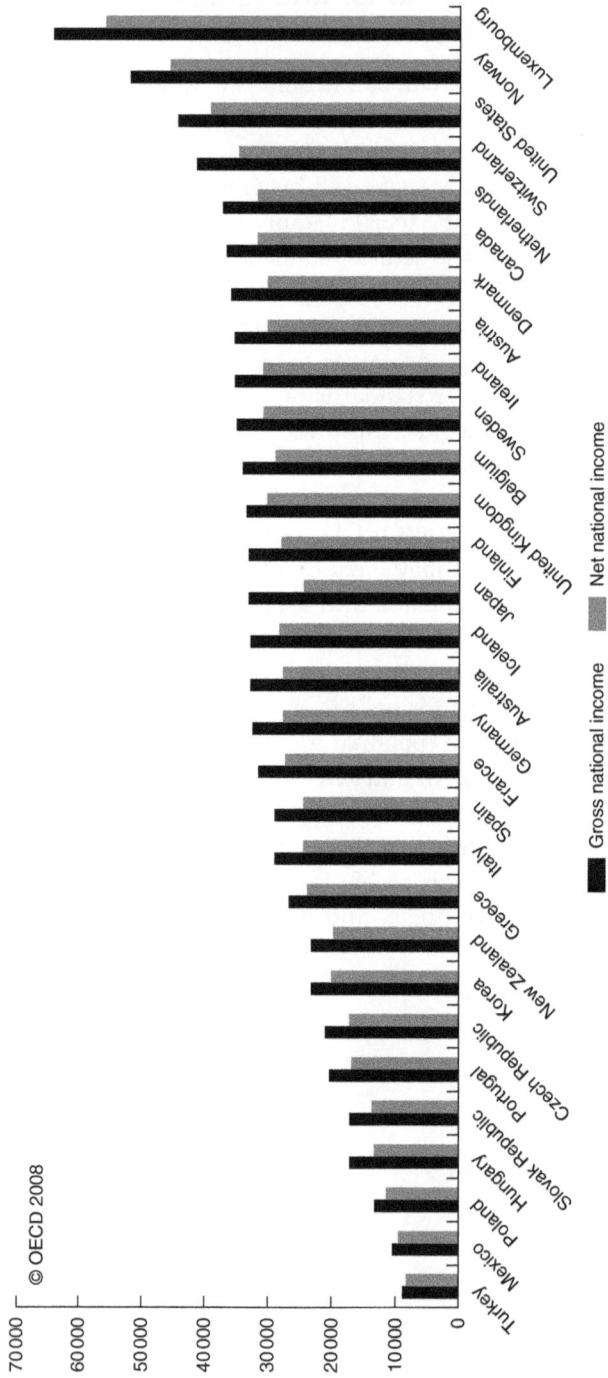

Fuente: OECD Factbook 2008, April 2008.

Graph 8.5. Distribution of Household Disposable Income among Individuals (*Measured by Gini coefficients*).

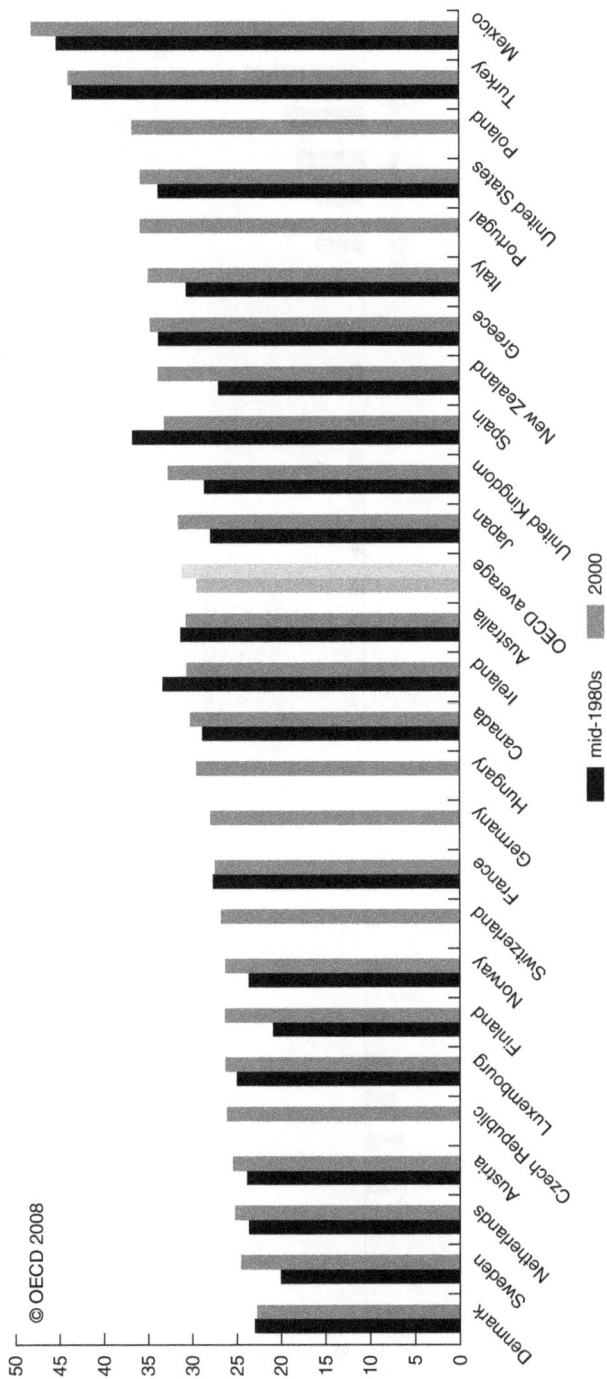

© OECD 2008

Legend: mid-1980s ■ 2000 ▨

Fuente: OECD Factbook 2008, April 2008.

Graph 8.6. Performance on the Reading Scale in PISA 2006 *(Mean scores)*.

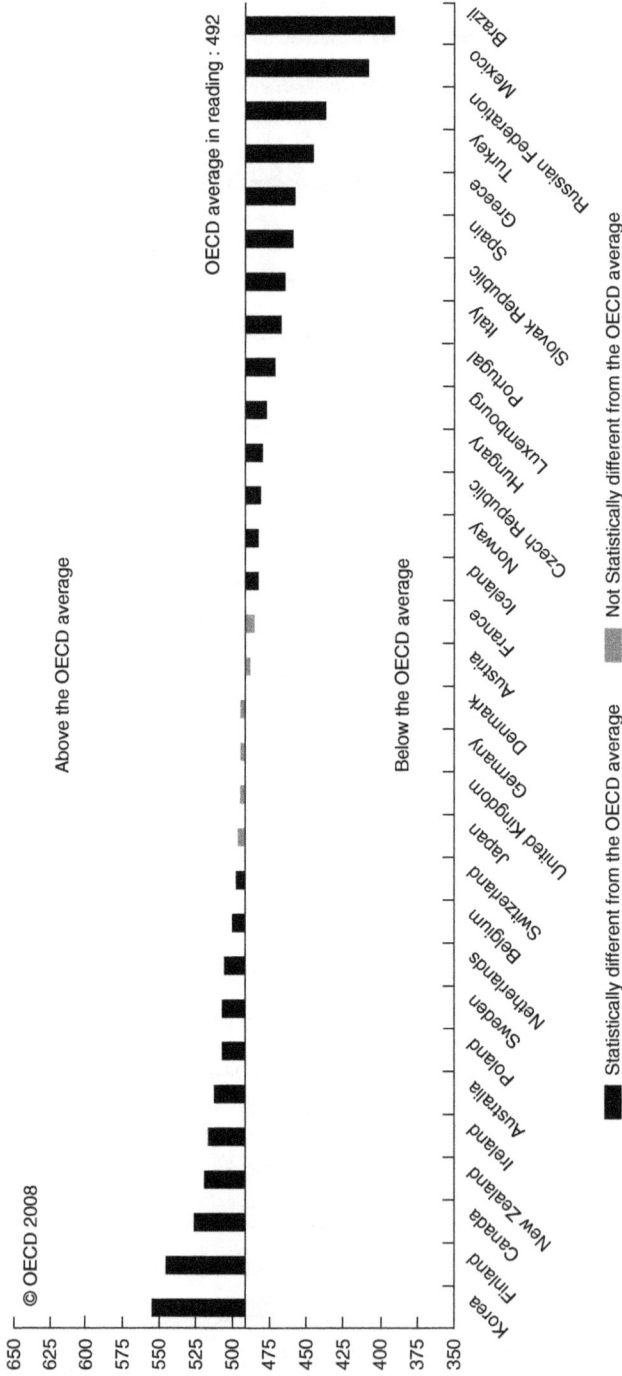

© OECD 2008

Above the OECD average

Below the OECD average

OECD average in reading : 492

Statistically different from the OECD average

Not Statistically different from the OECD average

Fuente: OECD Factbook 2008, April 2008.

Graph 8.7. Growth in GDP per Hour Worked (*Average annual growth in percentage, 1995–2000 and 2001–2006*).

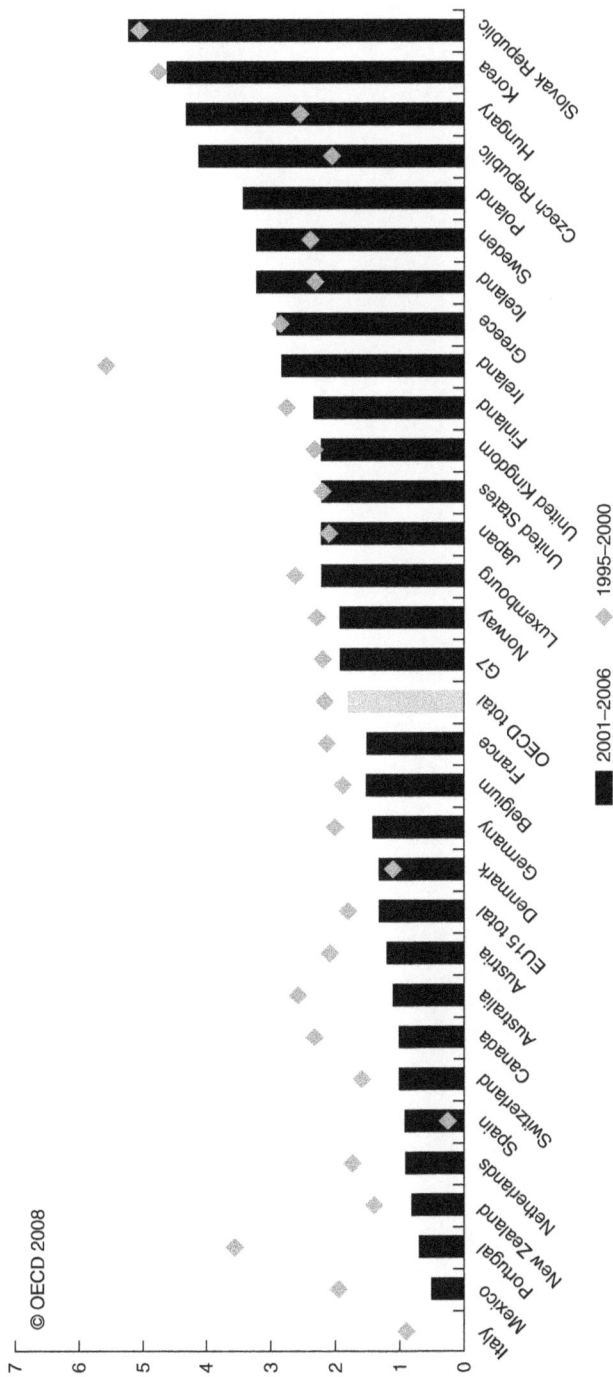

© OECD 2008

■ 2001–2006   ◆ 1995–2000

Fuente: OECD Factbook 2008, April 2008.
International Monetary Fund. 2007. World Economic Outlook Database. OECD. 2008. Factbook.
National Institute of Statistics, Geography and Information INEGI Database.

Chapter 9

TRILATERAL RELATIONS AMONG AFRICA, CHINA AND EUROPE: A CHINESE PERSPECTIVE

Tiejun Zhang

Introduction

Europe has long history of engagement with Africa after the Second World War and invested hugely politically and economically on the continent. China has also been engaging for decades with African countries, but the present Chinese approach to Africa shows its nuance, with more and more priorities in economic domain. The new Chinese engagement with Africa, especially its focus on resource extraction and non-interference principle that relates to the governance issue of Africa, has been raising serious concerns in European capitals.

This chapter is an attempt to analyse the trilateral relations among Africa, China and Europe, with Sino-European relations as a starting point. The chapter begins with an analysis on the dualities and thus also complexity of China, relevant to the trilateral relations. Secondly, I will describe the static and dynamic features of the trilateral relations. Thirdly, I will discuss the ideological background of the Chinese and European approaches to Africa. Fourthly, I focus on the Chinese engagement, with particular reference on the motivations and attractiveness of China in Africa. Fifthly, I will make a contrast between the Chinese and European approaches to Africa, in the dichotomy of good governance vs. effective governance. In conclusion, I argue that though on the surface the Chinese and European approaches to Africa show the contradiction between each other, they in fact can be complementary to a certain extent, and more coordination and cooperation are needed in this area.

Dualities of China and Implications for the Trilateral Relations

Dualities Internally—Dual Economy and Dual Society of China

Like other large rising developing countries such as India and Brazil, there is an evident dualistic economic structure within China. On the one hand, we see a relatively advanced and modernized urban and coastal economy, especially in the Beijing-Tianjin area of the North, Yangtze Delta region of the East and Pearl River Delta region in the South. On the other, many of China's rural areas (and some urban areas) are still very underdeveloped, focusing mainly on agricultural and primary production.

Such an economic structure has two implications relevant to the trilateral relations among Africa, China and Europe: firstly, while China competes at the low end of the global value chain with many other developing countries (including African ones) in low cost, labour-intensive products, it increasingly competes with developed countries (like European ones) at the high end of the global value chain. Secondly, there is a serious limit in terms of 'domestic driven' economic development due to the fact that large number of people are still living in a poverty or near poverty condition. This means that the Chinese economy will still substantially depend on the world market, including European and African markets.

Equally evident is the dualistic structure of the Chinese society. One of the priorities of the Chinese economic reforms initiated in the late 1970s was to 'get some people rich first'. Partly as a result of that effort, while China has been experiencing a highly growing economy, the gaps between different social groups, such as urban dwellers and rural dwellers, and employees of monopolized enterprises and non-monopolized ones, have been ever enlarging as well. A clear indicator for such is the Gini coefficient for income in China. The figure for 2004 was 0.447, approaching Bolivia (one of the most unequal in the world), while it was only 0.28 (slightly higher than Nordic countries) in the late 1970s. Accompanied with these income gaps are many potential social problems and unrest. That is also why the present Chinese government is proposing creating a 'harmonious society'.

Dualities Externally—Gaps in China's Foreign Relations

Here, we witness an officially constructed dual identity of the present China as both a developing country and a potential world power. This identity is not only a constructed reality of China itself, but to a certain extent acknowledged by the outside world, Europe in particular.

China as a developing country in the globalization era, one side of the dual identity highlights the weaknesses China endows, the resulting necessity and urgency of economic development and the common interests China shares with many other developing countries, African countries in particular.

The other side of the dual identity is China as a potential world power. Chinese leaders' frequent assertion on China as the largest developing country most frequently goes together with the admittance to the US as the largest developed country to emphasize China as an influential player on the international arena. Among other attributes that emphasize China's increasing international influences are the country as a standing member of the UN Security Council, the most populous country of the globe and a nuclear power. While the Chinese leadership has never openly claimed that China is a world power, China's strong appeal for creating a multipolar world order in which China itself would constitute one pole, the country's determination to oppose decisively hegemonism, and especially its mission to become a 'medium developed' country by the mid twenty-first century, all suggest a vision among the Chinese elites to make the country a world power in the future.

This dual identity gives rise to an immediate gap in China's foreign relations, i.e. the gap between developing country reality and world power aspiration.

This gap implies that China should not only be responsive to the developing countries, as the champion of the developing world (or put more modestly as the Chinese leaders repeatedly say, the largest developing country in the world), but to the developed world as well, as among the leading countries of the globe.

Parallel to this is the second gap in China's foreign relations, that is, the gap between increasing international cooperation needs and sovereign concern. Chinese engagement with Africa, among others, is a case here.

To dig even deeper, we witness the third gap, the one between national interests and foreign policy principles, in which the most debated one being non-interference in domestic affairs (a direct link to the sovereign concern).

Among China's national interests, we observe the fourth gap, that between issue-related national interests (such as China's energy needs) and relational national interests (like Sino-European relations). In many cases, the two are in conflict with each other. Africa is again a case here.

Related to the dual identity and all the gaps identified earlier, the final gap that has the closest reference to Sino-European relations is the one between increasing external expectations and the Chinese capacity to fulfill them. Back in China, we call the increasing demand or expectation from outside world (especially from developed world but also from developing world) as the 'thesis of responsibility' (*zherenlun*). Compared to the 'thesis of China threat' earlier, China feels at least equal amount of pressure, though from a different and more positive direction. The peaceful rise doctrine was a delayed response to the thesis of China threat, what could come out as a response to the thesis of responsibility? Something has to come out, we do not know what exactly.

Among the European demands on China, we can notice very frequently distinct signals, some reflecting China as a developing country, and others as a developed one. This fact suggests that the dual identity is not only a constructed 'reality' of China itself, but to a certain extent, acknowledged by the outside world, Europe in particular.

General Features of the Trilateral Relations

Static

Concerning the general features of the current trilateral relations among Africa, China and Europe, a contrast can be made between this triangle and the one between China, Europe and the U.S..

In the China-Europe-U.S. triangle, we observe, firstly, that the three sides are of distinct nature: the U.S., the only remaining superpower of the day, intends to prolong the 'unipolar moment'; China, as the largest emerging power of the world, is increasingly becoming both a reactor to the existing global system and shaper of the very system; Europe, being the largest economy of the world, is struggling between enlargement of the EU and deepening of European integration, and yet, at the same time, trying to form a common foreign and security policy of the Union.

Secondly, we see clearly the asymmetry in the trilateral relations: for both China and Europe, the relations with Washington are much more significant than the one between China and Europe, while Washington, especially the Bush administration, very frequently invoked its unilateral approaches in its dealing with both China and Europe for getting its agenda forward. China and Europe's relationships with the U.S. are comprehensive in nature. While there emerges a comprehensive relationship between Beijing and Brussels, for obvious reasons, Europe still plays a minor role on crucial issues such as Taiwan, which China considers as part of its core national interests, and Washington plays an indispensable role there. China is still not strong enough to be a fully-fledged global player, and Europe is still not united sufficiently to be such either. Then it is only natural that both lay great emphasis on the future potential of each other.

In the Africa-China-Europe triangle, on the other hand, Africa is the weakest among the three parties, and there are big differences between China and Europe on how to engage Africa, with the Chinese more pragmatic in nature, and the European more value-laden (see the next section for more details). In the Africa-China-Europe triangle, we see clearly that Europe very often uses its soft power in its foreign policy, and China, in recent years, practising both types of powers in its regional and global strategies, including in its African policy. There is an issue of perception on soft power. For those African countries that appreciate it, China's engagement with emphasis on non-interference is sort of Chinese soft power; seeing from European perspective, probably, it is a 'soft weakness'. By the same token, seeing from Europe, European engagement with conditionalities and interference is most often considered as a kind of soft power for Europe; but for many in Africa, it is a different case.

The importance and changing dynamics of the Africa-China-Europe triangle can never be so vivid and relevant as the present. For the first time since the Opium War in the mid-19th century, Europe takes China seriously, for China's own sake, due to the rise of China and increasing impacts of the country in a variety of issue areas, not the least Chinese engagement with Africa. In the late Cold War era, Europe treated China relatively seriously, mainly for third party reasons, i.e. the Soviet threat and the so-called U.S.-USSR-China strategic triangle. Under that circumstance, China-Europe relationship was secondary in nature. The current rise of China is making this secondary relationship to a primary one.

Interesting enough is the fact that for the first time in history, Africa is so significant for China, for China's own sake. The old Chinese engagement with Africa in the late Cold War era was more for competition with the Soviet Union and so on.

In an article published on 26 November 2007 and several other occasions, David Shambaugh, claimed that China-EU honeymoon was over and early marriage had started and thus problems followed (Shambaugh 2007). If there is a kind of 'marriage' between China and Europe, what nature is that? Is it the merely a marriage of convenience? Are China and Africa experiencing a 'honeymoon'? Has that 'honeymoon' matured into early marriage too?

Personally, I believe that there was no 'honeymoon' (thus also no marriage) between China and Europe as a whole. What we had was only sort of 'honeymoon' and probably 'early marriage' between Chirac's France, Schroder's Germany and the Chinese government. But even here, we know that this kind of 'marriage' was not based on love, but based on interests and thus a marriage of convenience. At the moment, because interests have been changing, so the problems come.

Contrary to EU-China relations is China's relations with some African countries, which share the basic value concerning how the international and domestic society should be organized. These African countries are in favor of the so-called Beijing Consensus about domestic authoritarianism and most importantly, appreciate China's foreign policy principle of 'non-interference'. As such, if there is 'marriage' between China and Africa, it would be a kind of 'marriage' based more on love than the EU-China one, because of the factor of value-sharing. However, I would like to indicate the limited relaxation from the Chinese government in terms of 'non-interference', and we can probably now say that China is now beginning to have sort of 'persuasive intervention', as exemplified by the Chinese moves on the Darfur issue and the more general active Chinese participation in UN peace keeping.

Dynamic

Here, we witness the widening bases and enriched ingredients of the two bilateral relations, China-Europe and China-Africa.

The current dynamics of EU-China relations can be described as 'from the height to the width'. In the immediate aftermath of the Cold War and throughout the 1990s, China had very high expectations from Europe, hoping that Europe would constitute a pole in the Chinese-conceived emerging multipolar world. In the 1990s, concerning Sino-European relations, in Chinese eyes, the US was always the greatest background while at the same time the biggest target. When visiting European capitals, the then Chinese president Jiang Zemin repeatedly appealed that China and Europe should see their relations from the 'strategic height'. The most significant hidden message there was clearly the vision of world multipolarity. He got some applause from certain European leaders, but only few, such as Chirac.

Time has passed and the U.S. remains the single superpower. In a comprehensive way, the world is still not multipolarized. What is more, the greatest background and biggest target (the U.S.) does not sit idly. It is acting proactively to prevent its European allies to get too close to China, exemplified in particularly by American lobbying activities in European capitals to persuade European countries not to lift the arms embargo against China.

The Chinese, after all, are pragmatic. With futile efforts on creating a multipolar world and increasing national interest needs accompanied by the growing economy, China began a tactical change away from the promotion of world multipolarity instead to concentrate on the more tangible issues and needs. China's new engagement with Africa and outsourcing for natural resources are two of the illustrations here.

This time, it is Europe's turn to have higher expectation from China on a wide range of issues, seeing from a Chinese perspective. After French and Dutch referendum refusing EU constitution, Chinese media and academic writings frequently portraited a dark picture for the future of European integration, at least for the short and medium terms. The Europeans expect China to have more sustainable and responsible behaviour in Africa, on environmental and energy issues, and to open the Chinese market and change the development mode of the country to be more domestic driven. Some of these are beyond the Chinese capacity to fulfill.

In this dynamic of Sino-European relations, economic relations are still the main foundation of the bilateral relations, and it goes deeper to include RMB exchange rates, for instance, while other factors (like environment, energy and Africa) are becoming more and more visible and significant in the relationship. Widening bases of the bilateral relations also mean more shared interests and more areas where the two sides have differences and disputes.

As for the Sino-African relations, three kinds of changes can be observed, from a Chinese perspective, as follows: the first is a transformation from class interests in the old engagement to national interests in the new engagement (and related, from class identity to national identity); the second is a shift from political oriented relations to comprehensive relations; and the last is a change from elite diplomacy to diplomacy of all levels.

Issues that Need to be Taken into Account in the Trilateral Relations

Here, three kinds of issues need to be taken into account. The first is, from a Chinese foreign policy perspective, two gaps that existed in China's foreign relations: the one between foreign policy principles and national interests (in many case, the former prevails); and issue related national interests and relational national interests (a compromise more difficult to make). The second is from the point of foreign demands on China, and here we witness a change from 'China threat' to 'China responsibility'. Here, the questions are: who sets the standards for being responsible? Is China the only international player that needs to be responsible on a variety of issues? Responsibility issue is not only relevant to China, but to other emerging powers as well, even to the primary powers like the EU and the U.S. The third issue is the one that has been debated much in terms of European and (recently) Chinese engagement with Africa. Back in East Asia, we see that the Asia-Europe Meeting (ASEM) process has been promoting East Asianness or East Asian regionalism (regional identity). The question is: would EU-African Dialogs and the Forum on China-Africa Cooperation (FOCAC) promote Africanness or African identity, and African Unity?

European and Chinese Engagement with Africa: Soft Imperialism vs. Pragmatism

The EU takes four different forms of foreign policy: enlargement in the core area of Europe; stabilization in the neighbourhood area; bilateralism with great powers; and inter-regionalism with other organized regions. In the last decade, inter-regional cooperation has become an important component of EU foreign policy and external relations. This form of EU foreign policy is partly realized through a large number of inter-regional arrangements with other regions around the globe, particularly in Africa, Latin America and Asia.

As Bjorn Hettne and Fredrik Soderbaum argue, the type of power exercised by the EU is of the 'soft' rather than the 'hard' type and is based on economic instruments, dialog and diplomacy, but even this kind of power can be used in different ways (Hettne B. and F. Soderbaum, 2005) A distinction is made between 'civilian power' and 'soft imperialism'. The former implies (soft) power without the hard option, the latter refers to soft power applied in a hard way, that is an asymmetric form of dialog or even the imposition or strategic use of norms and conditionalities enforced for reasons of self-interest rather than for the creation of a genuine dialog.

Both civilian power and soft imperialism are helpful in explaining EU inter-regional relations towards Africa, Latin America and Asia. The relevance of these two models is closely linked to the relative strength of the counterpart region. It is particularly interesting to note the various ways in which the EU promotes inter-regionalism towards different counterpart regions. In the case of ASEM, there is a pragmatic approach based on civilian power consisting of a reasonably symmetric dialog among 'equals' in combination with a cautious stress on norms and good governance, at least to less significant states like Myanmar. This sharply contrasts with the EU-African relations that is more asymmetrical, dominated by the strong and built on conditionalities and imposition of norms for material self-interests. Thus, civilian power may have the most relevance in the case of ASEM and soft imperialism describes EU foreign policy relationships towards Africa, while EU-Latin American (such as Mercosur) relations lie in between. As some European politicians and analysts argue, the European approach to Africa emphasizes to make Europe as model for Africa, regardless the local conditions of the latter. While doing this the Europeans do not even want to understand Africa and just make Africa as 'black Europe' (Interview 2007).

China has long historical links with African countries, dating back to the era of independence of African states in the 1950s and 1960s. This kind of links emphasized, among other factors, the solidarity of the developing world. Later on, China has strived hard to secure African countries' diplomatic recognition away from Taiwan. During the late Cold War era, China built infrastructure for African nations and helped them in other aspects. Nonetheless, the more recent Chinese engagement, or new engagement of China in Africa, concentrates more on resource extraction for fuelling the growing Chinese economy, together with infrastructure building and other trade and investment activities.

Motives and Attractiveness of China in Africa

While Taiwan remains part of China's core national interests, Africa is becoming more and more important. However, it seems Africa has yet to be added to the list of core national interests and would best be described as a new policy frontier for China.

From the messages of Chinese leaders to Africans, we can observe two important factors behind Chinese policy towards Africa: on the one hand, although China itself is a developing country with low level of productivity, China is willing to help African countries; on the other, the assistance that China provides to Africa is without conditionality and for no selfish motivation.

The official statement aside, the new Chinese engagement does have a number of motives that are driven by Chinese national interests. First of all, gaining access to African raw materials, especially oil and natural gas, is certainly the most important reason for the recent Chinese interest in Africa. With continuous high economic growth, China is increasingly facing the problem of energy shortage. Since 1993, China has become net importer of oil, and by 2003, China has been the second largest energy consuming country in the world after the U.S. China accounts for 31 per cent of global growth in demand for oil. Diversifying and increasing its energy and other raw materials importing sources is one of the priorities for the sustained economic growth of the country, which, in turn, would have profound impacts on domestic well-being and social stability. Secondly, being a developing country, one side of the Chinese self constructed dual identity, China does share a host of common interests with African countries. The close links and common interests between China and Africa have been formulated ever since the independent movement of African countries in the 1950s and 1960s. Thirdly, to secure the other side of the Chinese dual identity (a potential world power), China needs assistance and support from Africa in a number of international institutions, such as the United Nations (UN) and World Trade Organization (WTO), especially when considering the large number of countries on the African continent. Last but not the least, Africa is also significant for the Chinese efforts on limiting the 'international space' of Taiwan. If there are conditionalities behind the Chinese aid to Africa, dropping off diplomatic recognition to Taiwan is probably the only one.

A related issue here is the Chinese attractiveness to Africa. This attractiveness comes from the following factors, as compared (or rather, contrast) to Europe.

Firstly, China sets no conditionality for its aid to African countries no matter what the political situation is there, except for the requirement that recipient countries do not recognize Taiwan diplomatically. Most African elites welcome China's strong willingness of avoiding the conditions for human rights, better governance and so on. The ambassador of Sierra Leone to China, referring to the Chinese rebuilding of a stadium in the country, once commented that 'There are no benchmark, and preconditions, no environmental impact assessment. If a G8 country had offered to rebuild the stadium, we'd still be having meetings around it'. (Johnny S. 2005)

Secondly, being a developing country itself, China often emphasizes the Third World solidarity, which has been well-received in Africa.

Last but not the least, the Chinese engagement in Africa gives new sources of income and assistance to African countries, which provides an alternative to Western aid. Africa has benefited from the dramatic rise in prices for its natural resource exports. Not only oil, but copper, zinc, platinum and other minerals are at record or near record high, largely due to the heavy demand from China and other fast growing Asian countries.

European and Chinese Engagement with Africa: Good Governance vs. Effective Governance

Four years back, a paper from Survival depicted China's new engagement in Africa and warned that it had gone 'little noticed in the West' (Alden C. 2005). Since then, however, there have been increasing research and policy analysis on the subject in the West, and Europe in particular.

Are China's increasing activities a major challenge to European countries that have long been engaging in the continent? How competitive is the Chinese and European engagement in Africa?

Here we need to distinguish between 'good governance' and 'effective governance'. The former is a value-based approach, and sometimes idealized, more in the case of modelling other countries off of the democratic governance of Western democracies. The foreign aid policies of Europe to Africa, to a large extent, reflect such a trend. The latter (effective governance) is an end-oriented approach. The Chinese engagement in Africa is a case here.

My view on the differences between effective governance and good governance is as follows. Effective governance denotes, in principle, the functioning of an efficient governing system. Good governance, in conventional sense, is always connected to Western rules and norms and associated with Western democratic political system, which, in the Western context, is effective. Commenting on that, a former member of German parliament once said that the Europeans wanted to make the Africans as black Europeans. Effective governance, on the other hand, does not have a democratic system as a precondition. It is not value laden, but has a pragmatic orientation. The most important requisites for effective governance are to ensure political stability and a suitable environment for economic development. The governing system of Singapore is an example here.

Then, what are the main reasons behind which China wants to promote effective governance in Africa? I argue the three points below: firstly, you cannot expect China to promote the Western value-based good governance practices in Africa because China itself does not subscribe to it domestically. Secondly, without effective governance, a certain degree of anarchic or chaotic society might follow, which would certainly be harmful to Chinese business and other activities in Africa. Lastly, one of the prerequisites for a sound investment environment is an efficient governing system. When addressing the issue of Afro-Asian cooperative partnership, Zhou Xiaochuan, head of China's central bank, in the press conference after the Annual Conference of African Development Bank, in May 2007, proposed three key aspects for promoting the partnership and one of them is to improve investment environment that requires 'enhancing governmental governance' (Zhou 2007).

In foreign aid, China prefers the language of mutually beneficial economic cooperation to that of 'aid' or development assistance. When China does pronounce about development cooperation, it avoids the language of donor and recipient. Instead, the discourse has a strong emphasis on solidarity, deriving from a claim about China and Africa's shared 'developing country' status and it is weathered by several decades of working together.

From the perspectives of the African aid-recipient countries, this framing of language is comfortable, since it probably gives an alternative for African countries to the mere Western donation.

While taking care of its legitimate national interests needs, China does care about African peace and stability and how unstable countries could cause harm to them. At issue here is that while we all agree that poor performance in both economic and governmental aspects lead to the problems in Africa, the Chinese approach to Africa shows that China believes that the problem of Africa is more the lack of development than lack of better governance. Chinese workers build infrastructure for many African countries and help African countries to develop their own manufacturing capacity. China believes that with development more effective governance might follow.

Conclusion

As analysed earlier, it seems to be that while there are substantial differences between the Chinese and European approaches to Africa, they are nonetheless not irresolvable. The European approach emphasizes good governance in Africa and seeks to build a better framework for governance on the continent, while the Chinese one stresses on effective governance and tries to build an improved economic basis for political governance in Africa. In my mind, both of them are needed for Africa, and both approaches should not be in so sharp contradictions with each other as it seems to be now on the surface. In order to be so, more dialogues between China and Europe are needed on various levels, and policy and activity coordination of various kinds are necessary. China is still very inexperienced with its new engagement in Africa. Learning from Europe of its success and failure in engaging Africa would be a great benefit for China, and an incentive that the country might consider as valuable. Like many other countries, Chinese foreign policy can be defined as centring on satisfying national interests. In this case, China needs to have a balance between its issue-related national interests, such as energy needs, and relational national interests, like its important relations with African and Western countries. The latter requires that China, in formulating and enforcing its African policy, accommodates, to a large extent, Western and African interests. In its activities in African countries, China should have a thorough understanding on how African countries are different from each other, and dealing with them case by case. Towards the Europeans, China's increasing influences, especially in resource-extracting in Africa (and European concerns about Chinese engagement with so-called resource rich African 'failed states') can be used as leverages to persuade European countries to collaborate with China as energy consumers, a consumers' cartel of petroleum could be an option. To enhance dialogues and coordination, on the one hand, there should be a realization from both sides that the Chinese and European engagement in Africa is and should not be a zero-sum game for each other. On the other, coordination between the two sides could start with more simple things, for instance, to decrease the duplications in the Chinese and European infrastructure projects in Africa and then move on to more difficult ones such as building donor association or the like.

References

Alden C. 'China in Africa', *Survival*, 37/3, 2005.

Hettne B. and F. Soderbaum, 'Civilian Power or Soft Imperialism? The EU as a Global Actor and the Role of Interregionalism', *European Foreign Affairs Review*, Vol. 10, No. 4, Winter 2005.

Interview with Christoph Moosbauer, advisory board member of the Committee for A Democratic UN, and former member of German Parliament, May 18, 2007.

Johnny, S. *'interview by BBC reporter Lindsey Hilsum'*, May 20, 2005, quoted in Stephen Marks, *China in Africa—the new imperialism?* Pambazuka News, http://www.pambazuka.org/en/category/features/32432

Shambaugh, D. 'The "China-EU Honeymoon" is Over', *International Herald Tribune*. 26 November 2007.

Zhou, X. *answering in the press conference for the African Development Bank annual meeting*, May 17, 2007, Shanghai. http://finance.sina.com.cn/g/20070517/10093601880.shtml

Chapter 10

SOUTH AMERICA AND US RELATIONS: IMPLICATIONS FOR REGIONAL SECURITY

Rafael Duarte Villa

Introduction: The Securitization of New Threats

Studies regarding international governance rarely dedicate room for reflection about the link between international security and governance[1]. There are three main categories of actors that engage in the international regulation of new types of conflict: international organizations, whose best known mechanisms are UN's peace and humanitarian missions; states, especially medium and great powers, that interact in UN's multilateral forum and regional organizations such as North Atlantic Treaty Organizaion (NATO) or through unilateral or bilateral means; finally, in a third level of action, we cannot ignore the important role played by non-governmental organizations (NGOs) in humanitarian operations around the world.

Security and governance structures not only face traditional forms of military conflicts existing since the Cold War period, but also 'new wars'. War on terror, war on drugs, war on organized crime, war on hunger - all of these categories of conflicts are part of what Mary Kaldor called 'new wars'. According to Kaldor, these are: 'conflicts in which frontiers can not be well defined between war, organized crime and massive violation of human rights'. These wars happen 'in a context of erosion of State's autonomy and in extreme cases of State's disintegration. Particularly, they occur in the context of the erosion of the legitimate and organized violence' (Kaldor 1999, 4).

Still, with Kaldor's study in reference, new wars differentiate themselves from the traditional ones in terms of goals, forms of organization and funding and, above all, in terms of articulation between internal and external. Their goals are not associated with geopolitical or ideological reasons, but identity ones – in the sense of a fight for power linked to a particular identity, whether national, clan-like, religious or linguistic. Many times, these identities appear to occupy the vacuum left by socialism or nationalism as a tool for the maintenance of social cohesion and legitimacy.

The new security agenda, in this perspective, would be more decentralized and would have a stronger emphasis in regional aspects. Furthermore, it incorporates, along with political and military traditional sectors, three other areas: economical, environmental and societal. Putting in another way, the argument is that these three areas pass through a process of progressive securitization. By this way, the reflection about security has to answer the following question: can we keep on thinking state causality with explicative efficacy in face of tensions that generated threats whose nature is not necessarily found in the state? Barry Buzan and his team[2] have emphasized that securitization supposes that a securitization actor (the one who perceives a threat) transforms a political problem in a security problem, that is, he depoliticizes what, initially, should be treated by political means, for instance, policies. The securitization is a process or 'movement that takes established rules of the game and defines the issue as a special type of politics' (Buzan, Waever & Wlde 1988, 19). Securitization is an extremely subjective perception about what is an action made by a securitization actor and whose perception supposes objects of reference that are threatened (whether a territory, nation, nations' values, among others). Buzan and his team, however, recognize that the movement of depoliticization is not irreversible: it can be politicized again, since, as every reality, security is a social construction; thus security is also 'what states make of it'.

In the following pages, we will focus on how American security policies towards South America are imbued with a strong security conception, especially in the case of anti-drug policies in Andean countries, namely in Colombia.

An Overview of US Security Initiatives Towards South America

The US hemispheric agenda on governance towards Latin America has stressed three points during the post Cold War period: democracy, trade and security.

According to the literature (Goldberg 2001; Santiso 2001; Farer 1996), democracy issue emerged in the Inter-American system as a concept of collective defense of democracy, which takes into account the American concern with the stability presented by the institutions of the region. In the 90s, the Organization of the American States (OAS) was used by the American government as a forum that developed an intense diplomatic activity in order to apply democratic clauses, basically the 1080 Resolution, for several cases in

Latin American countries in which democratic institutions were seen as threatened. The 1080 Resolution was applied during the decade of 1990 in the cases of four countries: Haiti (1991), Peru (1992), Dominican Republic (1994) and Paraguay (1996).

As for the second point of the hemispheric agenda, the American government since Bush senior's administration stressed the negotiation of a wide zone of free trade, goods and services. Still in this period, initial steps were given towards the so-called 'Initiative for the Americas' (Martins 1992). In 1994, at the Miami Meeting of Rulers of America, the proposal of the Free Trade Area of the America (FTAA) was launched. For several years, after intense rounds of negotiation, we have watched a period of structural deadlock in 2004, as a product of the differences between the US and Brazil (for a reconstruction of these negotiations, see Lopes & Junior 2004; Cortes 2004).

As regards the security issue towards South America, the researched bibliography is almost consensual in stressing that since the Reagan's governments (1980–1988) there has been a continuous predominance of concerns not related with traditional threats. Since that time, the problem of drug production and traffic has been defined as a problem of national security. According to this logic, the combat to these kinds of threats should involve a strong attack in locus to the offer of drugs, that is, attacking the source of the production in countries such as Bolivia, Peru and Colombia. It is not by chance that American policy makers incorporated to its diplomatic vocabulary the expression 'war on drugs' (Cimadamore 1997, 21). Let's examine this last point with a closer lens.

In general, this assertion is correct, but it's important to mention that it neglects one important consideration: although Latin America does not have the same strategic importance in comparison to other regions, such as the Middle East, Western Europe and Asia, since the Cold War the US has kept a coherent security policy for Latin America. This policy is based on a solid consensus among Democrats and Republicans that guarantees the continuity of goals.

At the same time, differently from the past, the US has to deal now with several threat perceptions of distinct nature in the region: almost all of them are of non-estate nature. Communist states, parties or movements are not perceived as actual threats anymore, but actors and processes, such as drug traffickers, migrations, political instability, traffic of weapons, money laundry, terrorism, all of them of non-estate nature. In order to fight those challenges, the US government has promoted the signature of both anti-drug and anti-money laundry agreements in the Inter-American system. At the same time, it has promoted military initiatives as 'Plan Colombia' and the installation of military bases, like Manta in the Ecuadorian Pacific, and developed operation bases

(Forward Operating Locations, FOLs) as a way of advancing the support to tactical operations against drug traffickers and other agents considered to be terrorists.

In this last case, Washington is also worried about the remainder (mainly in Colombia and to a much lesser extent in Peru) of a very active guerrilla such as the Revolutionary Forces Armed of Colombia (FARC). American decision makers of the Departments of State and Defense suspect that these groups may occupy more strategic positions like what happened at the end of the 1990s, when the FARC managed to control 40 per cent of Colombian territory. The American unusual military activism in South America is highly related to these perceptions of the decision makers, who describe these groups as possible threats against the national security.

However, in the US perspective, the main perception of threat is undoubtedly related to the drugs production, consumption and traffic. It is noteworthy that the US, since the early 80s, has defined the problems derived from domestic drug consumption as a problem of national security. According to the data showed by Paul Kennedy (1993), in the beginning of the 90s, the US consumed fifty per cent of the cocaine produced around the world with just five per cent of the population of the world.

Although the United States government admits that producers and consumers must share responsibility, the idea of some of the American decision makers that the solution of the problem is found in its source is still predominant. The policy of 'going to the source', that prevailed at the beginning of the 1990s, continues to be very strong. The main argument is that countries such as Bolivia and Peru together produce 80 per cent of coca-leaf while Colombia produces 80 per cent of the world's cocaine. In relation to these two last countries, the strategy adopted by the US has been the eradication of coca-leaf plantations. Certainly, it has led the American government to invest resources in military and technical aid. On the other hand, this kind of assistance has been complemented with a program of substitution of plantation of coca by alternative plantations, such as haxixe.

Nevertheless, the main characteristic of the American anti-drugs policy has been the gradualism found in the means of combat, including eradication of coca-leaf plantations, military advices to dismantle the biggest cartels of drugs in Colombia, extradition of drug traffickers to the US and a certification policy to countries that the Department of State considers to be non-cooperative in the anti-drug initiative, as it happened with Colombia in the middle-90s. The last stage of anti-drug policy that started under Clinton's second administration included an improvement of military means in the drug combat. This phase was divided into two important stages: 1) the allocation of an enormous amount of financial resources to purchase military equipments to be used in places like the South of Colombia, where the large part of plantations and coca paste processing labs are located, besides serving as a shelter drug traffic groups; 2) installation of military bases that monitor countries such as Ecuador, Panama, Paraguay and Venezuela. Those countries are considered escape routes for drug traffic and money-laundry.

As regards the first phase mentioned above, the most controversial strategy has been the Plan Colombia, implemented in 1999. It is a package of US$ 1 billion and US$ 200 million. At first, the plan aimed at combating drug traffickers. Seventy per cent of Plan Colombia's resources are directed to military aid, including purchasing of military equipment, training of troops and eradication of coca-leaf plantations and cocaine processing labs. Moreover, during Álvaro Uribe administrations (2002–present), the US has taken advantage of the ideological convergences between both governments as for security issues in South America. Quoting Luis Alberto Restrepo, 'Uribe has put all the foreign policy to the service of the security. And even though he has scored important politics, financial and military victories, on the other hand, his strategy complicates the relations of Colombia with the neighborhood countries' (Restrepo 2004, 50)

September 11 also impacted American security policy towards South America. Indeed, one important change after September 11 was the emergence of conceptual and political shifts in the way American decision makers perceived the relations between threats and terrorism. As part of its global strategy after September 11, there was a conceptual and practical overlapping between the war against narcotraffic and the war against terrorism. Therefore, from the conceptual and practical perspective, Colombian guerrillas, as well as paramilitary groups, became synonyms to terrorists.

Thus, issues such as drug, terrorism, military assistance and economic aid started to be treated globally. In this sense, in 2001, George W. Bush government launched the Andean Regional Initiative. This program aimed to direct funds not only to Colombia, but also to all the Andean countries, Brazil and Panama. The American Congress approved a budget for this program, renaming it as Andean Counterdrug Initiative. Repeating the budget distribution of Plan Colombia, more than 70 per cent of the resources of this new plan are directed to the military use.

As for the second phase, which started during Clinton second government, there are signs that over the last ten years the US Department of Defense has been interested in negotiating the installations of a FOL in some South American countries. In 1998, the Ecuadorian government conceded the Manta air base in the Pacific Ocean to the US. This base was strengthened by the Larandia base and Puerto Legizano in the south of Colombia, units coordinated by the sophisticated radars at Guaviare and Leticia, both located in Colombian territory. The US is also negotiating the installation of another base in Peru and in the Amazon jungle of Iquitos. The negotiations with Paraguay, in 2006, could be the last round of these moves. What is new in this case is that the Paraguayan Congress itself has approved the presence of Americans FOLs, a decision that undoubtedly adds a certain level of legitimacy to the North American presence in that country as well as the fact that these troops will be immune to the consequences of their future actions.

On the other hand, it is probable that the displacement of troops and the installation of bases in South America arise as a kind of preventive policy that the last American governments have established. If we take a look at the map of South America, we can observe that all of these bases, FOL and troops allocated have been set up close or inside countries of political instability in the last fifteen years, such as Paraguay in the Southern Cone, and Ecuador, Colombia, Peru and Venezuela in the Andean region.

Drugs and Security: Dealing with Andean Countries' Case

As regards security aspects, US administrations since Reagan (1980–1988) have prematurely securitized the agenda related to drugs, when American policy makers defined narcotraffic as a 'problem of national security'. If national security is a public problem – and, in this sense, derived from what we perceive as a real 'existential threat' that demands public responses – securitization is a speech resource that depoliticizes the public character of security. 'Security is the move that takes politics beyond the established rules of the game and frames the issue either as a special kind of politics or as above politics. Securitization can be seen as a more extreme version of politization (...) [To be securitized, something that has to be presened] as an existential threat, requiring emergency measures and justifying actions outside the normal bounds of political procedure (...) Thus, the exact definition and criteria of securitization is considered by the intersubjective establishment of an existential threat with a saliency sufficient to have substantial political effects. Securitization can be studied directly; it does not need indicators. The way to study securitization is to study discourse and political constellations" (Buzan, Waever & Wilde, op.cit, pp. 23, 24 25).

The war on drugs as a doctrine had as its basis what the US Department of State called 'Andean Strategy' in Bush senior's administration, approved through the National Security Decree (NSD) No. 18. At the same time, in 1989, the Bush administration launched the 'National Drug Control Strategy' which 'made explicit the externalization of fight through the use of foreign policy' (Cimadamore 1997, 21; author's translation). The Andean Strategy had three main pillars: i. strengthening political institutions of key countries in the offer of illicit drugs (Bolivia, Colombia and Peru); ii. operational strengthening of political and military units in charge of combating the circuit of drugs (eradication of crops, trade of chemical precursors, laboratories destruction, drug interdiction, routes identification and money laundry penalties, as well as military and police direct advising to Andean countries for the dismantling of drug cartel (Colombia) and *firmas* (Peru), which include, in the case of Colombia, a drug dealers extradition policy). Finally, there was commercial and fiscal assistance to those Andean countries, plus Ecuador, to attenuate the social consequences that emerged, as they did, from the privatization of subsistence means of local communities.

In practice, the first point of Andean Initiative was neglected. There was no specific program aimed at strengthening democratic institutions in the region. Among the thirteen programs towards South America financed by the Department of State, only the one called 'Transition Initiatives' funds the strengthening of democratic institutions. As we will see, not even the change in global plans, as Plan Colombia, altered this situation: only 25 per cent of Plan Colombia funds (equivalent to more than US$ 1,3 billion) are dedicated to the strengthening of democratic institutions, as the judiciary and human rights NGOs. Truly, the greater attention that it dedicated to South America in terms of strengthening democratic institutions is indirectly related to the hemispheric strategy of consolidating and evoking the multilateral system of democratic clauses institutionalized by OAS since the end of the 80s.

The US concentrated its attention on the second point of the Andean Initiative, that is, operational strengthening of military and police units in charge of combating the drug circuit. Since Reagan's administration, the US has defined drugs as a 'problem of national security'. And combating the threat of national security should stem from an incisive *in locus* attack to drugs, in other words, attacking the production in source countries such as Bolivia, Colombia and Peru. Indeed, the greater amount of resources of Reagan's administration was directed to combatting the problems of drugs in the source: 61 per cent of 1982 total resources and 69 per cent in 1989.

Additionally to these policies aimed to reduce the drug offer, Reagan promoted two fundamental political measures: the mobilization of American Armed Forces to a foreign territory action; and the use of retaliation diplomacy, which, among various mechanisms, applies economic sanctions, denies authorization for exports towards the United States and exerts a strong pressure on international organisms looking forward to boycott the country retaliated (Cf., Procópio Filho & Vaz 1997; Guzzi 2007).

In the context of new wars, 'conflicts in which frontiers can not be well defined between war, organized crime and massive violation of human rights' (Kaldor 1999), the US has turned into the main state mediator of Andean countries since the middle 80s. American policy regarding drugs in the Andean

Amounts Directed to Anti-Drug Strategies During Reagan's Fiscal Years (1982–1989)

Fiscal Year	Total Amount (in US$ million)*	Amount Directed to the Reduction on Offer	% Directed to the Reduction on Offer	Amount Directed to the Reduction on Demand	% Directed to the Reduction on Demand
1982	2,903.4	1,768	61%	1,135.4	39%
1983	3,268.4	2,044.9	63%	1,223.5	37%
1984	3,707.3	2,464.8	66.5%	1,242.5	33.5%
1985	4,167.1	2,856.6	68.5%	1,310.5	31.5%
1986	4,284.8	2,976.5	69.5%	1,308.3	30.5%
1987	6,876.3	4,825.9	70%	2,050.4	30%
1988	6,486.7	4,413.5	69%	2,073.7	31%
1989	8,759.5	5,993.5	69%	2,766	31%

Source: Transactional Records Access Clearinghouse (TRAC) (available at: <http://trac.syr.edu/tracdea/findings/national/drugbudn.html>).

region will be developed in accordance to this concept. And after more than two decades, the problem of drug production and traffic continues to be defined as a problem of national security. Indeed, the American government affirmed in *2002 National Security Strategy*'s document this same conviction: 'Parts of Latin America conflicts specially arising from the violence of drug cartels and their accomplices. The conflict and the unrestrained narcotics trafficking could imperil the health and security of the United States' (National Security Strategy 2002, 15). The means applied by the US through agencies of the Department of State give priority to two mechanisms to face the problem: militarization (technically called interdiction of crops) and eradication and fumigation:

> Interdiction refers to the displacement of American effectives in foreign basis and a straight cooperation with local security forces, with the objective of identifying centers of drug production and detaining drug loadings by terrestrial, maritime or aerial means. On the other side, the eradication is related to the use of herbicides whose function is to destroy as much as possible coca and poppy crops. (Isacson 2005, 44)

As for the interdiction, as Bagley defends, the National Defense Authorization Act (NDAA),[3] approved in the first year of Reagan government, authorized the raise in the American Armed Forces participation in the anti-drug strategy, as well as permitted its action in foreign territory (Bagley 1993, 183–184). This law operated under three fundamental conditions: i. the existence of an official allowance from receptor country; ii. the acceptance that these Forces should be corrected and coordinated by US agencies; and iii. the role of American militaries should be restricted to giving support for local militaries.

American Institutional Structure for Anti-Drug Policies

In the same time, interdiction and eradication policies in Andean countries assumed that there was a significant change in the operational way found in foreign policy and security and defense agencies: their action did not claim autonomy in the coordination of actions anymore. In this sense, the US government, aiming to coordinate the military assistance, began to count on the integrated effort from agencies such as International Narcotic Control (INC) from the Department of State, the Drug Enforcement Administration (DEA) from the Defense Department and the Department of Justice.

The participation of the Department of State, up to INC, in anti-drug strategies, gave greater relevance to the theme in Washington and in the American embassies located in the affected countries (Freeman et al. 2005; Guzzi 2007). Despite this growing role of the Pentagon (State Department or DOD) in anti-drugs policies during the 80s and 90s, the INC[4] continued to be the main source of military and police assistance to all American countries (Freeman et al. 2005). Nevertheless, according to Bagley, the more discrete role in the DOD's 'anti-drug war' has been calculated: 'For its part, the Pentagon has systematically expressed its reluctance to get involved in the war on drugs, in part because of concern that the drug effort would divert funding away from its central mission of defending US interests abroad, and in part out of concern that an expanded military role might expose US armed forces to corrupting influences' (1993, 168).

Despite this, DOD's role is not irrelevant. After the promulgation of the law's Section No. 124 (1988), which defines the role of Armed Forces in the defense, DOD monopolizes activities such as controlling illegal drugs traffic on the US by air and marine forces, and in this sense, it is authorized by the Section to carry out drug interdiction operations, such as radar installations, air reconnaissance, Navy Coast Guard maritime patrolling and intelligence meetings throughout Latin America and Caribe. The Section No. 124 also allowed the presence of American militaries in anti-drug operations led in Latin America. DOD's power was even more strengthened in 1991, when the Bush administration approved Section No. 1004 of NDAA, which allowed that the DOD uses its budget for different types of military assistance (training, intelligence, equipments supply) aiming to combat drug trafficking without the participation of the State Department (Freeman et al. 2005; Guzzi, 2007).Differently, the Drug Enforcement Agency (DEA) subordinated to the Department of Justice, dedicates to operations directed to combating illicit substances traffic. Although its goal is to coordinate anti-drug information and intelligence abroad, it does not have the legal authority to put investigations and detentions in practice in other countries. For this reason, its action occurs only through bilateral agreements with intelligence and police agencies from other countries willing to cooperate (Freeman et al. 2005).

Finally, Andean Strategy, specially its policies regarding interdiction, found its funding in specific programs of the State Department: Military Assistance Program (MAP), Foreign Military Financing (FMF) and International Military Education and Training (IMET) which had their apogee in the 90s.

> Created in the 70s and 80s, these three programs (MAP, IMET and FMF) were the principal means of US military assistance transfer during the Cold War, including the greater military programs of Reagan administration towards Central America in the 80s. [...] Between 1980 and 1991, the MAP and FMF contributed with more than US$ 2 billion to West hemispheric security Forces and the IMET contributed with US$ 110 million. (Isacson 2005, 33)

The coordination between agencies from different states in the anti-drug strategy was followed by a pressure towards source countries. This interaction led to the substitution of police forces internally in charge of this task by Army special forces, as it happened in the case of Bolivia anti-drug force, Unity of Anti-Drug Fight (UMOPAR) strategy supported by the US government simultaneously to *Plan Dignidad* ('Dignity Plan'), an eradication program that promoted a fast decline in the production of coca leafs – until it achieved a 'zero production' in mid-90s, during Hugo Banzer administration. Peru also created his own anti-drug force, called *División Nacional Anti-drogas* – DINANDRO (Anti-drugs National Division), besides promoting assistance to the National Intelligence Service (SIN). In Colombia, the US' total investment was directed to the National Police of Colombia, elite squads and spray herbicide campaigns.

Extradition Policy

Still, concerning the second pillar of the Andean Initiative, American administrations have made use of the narcotraffickers extradition strategy, as well as of the certification mechanism to put pressure on Andean countries. Mainly, Colombia has been the target of these policies. A bilateral agreement, the Treaty on Extradition, signed in 1979 between Colombia and the Unites States, entered into force in 1984. According to Arbex (1993, 41), until 1991 approximately

49 Colombians involved with drug traffic were deported. The American Congress transformed the certification policy into a law (Law No. 490, Foreign Assistance Act (FAA), 1961) at the beginning of the second Reagan administration (1986). This policy allows the American president to define annually the production and transit countries, besides determining if their respective governments do or do not cooperate with American measures regarding illicit drugs combating. In this sense, the president makes the major list known each year, that is, a list of countries that, under Washington's understanding, are not sufficiently cooperative in combating illicit drugs production. Submitted to a logic of punishment and reward, the countries whose anti-drug efforts were evaluated as insufficient could see their commercial, fiscal and military aid policies suspended by American government, as well as face difficulties in obtaining financial aid from organizations such as IMF.

However, these unilateral actions were object to considerable tension in some Colombian governments in the 90s. During César Gaviria administration (1990–94) a new Constitution entered into force (1991), which established an end to Colombian citizens extradition policy. Certainly, this fact raised the tension between Washington and Bogota, and the situation became critical when Pablo Escobar, one of the narcotraffic leaders considered the target of Colombian and American authorities ran away. This originated a strong reaction in Clinton administration, which asked President Gaviria to create a constitutional mechanism that could permit the extradition of Colombian citizens in delicts undertook outside Colombia, as well as to intensify anti-drug actions in order to achieve narcotraffickers' capture. The drug cartels, in retaliation, initiated a strong terrorist assault in Colombia, attacking public buildings, especially from legislative and judiciary powers (Villa & Ostos 2005). Obviously, Cali cartel's strategy to exert greater influence in the national government, creating a very complex situation with the recently elected President Ernesto Samper (1994–1998), who was accused by *the* DEA of having his campaign financed by narcotraffic and of governing a *narcodemocracy*, and, for these reasons, the country was decertified in two occasions during his mandate.

Doctrinaire Shifts

The new millennium brought important changes in the doctrinaire aspect of the war on drugs. In this sense, the document titled *The National Drug Control Strategy* (2007), formulated during President George W. Bush's mandate – which has as its basis the Section No. 201 of the *Office of National Drug Control Policy Reauthorization Act* (2006) – is also the indicator that the original strategy is changing. In this report, the strategy is presented with three main elements: drug consumption prevention; intervention and recuperation of former consumers; and the disarticulation of the illicit drugs' market. The principal actions that sustain the third point of the strategy – to eradicate illegal crops, interdict illicit drugs' circulation and attack the organizations that finance the drug market – were conceived in order to reduce the drug offer, inside and outside the country's boundaries. But the main change observed is, perhaps, related to the first pillar, that is, to identify the drug consumption found in the US as a problem, once it gives strength to this market.

This shift occurs in contrast with the Andean Initiative, which was expected to raise the costs of trade for drug dealers. Through interdiction and eradication initiatives led by the United States and Andean countries, the contemporary *National Drug Control Strategy*, in facing the drug traffic as a transnational threat to security, aims to raise the costs of illicit trade for dealers and consumers. In other words, this doctrine admits what was not admitted in the Andean Strategy: that the problem was not found solely in the source, but also in American drug consumers. This new strategy focused on the reduction of consumption, with expectations that this could lead to a reduction in illicit drugs on offer in the United States (Viggiano 2007).

Nevertheless, in retrospect, this shift is also explained by the role that some Latin American countries have performed. Still during the Bush administration, there were two meetings with South American chiefs of state accused of having links drug production – Cartagena (1990) and San Antonio (1992) summits – aiming at creating a hemispheric regime to face the drug problem (Tokatlián 1992), as well as convincing the United States to adopt a 'shared responsibility' position. However, these summits presented no consensus as regards the most efficient measures to combat drug traffic in Americas, which evidenced the interest disparity between the White House and Latin American governments[5] (Guzzi 2007).

Similarly to the Vienna Convention, those who were considered to be drug producers raised the question about 'collective responsibility' to criticize the Certification Policy. Furthermore, they mentioned the growth in synthetic drugs' production in American territory, as well as the excessive military means to combat drug production in Andean countries. During the San Antonio Summit, Latin American countries insisted once again that the US should be more devoted to policies related to reduction on demands. The American government, in turn, proposed a regional coordination mechanism so that Latin American countries could discuss and promote anti-drug initiatives even in the absence of American representatives. However, in harmony with this regional coordination, the American leaderships proposed a operational regional action, which was not welcomed by Latin American countries, once interpreted as a American unilateralism in the region (Guzzi 2007).

Punctual Initiatives towards Global Mechanisms:
Plan Colombia and Anti-Drugs Andean Strategy
in the Security Aagenda

American doctrinaire shifts have been followed by strong changes in the content of anti-drugs programs. Precisely, one of the most notorious shifts observed on the war on drugs is due to the creation of global programs, such as Plan Colombia since 2000, and also a change on the attention directed to various Andean countries in order to focus on the impact of Colombia's internal conflict for the anti-drug strategy. In Colombia's particular situation, that of a fragmented country in the end of the 90s, the US directed its strategy to an action more direct, with greater financial and military involvement. Individual programs financed by the Department of State, especially International Military Education and Training, lost relevance considerably. Others, like International Narcotics Control and Law Enforcement and International Narcotics and Crime, have very low budgets (as in the Bolivian case) or are deactivated.

This does not imply that the US has lost interest in financing anti-drugs militarized mechanisms. Indeed, since the end of the 90s, there has been a minor preoccupation as regards financing isolated programs in agencies as the Department of State, and a stronger preoccupation towards initiatives with a global character, and not isolated, such as Plan Colombia and Anti-Drugs Andean Initiative. On the other side, decision makers of that agency were filled with a feeling that coca production was controlled in Bolivia and Peru by the end of the 90s. Then, they turned their attention to Colombia. The multiplicity of actors engaged in Colombian armed conflict made it clear that there were other problems for US security, which were independent of the problem of illicit drugs production and traffic.

After a diagnosis of the changes emerged from the end of the Cold War, the second Clinton administration elaborated, in 1996, the *National Security Strategy of Engagement and Enlargement* (NSSEE), that aimed to[6]: 1) update and restructure the conditions of military and security efficiency with basis on a strong defense capacity, as well as the exercise of a diplomacy that promotes cooperative measures towards the issue; 2) emphasize the importance of economics in international relations, motivating market opening and the expansion of economical global growth; 3) expand and promote democracy and human rights abroad (Cf., Guimarães 2000).

As regards to defense and security issues, the American government, up to NSSEE, defended the idea that, in the post-Cold War era, US security was threatened by various problems and, as a global power, the country should direct efforts to combat them. An interesting aspect of NSSEE was the great importance that it gave to a set of issues that were perceived as a threat, not necessarily a traditional threat. Among these problems, Clinton's Doctrine mentioned ethnic-religious conflicts, the reemergence of nationalisms, arms and drug trafficking, environmental degradation, accelerated population growth, proliferation of arms of mass destruction and terrorism (Guzzi 2007).

As regards drug traffic, the Clinton Doctrine gave continuity to the securitized discourse of threats to United States' national security, for two main reasons:

> [...] first because, even with the growth in internal production, the greater part of the drug consumed by American citizens was produced abroad and, second, because both the production and the traffic were activities that made not only the United States unstable, but also its inter-relations. (Scheer 1996)

These anti-drug strategies were not different from the former administrations: they used the demand and offer reduction measures to fight the drug traffic. In the beginning of his first mandate, the Democratic President aimed to centralize his efforts on the domestic sphere, promoting internal education and treatment, arguing that, despite Reagan and Bush's efforts to reduce the offer, there were few advances on the war on drugs and the US was still the main consumer cocaine market of the world (Diaz-Callejas 1997, Guzzi, 2007).

Even using the same strategies as those of Republican governments, the Clinton administration presented limited results as regards the reduction on demand. This led to a series of critiques in the domestic sphere, especially in Congress – including congressmen of the Democratic Party. Possibly sensible to these critiques, Clinton approved stronger measures to contain the illicit drugs' traffic, namely he asked for the authorization of Congress to use the International Emergency Economic Powers Act (IEEPA),[7] which permitted to block financial transfers that used to benefit the organizations responsible for the drug traffic. Additionally, he used more often the *Major Lists*, as in the above-mentioned Colombian case.

Although American anti-drug strategies were mainly directed to Andean countries, Colombia was identified as the major cocaine source in the world by Internal Narcotic Control's (INC) reports (75 per cent of world production, using the coca leaf produced in its territory but also in Bolivia's and Peru's). Colombia is also pointed as a major heroin and marijuana supplier to the American consumer market, as well as a focus of activity related to money laundry and international crime.[8] Finally, the US government alleged that multiple small traffic organizations emerged after the dismantling of the two major drug cartels during the 90s – Cali and Medelín cartels. This turned difficult the task to control the drug traffic activities. In addition, part of the activity began to be controlled by left guerrillas that obtained their resources by charging 'taxes' of coca producers and dealers (Guzzi2007).

With these justifications presented in INC reports, American military assistance to South American countries began to be announced as having the following goals: i. to reduce coca leaf and poppy crops to a non-commercial level; ii. to dismantle the major organizations responsible for the drug traffic; and iii. to eliminate the dissemination of chemical precursors and money laundry (Guzzi 2007). However, achieving these goals required a global strategy, what would emerge with Plan Colombia.

Plan Colombia was approved by United States Congress in 1999 after a solid consensus between Democrats and Republicans. Projected to count with US$ 7.5 billion, the Plan presents three components: component A, which consists in the approximation between the Colombian State and the population affected by violence through social investments and the substitution of coca crops. To achieve this goal, the Colombian State should raise US$ 4 billion. The B component, totalizing US$ 1.3 billion, is associated to American technical, military and financial anti-drug assistance in the Andean region, especially Colombia. As for the component C, approximately US$ 1.7 billion, it refers to the European contribution for peace (Tokatliatán 2001, 81). In fact, only US$ 329 million in 2000 fiscal year were directed to the neighbors (namely Bolivia, Peru and Ecuador) to assist in the eradication of coca crops, in the creation of areas of control along Colombian boundaries, in the development of social programs and in the increase of local polices' military arsenal (Rippel 2005). On the other hand, 'not all the financial resources of American assistance will enter the country. A major part will be reserved to warcraft procurement with American enterprises and hiring mercenaries from the United States to go on combat in Colombian soil' (Anzola 2000/2001, 79; author's translation).

In 2000, the US Congress approved a contribution of US$ 1.3 billion for the Plan. From this amount, US$ 860.3 million were directed to assistance to Colombia. The other US$ 329 million, approved for the 2000 fiscal year, were directed not only to Colombia, but also in Bolivia, Peru and Ecuador, aiming at assisting in the eradication of coca crops, creating areas of control along Colombian boundaries, developing social programs and increasing local polices' military arsenal (Rippel 2005).

On official grounds, although Plan Colombia was elaborated and approved unilaterally by United States' executive and Congress, President Pastrana accepted the design of the strategy, which presented five pillars: i. the peace process; ii. Colombian economy; iii. social and democratic development; iv. war on drugs; v. the reform on the judicial system and human rights protection.

Plan Colombia – Assistance for Colombia

	Amount (in US$ million)	% of Total Amount
Military assistance	519.2	60,3%
Police assistance	123.1	14,3%
Alternative Development	68.5	7,9%
Refugee Assistance	37.5	4,3%
Human rights	51.0	6,0%
Judicial reform	13.0	1,6%
Law Enforcement	45.0	5,3%
Peace process	3.0	0.3%
Total	860.3	

Source: Center For International Policy (CIP) (available at: www.ciponline.org/colombia/).

From Plan Colombia to Anti-Drugs Andean Strategy: The Overlap Between War on Drugs and War on Terrorism

According to the 2002 National Security Strategy, when it comes to possible threats in Western Hemisphere, there are explicit references to the relation between Andean countries and the drug traffic, especially Colombia: parts of Latin America confront regional conflict, especially arising from the violence of drug cartels and their accomplices. This conflict and unrestrained narcotics trafficking could imperil the health and security of the United States. Therefore we have developed an active strategy to help the Andean nations adjust their economies, enforce their laws, defeat terrorist organizations, and cut off the supply of drugs, while—as important—we work to reduce the demand for drugs in our own country.

In Colombia, we recognize the link between terrorist and extremist groups that challenge the security of the state and drug trafficking activities that help finance the operations of such groups. We are working to help Colombia defend its democratic institutions and defeat illegal armed groups of both the left and right by extending effective sovereignty over the entire national territory and provide basic security to the Colombian people. (National Security Strategy 2002)

There is no other similar preoccupation towards another region in the hemisphere as there is towards the Andean region, and this is a signal of the high degree of securitization that the perception of drugs as threats have reached in American policy makers on foreign policy and security in the region.

How did this process of securitization happened? September 11 had a great influence over United States-Colombia and –Andean countries relations. But some of the conceptual changes that led to a global treatment of guerrillas and narcotraffic as 'terrorists' had already been developed before September 11. In this sense, the Colombian domestic environment helped in this conceptual transition. Since the mid-90s, both American and Colombian governments have been insisting in the straight links between Colombian guerrillas and narcotraffickers. In President Ernesto Samper's (1994–1998) words, the FARC and National Liberation Army (ELN) were 'narcoticized' (Samper, 1997, pp. 96–97), that is, part of their financial support stemmed from 'the war taxes' and the payment for protection of crops, laboratories and shipments of narcotraffickers. This bizarre link between guerrillas and narcotraffickers was incorporated in the political vocabulary of Washington and Bogotá policy makers as 'narcoguerrilas'. Not even when the militarization of repression in Colombia and Peru aimed at combating insurgent groups, was this objective put in so explicit terms.

The Bush administration had made an alert, since the beginning of his government, in 2001, as regards the lack of attention by his predecessors towards the armed conflict in Colombia. Thus, it was clear that his participation in this conflict should contribute to finish with the drug traffic, detain guerrillas and put an end in the violence in the region known as the 'Radical Triangle'.

In addition to that, the Bush administration meant a shift of emphasis and, above all, of direction in the treatment of the Colombian issue once the conflict began to be viewed more as a global issue than something restricted to the Andean region. In concrete terms, the Bush administration, in an evolution of Plan Colombia, implemented the Andean Regional Initiative, which directed funds no only to Colombia, but also to other Andean countries, as well as Brazil and Panama. Afterwards, renamed as Andean Counter-drug Initiative (ACI), the program was approved by the US Congress with a budget of US$ 700 million for 2003 and US$ 731 million for 2004. However, in both budgets the priority given to Colombia was evident: 63 per cent of total amount accounted for eradication and fumigation programs in large scale, as well as for training and buying military equipment, while the rest of the funds were divided between Peru, Bolivia and Equator, in this order.

From the total US$ 731 million of the Initiative, 49 per cent were directed to Colombia. From this amount, 36 per cent accounted for economical, social and governance purposes and the other 64 per cent accounted for anti-drug and security strategies. In the Peruvian and Bolivian cases, the amount directed to economical and social sectors was grater: 61 per cent in both countries. As for 2003 fiscal year, Bush government sent to Congress a request of US$ 980 million for a ACI fund, of which 55 per cent would be directed to Colombia. In the following fiscal year, the request corresponded to US$ 990.7 million, being US$ 463 million to fund anti-drug programs in Colombia (Perl 2006; Guzzi 2007). In comparison, ACI 2002 funds totaled US$ 292 million to Colombian neighbors. Peru received US$ 132 million; Equator, and even Venezuela and Brazil, which opposed to United States anti-drug measures towards the region, received, US$ 37 million, US$ 8 million and US$ 12 million, respectively, (Urigüen 2005, 85). Urigüen (2005, 86) offers an interesting analysis of the concrete measures related to ACI: i. there was an increase in the assistance to Peru – through interdiction and alternative development programs – in order to avoid the resurgence of coca crops and strengthen Ecuadorian efforts to protect its boundaries with Colombia; ii. the control of Venezuelan and Brazilian boundaries, as well as its judicial systems and its anti-drugs programs also increased; and iii. there was an expectation that the program operated a balance in the region between law enforcement, security programs and social and economical development.

In addition to strengthening financial aid to Andean countries, ACI also had various political goals, such as giving assistance to its 'allies' (namely, Colombia, Equator and Bolivia), convincing 'doubtful' countries (Peru) and putting pressure over the 'opponents' (Venezuela and Brazil). The goal was to establish a common policy against narcotraffic in Colombia. However, the initiative meant a more intense fumigation of marijuana, coca leaf and poppy crops, the prohibition of shipments directed to United States and Europe, the extradition of condemned for links with narcotraffic and a greater vigilance along the boundaries aiming at stopping the move of terrorist actors from one country to another, fact that generated risks to the national security.

In this sense, the strategy to 'push in Southern' adopted by the Clinton and W. Bush governments towards Colombia was translated into the creation of three anti-narcotic battalions in the forests of Putumayo, Caquetá and Guaviare. The goal was to promote a campaign of massive interdiction and eradication of coca leaf and poppy crops, which up to 1992, simply quadruplicated (from 38.000 ha. to 136.000 in 2000). This policy had serious consequences to the local population as well as to the environment, and it was responsible for the disappearance of more than 8.100 ha. of tropical forests. On the other side, the area of narcotraffic crops expanded beyond Colombian boundaries, generating problems to neighbor countries.

Thus, innovation of ACI can be understood in terms of its goal to erase any trace of a differentiated strategy to combat the guerrillas, paramilitaries and narcotraffickers. All these actors were qualified as terrorist groups. The war on drugs corresponded entirely to the war on terror. This is explicit in the document of the 2002 *National Security Strategy*, when it refers to the specific case of Colombia. 'In Colombia we recognize the link between terrorism and extremist groups that challenge the security of the state and drug trafficking activities that help to finance the activities of such groups' (National Security Strategy 2002).

The 2001 list of terrorist organizations of the US State Department, constituted mainly by groups that operate in the Middle East, considered four Latin America armed groups, all of them located in South America: FARC, ELN and United Self-Defense Forces of Colombia (AUC) from Colombia, and Sendero Luminoso from Peru. Nevertheless, since 1997, the Department of State elaborates an annual list, known as Foreign Terrorist Organizations (FTO) to indicate international terrorist organizations understood as threats to American national security. While the FARC and the ELN were included in FTOs since 1997, AUC only began to be considered as a terrorist organization up to 2001 FTO (Cronin 2003; Guzzi 2007).

Conclusions

Plan Colombia's preliminary results on drug eradication seem to be positive in the first years of its implementation if we consider the data available at American and Colombian governmental sources as well as UN. Although some authors (Meza 2004) may disagree, this data show a reduction of more than half of the coca leaf crops in southern Colombia. In this region, the land extension for growing coca was about 80.000 ha. in 2001 and, in 2002, corresponded to 40.000 ha. According to UN data, there was a reduction of 30 per cent in the area used for growing coca in the whole country. Indeed, in 2004 the Colombian government announced that from the past 35.000 ha. near the Venezuelan border in 2001, only 3.000 ha. remained.

Despite some recent data of the National Drug Threat Assessment, elaborated by the National Drug Intelligence Centre (2006, 10&39) which shows that Colombia cultivated 114 mil hectares in 2004 and 144 mil in 2005, the cultivated area has grown again. And maps of this same report affirmed the presence of a net of narcotraffickers groups that stretched from the center of the US to the west side of the country.

In any way, despite these limitations, it is important to note that there was something new in the US security policy as regards the war on drugs. The two new global initiatives here analysed – Plan Colombia and Anti-drug Andean Initiative – mark this shift, once they differentiate from the past policies in two main points: first, for Plan Colombia's aspect of a military-diplomatic agreement between Colombia and US; and second, for they were the only plans of great variety of resources that faced a non-governmental actor, the narcotraffic, through military means. Above all, both initiatives – especially ACI – distinguish from the past ones for incorporating South America in the global strategy of 'war on terrorism'. American decision makers have a security perception towards the Colombian case that strongly mix new elements ('multidimensional threats') as well as classic components (conflicts based on boundaries or resources).

At least until September 11, narcotraffic was the subject of the main perception of hemispherical threat in the eyes of US policy makers. Although the use of force emerges as an element that we should take into consideration when coping with threats whose origins are found outside the state, as affirmed by the National Security Strategy and the National Military Strategy, Plan Colombia is centered on the traditional military action, in cooperation with the Colombian armed forces. This policy is different from the hemispherical bilateral agenda on security, once it considers long run strategies implemented by the US executive, both because of the amount of resources involved and the perspective of keeping such a policy into force (Viggiano 2007, 16).

As regards the anti-drug agenda, it is possible to say that the US has been relatively successful on engaging some regional actors, such as Colombia and, eventually, Bolivia and Peru. However, this symmetry between the US and some other countries of the region may be occasional, which means that the continuity of such an overlap will depend on the agreements (and also on the susceptibility to pressure) of local governmental elites, but this does not mean that there is a pattern of securitization among these elites, since their securitized vision is still not a policy of State in these countries, as in the case of the US. Changes in government, with different ideological content, can change the overlap.

Another important problem faced by the US is related to the nature of the security perceptions. This nature is transnational, whether it derives from the narcotraffic whether from the possibilities of terrorist presence in South American soil. But this similarity in nature does not turn narcotraffic into a functional actor (or threat agent) of the same intensity of terrorism. Thus, the conceptual shift that makes the perception of threat so uniform (every narcotrafficker, and every guerrilla member is a terrorist) imposes a problem on the US: this is, the duty to legitimate why both narcotraffickers and guerrilla are terrorist groups. It is, certainly, a very difficult conceptual task because the terrorist groups, in the most strict sense, shown with September 11 its potential to threat the US territory. But is very probably that narcotraffiker's groups and guerrilla could not show the same degree of threat to the US territory than the terrorist groups.

In fact, during the 90s narcotraffic was the object of stronger perceptions of threats, once this was a period of great activism of Cali and Medellín cartels. Even if we consider narcotraffic's potential for fragmentation of the Colombian state, we will have to recognize that during the 90s the fragmentation inside Colombia was greater and its elites were socially delegitimate on the ground of accusations of links with drug traffic.

References

Anzola, L. S. 2000/2001. 'O Plano Colombia e a economia política da guerra', *In: Política Externa*, São Paulo/USP/Paz eTerra 9(3).

Axworthy, L. 2001. 'Human Security and Global Governance', *Global Governance* 7(1).

Bagley, B. M. (1993). 'Los mitos de la militarización: las fuerzas armadas en la Guerra contra las drogas' in: P. H. Smith *El combate a las drogas en America*, México: Fondo de Cultura Economica.

Buzan, B., Weaver, O. and Wilde, J. 1998. *Security: A New Framework for Analysis*. United Kingdom: Lynne Rienner Publishers.

Cimadamore, A. D. 1997. 'La política antidrogas de EE.UU. Condiciones internas y efectos intra-hemisféricos', *Cuadernos de Nueva Sociedad* 1.

Cortes, M. J. 2004. 'O Brasil e a ALCA. Um estudo a partir da Argentina', *Contexto Internacional* 26(2).

Cronin, A. 2003. 'The FTO List and Congress: Sanctioning Designated Foreign Terrorist Organizations. CRS – Report for Congress. Online: http://www.fas.org/irp/crs/RL32120.pdf (accessed July 2007).

Diaz-Callejas, A. 2005. *Nueva Hegemonia: unilateralismo y certificacion. Colômbia bajo el garrote del império*. Online: http://apolinardiaz.org/verdocumento.php?id_tema=0&id_documento=17 (accessed September 2005).

Farer, T. 1996. 'Collectively defending democracy in the western hemisphere: introduction and overview' in T. Farer (ed.), *Beyond Sovereignty. Collectively Defending Democracy in the America* Baltimore and London: The John Hopkins University Press.

Freeman, L., et al. 2005. 'Una breve descripción de las leyes estadonidenses y de las agências relacionadas con las iniciativas para el control internacional de drogas' in C. A. Youngers and E. Rosin (eds), *Drogas y Democracia en America Latina*. Buenos Aires: WOLA, Editorial Biblos.

Golberg, D. 2001. 'Is there a democratic regime evolving in the western hemisphere? Some lessons from the 1990s'. Mimeo. Prepared for delivery at the 2001 meeting of the Latin American Studies Association, Washington.

Guimarães, S. P. 2000. 'Estados Unidos: visões Brasileiras' in S. P. Guimarães (ed.), Brasília: Instituto de Pesquisa de Relações Internacionais/ Fundação Alexandre de Gusmão.

Guzzi, A. C. 2007. 'A Relação EUA-América Latina: Medidas e Conseqüências da Política Externa Norte-americana para combater o Tráfico Ilícito de Drogas', in press.

Isacson, A. 2005. 'Las Fuerzas Armadas de Estados Unidos en la Guerra contra las Drogas', in C. A. Youngers and E. Rosin *Drogas y democracia en America Latina*, Buenos Aires: WOLA,Editorial Biblos.

Kaldor, M.1999. *New and Old Wars. Organized Violence in a Global Era*. Stanford: Stanford University Press.

Kennedy, P. 1993. *Preparando para o século XXI*. Rio de Janeiro: Editora Campus.

Lopes, D. B. and Joelson, J. V. 2004. 'Balanço sobre a inserção internacional do Brasil', *Contexto Internacional* 26(2).

Martins, L. 1992. 'A reformulação da ordem internacional', *Política Externa* 1(1).

Meza, R. V. 2004. 'Drogas, conflicto armado y seguridad global en Colombia', *Nueva Sociedad* 192.

National Security Strategy of the United States. 2002. Online: http://www.whitehouse.gov/nsc/nss.html (Accessed 10 October 2007).

National Drug Threat Assessment. 2006. Washington: National Drug Intelligence Center (US Department of Justice).

Passetti, E. 1991. *Das "fumeries" ao Narcotráfico*. São Paulo: EDUC.

Perl, R. 2006. *International drug trade and US foreign policy*. CRS – Report for Congress. Online: http://193.43.76.2/pdf/other/ RL33582.pdf (Accessed June 2007).

Procópio Filho, A. and Vaz, A. C. 1997. 'O Brasil no contexto do narcotráfico internacional', *Revista Brasileira de Política Internacional* 40(1). Online: http://www.aclessa.com.br/NewFiles (Accessed January 2005).

Restrepo, L. A. 2004. 'La difícil recomposición de Colombia', *Nueva Sociedad* 192.

Rippel, M. P. 2005. 'O Plano Colômbia como instrumento da política norte-americana para a América Latina e suas conseqüências'. Marinha do Brasil – Escola Naval de Guerra. Online: www.mar.mil.br/egn/cepe/trabalhosCurriculares/CpemCemos/ ensaioCcRippel.pdf (Accessed November 2007).

Samper, E. 1997. 'Ernesto Samper: gobernabilidad sin soberanía no vale la pena', in D. Archard and M. Flores. 1997. *Gobernabilidad: un reportaje de América Latina*. México:. Fondo de Cultura Económica.

Santiso, C. 2002. 'Promoção e proteção da democracia na política externa brasileira', *Contexto Internacional* 24(2).

Scheer, E. F. 1998. 'Objectivos Criticos', *Cuestiones Mundiales:* Publicaciones Eletrónicas de USIS 1(7).

Tokatlián, J. G. 1992. 'Seguridad y drogas: una cruzada militar prohibicionista' in H. Muñoz (ed.), *El Fin del Fantasma: las relaciones interamericanas después de la Guerra Fria*, Santiago: Hachette.

———.2001. 'El plan Colombia. De la Guerra interna la intervención internacional?', *Anuario Social y político de América Latina y el caribe*, FLACSO/Nueva Sociedad (4).

Viggiano, J. 2007. 'Percepções e Alternativas na Formulação da Agenda de Segurança Hemisférica nos Estados Unidos', in press, Departamento de Ciência Política / USP.

Villa, R. D. and Ostos, M. d. P. 2005. 'As relações Colômbia, países andinos e Estados Unidos: visões em torno da agenda de segurança', *Revista Brasileira de Política Internacional* 48(2).

Chapter 11

THE FUTURE DEVELOPMENTS IN GLOBAL GOVERNANCE – MULTILATERALISM & REGIONALIZATION PROCESS: INDIA'S ROLE

Vijaya Katti

The pursuit of the global common good is the core challenge for all concerned with governance today. It is a responsibility shared by different actors viz. individuals and companies, as well as states and their leaders who are motivated chiefly by their own specific interests. In the future world of globalization, mankind will need to accept new values in order to alleviate the plight of the poor.

Global economic interdependence has grown significantly. This development, generally called globalization, is the consequence of enormous technological progress and the determination, demonstrated by political decisions, to open national economies internally and externally to competition. This process is bound to continue. Thus far, globalization has brought improvements and opportunities for many people in many parts of the world. However, many have not been able to adapt to it and thus were excluded from its benefits. Consequently, they are disadvantaged. Globalization makes it possible to enjoy the experience of encountering a world of diversity and greater efficiency, but it raises fears about the loss of cultural identity. Global governance is the key to ensure that the positive impacts of globalization are enhanced and that its potentially negative effects are diminished.

Whilst economic interdependence has been reinforced in recent years, the absolute number of very poor people has grown worldwide. Material inequality between countries and within countries has also increased. The world now requires a coherent approach to reduce poverty and inequality. Open economies will not be sustainable without the willingness of states to open up politically as well. The world is now marked by growing interdependence.

The tectonic power shifts resulting from the explosive growth in the influence of the up-and-coming states in the south – particularly China and India – are taking the global system off the hinges. The supremacy of the West, which commenced with the Industrial Revolution at the end of eighteenth century, is beginning to falter. The G-8 today is no longer in a position to claim the sole leadership of the world economy. The outcomes of the 2007 G8 summit in Heiligendamm, Germany illustrate both the promise and the limitations of this elite global governance club.

In order to enhance dialogue with emerging economies, the G-8 summit in Heiligendamm agreed to launch a new form of cooperation called the Heiligendamm Process. The process aims to find common solutions in the following areas:

- Promoting and protecting innovation;
- Strengthening the freedom of investment by means of an open investment climate, including strengthening the principles of corporate social responsibility;
- Determining joint responsibilities for development, focusing specifically on Africa;
- Joint access to know-how to improve energy efficiency and technology co-operation, with the aim of contributing to reducing CO_2 emissions.

According to the summit website, the dialogue is to be launched in the second half of 2007. The Organisation for Economic Co-operation and Development (OECD) is going to provide a platform for dialogue and a first process report will be presented at the 2008 G-8 Summit in Japan.

There have been many different proposals for reform of the G-8. Five countries – China, India, Brazil, South Africa and Mexico – that are acting as major economic players and global actors have been invited by British Prime Minister Tony Blair to take a leading role to deal with central global problems by means of institutionalized co-operation. Thus, there is significant move to formalize the relationship of G-8 with the above 5 countries which have been called as Outreach 5 through the establishment of a structured forum for on-going dialogue.

The questions that now come to the forefront are as follows:

- Does the 'Heiligendamm Process' mean that the G-8 is willing to consider extending membership to Outreach 5?
- Alternatively, do these O-5 countries even want to be part of an enlarged club?

- What will be the future role of the universalist United Nations (UN) in the co-ordination of global politics?
- What will be the reaction of O-5 to the environmental and development policy issues?
- How will India react to these developments?
- What type of preparedness is required for India in this context?

Political arrangements in global systems are undergoing changes. Regional integration is coming into a special focus. The global framework for development cooperation is also undergoing changes. Development needs in the global contexts are also assuming different dimensions.

This paper tries to examine India's role in the regional economic integration process and in development cooperation in the context of Africa. The paper is divided in two sections. Section one covers India's role in regional integration and section two covers Indian development cooperation aspect.

An attempt is made to explore some of the above issues in this paper. As a number of emergent countries become increasingly engaged global actors, the rationale for widening the summit process has been strengthened. A broadened G-8 focus on social/development and environmental issues in turn reinforces the need for a more geographically and culturally representative membership. There is a general consensus concerning the regional and global role of China, India and Brazil.

By the 2007 summit, it was clear that major international challenges could not be addressed without ongoing co-operation of the large countries of the global south. From that viewpoint, it is necessary to look at the role of India in the regional integration process.

The G8 is showing signs of embracing an expanded membership, which its supporters hope will reinforce its legitimacy and efficiency in new international architecture. The simple acknowledgement that the G8 is incapable of creating a relevant strategy for climate change without the particular of major CO_2 emitters, such as India or China or leading alternative energy suppliers, such as Brazil, is certainly a step in the right direction.

UN's Intergovernmental Panel on Climate Change (IPCC) report published in April 2008 has warned that India will suffer acute water shortages, hunger and the continent's rivers running low. However, India will not take steps that would slow its economic growth.

India's primary concern is lifting its billion plus population out of poverty, and will not allow climate change limitations to hinder its economic advances.

As a developing economy, India does not have legally binding Greenhouse Gas (GHG) emissions reduction targets under the Kyoto Protocol. But, with the Protocol ending in 2012, a new global agreement is needed to curb emissions. Without the participation of countries such as India, China and the US any negotiations, let alone agreement, on climate change would leave us no further forward than Kyoto.

An international economic report by Goldman Sachs claims that the Chinese economy definitely, and the Indian economy possibly, will overtake that of the United States quite soon. The importance of India and China's contributions to the trade negotiations at the G-8 therefore cannot be underestimated.

India is an outspoken member of the G-20, the body that emerged during the failed World Trade Organization ministerial conference at Cancun in 2003.

India's Role in the Regional Integration Process

Three waves of regionalism have been experienced by the world since 1947. The first wave was experienced between 1950 and 1960 with the establishment of European Commission (EC), followed by the second wave marked with 'new regionalism' which involved United States' departure from the General Agreement on Tariffs and Trade (GATT) non-discriminating principle in the first half of the 1980s. The third wave of discriminatory trading arrangement started getting momentum in the 1990s characterized by North American Free Trade Agreement (NAFTA), Association of South East Asian Nations (ASEAN), Asia-Pacific Economic Cooperation (APEC), South Asian Association for Regional Cooperation (SAARC) and further consolidation of EC into the European Union (EU). This phase of regional integration witnessed a parallel development as the countries of the world started to form bilateral Free Trade Agreements (FTAs). India is no exception to it. Regional Trade Agreements (RTAs) are being embraced by many WTO Members as trade policy instruments and, in the best of cases, as complementary to the MFN (most favoured nation) principle. Economic considerations are only one facet of complex RTA strategies being pursued by individual or groups of countries which often include broader foreign policy aims such as political and security considerations. The promotion of free trade at a preferential level may help developing economies to implement domestic reforms and open up to competitive market pressures at a sustainable pace, thus facilitating their integration in the world economy. This may also benefit the multilateral process by exerting leverage for openness and competitive liberalization in international trade relations.

Article XXIV of WTO enables the establishment of FTA/RTA provided they satisfy the following conditions:

a) Any major sector not to be excluded.
b) The 'reasonable length of time' referred to in paragraph 5(c) of Article XXIV should exceed 10 years only in exceptional cases. In cases where

Members parties to an interim agreement believe that 10 years would be insufficient they shall provide a full explanation to the Council for Trade in Goods of the need for a longer period.

c) These arrangements should be reported in WTO.

Post 2005, certain RTA related trends are apparent. The new generation of RTAs, especially those involving developed countries, tend to go far beyond traditional tariff-cutting exercises and even beyond the realm of existing multilateral rules (Nataraj 2007).

- While old regionalism was essentially confined to RTAs between industrial economies or developing economies, the new regionalism does not seem to be limited to neighbouring economies. In recent times RTAs have been intercontinental. This may involve coordination problems but can be beneficial from the gains-from-trade perspective.
- Under the new arrangement RTAs are not exclusive, meaning thereby one country can simultaneously be a member of more than one RTA. This may eventually turn out to be an aid in promoting multilateralism through RTAs.
- While old regionalism was limited to shallow integration, the new regionalism is more ambitious. A number of recent agreements aspire for deep integration, with commitments to harmonization of regulatory measures, freeing factor movements and other close integrating measures. Such trade agreements include more and more regional rules on investment, competition and standards, in a few cases; they also contain provisions on environment and labour. Many more agreements today contain disciplines limiting the use of quantitative restrictions and subsidies among countries forming an RTA.
- Countries across the world, including those traditionally reliant on multilateral trade liberalization, are increasingly making RTAs the centerpiece of their commercial policy and for some countries, RTAs are on a par with multilateral trade objectives; however, for many others, RTAs have become the priority.
- RTAs are becoming increasingly complex, in many cases establishing regulatory trade regimes which go beyond multilaterally agreed trade regulations.
- Reciprocal preferential agreements between developed-developing countries are on the increase pointing to a decreasing reliance by some developing countries on non-reciprocal systems of preferences; also significant is the emergence of preferential agreements among key developing countries that may be evidence of a strengthening of so called south-south trading patterns.
- RTA dynamics show, in spite of regional idiosyncrasies, a general pattern of expansion and consolidation; on the one hand, we are witnessing a

proliferation of cross-regional RTAs, which account for a large proportion of the total increase in RTAs; on the other, regional trading blocks on a continent-wide scale are in the making.

The configuration of RTAs is diverse and becoming increasingly more complex with overlapping RTAs. The simplest configuration is a bilateral agreement formed between two parties. These account for more than half of all RTAs in force and for almost 60 per cent of those under negotiation. The most noteworthy development expected in the next five years is the emergence of a new category of agreement, namely RTAs where each party is a distinct RTA itself. Several agreements of this kind are currently under negotiation.

Asia-Pacific is a region currently undergoing significant changes with respect to its stance towards regional integration, with a number of countries shifting their long-standing policy of MFN trade liberalization to actively consider the regional option. Also, the 'open regionalism' typically associated with AEPC appears to be counteracted by a drive towards preferential trade initiatives. Japan, Singapore and the Republic of Korea have been negotiating and conducting feasibility studies for the establishment of several RTAs both among countries in the region and cross-regionally. Similarly, New Zealand and Australia are exploring the possibility of several RTAs with regional partners and with countries of the western hemisphere. Singapore and New Zealand already concluded a far-reaching RTA and discussions are being held for a closer economic partnership between New Zealand and Hong Kong, China. Japan and Singapore formed their own bilateral agreement in 2002. A notable development in the region has also been the agreement between the members of ASEAN and China establishing a FTA in 2005. Japan and the Republic of Korea have also initiated similar negotiations with ASEAN. These developments constitute an enormous change in East Asia. Prior to them, Japan and Korea, along with Hong Kong and one other country, were the only four members out of 151 members of the WTO that had not participated in a reciprocal regional trading agreement.

In economic terms, RTAs benefit member countries through trade expansion resulting from lower trade barriers. The member countries provide each other preferential market access for goods and services. As noted above, the current trend towards the conclusion of bilateral FTAs, rather than customs unions, has led to an ever-increasing number of criss-crossing and overlapping FTAs, each with its own tariff liberalization schedules and distinct rules of origin regime. If the parties to an FTA adopt a 'big bang' approach and liberalize all tariffs on all products on the date of entry into force of an agreement, there would be no need to negotiate tariff liberalization schedules. However, this is rarely the case. In general, FTAs contain a timetable for the progressive reduction of duties on

Figure 11.1. Growing Number of RTAs in World.

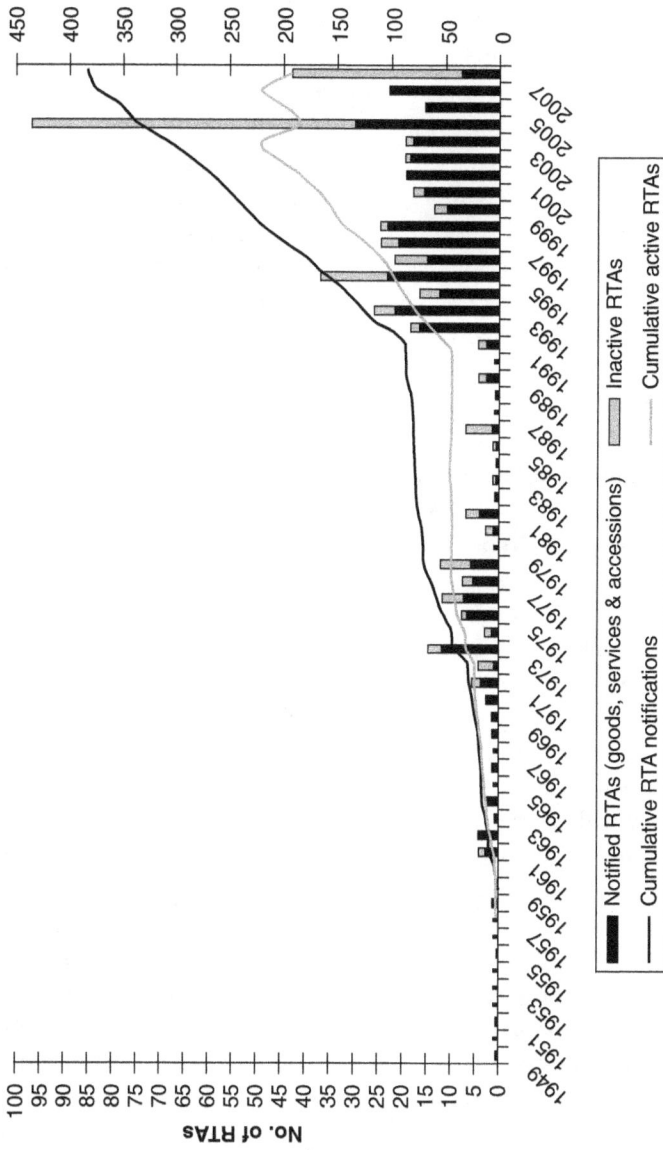

Legend:
- ■ Notified RTAs (goods, services & accessions)
- ─── Cumulative RTA notifications
- ▨ Inactive RTAs
- ─── Cumulative active RTAs

Source: *WTO Secretariat.*

a bilateral basis. Tariff liberalization schedules may be asymmetric, allowing one country a longer transition period to implement tariff reductions; most countries negotiate longer implementation periods or exclusions for their most sensitive products.

The key motivations for entering into FTA/RTAs have been both strategic and economic. India envisages Preferential Trade Arrangements (PTAs) as important foreign policy tools to forge new strategic alliances with the rest of Asia and to contribute to regional security efforts as well.

The PTAs are also expected to strengthen India's market-based economic integration with its neighbors and geographically proximate regions, viz. SAARC, ASEAN and East Asia. India also aims to increase cross-regional trade linkages with Latin American and Middle Eastern countries, as indicated by the initiatives to form similar agreements with the Mercosur, Southern Africa Customs Union (SACU), Gulf.

Cooperation Council (GCC), Egypt and Chile. With India planning to expand bilateral trade and investment linkages through economic partnership agreements and PTAs with a number of Asian countries, the pace of India's trade integration with the rest of Asia – not just in merchandise trade, but also in commercial services – is likely to increase in the near future.

India's growing web of PTAs with Asian countries indicates its willingness to engage the rest of Asia towards forming an Asian Economic Community that is inclusive in its approach. As most of India's PTAs that are in force are undergoing further negotiations, there is a distinct possibility of their becoming more comprehensive in the future – inclusion of services and investments are likely to be added. In particular, India is discussing comprehensive bilateral agreements with Japan and Korea. An economic agreement with China is also under discussion. Effective implementation of these PTAs and managing to reduce transaction costs due to possible trade and investment diversion created by diverse **ROOs** is crucial for realizing economic efficiencies and welfare improvement.

India has signed bilateral RTAs with Sri Lanka (1998), Thailand (2003) and Singapore (2005). All these RTAs are now operational. Seven member countries of SAARC signed the Agreement on South Asia Free Trade Area (SAFTA) in January 2004. Negotiations on all aspects of SAFTA were concluded and the tariff liberalization programme has been operational since 1 July 2006.

The Framework Agreement on CECA with ASEAN; Bay of Bengal Initiative for Multi Sectoral Technical and Economic Cooperation (BIMSTEC); Mercosur; South African Customs Union (SACU); GCC and Afghanistan on goods, services and investment are under negotiations. Joint Study Groups (JSG) were set-up for studying the feasibility of FTA with China, Japan, South Korea, Chile, Malaysia, Indonesia and other countries.

Figure 11.2. India's Regional Trading Arrangements.

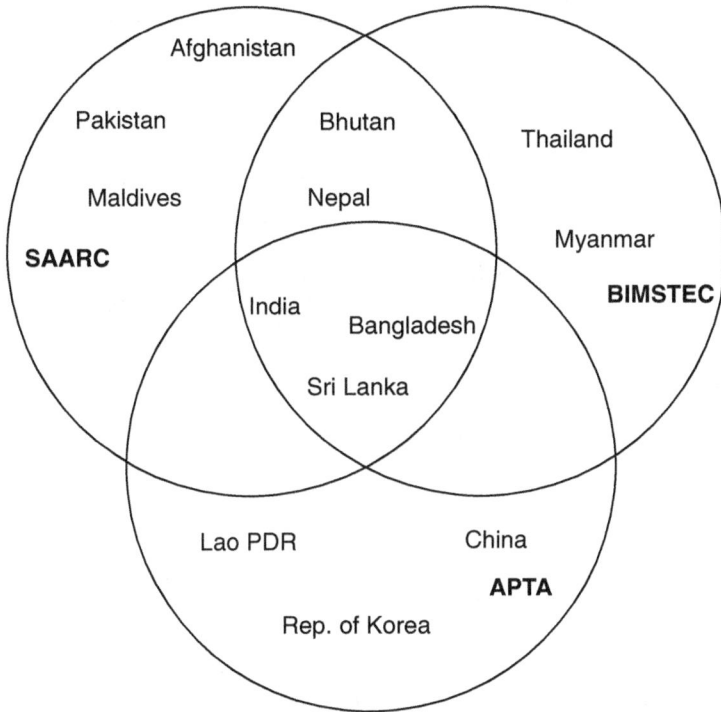

The JSG reports for China, Japan and South Korea have been finalized and negotiations have begun with South Korea and Japan.

The analysis of India's trade reveals that trade with RTA/FTA partners is increasing but at much slower pace compared to India's trade with the world. It has been further noticed that the pick up in trade with RTA/FTA partners has started only recently, 2003 onwards. The following tables furnish the detailed trend of India's trade with individual trading partners in different FTAs/RTAs.

India's Role in Regional and Cross Regional Economic Integration

To cope up with the new opportunities and challenges brought by the current era of liberalization, privatization and globalization, regional grouping for mutual economic benefits is a fast becoming phenomenon. India is actively engaged in regional economic integration process. India is a founding member of SAARC, which has recently entered into the 'Free Trade' stage

Table 11.1. **India's Trade with RTA Partners (Value in Million USD)**

Year	Trade with RTA/ FTA Partners	Trade with World	Share of RTA/FTA Partners
1990	2474.17	41804.4	5.92
1991	2341.80	37382.9	6.26
1992	3327.19	42429.2	7.84
1993	3883.45	42258.6	9.19
1994	5082.90	49682	10.23
1995	6511.29	65024.5	10.01
1996	7153.61	68380.4	10.46
1997	7891.5	75518.5	10.45
1998	8049.00	75827.3	10.61
1999	8438.34	83822.1	10.07
2000	9281.55	92961.9	9.98
2001	14182.35	104252.3	13.60
2002	13639.87	109408.7	12.47
2003	19809.47	135188.5	14.65
2004	27346.36	175220.5	15.61
2005	39416.46	232608.1	16.95

Note: The countries include belong to the SAFTA (Bangladesh, Bhutan, Maldives, Nepal, Pakistan and Sri Lanka) , BIMSTEC (Bangladesh, Bhutan, Myanmar, Nepal, Sri Lanka, Thailand), APTA (Bangladesh, China, Lao PDR, Korea, Rep., Sri Lanka), ISLFATA (Sri Lanka) and ITFTA (Thailand), ISCECA (Singapore).
Source: *IMF, DOTS – CD ROM, January 2007.*

(SAFTA). India is a full dialogue partner of ASEAN and have made arrangements with other regional groupings such as EU, SACU, Common Market for Eastern and Southern Africa (COMESA), Economic Community Of West African States (ECOWAS) etc. South Asia would ideally like to see the same level of economic integration as seen in European and this is indicated in the report of Group of Eminent Persons (GEP), i.e. to achieve a SAARC Customs Union by 2015 and a SAARC Economic Union by 2020. Given the current ground level reality in the SAARC region, it will be difficult for SAARC to achieve the goals of GEP report. India has an important role to play in economic connectivity of the region that will strengthen over the years via market integration and help achieve the targets. Various unilateral liberalization measures, measures taken by India and cross border trade and investment induced by high growth in the region will play a more prominent role in strengthening connectivity in coming years.

Figure 11.3. India's Trade with RTA Partners and World.

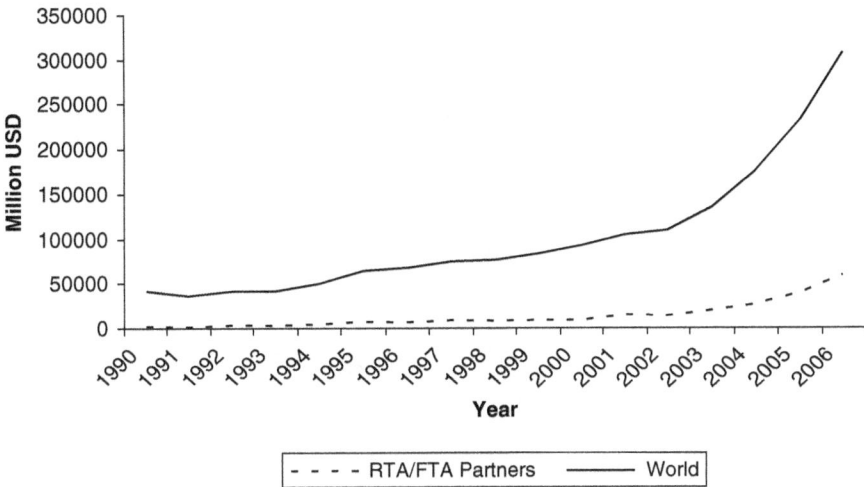

Note: The countries included belong to the SAFTA (Bangladesh, Bhutan, Maldives, Nepal, Pakistan and Sri Lanka), BIMSTEC (Bangladesh, Bhutan, Myanmar, Nepal, Sri Lanka, Thailand), APTA (Bangladesh, China, Lao PDR, Korea, Rep., Sri Lanka), ISLFATA (Sri Lanka) and ITFTA (Thailand), ISCECA (Singapore).
Source: *IMF, DOTS-CD ROM.*

India's high growth is good for the entire South Asian region for there will be spillovers from India's growth to the region. However, to capture the spillovers the other South Asian countries should work on their infrastructure and create a stable macroeconomic environment with good governance.

Indian Development Cooperation

Foundation

The foundations of Indian development cooperation were laid during the freedom movement. While fighting for independence, the visionary leaders were conscious of the fact that their struggle was a part of the general struggle to achieve complete decolonization in the world. Indian National Congress established an office for international collaboration in 1920s and participated in the International Congress against Colonial Oppression and Imperialism, Brussels 1927, and the Asian Relations Conference 1947. First Prime Minister of India Pandit Jawaharlal Nehru further emphasized this in his famous speech of 'tryst with destiny' on 14 August 1947. He said, '...dreams are not just for India, but they are also for the world. All the nations and peoples are

Table 11.2. **India's Trade with RTA Partners 1990–2006 (Annual Growth Rate)**

Year	Bangla-desh	Bhutan	China	Lao PDR	Maldives	Myanmar	Nepal	Pakistan	Korea, Rep.	Singapore	Sri Lanka	Thailand
1991	5.74		42.03	-91.52	4.36	-39.87	76.56	10.67	13.47	-30.05	50.55	-5.94
1992	9.89	101.80	171.44	30.00	57.79	96.63	-0.73	102.26	9.20	72.53	31.65	24.62
1993	21.93	118.66	189.85	127.13	-17.98	21.58	-1.61	-47.13	-1.69	9.71	7.79	20.33
1994	25.47	31.51	53.63	-66.13	152.32	9.69	4.43	1.89	63.25	10.41	38.10	40.06
1995	87.01	186.02	30.77	768.42	-21.79	25.84	36.77	1.15	14.25	21.56	15.84	16.76
1996	-14.25	-5.47	13.72	29.06	304.06	6.91	53.76	66.60	20.58	8.15	16.80	0.42
1997	-3.33	27.68	38.27	-23.69	-81.68	34.14	23.87	5.30	8.41	3.99	5.46	-2.61
1998	16.50	-45.70	-6.89	200.00	-7.77	-15.09	4.07	51.96	13.18	-3.65	-6.58	-0.70
1999	-20.19	25.34	9.29	38.46	-8.14	-7.23	20.58	-30.05	5.71	10.94	8.31	24.02
2000	17.47	-0.32	26.02	270.37	159.81	10.71	18.71	13.65	-16.81	8.29	23.44	15.55
2001	22.71	10.40	64.89	10.40	88.26	10.40	10.40	27.83	76.61	74.85	-3.65	35.07
2002	3.48	140.81	18.80	-62.05	-20.40	66.30	46.28	-17.64	-20.57	-32.80	49.11	-5.26
2003	40.15	102.68	49.17	-59.30	30.10	14.29	41.82	33.58	59.60	42.80	48.74	25.09
2004	0.72	9.58	58.99	151.50	7.44	5.87	18.94	67.11	24.06	50.73	20.07	20.26
2005	3.00	32.17	58.74	122.77	48.71	19.82	15.54	48.77	43.41	41.59	43.40	31.49
2006	20.74	23.41	57.09		23.56	23.68	63.59	23.61	48.28	55.87	23.61	62.54

Note: The countries included belong to the SAFTA (Bangladesh, Bhutan, Maldives, Nepal, Pakistan and Sri Lanka), BIMSTEC (Bangladesh, Bhutan, Myanmar, Nepal, Sri Lanka, Thailand, year of operationalisation of SAPTA in 1994), APTA (Bangladesh, China, Lao PDR, Korea, Rep., Sri Lanka- Launched in 1975. Second round-1990, Third Round-2006), ISLFATA-2000 (Sri Lanka) and ITFTA-2004 (Thailand), ISCECA-2005 (Singapore). Calculations based on data from IMF, DOTS-CD ROM.

too closely knit together today for any one of them to imagine that it can live apart'[1] These visions were reiterated in the foreign policy of independent India in 'Panchsheel Principles' and 'Bandung Principles'.

In the era of Liberalization, Privatization and Globalization (LPG) there is an increasing trend of regional and sub regional integration. Indian Foreign Policy makers have been consistently trying to cope with emerging trends. India was a founding member of SAARC, which has entered into the stage of free trade (i.e. SAFTA) very recently. India is also collaborating with other regional organizations like ASEAN, ARF etc. and is making efforts to support regional integration at a continental level and evolve infrastructure such as 'trans-Asian Highway' and 'trans-Asian Railways'. Today, Indian foreign policy firmly believes that regional arrangements can show the way forward to bring prosperity and development. Therefore, India is collaborating with various regional and sub-regional organizations (Katti and Gupta 2003–4).

Institutions for Development Cooperation

Indian development cooperation is implemented through various ministries, institutions, programmes, grants etc. Some of them are:

Indian Technical and Economic Cooperation and SCAAP:

ITEC was launched in 1964. Under ITEC and its corollary SCAAP 156 countries in Asia, East Europe, Central Asia, Africa and Latin America are invited to share in the Indian developmental experience. India spends about Rs. 500 million annually on ITEC activities. Since 1964, India has provided over US $2 billion worth of technical assistance to developing countries. ITEC is essentially bilateral. There have been occasions, however, when ITEC resources were used for financing trilateral and regional programmes under the Economic Commission for Africa, UN Industrial Development Organization (UNIDO) and Group of 77. Today, Afro-Asian Rural Reconstruction Organisation (AARRO) and G-15 are being helped by ITEC with Training and project support and a small beginning has also been made with cooperation with the Southern African Development Community (SADC). ITEC has five components viz.

(1) Training in India of nominees of ITEC partner countries;
(2) Projects and project related activities such as feasibility studies and consultancy services;
(3) Deputation of Indian experts abroad;
(4) Study tours.
(5) Aid for disaster relief (ADR).[2]

Focus Africa Programme

Focus Africa Programme was launched in 2002 with the aim to boost trade between India and countries of Sub-Saharan Africa. In the first phase of the 'Focus Africa Programme', the target countries identified were: Nigeria, South Africa, Mauritius, Kenya, Ethiopia, Tanzania and Ghana. These seven countries accounted for nearly 70 per cent of India's total trade with the Sub-Saharan African region during 2000–01. The target commodities to export were:

- Cotton yarn, fabrics and other textile items;
- Drugs & pharmaceuticals;
- Machinery & instruments;
- Transport equipment; and
- Telecom and information technology.[3]

Under this programme, the government of India extends assistance to exporters, Export Promotion Councils, etc. to visit these countries, organize trade fairs and invite African trade delegations to visit India. The initiatives taken under this programme have received an encouraging response from the Indian exporting community. As of now, the programme has extended to 24 Sub-Saharan African countries.

African Agenda

While India has little international leverage on aid to Africa, its contribution to the region should not be forgotten. For example, in 2003 India donated 5000 metric tones of food to the government of Namibia, and in 2004 did the same for Lesotho and Chad. India recently wrote off all Mozambique's government-to government debt.

India is also involved in peacekeeping operations in Africa. The 1,400 Indian military contingent is the largest component of the United Nations Mission in Ethiopia and Eritrea (UNMEE) and India also has over 3,000 troops in the Democratic Republic of Congo as part of United Nations mission there (MONUC). India has considerable experience in de-mining activities and has made significant contributions to the recent de-mining work in various missions in Rwanda, Mozambique, Somalia and Angola. In loans and banking, India is also leading the way. Total operative Lines of Credit (LOCs) extended to Sub-Saharan Africa by The Export-Import Bank of India (EIBI) is over US $550 million. In May 2006, EIBI extended a US $250 million LOC to the ECOWAS Bank for Investment and Development. The EIBI also signed US $10 and US $5 million LOCs with the West African Development Bank (BOAD) and the

Eastern and Southern African Development Bank (PTA BANK), respectively. The EIBI has also signed dozens of LOCs with individual African countries to finance Indian export.

TEAM-9

With a view to provide a special focus to enhancing commercial relations with countries in the West African region, the government of India has put in place the Techno-Economic Approach for Africa India Movement (TEAM9 Initiative). TEAM-9 Initiative envisages a special cooperation model amongst eight countries of West Africa, viz. Burkina Faso, Chad, Cote d'Ivoire, Equatorial Guinea, Ghana, Guinea-Bissau, Mali and Senegal along with India.

Under the TEAM-9 Initiative, a cooperation mechanism is envisaged which will operate at governmental, institutional and private sector levels sharing various types of expertise, intellectual and physical resources as well as economic opportunities for promoting welfare, growth and prosperity in these countries. It would thus involve, among others,

- providing opportunity for education and training in crucial sectors;
- transfer of critical technologies from India;
- undertaking specific projects in individual TEAM-9 countries which would have region-wide beneficial impact in the sectors critical for employment and growth, such as agriculture, small-scale industries, pharmaceuticals and healthcare, information technology, telecommunications, transport, energy, etc.
- putting in place LOCs and identifying priority sectors in the eight countries which would be financed out of the LOCs. The projects financed will increase bilateral trade between Indian and the select countries in West Africa.[4]

EXIM Bank in Africa

Export-Import Bank of India (Exim India) operates a number of financing and support programmes to facilitate and promote India's trade and investment in the African region.

Exim India extends LOCs to governments, parastatal organizations, commercial banks, financial institutions and to regional development banks to support the export of eligible goods on deferred payment terms. In total, the Bank has 27 operative LOCs amounting to US$ 540.87 million in the African region, including those extended with the support of Government of India. Exim India has a long standing working relationship with the International Finance Corporation (IFC) of the World Bank Group to facilitate the utilization of Indian consultants for initiatives/project facilities promoted and sponsored by IFC to develop private sector small and medium enterprises in Africa.[5]

Governmental Projects

The Indian government has undertaken several projects and joint ventures for mining, industrial and infrastructure development. Some of the recent examples are:

- The Oil and Natural Gas Corporation (ONGC) and Arcelor Mittal have entered into a $6 billion contract for industrial development in Nigeria, including oil exploration;[6]
- Rail India Technical and Economic Services (RITES) and IRCON, the public sector railway project companies, have acquired prestigious projects in Sudan, Tanzania and Mozambique etc.[7]
- The government of India has undertaken E-network project to link all African countries. This is a major initiative to provide benefits of information and communication technology to the African continent.[8]

Private Sector Investments

Several Indian companies are successfully operating in African countries on various sectors. Some of them are: groups like Tata and Mahindra, pharma majors Ranbaxy, Cipla and Dr. Reddy's, consumer firms like Marico and Emami, construction firms like Punj Lloyd and Shapoorji Pallonji and liquor maker UB Group etc. Indian companies are investing more and more in Africa. The Tata Group has stepped up its exposure in the continent. Several projects including a $1-billion investment in South Africa's Second Network Operator Telecommunications (SNO), a $100-million Ferro Chrome smelter in Richards Bay, also in South Africa, a $180-million investment in hotels, a $12-million coffee plant in Uganda and a 509-hectare farm in Zambia are now underway (Katti and Gupta 2003–4).

Indian Contribution to the Future Development Agenda

United Nations

India has been vocal supporter for the cause of the Third World since her independence. India was the brain behind Non-Aligned Movement (NAM), which was aimed at independent foreign policy and development without aligning with the two ideological blocks prevailing in the cold war period.

Table 11.3. **Indian Participation in the UNPKMs in Africa**[9]

Place	Operation	Duration	Contribution
Angola	UNAVEM I	1989–91	30 MOs
	UNAVEM II	1991–95	3 MOs
	UNAVEM III	1991–95	452 troops, 20 MOs,
	MONUA		11 civilian police
Mozambique	ONUMOZ	1992–94	940 all ranks in 1993
Somalia	UNOZOM II	1993–94	1 Inf. Bde., HQ staff: 4,967 all ranks
Liberia	UNOMIL	1993–97	20 MOs
Rwanda	UNAMIR	1993–95	Inf. Batt., 800 troops
Sierra Leone	UNAMSIL	1999–2000	3100 Troops
DRC	MONUC	2000–	29 MOs
Ethiopia/Eritrea	UNMEE	2001	1 Inf. Batt

From 'Agenda for Peace' to the demand for a 'New International Economic Order', India always stood for Third World in general and particularly with African countries. Now, in post-Cold War realities, India and countries of Africa are together at least in principle on the demand of 'restructuring the UN'. India is among the largest contributors to the United Nations Peacekeeping Missions.

NEPAD

The New Partnership for Africa's Development (NEPAD) is a vision and a strategic framework for Africa's renewal. The NEPAD strategic framework document arises from a mandate given to the five initiating Heads of State (Algeria, Egypt, Nigeria, Senegal, South Africa) by the Organisation of African Unity (OAU) to develop an integrated socio-economic development framework for Africa. The 37th Summit of the OAU in July 2001 formally adopted the strategic framework document. Objectives of NEPAD are:

a) To eradicate poverty;
b) To place African countries, both individually and collectively, on a path of sustainable growth and development;
c) To halt the marginalization of Africa in the globalization process and enhance its full and beneficial integration into the global economy;
d) To accelerate the empowerment of women.

India has contributed US $200 million for the implementation of various projects under NEPAD.[10] India has also announced a LOC of $ 200 million to assist the NEPAD. Many developmental projects in Senegal, Mali, Niger and the Democratic Republic of Congo worth over $ 80 million have already been approved under this programme. Besides, the development of the African Peer Review Mechanism (APRM) will help in creating the culture of good governance in African countries.[11]

E-Network Project (Pan-Africa Project)

India has started work on a connectivity mission in Africa which will support tele-education, tele-medicine, e-commerce, e-governance, info-tainment, resource-mapping and meteorological services. The seamless and integrated satellite, fiber optics and wireless network, to be provided by India, will connect 5 universities, 51 learning centers, 10 super-specialty hospitals and 53 patient-end locations in rural areas spread all over Africa and would put in place a network providing video conferencing facilities connecting all 53 heads of state/government in Africa. The Pan-African Network Project has been formally endorsed by the African Union and by an MoU between the government of India and the African Union in 2005. This is a landmark project, which will assist African countries in meeting MDGs in education and healthcare (Katti and Gupta 2003–4).

Conclusion and Future Scenario

India's development cooperation with developing countries in general and particularly with African countries has a golden past. Now, it is taking shape with the changing realities in the world. Recent initiatives taken by India are driven towards equal partnership instead of traditional relations of donor and recipients. It is likely that future cooperation will be based on India's desire for energy, capabilities of India to provide advanced but relatively low cost technology and the global issues of common importance. The first India-Africa Forum Summit concluded in April 2008 at New Delhi has taken various steps in deepening and widening cooperation between India and Africa. The Framework of Cooperation, exemplifying close, co-operative and multi-sectoral partnership encompasses political, security related, economic, science and technology, human resource development, social, cultural and other areas of mutual interest.

References

Katti, V. and Gupta 2003–4. *India's Development Cooperation* Working Paper, IIFT P. Ministry of External Affairs. 2003–4. *Annual Report, 2003–04*, Government of India.
Nataraj, G. 2007. *Regional Trade Agreements in the Doha Round: Good for India?*, ADB Institute Discussion Paper No. 67, ADBI.

Chapter 12

MANAGING SOCIAL ISSUES FOR SUSTAINABLE DEVELOPMENT: THE INDIAN EXPERIENCES

Ravi Shanker[1]

'Why can't you sell brotherhood like you sell soap?'

G. D. Wiebe (1958)

Introduction

Social marketing is becoming increasingly relevant to the developing world. The success of social programmes has significantly contributed to the process of development in the countries of the Third World and the failure of such programmes has resulted in tardy development. Their success has been attributed to the adoption of marketing approach to the social/development programmes. In promoting any social idea or issue, it is not enough to prepare the communication programme. Everything associated with the delivery system has to be taken care of. Let us take the example of the immunization programme. One cannot expect the success to come only through catchy advertising campaigns. The network of primary health centres, with proper staff, adequate stock of vaccines kept under prescribed conditions, quality of vaccines and the price one has to pay for immunization are significantly important. It is the marketing approach which helps in gaining an insight into these finer aspects.

Social marketing, as the concept evolved, acquired two different dimensions (Luck 1974). One dimension of it related to social responsibilities of marketers, mainly in response to consumer advocacy movement and also the pressures of government regulations. In this case, the focus is on economic benefits to business and social benefits to society that emerge from the adoption of socially responsible business policies by business organizations (Lazer and Kelley 1973). This expression was later titled as societal marketing (Takas 1974). Also, a large number of business organizations support programmes of societal concern like, culture — Sangeet Sammelans, sports, athletic meets, car rallies, balloon expeditions; environment — pollution control, deforestation, etc.

The second dimension of social marketing is the applicability of marketing philosophy and principles to the introduction and dissemination of ideas and issues of social significance like road safety by observing traffic rules; controlling child/infant mortality by immunization; better living by family planning, primary education and health care, hygiene and sanitation, etc.

In another words, a social issue is anything that affects human lives on a long-term basis can be called a social issue. Under the broad classifications of health, environment, education and civic issues you will find myriad subjects such as HIV/AIDS, Safe Motherhood, Malaria, Leprosy, Tuberculosis, Blindness, Iodine Deficiency Disorders, Diarrhoea, Family Planning (Health); Vehicular Pollution, Deforestation, Industrial Waste, Preservation of Biodiversity, Renewable Energy Sources (Environment); Traffic Sense, Household Waste disposal, Noise pollution, Drug Abuse (Civic Issues). Then there are other basic social issues like dowry, child rights and human rights, which cannot be classified at all.

The first to propound this aspect was Wiebe in 1952 and later the others (Fox, Kotler, Levy and Zaltman during 1969 and 1980) established this thought. In fact it was Kotler and Zaltman who defined 'social marketing' as the design, implementation and control of programmes calculated to influence the acceptability of social ideas and involving considerations of product planning, pricing, communication, distribution and marketing research. Thus, it is the explicit use of marketing skills to help translate present social action efforts into more effectively designed and communicated programmes that elicit desired audience responses. The marketing techniques are the bridging mechanisms between the simple processes of knowledge and the socially useful implementation of what knowledge allows' (1971).

They suggested that the role of marketing encompasses helping solve some of the fundamental problems being faced by a nation's economic and social environment.

To this extent, it can be assumed that the full import of the social marketing concept of developmental programmes has not been explored and in a sense, this is a need unique to the developing countries. The state being ascendant over society, it cannot remain a passive bystander while the society undergoes a natural evolution process. It has to intervene with a set of carefully designed social change strategies that would accelerate the pace of development.

Social Issues: Importance in National Plans

India's plan documents provide an insight into the magnitude and importance being given to development tasks.

	1st Five year Plan	5th Five year Plan	9th Five year Plan	10th Five year Plan (2002–07)
Social Services	3400 Million INR	4767+1284 = 60510 Million INR	1945290 Million INR	3473910 Million INR (Projection)

Under the first Five Year Plan Rs. 3400 Million (INR) was spent under the head social services which increased to Rs. 60,510 Million (including 12,840 Million INR in education) (INR) under the fifth Five Year Plan (absolute values, not inflation adjusted).

During the ninth Five Year Plan, the total amount spent was Rs. 1,945,290 Million (INR).

It was projected that the total amount spent under the social services in the tenth Five Year (2002–07) plan it would further increase to 3,473,910 Million (INR).

Under the head 'Social Services', there exists a plethora of developmental tasks ranging from education and health to labour welfare, housing, welfare of backward classes, employment, etc. Indian planners have also followed a strategy of 'target setting' in the 'plans'. This target orientation has its pros and cons, as pressures on performance have led to use of short-term strategies and the development task of providing a service delivery system directed at raising the standard of living and inducing social change remains unfulfilled.

Understanding Social Marketing

Social marketing is nothing but adaptation of the methodology of marketing to social imperatives with the objective of achieving social change.

Kotler (1985) identified four basic approaches to social change—the legal, technological, economic and informational approaches. To elaborate this point one can examine how these four factors apply to immunization. The legal approach in this case would be to pass laws that make immunization absolutely essential. The technological approach would be innovating high-quality single shot vaccines so as to reduce the number of visits a mother has to make to get her child properly immunized. The economic approach would be to make immunization free from any charge and the information approach would be to educate people about the ill effects of the diseases against which immunization is available.

Before we go in for more details, let us first develop clarity on the type of organizations that are engaged in social marketing.

If we plot a diagram (Figure 12.1) by taking 'organisational ownership and control' on 'X' axis and 'organizational purpose' on 'Y' axis we get the following matrix:

Figure 12.1.

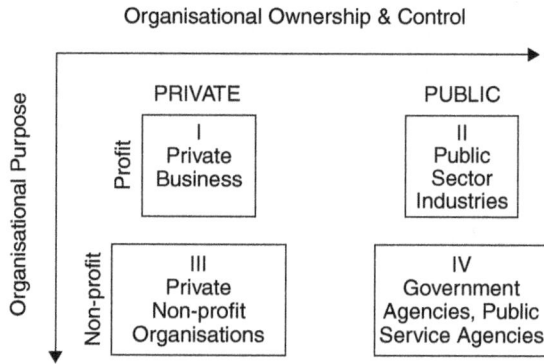

Organisational Ownership & Control

	PRIVATE	PUBLIC
Profit	I Private Business	II Public Sector Industries
Non-profit	III Private Non-profit Organisations	IV Government Agencies, Public Service Agencies

Organisational Purpose

The Scope of Marketing

Organizational Ownership & Control

It's either the non-profit organizations or public service organizations which are involved in social marketing. In practice public services marketing and social marketing are not taken much different from each other. (In this article the word social marketing is preferred and used rather than public services marketing).

Differences between Commercial and Social Marketing

There are obvious differences in commercial marketing and social marketing. In the case of commercial marketing, the major emphasis is on persuading the audience to buy the company's product and it pertains mainly to goods and services which can be even adapted to suit audience felt needs. Here the results are cognizable. Whereas in the case of social marketing, the emphasis is on persuasion to make the audience learn, adopt and change their ideas,

Table 12.1. **Differences Between Commercial and Social Marketing**

Commercial Marketing	Social Marketing
Felt need and cognizable rewards	Needs not perceived, rewards not seen
Pertains mainly to products	Pertains to ideas, behaviour and practices
Persuasion to make audience buy	Persuasion to make audience learn, adapt and change
Adapt products to audience needs	Adapt audience to larger social needs
Buyer, user main audience	Audience: Providers, Influencers
Price: Cost, Tax and Margins	Price: Performance cost
Distribution: Wholesaler to retailer	Distribution: Social network
Product: Goods and Services	Product: Added value
Competition: Competing brands/ substitutes	Competition: Existing behaviour, peer groups and pressure groups
Profit motive	Welfare objective
Talks to people who have money	Talks to needier sections
Success / failure hardly affect society	Major impact on society
Rarely needs to involve Government	Must work with Government to ensure achievements of national priorities.

behaviour and practices in keeping with the large social needs which are not clearly perceived by them. In social marketing the results are also not cognizable. There differences are summarized in Table 12.1.

Process of Social Marketing

The planning of social marketing programme involves six major steps. These are: (a) problem definition, (b) goal setting, (c) target market segmentation, (d) consumer analysis, (e) marketing strategy and tactics, and (f) implementation and evaluation.

(a) Problem Definition

The very first step in developing any social marketing programme is to define the problem. For example, all of us are aware that the use of drugs is deadly dangerous and even the ones who take drugs are aware of it. They perhaps want to give it up but they cannot. So in this case one can define the problem as 'how to help drug addicts actually stop taking drugs' rather than convincing them that drug addiction is bad for their health. Social marketing, therefore, must address itself to the right problem in order to be effective and successful.

(b) Goal Setting

The second step in developing a social marketing programme is to set measurable goals of performance and which can be hopefully accomplished. These goals will help in developing plans of action within the available budgets and also in evaluating success of the programme.

(c) Market Segmentation

For better performance and results it is desirable that the heterogeneous market may be divided into homogeneous market segments keeping in view various demographical, psychographical and geographical factors. First, the segmentation would help in selecting specific segments as the focus to channel the marketing efforts and, secondly, it would also help in studying the behaviour of each segment to develop suitable marketing strategies.

Bloom and Novelli (1981) have pointed out certain problems which social marketers have to encounter while segmenting their market. First, they face pressure against segmentation in general and especially against segmentation that leads to ignoring certain segments altogether. Secondly, they frequently do not have accurate behavioural data to use in identifying segments, and thirdly, their target segments must often consist of those consumers who are the most negatively pre-disposed to their offerings.

(d) Customer Analysis

There is a much greater need in social marketing to explore in depth customers' behaviour and attitudes in order to identify and develop suitable campaigns to change their behaviour and attitudes to desired levels. Therefore, it becomes essential to carry out consumer research about wants, needs, perceptions, attitudes, habits etc., to develop maximally effective marketing strategies. The major problems, as compared to commercial marketing, which a social marketer encounters as summarized by Bloom and Novelli are: (i) they do not have good secondary data available about their consumers; (ii) they have more difficulty in obtaining valid, reliable measures of salient variables in doing primary data collection; (iii) they have more difficulty in sorting out the relative influence of identified determinants of consumer behaviour; and (iv) they have more difficulty in getting consumer research studies funded, approved, and completed in a timely fashion.

(e) Developing Marketing Strategies

A product is something that has the ability to satisfy customers' needs and wants. The test for whether a thing is a product or not lies in its exchangeability. This broader meaning of product permits inclusion of concepts that have been referred to by various other appellations. Public goods are involved in those transactions where the governmental agencies are the marketer and the public at larger are direct consumers because they are affected by 'consumption' of these goods, which include flood control, energy conservation programmes, etc. They are purchased in exchange for the price of taxation. There are certain public goods which are meritorious and are produced at considerable costs, but offered at a notional price such as education, health care etc. These goods are called merit goods (Wish and Gamble 1971) and Phelps (1975) called respect, love and status impalpable goods. Dewey (1939) referred to ready made intellectual goods as information provided by mass media. However, irrespective of the name the product continues to be a 'thing' that is to satisfy needs and wants of the market.

Product strategies include branding, packaging, product positioning, product differentiation etc. Like commercial marketing, these concepts are equally relevant in social marketing. People choose products, including political candidates, based on the familiarity of name (*Newsweek* 1976). However, in developing product strategies, a social marketer encounters three major problems: (i) they tend to have less flexibility in shaping their products or offering (Lovelock and Weinberg 1975); (ii) they have more difficulty in formulating product concept; and (iii) they have more difficulty in selecting and implementing long-term positioning strategies.

The social marketing price includes money costs, opportunity costs, energy cost and psychic costs. For example, the cost of using helmets is the charge for buying them, the effort to wear it and strap it, and the psychological cost of not being completely sure one is better off in an accident wearing it or not wearing it. Developing a pricing strategy (Bloom and Novelli 1981) primarily involves trying to reduce the monetary, psychic, energy and time costs incurred by consumers, when engaging in a desired social behaviour. It is rather difficult to measure all the costs (Rothschild 1979) and, therefore, the effort should be to reduce them.

Kotler and Zaltman (1971) have suggested that the poor result of many social campaigns can be attributed to their failure to suggest clear action outlets for those motivated to acquire the product. The effectiveness of current campaigns on controlling infant mortality can be enhanced manifolds by ensuring proper vaccination facilities at every village. The challenge for social marketing lies in utilizing and controlling desired intermediaries.

The most significant component of social marketing strategy is the communication strategy, which is persuasive and makes the product or programme familiar, acceptable and desirable to the audience. The challenge in social communication is that it is not always possible to use advertising but yet the message has to be put across. The other constraint is that in social communication and advertising there is pressure not to use certain types of appeals (Houston and Homans 1977). For example, fear, humour or hard selling appeals are rather undesirable. In social advertising, as compared to commercial advertising, a large amount of information is to be given and this poses another set of challenges before the social advertiser. Rothschild (1979) has suggested that before developing a non-business or social communication campaign, one must consider the following:

The involvement of situation and relevant segments: Due to the potentially very low levels, traditional promotion tools may be inadequate. Given the current state of the art of marketing communications, one must conclude that what can work reasonably well in private sector consumer goods cases may not work at all for non-business cases. While most consumer goods exist within a broad range of middle level involvement, many non-business issues exist in either very high or very low involvement environments. These environments may call for an enlarged set of communication tools and strategies.

The available positive and negative reinforcers: Since the benefits of non-business issues may be less apparent to the message recipient, it is incumbent upon the sender to consider all possible behaviour reinforcers. This especially would be the case where the more apparent benefits are societal rather than individual.

The non-monetary costs: The cost associated with behaviour towards non-business issues may include several non-monetary costs which raise the cost of behaving beyond the level of the perceived benefit. In such a case, communication tools will be hard pressed to present a convincing case for elicitation of the desired behaviour.

The level of latent demand: Many non-business marketing campaigns exist as a result of the efforts of a small group of individuals. When little latent demand exists, then little desired behaviour will follow.

The relevant segments: For virtually all issues, there will be at least a small segment of society for whom the issue will have positive value, another segment for whom compliance with the law will be sufficient motivation and another segment for whom engaging in the socially beneficial act will be sufficient motivation. For many issues, there will remain a large segment for whom a direct personal benefit must be shown if appropriate behaviour is to result. The manager must, of course, consider the trade-offs of using segmentation strategies and whether or not segmentation is a permissible strategy.

The wide range of communication alternatives: Given the limitations of traditional marketing communication tools, one also must consider alternatives such as movies and television programmes, or even broader alternatives such as in-school or in-home educational communications. It is generally felt that public service spots are not very effective. Perhaps the money spent on their production could be used more efficiently in one of the non-traditional media.

(f) Implementation and Evaluation

Most good plans fail at the implementation stage. Proper care should be taken while developing the plans by anticipating the problems which might crop up at the implementation. Periodical evaluation system would help in identifying the achievements and pitfalls to take corrective measures. Although it is difficult to define effectiveness measures, an effort to establish performance standards would go a long way towards making the social marketing programme successful.

Case I: The Family Planning Programme

India's population is fast chasing a 1,000-million mark. In spite of all efforts, the population is increasing almost at the same rate as that of before. So far, only a fractional decline in the population growth from 2.2 per cent to 2.1 per cent has been achieved. The picture on the population density is rather gloomy as the density has increased from 216 to 267 people per kilometre. The situation in urban areas is even worse. Similar is the situation in the rest of the developing world which has led to environmental imbalance, poor living conditions and an inferior quality of life.

The recent UNFPA (1991) report on 'State of World Population' lays down targets to be achieved to curb population explosion. It suggests that the number of couples in the developing world using voluntary family planning methods showed a 50 per cent increase from 381 million in 1990 to 567 million by the year 2000. The report also goes on record that 'reaching the target will be critical for development and even the human survival in the next century'. Such is the gravity of this problem and to combat it one can anticipate the kind of efforts required, especially to achieve a 50 per cent growth in the targets.

In India, the need for family planning programme during the early fifties. Family planning was then taken up at a mass scale but till date limited success has been achieved. It is only the non-termination methods which have become popular to some extent, but termination methods have yet to take off. One of the reasons for the failure of the family programme was that the campaign on family planning has been faulty. The symbol of this campaign which is inverted red triangle on a yellow background with the slogan 'Do Ya Teen Bachee Bachhe' (meaning two or three children) was quietly changed to 'Hum Do Hamare Do' (meaning we two and ours' two) and later the visual showed only one child with a slogan 'Larka Ho Ya Larki.....' (meaning no matter whether there is a girl child or a boy child). Then came the 'Emergency' during which people were forced to undergo terminal methods. The impact of these measures which were, no doubt, in the larger interest of society, became negative to the extent that the people were alienated. Those who underwent vasectomy were laughed at. This happened because of the arbitrary approach and there is hardly any implementation of these campaigns as the basic problem lied in the communication with the change in the slogans very frequently.

Scarlett Epstein (1990), who has spent three years in the interior of Karnataka and carried out evaluation studies on developmental programmes, has categorically pointed out that the poor success rate of the developmental programmes is due to two reasons. First, without any exception most of our development programmes are top-down and not bottom-up, which is the essence of marketing. In fact, the recipients are never aware of what they are getting. Secondly, lack of social marketing research skills to develop an insight into the key sets of social, cultural and anthropological variables to understand people's behaviour which would help in an understanding of the form in which any social programme is to be packaged and delivered.

Epstein's observation very aptly emphasizes the need for a marketing approach for promoting social programmes which should begin with a deeper and detailed marketing research. People's behaviour must be analysed in detail. Perhaps, a lack of such insight led to the failure of the programme in the seventies. Although it is difficult to substantiate the observation with empirical support, the failure of the family planning programme is perhaps due to the failure in understanding the psyche of the masses. What is perhaps required is to convince the masses on 100 per cent survival of every single child coming to the family and then promoting the idea of a smaller family norm. There is a requirement of 100% immunization which can be achieved through immunization, general hygiene, balanced diet, education etc.

It would be appropriate to first research the factors causing resistance of the masses in adopting the programme, which results in its poor performance. Secondly, what is important is the position of the programme. What is required is that people should feel motivated to come forward voluntarily. Thirdly, better, newer and foolproof non-termination methods should be found out. The UN Population Fund Report on World Population (1990) suggests that special attention is required to scientific and commercial research to develop better methods for men. This would encourage them to take more responsibility for family planning. Fourthly, instead of promoting the concept of a smaller family, the emphasis should be on healthier, happier and better living. If the earlier mentioned psyche of the people is correct, then the efforts must be focused on encouraging cent-percent survival of every single child, which can be achieved through education. This in turn means packaging the programme by understanding the psyche on one hand and linkages between various social programmes (like, family planning, immunization, home management of diarrhea, nutrition, sanitation and hygiene etc.) on the other hand. Fifthly, the delivery systems should be made effective and efficient. At present, the system at the grassroots level is excelling in imperfection. The conditions at the Primary Health Centres (PHCs) need considerable improvement. The lowly paid Village Level Workers (VLWs) need proper briefing about their job and the need to be motivated to work for the programme wholeheartedly (Shanker 1987). Needless to say, both PHCs and VLWs are the immediate contact points at the grassroots level and any step to improve their efficiency would improve the efficiency of the programme. Lastly, due attention is to be paid to the evaluation and control mechanism to ensure that whatever is spent on the programme is well spent (Shanker 1991).

Case II: Population Services International (PSI)

PSI a registered non-profit organization and was associated with the effort to promote the cause of family planning, thereby providing support to the government programme. PSI was marketing the 'Masti' brand of condoms and the 'Pearl' oral contraceptive pill in the northern region.

Thus the entire market was segmented into two groups. First, those who transmit the virus through unsafe sex, and second, those who transmit the virus through any form of intra-vinous transfusion weather, blood, medicines or drugs — and the use of infected needles. PSI went for the first, as the second can be checked through educating medical practitioners about the use of disposable syringes.

In the first segment there were clearly identifiable sub-segments. They showed distinct behavioural patterns and therefore these sub-segments required separate treatment. On the one hand, there were prostitutes, and on the other, the sex buyers.

PSI decided to run a programme in the three major red-light areas of Bombay where there are 100 thousand prostitutes. PSI, although a Delhi based organization, did not go for the red-light areas of Delhi, as there are only 82 brothels in Delhi and not more than 2,000 prostitutes.

The programme had both communication and distribution components built around the behaviour patterns of both prostitutes and customers.

Studies carried out by the All India Institute of Medical Sciences (AIIMS), UNICEF and other organizations revealed the following facts:

1. Without exception, prostitutes are in the flesh trade not out of choice but due to the miseries of poverty.
2. Prostitutes are frequently sold and resold by the brothel owners and as a result, it is very difficult for an interpersonal communicator to keep track of.
3. More than 50 per cent of the prostitutes share sex even during the mensturation period, increasing the probability of getting infected if the customer is carrying the virus, or transmitting the virus to the customer if she is carrying the virus.
4. Use of the condom can prevent the transmission provided it is put on properly to prevent bursting or leakage. A large majority of the people do not know how to put the condom on.
5. As far as the customers are concerned, they come in groups in the red light areas and most of them are drunk. They normally go for an extended meal near the red light area or in the red light area before walking up to a brothel.

The communication strategy adopted was to create awareness about the disease and educate people on how it can be prevented with the use of a condom. It was observed that the use of a condom largely depends on the sex buyer and there is general resistance. The campaign aimed at converting this negative into an opportunity for a prostitute to get some more money if she not only insists on the use of the condom, but also puts the condom on. During the process, there would be foreplay game and the prostitute can charge for it. Innovative media vehicles were used to communicate with both the segments.

Realizing that the brothel culture is more film-based and all the time film music keeps playing, PSI came out with film-magazines on audio cassettes full of film gossip. In between, there were messages on AIDS, AIDS prevention, use of a condom, etc. These cassettes were priced and became quite popular.

PSI also arranged film shows for the prostitutes. Free passes were distributed. In between, the film was stopped and the messages on AIDS were shown, apart from a small clipping on how to put a condom on. The film shows were packed to capacity.

To communicate with the customers at the restaurants, the PSI arranged the supply of TV & VCR sets on interest-free installments for the restaurant owners and supplied video cassettes of the so-called hot-dances from Hindi films. In between, after small intervals, messages on AIDS, AIDS prevention, use of condoms, etc., were included.

Interpersonal communicators were also appointed from among the prostitutes or their children. They had access to the prostitutes and were able to communicate for support of the cause. Stage shows were arranged everyday and wall posters were extensively used.

The distribution strategy was to supply condoms to restaurant owners, pan-shops, local medical shops and prostitutes. The same retail margins were given to each of them.

Although the evaluation study on the success of the programme is yet to begin, there is considerable awareness about AIDS in the red light areas of Bombay.

Case III: The Immunization Programme

The Immunization Programme was started in India in 1978 with the objective of reducing the morbidity and mortality due to vaccine preventable diseases. Immunization coverage levels in infants and pregnant women have increased substantially over the last decade. Immunization coverage levels of 69 to 82 per cent with various vaccines were reported in 1989–90. There is, however, a wide disparity in the coverage levels in states and in the districts. While the priority remains to increase immunization coverage levels, surveillance of vaccine preventable diseases is receiving high priority to identify weak pockets for intensification of immunization services and to document impact. Besides completeness of reporting, emphasis of the surveillance system in many areas has shifted to obtaining information on cases as early as possible to allow epidemiological investigations and effective follow-up action. The achievements in a large number of districts show that the goal of universal immunization, while difficult and challenging, is attainable.

The Expanded Programme on Immunization (EPI) was launched in India in 1978 to control other vaccine-preventable diseases (VPDs). Initially, six diseases were selected: diphtheria, pertussis, tetanus, poliomyelitis, typhoid and childhood tuberculosis. The aim was to cover 80 per cent of all infants. Subsequently, the programme was universalized and renamed as Universal Immunization Programme (UIP) in 1985. Measles vaccine was included in the programme and typhoid vaccine was discontinued. The UIP was introduced in a phased manner from 1985 to cover all districts in the country by 1990, targeting all infants with the primary immunization schedule and all pregnant women with Tetanus Toxoid immunization. The UIP envisages achieving and sustaining universal immunization coverage in infants with three doses of DPT and OPV and one dose each of measles vaccine and BCG, and, in pregnant women, with two primary doses or one booster dose of TT. The UIP also requires a reliable cold chain system for storing and transporting vaccines, and attaining self-sufficiency in the production of all required vaccines.

In 1992, the UIP became a part of the Child Survival and Safe Motherhood Programme (CSSM), and in 1997, it became an important component of the Reproductive and Child Health Programme (RCH). The cold-chain system was strengthened and training programmes were launched extensively throughout the country. Intensified polio eradication activities were started in 1995–96 under the Polio Eradication programme, beginning with National Immunization Days (NIDs) and active surveillance for acute flaccid paralysis (AFP). The Polio Eradication Programme was set up with the assistance of the National Polio Surveillance Project.

India's Immunization Programme is one of the largest in the world in terms of quantities of vaccines used, numbers of beneficiaries, the numbers of immunization sessions organized, the geographical spread and diversity of areas covered. Under the immunization program, six vaccines are used to protect children and pregnant mothers against Tuberculosis, Diphtheria, Pertussis, Polio, Measles and Tetanus. It is also proposed to include Hepatitis B vaccine in UIP in phased manner. To help the parents keep a record of the immunization, including the booster dose a very innovative record card was developed by the Public Health System in India and promoted extensively through the advertising campaign. This record card was called in the local dialect as the Suraksha Card (Safety Card) and it became so successful that the private pediatricians imitated it. One of the major behavioral change which this card brought out was that parents used to carry that card all the time as and when they visited the hospital / doctor and they were reminded to come after a fixed period for the next vaccine or the booster dose. Parallel to this campaign, the polio campaign was run using celebrities, including movie stars. Typically, in health related campaigns, a fear or a negative appeal is used suggesting that if you do not go for vaccination you may have to suffer from the ill effects of the disease. However, the polio campaign used gave a very positive stroke to the parents wherein the theme of the campaign was communicated in such a way that it revealed that nobody can harm our children in any way.

The programme also had challenges of implementation, supply chain management (cold chain management) and management information system for proper monitoring. For a complex and extensive programme on immunization, an efficient management information system was necessary to get timely reports at and national levels.

At present, the programme has to depend upon routine reports received as part of the reporting under the Reproductive and Child Health (RCH) programme. This system provides feedback on coverage data only. Important information regarding the vaccines and cold chain logistics which are high cost areas does not get captured in the present system and a lot of effort and time is required in getting the critical data on these issues for planning and forecasting requirements and monitoring the status of vaccine supply and availability. To address these issues now and to collect data from District/PHC level a computer based monitoring system called Routine Immunization Monitoring System (RIMS Software) is under development for implementation throughout the country. A prototype of this software to assess practical applicability in the field has been developed. RIMS is a computerized implementation to enter data, generate reports and perform queries. The system is presently developed in Microsoft ACCESS as a standalone CD version. It is user friendly and no special training is required to operate the system. Online system is under development in a different platform using other database and programming tools.

The data are collected at district level from PHCs /Reporting Units in the standard pre-designed UIP format and entered on five broad categories namely (A) Immunization & Vitamin A, (B) Vaccine Supply, (C) VPD Surveillance, (D) Status of Cold Chain Equipment and (E) AEFI (Adverse Event following immunization). The system is capable of performing data analyses and generating useful reports for the use of UPI managers at all levels i.e. district, state and national. RIMS will be very useful tool to monitor UIP program as reports from all the 600 districts will be collected in a short period and then analyzed automatically by the software.

Conclusions

Anything that affects human living on a long-term basis can be called a social issue. Under the broad classifications of health environment education and civic issues, there are many issues that are important for social development in the developing countries, like India.

The national five year plans in India have given tremendous importance to social development and increased the expenditure in the social sector significantly in every successive five year plan. However, implementing such social programmes requires a strategic approach.

Social marketing is a half a century old concept that says that the concepts of marketing (which conventionally being seen as an instrument in promoting different goods and services) can be successfully applied to a social programme. In India, there have been some social programmes for which an adhoc approach was used and the programme was not successful. The family planning programme is one such programme. On the other hand, there have been experiences wherein a proper planning was undertaken and at the implementation stage the programme was tailored to the social and cultural aspect of different regions of the country, making the programme successful, clearly suggesting that marketing concepts can be applied to social programmes as well.

It is heartening that in 2008 the American Marketing Association has redefined marketing as 'the activity, set of institutions and processes for creating, communicating, delivering and exchanging offerings that have value for customers, clients, partners and society at large'.

References

Bloom, P. N. and Novelli, W. B. 1981. 'Problems and Challenges in Social Marketing', *Journal of Marketing* (45).

Census of India. 1991. *The Economic Times*, New Delhi, April 18, 1991.

Dewey, J. 1939. *Freedom and Culture*. New York: Putnam.

Fox, K. and Kotler, P. 1980. 'The Marketing of Social Cause – The First 10 Years', *Journal of Marketing*, (44).

Houston, F. S. and Homans, R. E. 1977. 'Public Agency Marketing -Pitfalls and Problems', *MSU Business Topics* (25).

Kotler, P. and Levy, S. J. 1969. 'Broadening the Concept of Marketing', *Journal of Marketing* (35).

Kotler, P. and Zaltman, G. 1971. 'Social Marketing – An Approach to Planned Social Change', *Journal of Marketing* (35).

Kotler, P. 1985. *Marketing For Nonprofit Organisations*. New Delhi: Prentice Hall.

Lazer, W. and Kelley, E. 1973. *Social Marketing Perspectives and Viewpoints*. Homewood, Illinois: R. D. Irwin.

Lovelock, C. H. and Weinberg, C. B. 1975. 'Contrasting Private and Public Sector Marketing,' in R. C. Curhan (ed.), M*arketing's Contributions to the Firm and Society*, Chicago, IL: American Marketing Association.

Luck, D. 1974. 'Social Marketing – Confusion Compounded', *Journal of Marketing* (38). *Newsweek*, Sept. 27, 1976, p. 36.

Phelps, E. S. 1975. *Altriuns, Mortality and Economic Theory*. New York: Basic Books.

Rothschild, M. L. 1979. 'Marketing Communication in Non-Business Situations or Why It Is So Hard to Sell Brotherhood Like Soaps', *Journal of Marketing* (Spring).

Sadak, N. 1991. UNFPA-World Population Report. *UNFPA, United Nations Population Fund, US*.

Scarlett Epstine 1988: *A Manual Social Marketing Research (CMR) in the Development Process*, Bexhill-on-Sea:RWAL Publications.

Shanker, R. 1989. 'Social Marketing: Concept and Process', *Communicator.*–. 1991. 'Marketing Approach to Social Campaigns', *The Financial Express*.

Takas, A. 1974. 'Societal Marketing – A Businessman's Perspective', *Journal of Marketing* (35).

Wiebe, G. D. 1951–52. 'Merchandising Commodities and Citizenship on Television', *Public Opinion Quarterly* (15).

Wish, J. R. and Gamble, S. H. 1971. *Marketing and Social Issues* New York: Wiley.

Part Three:

CASE STUDIES IN GLOBAL GOVERNANCE

Chapter 13

UNITY IN DIVERSITY: SOUTH COALITIONS AS GOVERNANCE ADAPTION VEHICLES IN GLOBAL TRADE GOVERNANCE

Vicente Paolo B. Yu III*

Introduction: Rapidly Changing Global Economic Scene

The geo-political and economic map of the world is rapidly changing. Global institutional arrangements borne out of the historical experiences of the mid- to late twentieth century will need to adjust to the new global political and economic context that is now evolving, even as the post-World War II issue of promoting the development of developing countries[1] continues to remain at the centre of international economic policy debates.

A major aspect of this new context is the development of new international policy regimes and the institutional architecture relating to these regimes that have an impact on developing countries' development policies and prospects. These include a new institutional architecture on global trade policy represented by the World Trade Organization (WTO), complete with a more comprehensive set of trade rules that are binding on countries, and whose work both influences and is influenced by the work of other existing trade-related global institutions such as the UN Conference on Trade and Development (UNCTAD).

Another aspect of this new context is the increasing share and influence of developing countries in global economic affairs – both in terms of shaping global economic policy and in terms of actual weight in the global economy. While global economic policy-making continues to date to be largely shaped by the institutions that were set up after World War II, such as the Bretton

---

* The contents of this paper are personal to the author and do not reflect the official views or positions of the South Centre, its Member States or other developing countries. The usual disclaimers apply.

Woods institutions, and by individual developed countries and their collective institutions (such as the G-8), the long-standing assertiveness of developing countries in seeking to influence policy discourse has become even more pronounced in recent years. This has been clearly evident in both the WTO and UNCTAD, especially since the start of the current decade. This assertiveness is based on the spectacular performance of many developing countries to grow their economies in recent years.

The current decade has seen a significant shift in the global economic environment. Developing countries as a group (including China and India) have achieved an average of 5–6 per cent growth between 2002 and 2007, 'although not all countries or segments of the population are beneficiaries of this growth...' (UNCTAD 2007). In addition to the economic growth spurt experienced by developing countries as a whole, some large developing countries such as China and India are now 'engines of growth for the world economy ... [and] the share of South-South trade is increasing in the world economy, making inter-South trade a veritable locomotive of growth' (UNCTAD 2007).[2]

The increasing economic share of developing countries in the global economy has been an integral part of the global economic recovery that has taken place since 2001, stimulated to a large extent by the rapid increase of exports from developing countries.[3] The fast-growing economies of China, India, Brazil, South Africa and other developing countries have also helped create new trade opportunities for both developed and developing countries, especially in terms of increased demand in these growing economies for primary commodities and intermediary inputs (TDR 2006). (Figure 13.1)

Figure 13.1. Per Capita GDP Growth by Region and Economic Grouping, 1981–2007 (Per cent).

	Average Annual Growth			Overall Growth
	1981–1989	1990–2002	2003–2007	1981–2007
World	1.4	1.2	2.3	41.4
Developed economies	2.5	1.8	2.0	67.5
Economies in transition	1.9	−4.0	7.3	−25.8
Developing economies	1.7	3.0	5.0	112.5
Of which:				
Africa	−0.5	0.3	3.0	16.4
America	−0.3	1.1	3.5	22.7
West Asia	−1.7	1.1	4.1	16.0
East and south Asia	5.1	5.3	6.3	3175.5

Source: UNCTAD secretariat calculations, based on UNCTAD Handbook of statistics: and Table 1.1.

The Continuing Challenge of the Widening Development Gap

But also very evident in this new context is the continued widening of the development gap (as measured in terms of income inequality) between developed and developing countries, in many respects, even as some developing countries are able to put their economies on a sustained growth path. The continued existence of global income inequality matters not only in terms of the long-term economic and social instability that it implies for the global community, but also because it affects how the global economic governance structures that exist function. As a UN report points out, 'economic power and political power tend to be reinforcing. Also, in this sense, the rules governing global markets are likely to be less advantageous for developing countries, as these countries tend to have less of a voice in the negotiation processes leading to the establishment of those rules'[4] (WESS 2006).

Systemic global economic inequality looks set to continue in the medium- and long-term. There are many more developing countries that continue to languish at low levels of economic development, in Africa, South Asia and the Pacific, and Central and South America.

The UNDP has pointed out that on 2000 to 2005 growth trends, 'it will still take India until 2106 to catch up with high-income countries. For other countries and regions convergence prospects are even more limited. Were high-income countries to stop growing today and Latin America and Sub-Saharan Africa to continue on their current growth trajectories, it would take Latin America until 2177 and Africa until 2236 to catch up'(HDR 2005).

In fact, except for some Asian developing countries, most other developing countries are falling behind, rather than catching up, with developed countries in terms of income growth, with Africa's share of the income poor projected to increase (see Figure 13.2).[5]

Unsatisfactory fulfilment of the development imperative becomes even clearer when one looks at the increasing development gap between the developed and developing countries (as measured in terms of income inequality) between developed and developing countries.

While income levels have risen steadily in developed countries over the past half-century, they have not done so as steadily in most developing countries especially over the past 25 years (WESS 2006). Leaving out China's and India's (together accounting for almost half of the global population) exemplary progress in increasing their people's incomes reveals a picture in which global income inequality is in fact increasing (WESS 2006; see Figure 13.3).

A major part of the problem is that income inequality between countries remains extremely high and whatever income convergence with developed countries might take place will likely be concentrated in only some developing

Figure 13.2.

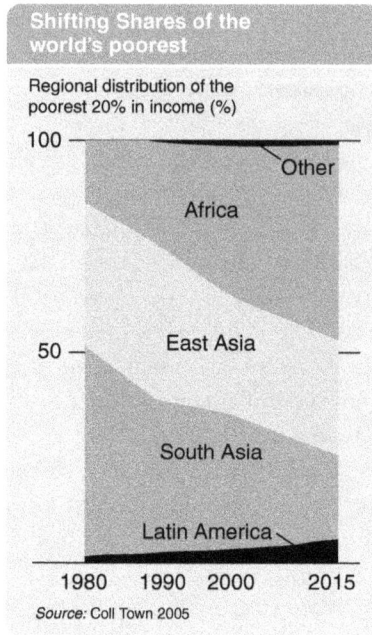

Source: HDR 2005, p. 35.

Figure 13.3.

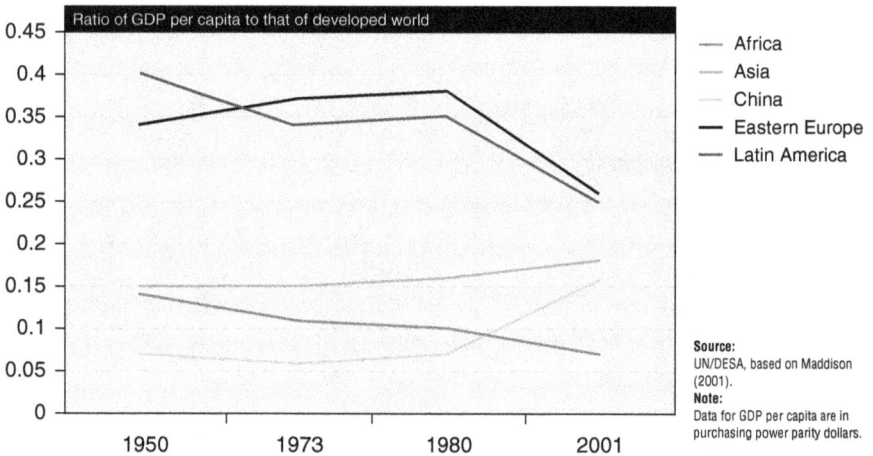

Source: WESS 2006, p.1.

Figure 13.4.

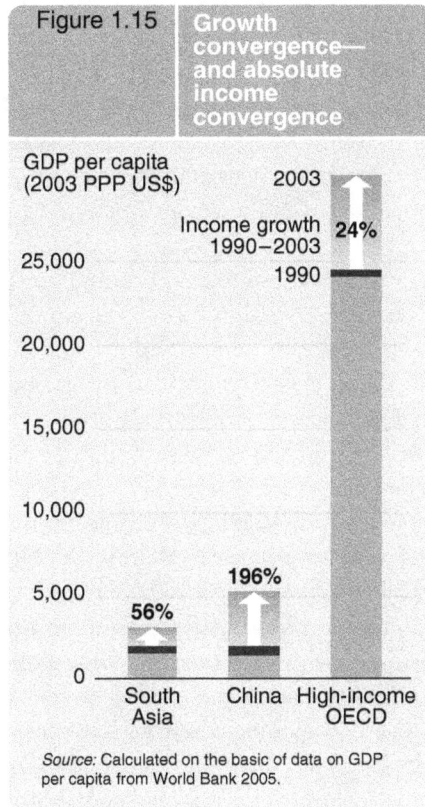

Figure 1.15 — Growth convergence—and absolute income convergence

GDP per capita (2003 PPP US$)

25,000
20,000
15,000
10,000
5,000
0

South Asia — 56%
China — 196%
High-income OECD — 24%

Income growth 1990–2003 · 2003 · 1990

Source: Calculated on the basic of data on GDP per capita from World Bank 2005.

Source: HDR 2005, at 37.

countries rather than be broad-based across all developing countries.[6] Even when developing countries have higher growth rates, the absolute income gap with developed countries on a per capita purchasing power parity (PPP) basis will continue to increase 'precisely because the initial income gaps are so large … If average incomes grow by 3% in Sub-Saharan Africa and in high-income Europe, for example, the absolute change will be an extra $51 per person in Africa and an extra $854 per person in Europe' (HDR 2005; see Figure 13.4).

Developing Countries and Imbalances in Participation in Global Economic Governance

Inequities in economic terms often reflect political inequities, and vice versa. The current global trading system exemplifies 'some historical and structural inequities' (UNDP 2003) in which the rules are 'less advantageous for developing countries'. Changing the rules of the trading game to make them more equitable and capable of supporting developing countries' development interests will require addressing the flaws in the institutional architecture which shapes and implements those rules. This means looking at how the institutions that form part of such architecture operate in terms of their ability to put in place rules that reflect and promote, in a pro-active manner, the needs of the disadvantaged in their constituency.

Cognizant of the difficulties and imbalances that they face in participating effectively and fully in various global economic institutions, developing countries have been consistently calling for governance reforms that would allow for their increased participation and representation in such institutions. These calls have been made in the context of, for example, the World Bank and the International Monetary Fund (IMF) vis-à-vis voice and quota reforms, the UN Security Council with respect to its permanent membership, international financial institutions such as the Bank of International Settlements (BIS), international standards-setting organizations such as the Codex Alimentarius and the International Standards Organization (ISO) and in the WTO itself. Parallel to these initiatives, developing countries have also been active in establishing mechanisms designed to improve both their ability to cooperate and coordinate with each other in these international institutions and to bolster their substantive capacity to participate.

In all of these initiatives, developing countries have been consistent as well in stressing a clear development-oriented perspective in that development should be the main priority and focus for international cooperation and global action. These past few years of robust (although unequal) growth among many developing countries, especially among the big emerging economies of Brazil, India, China and South Africa, have spurred an increasing sense of confidence, self-reliance and optimism not only in terms of national prospects for development, but also with respect to enhanced South-South cooperation and solidarity and the utility of working together in different institutions, such as the WTO.

Unfortunately, effective developing country participation in most of the international economic institutions, such as the World Bank, the IMF and the WTO, is often very much lacking. This is an institutional global governance problem that has been consistently pointed out by developing countries,[7] especially with respect to the World Bank and the IMF,[8] the WTO,[9] the United Nations,[10] as well as with respect to international standards setting.[11]

This problem of unequal levels of participation may, in fact, be deeply rooted in the very architecture of these institutions that reflect the power balance existing at the time that such institutions were created (Barnett and Duvall

2005).[12] While these institutions' official mandates stress the promotion of the interests of the weaker members of their constituencies, it was often the case that the policy orientation, agenda, and organizational bias of the institution tended to favour the interests of some, mostly the more powerful, members over others and limited the ability of weaker members to effectively participate in both agenda-setting and decision-making (Barnett and Duvall 2005).[13]

Developing Country Participation in the World Trade Organization

Participation Issues in the WTO

The issue of effective participation by developing countries in the WTO and in UNCTAD is particularly important because of the key roles that these institutions play in shaping global trade rules. In the trade area, the WTO and UNCTAD are the most prominent in the trade area in terms of policy setting and implementation. As such, they serve as the multilaterally agreed framework through which multilateral rules and disciplines relating to cross-border trade are discussed, designed, implemented, enforced and managed to ensure that there is a smooth interface between different national systems.

Issues relating to internal WTO institutional governance processes have long been recognized by, and been placed on the agenda of, the WTO.[14] This is due primarily to the fact that the institutional governance mechanisms and processes currently used in the WTO have led to problems of transparency, inclusiveness, participation, and efficiency in decision-making in the organization.[15] In this connection, there are two (2) major issues that bear importantly on the ability of developing countries to participate effectively in the negotiations:

(1) the decision-making process and
(2) the capacity to participate.

The decision-making process is important because of the impact that it may have on the actual outcomes. For example, the difficulties inherent in complying with the requirement in Article IX:1 of the WTO Agreement for formal consensus as the basis for decision-making has pushed the WTO to engage in and rely more and more on informal processes for building such consensus (UNDP 2003), which in turn have historically tended to reflect, in terms of both process and outcome, the differential power relations among members that exist in the organization.

The difficulties faced by developing countries in the context of the WTO's decision-making processes are now well-recognized as an institutional problem faced by the WTO, as can be seen from the following statement from UNCTAD's 2006 Trade and Development Report:

> WTO negotiation procedures have often given the impression of less than full transparency and participation, so that some countries appear to have stronger influence than others. Decisions taken in so-called "green room" meetings or in other gatherings of a limited number of members are often presented to the entire membership as fait accompli. These procedures may have resulted from well-intentioned attempts to preserve practicality and efficiency in complex decision-making. However, they have prompted concerns about unequal influence and unequal representation of national priorities in processes the results of which affect all participants. (TDR 2006)

This does not mean, however, that WTO negotiating outcomes are predetermined by the power relations among members. The ability of developed members to agree on the terms of agreement and expect that agreement to be ratified by the rest of the membership now seems to be fast diminishing as other developing members both individually and collectively become more able and willing to assert and defend their own perspectives and views.

In addition to the process issue which affects the qualitative nature of individual developing country participation in WTO decision-making, an associated issue is the participation capacity question – i.e. effective participation is also a function of the size and expertise of the member's delegation in Geneva and the extent to which such delegation is provided with adequate and effective technical and policy support from their capital (South Centre 2003).[16]

In sum, the WTO's institutional decision-making process, individual negotiating capacity limitations and information asymmetries are, among others, constraints to the actual effectiveness and mode of participation by developing countries in the WTO's decision-making system. In response to these constraints, developing countries have increasingly turned to forming informal groupings or coalitions and to strengthening existing groupings with other developing countries. This response has been particularly evident since the launch of the WTO's Doha negotiations in late 2001.

Governance Adaptation by Developing Countries in the WTO: Coalition-Building in Pursuit of a Development Agenda

It can be argued that a fundamental ideational shift has indeed taken place in terms of how developing countries view the WTO, its role in their respective development processes and their role as participants in its governance system, and underlies the basic negotiating positions of today's WTO developing country coalitions. This ideational shift can be clearly seen in the increasingly development policy-oriented thrust of the negotiating positions of the various developing country coalitions, in which the concept of increased levels of development policy choices and flexibilities is sought to be reflected in operational terms as part of the negotiated outcomes.[17]

As a result, developing country participation in the Doha negotiations now take place both directly – as individual members – and indirectly – as members of various groups or coalitions. In the major negotiating issues of agriculture, NAMA and trade facilitation, this trend is much more evident (the services negotiations, with its bilateral request-offer negotiating format, are not as conducive to group-based negotiations as the others).

More than simply viewing the WTO as an international negotiating forum where trade concessions may be negotiated and exchanged, developing country coalitions now view the WTO as a negotiating forum in which the development implications of trade concessions will need to be considered as part and parcel of the philosophical moorings and values underlying the multilateral trading system. The G-20, the G-33, the NAMA-11, the Core Group on Trade Facilitation, the African Group, the ACP Group, the LDCs Group and the Small Vulnerable Economies Group all have clearly and distinctly pegged their positions in the WTO to a clear ideational preference for linking negotiated concessions to their respective longer-term strategic development objectives and ideas.[18] This developing country insistence on viewing the WTO as not merely a trade institution but as a development and trade institution has been clearly evident in all of the ministerial conferences since Seattle in 1999, and indeed was instrumental in ensuring that the mandate of the Doha negotiations is contextualized within a broader development discourse.

Working together and forming coalitions is a rational response by developing countries to both the issue of negotiating constraints and the issue of being better able to advance their development agenda. Coalitions enable developing countries to pool together resources, find strength in numbers, be represented (directly or indirectly) in various negotiating formats, and have a vehicle through which they can inject their agenda into and influence the negotiating outcome. In essence, working together in coalitions helps developing countries in the WTO to increase their power and consequently their ability to influence outcomes despite the complexity of the issues and the political dynamics that occur in the negotiations.

Learning from their experiences during the Uruguay Round – in particular from the experiences of the G-10 and the Café au Lait groups, their individual country-based negotiating experiences and the results of the negotiated

Table 13.1.

A. Regional Groups or Coalitions	B. Issue-Based Coalitions	C. Groups or Coalitions Based on Common Characteristics
• African Group	• Cotton-4	• Least-Developed Countries (LDCs)
• African, Caribbean, Pacific (ACP) Group	• Core Group in Trade Facilitation (CGTF)	• Landlocked Developing Countries (LLDCs)
• Association of South East Asian Nations (ASEAN)	• G-20	• Small Vulnerable Economies (SVEs)
• Caribbean Community (CARICOM)	• G-33	
• Pacific Islands Forum (PIF)	• NAMA-11	
	• Paragraph 6 NAMA countries	

outcomes for developing countries – and taking into account the governance challenges they face in the WTO context, developing countries now tend to work together and negotiate in the WTO on the basis of voluntary developing country-only coalitions – whether organized along regional, cross-regional or issue-based lines.

There have been studies on the kinds of collective action-focused coalition building that developing countries have undertaken in the WTO (Narlikar 2003; Wolfe 2006; Draper and Sally 2005; Bernal et. al. 2004). These have looked at the mechanics, internal dynamics, and the role that these coalitions play in WTO decision-making. These studies all point to the same overall conclusion – developing country coalitions are, per se and whether in their formal or informal sense, becoming an integral and important of WTO decision-making. They have become the de facto preferred response of developing countries to imbalances in power, process, and participation that existed in the GATT and which persisted into the WTO. They help harness the power of numbers in favour of those who join the group, and help improve the negotiating ability of their members by allowing them to put together a more proactive and defensive negotiating position.[19] As such, they are becoming the vehicles through which some of the worst aspects of such imbalances may be remedied on an operational basis and through which developing countries can enhance their role in shaping and influencing decision-making.

They also represent a clear recognition on the part of developing countries that negotiating success in the WTO lies in improved levels and modes of coordination with other developing countries in order to effect more effective and active participation in the WTO decision-making process. As a result, developing countries have shown dramatic improvements in their ability to establish and maintain their coalitions in the context of the WTO negotiations, and they have become more strategic in doing so.

Of the 112 WTO members who are commonly recognized as, or who ascribe to themselves the designation of, 'developing countries', 99 (or 87.61 per cent) developing countries are members of one or more developing country-only groups or coalitions. 67 developing countries (or 58.77 per cent of developing WTO members) have joined one or more informal issue-based developing country coalitions. 61 developing countries are members of a regional group (including 35 which are also members of one or more issue-based groups and 37 which are members of one or more common characteristic groups). 51 developing countries have joined one or more common characteristic group. 19 countries have membership in all three types of developing country groups or coalitions.

As can be seen above, while region-based or common characteristic-based groups (such as the African or ACP Groups for the former and the LDC Group for the latter) continue to be major vehicles for coalition-based action by many developing countries, informal issue-based groups or coalitions such as the G-20, the G-33 and the NAMA-11 have now become the primary means for group-based action by developing countries.

The use of both formal and informal coalitions by developing countries as vehicles for their participation in the negotiations naturally leads to overlapping memberships by individual developing countries in various groups. For example, all members of the African Group and the CARICOM are members of the ACP Group. All 32 LDC WTO members, except for Bangladesh, Cambodia, Haiti, Maldives and Nepal, are also members of the ACP Group.

Overlapping memberships can be both a source of weakness and of strength for developing country coalitions. For the most part, however, over the course of the Doha negotiations, developing countries have managed to maximize the strengths that overlapping memberships give to their respective groups and coalitions. Countries that are members of two or more coalitions often play key roles in ensuring that inter-coalition dynamics remain positive and mutually complementary to the maximum extent possible.

The extent of overlapping memberships among the various developing country coalitions can be seen below:

Developing Countries in the WTO: Groups and Overlapping Memberships.

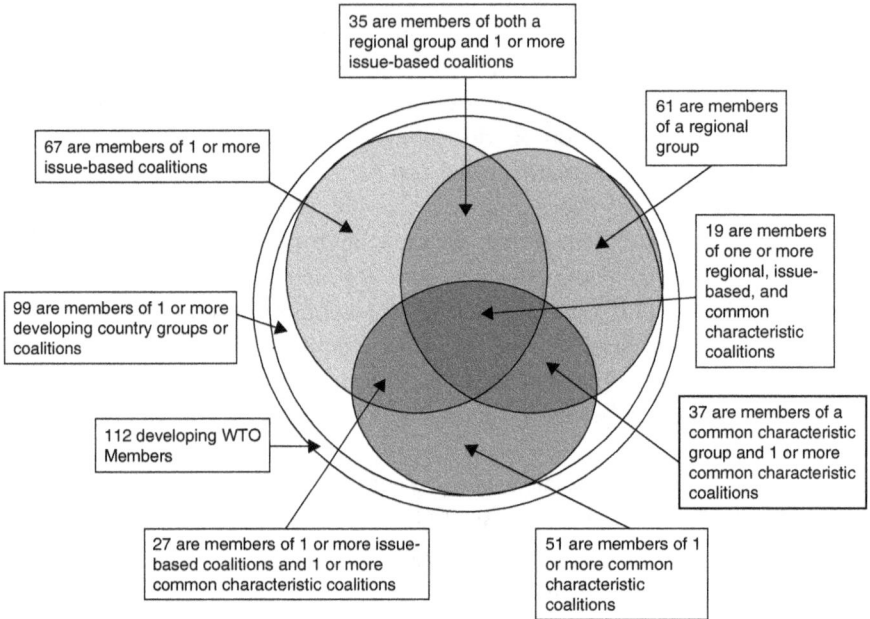

35 are members of both a regional group and 1 or more issue-based coalitions

61 are members of a regional group

67 are members of 1 or more issue-based coalitions

19 are members of one or more regional, issue-based, and common characteristic coalitions

99 are members of 1 or more developing country groups or coalitions

37 are members of a common characteristic group and 1 or more common characteristic coalitions

112 developing WTO Members

27 are members of 1 or more issue-based coalitions and 1 or more common characteristic coalitions

51 are members of 1 or more common characteristic coalitions

Coalitions with a diverse constituency – whether cross-regional or inter-group – have the tendency of participating more actively on issues in which exists a previous general common understanding and abstaining from sensitive issue-specific negotiations in which consensus would be much harder to achieve. In addition, the greater cohesiveness shown by regional coalitions across virtually all the negotiating areas in the WTO suggests that greater levels of similarities among group members result in improved group cohesiveness and negotiating weight.

As a result, more emphasis is now generally placed on establishing and maintaining stable and sustainable intra-group coordination mechanisms, whether through a systematized system of rotating group coordination, or through group acceptance of a member taking on the coordination functions of the group. Group cohesiveness has become a key priority in terms of coalition building.

Rotating group coordination mechanisms remain the primary mode for group leadership of the African, ACP and LDC Groups. The task of coordinating the overall actions and positions of the members of these groups is rotated among group members who are both willing and able to provide the necessary human, administrative and logistical resources in their missions in Geneva for such coordination. Overall, group coordination is usually done by the ambassador of the country acting as the coordinator, supported by the Geneva-based staff of his or her mission. The task of coordination is made easier through the practice of selecting 'issue focal points' – basically another member of the group willing and able to take the lead for the group on specific negotiating issues by assigning one of their technical-level experts or delegates in the Geneva missions to take charge of suggesting, formulating and coordinating group positions and actions on such specific issues.[20]

On the other hand, other coalitions agree on having specific members provide both coordination and leadership functions. In their case, strong leadership by some members of the group coupled with willing acceptance of such leadership on the basis of perceived commonalities of interest is seen as essential in ensuring group success, especially in the case of the bloc-type or issue-based groups. For example, the leadership roles of Brazil and India ensured that the G-20 would not collapse after the Cancun Ministerial Conference. In the case of the G-33 (the "Strategic Products/Special Safeguard Mechanism (SP/SSM) group), the leadership of Indonesia and the Philippines were and continues to be instrumental in keeping the group together.

Developing countries are now more conscious about engaging effectively with other developing country groups to form mutually supportive ad-hoc inter-group alliances. For example, the G-90 (composed of the African, ACP, and LDC Groups) has become the vehicle of choice among many developing countries belonging to these groups to express common views from a position of numerical strength at critical times of the WTO negotiations – together with the G-20, SVEs, and the G-33, these become the G-110.

The recognition that coalition-building may work best in situations where the group constituents share common and clearly articulated perspectives on specific issues resulted in an adaptative move on the part of developing countries to develop issue-based coalitions. Their articulation of their positions on specific issues has also become more strategic. For example, developing country coalitions are now generally both defensive (in the sense of responding to perceived negotiating pressure from other Members) and proactive (in the sense of seeking to advance a specific negotiating agenda) in their areas of interest – e.g. the G-20 that was formed during the Cancun Ministerial Conference has a clearly articulated agenda containing both defensive and proactive elements in the context of the WTO agriculture negotiations (Aggarwal 2005).

Finally, the working relationships of individual delegates with each other also play an important role in developing country coalition building and cohesion. While the decision to join a particular group – especially an issue-based coalition – is a political decision that is made by the capital-based decision-makers (e.g. the trade minister) of the country concerned, such a decision is often based on the recommendations of their delegations in Geneva. In this regard, the personal and working relationships and contacts that these delegations have with each other play an important role in shaping the decision to join a coalition or not. Just as important is the role that shared personal perspectives and experiences on certain issues may have in encouraging delegations to work with each other.

For example, in many cases, developing country delegates often find it much easier to relate to each other on a personal and working level than with their developed country counterparts – whether because of common negotiating experiences or shared perspectives about issues. This engenders mutual confidence and positive inter-personal dynamics with each other, and makes it easier for them to work together in ensuring that intra-group and inter-group dynamics are made smoother. This is not to say that differences do not exist among developing country delegations on both a personal and working level, or that intra- and inter-group developing country dynamics are free of friction and disagreements. Such differences and friction do exist, but resolving or surmounting these are often made easier because delegates – especially when they come from the same region or when they perceive that they have common interests with respect to certain development issues such as special and differential treatment – may then find it easier to find bases for common agreement and action.

Developing countries are now more aware of the need to ensure that their negotiating positions are supported by arguments grounded on a good body of research, data analysis, and intra-group information sharing, whether done by their members or else provided by external institutions supportive of their positions. This research and analysis becomes the basis for more strategic approaches to negotiating strategy.

Many developing country coalitions are now also including a more proactive approach to engaging with external actors that can help them promote their issues such as international organizations, civil society, and international media. The G-33 and the G-20 have become more media-savvy, issuing press releases and making their spokespersons available when needed. They have become more open to having the support of civil society advocacy and campaigning organizations on specific issues. Much more use is made of the technical-level direct negotiating and policy research assistance made available by developing country intergovernmental organizations such as the South Centre.[21] The Geneva-based support missions of regional organizations such as the African Union and the ACP Group of States also play important roles in supporting the work of these groups in the WTO negotiations. Support to various developing country groups, in various forms including the organization of workshops and the provision of substantive input, has also been sought and provided by other organizations such as UNCTAD, UNDP, the Commonwealth Secretariat, the UN Economic Commission for Africa (UNECA). Civil society organizations with offices in Geneva such as the International Centre for Trade and Sustainable Development (ICTSD) and TWN also became resources, to varying degrees, which developing country groups could tap for substantive input.

But while external input and support are important for developing country groups, they are conscious of the need to ensure that such external support and input must be demand-driven and, on the basis of their own assessment, be consistent with their own negotiating interests and positions. The best form of technical policy input and support is one that is iterative and undertaken in close consultation with the group concerned, to ensure that such input meets the group's needs.[22]

To summarize, there has been a distinct change in the negotiating dynamics among WTO members. Developing countries have learned to work together in cohesive groups or coalitions based on their self-identified interests in a much better and more coordinated way as compared to, for example, the way in which they interacted prior to the Seattle Ministerial Conference in 1999. The development of more cohesive regional, cross-regional, common characteristic, and issue-based purely developing country groupings in the run-up to the 2003 Cancun Ministerial Conference was followed up by more consistent efforts on the part of these coalitions to work together more closely and in a more coordinated fashion both internally and with other groups. This trend is clearly reflected in the 15 November 2007 joint statement by the various major developing country-only groups in the WTO as follows:

The Ministers and Senior Officials of the G-20 and the coordinators of the G-33, the NAMA-11, the ACP Group, the Least Developed Countries (LDCs), the African Group, the Small, Vulnerable Economies (SVEs), and the Cotton-4 met in Geneva on 15 November 2007 to review the situation in the Doha Round and to discuss ways to enhance coordination among developing country groups on issues of mutual interest.

They welcomed the engagement and solidarity demonstrated by developing country groups. They noted that developing-country coordination and contribution increased the efficiency and legitimacy of the negotiating process. Developing countries have shown an unprecedented level of participation in this Round. They are ready to continue playing an active role in the WTO commensurate with the growing importance of developing countries in international trade.

The Groups pledged to maintain the unity and cooperation among developing country groups. They reasserted their readiness to engage with other WTO Members with a view to achieving an outcome acceptable to all in the shortest possible time.[23]

The result has been a marked improvement in the extent of overall developing country participation in the WTO negotiations, albeit indirectly. And a stronger ability to influence WTO decision-making on the part of developing countries can be concluded from the fact that developing country issues now form part of the central negotiating agenda of the WTO.

Developing Country Participation in the UN Conference on Trade and Development

Participation Issues in UNCTAD

The current role of developing countries in UNCTAD is in some ways similar to that in the WTO, in the sense of these countries being seen as primary stakeholders whose consent to a decision is always needed, but in some other ways quite dissimilar to that in the WTO. This is not surprising considering that the WTO (including its institutional precursor, the GATT 1947) and UNCTAD were both separate historical institutional responses by the international community to the non-birth of the International Trade Organization (ITO).[24]

UNCTAD has historically had much greater internal transparency with respect to its intergovernmental processes as compared to the WTO. Coupled with the long-standing use of the group system as a means for intergovernmental interaction within UNCTAD, there has traditionally been much more informed and systematic developing country participation in UNCTAD's governance processes as compared to the GATT or the WTO.

In many ways, the imbalances among the political power and influence among different countries that exist in the WTO as a result of the use of informal processes seem to have been much less evident in UNCTAD, especially during its first two decades and, it seems, is becoming so again in recent years mainly as a result of: (i) the use by developing countries of group-based dynamics; and (ii) relatively greater transparency in terms of the processes used in UNCTAD.

Governance Adaptation in UNCTAD: The Role of the G-77 as the Primary Developing Country Coalition Actor

Group-based dynamics have had a long history in terms of UNCTAD's intergovernmental processes. Negotiations in the various UNCTAD conferences historically (at least until the late 1990s) were not carried out by individual countries but by groupings of countries acting together with a common platform and a main spokesperson.

Developing countries have historically participated in any negotiations – e.g. on international commodity agreements, the ministerial declaration of the UNCTAD conferences, etc. – through the vehicle of the Group of 77 and China's (G-77 and China) Geneva chapter. The members of this chapter include all the current 132 G-77 members,[25] including China. Developed countries operated through, while Group D was composed of the then-socialist countries within the Soviet Bloc. These blocs continue to exist and play major roles in today's UNCTAD, although with some more recent permutations in that European Union (EU) member States also tend to speak as a bloc (both within and outside of Group B), while Group D's current membership also includes countries that are now EU member States.[26]

The G-77 as an intergovernmental developing country coalition was formed on 15 June 1964 by seventy-seven developing countries that were signatories of the 'Joint Declaration of the Seventy-Seven Countries'[27] issued at the end of the first session of UNCTAD in Geneva. It originated from the 'merger of Afro-Asian countries (Group A) and Latin American countries (Group C) for the purpose of UNCTAD negotiations' (Iida 1988).

Beginning with the first G-77 ministerial meeting in Algiers in October 1967, the G-77 gradually developed a permanent institutional structure that eventually led to the creation of Chapters of the Group of 77 in Geneva (UNCTAD), Nairobi (UNEP), Paris (UNESCO), Rome (FAO/IFAD), Vienna (UNIDO) and the Group of 24 (G-24) in Washington DC (IMF and World Bank). Although the members of the G-77 have since increased to 132 countries, the original name was retained because of its historic significance.[28]

From its origins with the birth of UNCTAD, the G-77 has now become the premier intergovernmental developing country group working together within the UN system, being very active on most issues being discussed within the UN.[29] It 'provides the means for the countries of the South to articulate and promote their collective economic interests and enhance their joint negotiating capacity on all major international economic issues within the United Nations system, and promote South-South cooperation for development' (South Centre 2004).

The various G-77 chapters have some common operational features, such as having the same organizational set-up. A chapter chairman, serving for a year, coordinates the work of the chapter and the position of chairman rotates among the G-77's three regional groups – Africa, Asia, and Latin America and the Caribbean. A country does not normally chair more than one chapter at a time. The chapter chairs try to meet at least once a year to coordinate the work of their respective chapters with each other. The South Summit, which convenes once every five years (with the next one in 2010), is the G-77's highest decision-making body, while ministerial-level meetings by the foreign affairs ministers of the G-77 take place annually at the start of the regular session of the UN General Assembly. Special or sectoral ministerial meetings of the G-77 may also take place.

The G-77 has become a key institutional international actor that carries great political weight. It displays institutional features such as some norms, regularity of interaction, and formal rules of procedure. But a serious institutional shortcoming that the G-77 has faced and continues to face in the context of its operations and its policymaking is that it has no real secretariat of its own to provide it with substantive policy analysis and technical support on a day-to-day basis. Instead, each chapter would be supported by a generally small logistical liaison unit hosted by or in the main UN agency in which the chapter is active – e.g. UNCTAD in Geneva, UNEP in Nairobi, UN Headquarters in New York, UNESCO in Paris, UNIDO in Vienna. Substantive policy research and analytical support on specific issues handled by each chapter would be done by the permanent mission staff of the chapter's coordinator, by individual delegates of G-77 members on an ad hoc basis, or by other agencies on a demand-driven basis (e.g. UNCTAD, the South Centre, NGOs).[30]

In some ways, the establishment of the G-77 in UNCTAD and their ability to generate and push cohesive and united negotiating positions was both the effect and cause of developed country actions. Developing countries in the early 1960s (especially from Africa and Asia) were becoming increasingly frustrated at the way in which developed countries were not responding favorably to their requests for increased levels of international cooperation to restructure global economic relations to promote the development of developing countries. As a result, they felt that only a united and cohesive front vis-à-vis developed countries could enhance their leverage and effect changes in terms of their economic relations with developed countries. This eventually led to the creation of the G-77. During and after UNCTAD I, as the G-77 started operating and presenting cohesive and united group positions, developed countries started responding by also adopting joint negotiating positions that were previously discussed and coordinated through their organization, the Organisation for Economic Co-operation and Development (OECD).[31]

Developing countries saw UNCTAD as a forum that 'would have some quasi-legislative traits and make at least certain decisions – however they might be called – that would commit the developed countries to a given course of action'(Ricupero 2004). However, developed countries 'tended to regard the UNCTAD forums as deliberative meetings where countries could exchange viewpoints and engage in general discussions' in which 'the decisions made through this process [were] irrelevant to themselves (in contrast to the GATT negotiations) and possessing at best a declaratory value (Boutros-Ghali 2006).

In the context of UNCTAD in Geneva, the leadership and actual coordination of the work of the G-77 Geneva chapter is done by the chapter chair – usually the ambassador and his/her team in their Geneva permanent mission of the country selected to be the chapter chair for that year. As pointed out above, the responsibility to coordinate the chapter rotates annually among the members on the basis of their regional origin – i.e. Africa, Asia, and Latin America and the Caribbean.

The G-77 Geneva chapter's regional coordination mechanism also does not prevent it from making decisions as a whole, nor prevent any of the G-77's members from raising issues individually that may not have been covered or raised by the relevant regional group (Gosovic 1972). Finally, specifically in the context of UNCTAD, the G-77 also includes States which are not members of the G-77 in other chapters such as in New York because for the purposes of UNCTAD intergovernmental processes, the G-77 is composed of the Member States that are listed in Lists A and C annexed to UN General Assembly Resolution 1995 (XIX).[32]

Institutional leadership within the G-77 is also often a function of different factors. These include economic strength and size; having clear political objectives; having a defined program, technical preparedness and a delegation with clear instructions; specialization in a particular issue; membership in a formal UNCTAD body such as the Trade and Development Board; having a competent permanent mission in Geneva; the personality, individual skills, and negotiating diplomatic flexibility of their delegates (Gosovic 1972). These factors generally militate against any one country acting conspicuously as 'the' G-77 leader, which essentially means that leadership in the G-77 context – i.e. the ability to have a certain degree of political and intellectual influence in shaping G-77 positions – often comes from individual countries in the context of their influence in their regional groups (Gosovic 1972).

Based on its philosophical orientation, understanding of the systemic imbalances in the international economic order, and views on the institutional role of UNCTAD, the G-77's negotiating positions during the hey-day of UNCTAD's years as a negotiating forum were often maximalist – that is, based on the maximum common denominator of demands from G-77 members. This also enabled the G-77 to maintain group cohesion despite their internal differences that formed the internal context for the development of G-77 negotiating positions from its early years.

Of course, as may be expected from a coalition the size of the G-77, with a membership of countries that have widely varying economic policies, development conditions, and economic and political ties to developed countries, a major aspect of the G-77 coordinators' job is to try to mediate and settle the differences among the G-77's members in order to arrive at a common position.

These differences were of three main types, as an observer pointed out: '(1) those that are political and ideological in nature, (2) those between the more and the less advanced countries in the group, and (3) those resulting from the links of certain developing countries with certain developed ones' (Gosovic 1972).

G-77 negotiating unity and cohesion during the 1970s and early 1980s were fostered to a large extent by their common agreement on the right of each state to determine its own development strategy on the basis of the unique cultural, social and other characteristics of each country (Lavelle 2001). They argued that there is no one single universal model for development, no one-size-fits-all approach to development. This philosophical perspective found itself reflected some of the principles that came out from the first session of UNCTAD.[33] Developing countries, by and large, during this period were critical of the package of market-oriented economic reform policies that, by the early 1980s, were already being promoted by developed countries and the Bretton Woods institutions as constituting "the" development policy approach applicable to all countries regardless of development context.

But as more developing countries changed their economic policies to conform to the Washington Consensus model in order to try to adapt to and deal with the debt crisis of the early 1980s, UNCTAD began to decline in terms of relevance for both developed and developing countries alike. Also, from the mid-1980s and well into the 1990s, developed countries sought to 'rollback the international development agenda, which had been laboriously crafted in the U.N. framework during the previous decades. They interrupted the North-South dialogue and effectively kept the issues of international economic environment and its impacts on development off the agenda, thus frustrating those processes where the Group of 77 had played a major role in the past'.

As a result of the factors above coming into the 1990s, the G-77's internal cohesion and unity in UNCTAD started to break apart (Lavelle 2001). This situation was further aggravated when the Soviet Union, and along with it 'the Socialist alternative', broke up in the early1990s (Ricupero 2004). By the time of the 1992 Cartagena session of UNCTAD (UNCTAD VIII), the G-77 in UNCTAD was virtually moribund as a united and cohesive group.

The G-77's internal difficulties in negotiating as a cohesive and united group in UNCTAD in the 1990s were compounded by the fact that the UNCTAD secretariat was, by the early 1990s, no longer providing it with secretariat-type support.[34] Neither was the UNCTAD secretariat, during the 1990s, able to provide the G-77 with the systemic analysis and critique that was the hallmark of the Group's approach to UNCTAD discourse as the UNCTAD secretariat started focusing instead on providing developing countries with technical negotiating advice and support in the context of their participation in the GATT 1947 Uruguay Round of negotiations (which took place from 1986 to 1994) and thereafter (Lavelle 2001).[35] The G-77's low point in terms of organizational unity and cohesion during the 1990s is reflected in the fact that the G-77, as such, was not active at all in the Uruguay Round negotiations and thereafter.[36]

However, by the end of the 1990s and the early 2000s, coming out of the various financial and developmental crises that adversely affected the development prospects of developing countries during the 1980s and 1990s, G-77 unity and cohesion in the UNCTAD context started recovering,[37] spurred in part by the success of collective group action by developing countries in promoting a more development-focused trade agenda in the WTO. There was also an increasing recognition among developing countries that fundamental development challenges continue to remain that required developing countries to re-exert a collective effort to get their development partners to cooperate with developing countries to address these challenges effectively. The G-77's analysis and critique of the impacts of globalization and the role that the existing system of international institutions and policies play with respect to developing countries' development prospects also became clearer. This analysis and critique became the basis for a renewed interest in the recovery of the G-77 in UNCTAD as a major political actor in UNCTAD intergovernmental dynamics.

By the time of UNCTAD XI in Sao Paulo, Brazil, in June 2004, the G-77's preparatory process had become stronger, with the result that once again, UNCTAD negotiating dynamics became focused on inter-group dynamics involving the G-77 as the sole negotiating vehicle for developing countries.[38] Since UNCTAD XI, G-77 unity in the UNCTAD context has further strengthened. The 2006 process for the UNCTAD XI Mid-Term Review of the implementation of the Sao Paulo Consensus saw a G-77 that was more pro-active and able to effectively table and articulate group negotiating positions.

Regional groups within the G-77 were more active as well. One key factor that stimulated the re-emergence of the G-77 as a strong actor in UNCTAD negotiating dynamics was the formation of an active small ad hoc group of G-77 countries (represented by active and articulate delegates) coming from the various G-77 regions to support the G-77 Chair.

The intergovernmental preparations for the April 2008 twelfth session of UNCTAD (UNCTAD XII) in Accra, Ghana, are now seeing the G-77 also playing a major role in shaping the process and its negotiated outcomes. The G-77 has designated one of its member countries, Brazil, to serve as its coordinator and the lead G-77 spokesperson for the UNCTAD XII process. The coordinator for each of the G-77 regional groups (in 2008, Philippines for Asia, Argentina for Latin America and Caribbean, and Ivory Coast for Africa) work to ensure that regional group positions are developed for integration into the overall G-77 negotiating position after intra-G-77 discussions. Some regional coordinators, such as Ivory Coast for the African Group, are assisted by issue-specific "focal points" from other countries in their regional groups to assist them in managing intra-group discussions with respect to such issues. The regional coordinators sit and work with the G-77 UNCTAD XII coordinator during the intergovernmental negotiations. The lead G-77 coordinator and the regional coordinators are supported by the active involvement of many other G-77 members in drafting and discussing G-77 positions. At the same time, G-77 processes are flexible enough to also allow individual G-77 members or regional groups to also present their own positions if no intra-group consensus could be achieved on such positions.

Hence, as of this writing, the G-77 has come nearly full circle from its early beginnings in terms of being a major collective actor in international trade-related policymaking in the UNCTAD context. The revitalization of UNCTAD very much depends upon the unity, dynamism and the sense of purpose of the G-77. The recent effective functioning of some of the groups of developing countries in the WTO context is a good example for the G-77 in UNCTAD. The G-20 and G-33 have functioned effectively in WTO mainly because of the perception of the countries that are members of these groups of the threat posed to their economic interest by the aggressive stance and the rigid positions of developed countries. These groups joined with G-90, consisting mostly of LDCs, and formed the wider G-110 to safeguard their interest. The developing countries have realized that the most effective means of safeguarding their interest is to confront the dominant ideology moving WTO and developed countries individually as well as collectively, and to put forward alternative ideas and policy approaches.

Conclusion: Developing Country Group Action as an Essential Component in Global Trade Governance

As can be seen from the discussion above, the ways in which developing countries participate in the governance of the WTO and UNCTAD, the two premier multilateral trade governance institutions, reflect their adaptation to perceived and real imbalances of economic and political power, both in terms of the bigger international economic system as well as with respect to the institutional governance mechanisms of these organizations.

The experiences of developing countries in both the WTO and UNCTAD clearly show that in the face of such imbalances, stemming from and resulting in the widening development gap discussed above, further enhancing developing country participation and influence in global trade policy-making and governance will require the following:

• *Clear policy issue and agenda articulation* – Strong group action can only take place on the basis of a shared perception by the group members of having shared issues and a shared agenda that they are committed to and which they are willing to promote. In the case of the WTO, the rise and prominence of issue-based developing country coalitions and the ability of various developing country groups to work together across different issues in pursuit of a common development-oriented negotiated outcome clearly point this out. An important aspect in triggering collective group action in the WTO by developing countries was a generally shared perception of the imbalances that exist in the WTO's legal and institutional framework. In the case of UNCTAD, the continued relevance and legitimacy of the G-77 as the developing countries' negotiating vehicle to push and articulate their common systemic critique of the imbalances and inequities of the current international economic system also reflect this point. Furthermore, in both WTO and UNCTAD, developing country group action is based on a shared understanding of the need for a more development-oriented approach that addresses systemic problems to be undertaken in both institutions.

This shared understanding is important, especially in terms of continuously updating, fine-tuning and articulating a clear policy framework, a set of well-articulated policy objectives, and a clearly defined action agenda, that can be promoted in both institutional contexts. This represents an essential foundation and reference point for collective developing country group action in both the WTO and UNCTAD. This is a vital step in trying to overcome the intellectual and conceptual dependence vis-à-vis the North in which the developing countries have been entrapped. Today, the South faces the challenge of "intellectual liberation", which has to be undertaken collectively, as a serious, systematic and sustained effort by developing countries.

• *Coordination and leadership* – Strong groups in both the WTO and UNCTAD show that having institutionalised coordination and group leadership mechanisms are vital to the long-term survival of the group. This is clearly seen in the way that in the WTO, all of the developing country groups have established internal coordination mechanisms that allow them to designate individual members to be the focal point or lead for the group with respect to specific issues, and to report back to the group on such issues and suggest the actions that need to be taken. This is particularly visible in the regional or cross-regional groups in the WTO such as the African Group, the ACP Group, and the LDCs Group. The G-77 in UNCTAD, with its internal regional coordination system and the use by some of its regional groups of issue-specific focal points when needed, provides another example of how important good internal coordination mechanisms are for developing country groups.

Leadership patterns are more complex when comparing WTO groups to the G-77 in UNCTAD. In the WTO, developing country groups often tend to have no single identified "leader." Instead, "leadership" is often linked to the internal coordination mechanism of each group, especially for the regional and cross-regional groups. However, issue-based groups often tend to have de facto recognized "leaders" – i.e. those countries that are most active and provide much input and influence into internal group dynamics, such as Brazil and India for the G-20, Indonesia for the G-33, South Africa for NAMA-11. In the G-77 in UNCTAD, institutionalised nominal leadership comes from the G-77 Chair (which rotates automatically every year among the three regional groups) but in actual practice, the regional coordinators (which rotate among regional members) and various individual members often also play important roles in shaping G-77 negotiating positions and policies.

- *Working relationships* – Given the relatively greater role that human resource constraints play in determining the extent of developing country participation, the working relationships that individual delegates have with other developing country delegates in the context of group dynamics become very important factors in ensuring smooth intra- and inter-group coordination and action. Since most of the WTO's developing country groups are ad hoc formations, the establishment of such working relationships – which in turn often depends on the personal skills of the delegate concerned – become the basis for internal group trust and coordination. And although the G-77, as compared to the WTO groups, is far more institutionalised and established as a group, such working relationships are still nevertheless very important in ensuring that the G-77's internal coordination and dynamics go smoothly.

- *Having institutional support* – Full and continuous institutional support of the highest professional quality is essential for any multilateral endeavour, especially in a multilateral setting such as the WTO and UNCTAD, where developing countries are confronted with a complex, overlapping and interrelated agenda. This continues to be one of the weakest links in strengthening collective group action by developing countries. Creating, financing, staffing and running such an institution presents a number of problems that have earlier frustrated proposals of this kind. For example, despite the decision of the South Summit in 2000 to upgrade the existing arrangement of the Office of the Chairman of the Group of 77 in New York into a 'compact executive secretariat' and to increase the annual contribution of each member state from $1,000 to $5,000, less than a quarter of the 132 member of the G-77 have met their financial obligations and the secretariat support has not been strengthened. In UNCTAD, the G-77, as stated before, benefits from a small logistical support unit being provided by the UNCTAD secretariat and can also call, on an ad hoc basis, on technical advice and support from UNCTAD. In the WTO context, institutional support for group action is very much dependent on the willingness and resources of individual countries – especially those coordinating the groups – and a few organizations (such as the South Centre). Developing country institutions such as the South Centre, the African Union, and the ACP Group (all of which have small offices in Geneva) try to cover the gap in terms of providing institutional support to developing country groups in both WTO and UNCTAD, but are themselves hampered by a lack of sufficient human and financial resources. The underlying policy rationale which inspired the formation of the G-77 in UNCTAD in 1964 has essentially remained unchanged, and has been reconfirmed by events and developments during the last 40 years, especially during the last decade or so in both the WTO and UNCTAD. Indeed, today the need for collective and group action by developing countries is greater and more urgent than ever, for a number of reasons, including:

- The greater weight and importance of the world economy, and the related processes, for their national development and in general their economic policy and environmental space and sovereignty;
- The increasing complexity and scope of the development process, which no longer allows for sectoral and narrow approaches, and the multiplication of issues and challenges that concern all countries;
- The continued efforts by developed countries to dominate multilateral processes, institutions and outcomes, and, via these, the developing countries, their political and economic space, and their natural resources and endowments.

The experience of developing countries, individually and collectively, during the more recent period of globalization has only confirmed that developing countries need to be consistent and united in promoting their views and interests, and that to succeed it is also essential for them to join forces and pursue group action in most domains on the development agenda, including in the trade area.

In a world which is becoming increasingly interconnected and interrelated, and with a number of developing countries having made important progress and strides in development and economic growth, the collective weight of the South that can be mobilized today is significant and should be put to good use, both for launching major policy initiatives, as well as to counter the systemic economic and political imbalances that continue to exist in favor of developed countries.

References

Aggarwal, R. 2005. 'Dynamics of Agriculture Negotiations in the World Trade Organization', *Journal of World Trade* (39)4.

Barnett, M, and Duvall, R. 2005. 'Power in International Politics', *International Organization* 59.

Bernal, L, et al. 2004. *South-South Cooperation in the Multilateral Trading System: Cancun and Beyond*. South Centre TRADE Working Paper No. 21, May 2004.

Boutros-Ghali, B. 2006. *Reinventing UNCTAD*, South Centre Research Paper 7.

Draper, P. and Sally, R. 2005. 'Developing-Country Coalitions in Multilateral Trade Negotiations' South African Institute of International Affairs.

Gosovic, B. 1972. UNCTAD Conflict and Compromise: The Third World's Quest for an Equitable World Economic Order through the United Nations.

Iida, K. 1988. 'Third World Solidarity: the Group of 77 in the UN General Assembly', *International Organization* (42)2.

Lavelle, K.C. 2001. Ideas with a context of power: the African group in an evolving UNCTAD, 39:1 The Journal of Modern African Studies (2001).

Narlikar, A. 2003. *International Trade and Developing Countries: Coalitions in the GATT and WTO*. London: Routledge.

Ricupero, R. 2004. Nine Years at UNCTAD: A Personal Testimony – Preface to UNCTAD, Beyond Conventional Wisdom in Development Policy: An intellectual history of UNCTAD 1964–2004.

South Centre 2003. Institutional Governance and Decision-Making Processes in the WTO (SC/TADP/AN/IG/7).

———.2004. The Group of 77 at Forty: Championing Multilateralism, A Democratic and Equitable World Order, South-South Cooperation, and Development.

UNCTAD. 2006. *Trade and Development Report 2006: global partnership and national policies for development*.

———.2007. *Report of the Secretary-General of UNCTAD to UNCTAD XII – Globalization for development: Opportunities and challenges*. TD/413.

UN DESA. 2006. *World Economic and Social Survey 2006: Diverging Growth and Development*.

UNDP. 2003. *Making Global Trade Work for People*.

———.2005. *Human Development Report 2005: International cooperation at a crossroads – aid, trade and security in an unequal world*.

Walters, R. 1971. International Organization and Political Communications: The Use of UNCTAD by Less Developed Countries, International Organization 25(4).

Wolfe, R. 2006. *New Groups in the WTO Agricultural Trade Negotiations: Power, Learning and Institutional Design*. CATPRN Commissioned Paper CP 2006–2.

Chapter 14

IN THE FOGGY MIDDLE EAST: JUST WARS REMAIN THE NAME OF THE GAME

Ibrahim Saleh

Introduction

Throughout history, 'wars of religion' have served to obscure the economic and strategic interests behind the conquest and invasion of foreign lands. 'Wars of religion' were invariably fought to secure control over trading routes and natural resources. Islam has always remained in the eyes of the West as a totally strange culture. Similarly, the 'war on terrorism' purports to defend the American homeland and protect the 'civilized world'. But, in fact, it attempts to secure control and corporate ownership over the region's extensive oil wealth, while also bringing it under the helm of the International Monetary Fund (IMF) and the World Bank (Michel Chossoudovsky 2007).

Arabs themselves have perpetuated the idea of unilateral cultural import. Such preserved original identity can only exist within an impermeable cultural environment that is cut off from foreign influences – an idea that still exits among Arabs today and can explain many of the phobias related to globalization. This complicated situation has caused two parallel wars to be going on in the Middle East.

One is the military conflict and the other is the media mobilization affair. While the media covers falling bombs and fleeing civilians and from time to time puts a human face on the agony of a war so far directed mostly at civilians, it rarely covers its own reporting with anything like a self-critical eye. In this context, news media has emphasized the inability to process the crisis, with charges of bias on all sides; the media itself has become a battleground of warring narratives and interpretations. The question is not just of how to know what's true, but what you need to know to put rapidly changing events into context in order to make sense of them. This obvious chaos is now unfolding in the Middle East, both in the 50 year Arab–Israel conflict, or the five-year conflicts in Afghanistan, Sudan and Iraq, and the yet again in the dangerously unstable stalemate between Israel and its Arab neighbours. Decisions made in this haze often have unexpected consequences that make the struggles even more vehement. And within this current 'Grapes of Wrath in the Middle East', the term 'fog of war' is now routinely used to describe a state where political, strategic and moral choices in areas of conflict become shaded by the exigencies of human response to violence and an abandonment of an ethical compass that determines policy and behavior.[1]

'Fog' is the watchword of this war, with the lines between fact and propaganda being blurred on a daily basis. The demands of round-the-clock news ensure that military claims are being relayed instantly to millions without being confirmed or verified – only to be refuted later by reporters on the ground or by fresh military updates (Lawson, O'Carroll, Tryhorn and Deans 2003).

The 'fog of war' refers to the uncertainty that descends over a battlefield once fighting begins. The concept of 'fog of war' is attributed to Clausewitz, who receives the credit for the alliterative 'fog and friction', where friction refers to a physical impediment to military action, and fog emphasizes the lack of clear information (Kiesling and Eugenia 2001). However, the situation is further jeopardized by the use of both parties of a 'fog of war' approach to entangle news media in the struggle (to their own detriment, as the two rivals are intolerant and cannot survive actual exposure through media to the will of their populations) through weaving a web of dissemblance to moderate voices in each camp, while retaining strong control over media to divert the attention of the public on external factors, rather than their own oppression.

This is especially true when the repercussions of the just war media, a situation that occurs when media becomes a platform for justifying wars, and mobilizing the public towards killing, has often led to 'one vote, one time' in a region, where the majority of its media is quasi-governmental and distort news coverage in ways that advance government agendas; yet it has resulted in further escalation of the current hawkish extremism instead of fostering tolerance.

Note this example "And, to our dear nation in the Islamic Maghreb in general, and our people in Mauritania; the people of knowledge, patience and Jihad, in particular, I say: carry Jihad forth against the new crusader campaign with your money, selves, and tongues, and stand in one rank with your Mujahideen Qaida Organization in the Islamic Maghreb, and may you support and uplift them as they are the hope and the spear head that'll defend you and your religion (Saleh 2007)."

Such mass mediation of political propaganda framed in a religious discourse has turned the Middle East into a real hotbed of extremism and appalling deeds (presented through media platforms under the name of religion) by killing others and disseminating hate crimes and xenophobia.

Kimmage and Ridolfo argue in their report on the 'Iraqi Insurgent Media: The War of Images and Ideas' that insurgent media seek to create an alternative reality to win hearts and minds, and they are having a considerable degree of success. It is noteworthy that the insurgent media efforts have created an exaggerated distorted reality to convince the audience in the region that those insurgent groups serve their goals and get back to the bad guys. (Kimmiage and Ridolfo 2007).

There is a pressing need to explore this thought-provoking and challenging *Just War Theory* within the current foggy Middle East, by investigating the mechanism of 'slippery slope', when individuals and governments betray their innate moral frameworks to camouflage the real objectives of the military operations, while providing a moral and principled image to the invaders.

The *Just War Theory* has become the common dominator in any kind of socio-political and religious conflicts in the region. Such *just war* has its own dynamics; and new purposes, which were not heard of before. At this point, after years of contrasting and overlapping *just wars*, it became only 'natural' for the public to ask, 'Then, what?' In its contemporary version, the implication of the phrase *just war* faces a dichotomy between the western interpretation that calls for military intervention on ethical and moral grounds against 'rogue states' and 'Islamic terrorists' on the one hand, and the extreme fundamentalist movements' call for a real *Islamic State* that stops the western civilizing missions in the Middle East.

A major cause for the current dilemma is that only a few lay people are well-versed in the background and rationale of the controversial issues that non-Muslim polemicists or those curious to know about Islam usually raise. Being weighed down by life obligations, the majority of lay Muslims are not ready to research issues and prepare adequate answers substantiated with proofs from Scripture and authentic Islamic sources. In addition, the majority of the media have no patience and tolerance to listen to, and search for the truth as a result of the fierce competition, or out of ignorance. The result is that if ever any encounter happens to take place, it is beset with impatience, digressions, and disputes that lead nowhere.

The problem inside the Arab/Muslim world is aggravated because those who should be qualified enough to educate others are doing less than an adequate job, if not a really a bad one. Many Imams and volunteers who are in charge of giving the *khutbas* (sermons) at mosques or who act as spokesmen for Islam on occasions are amateurs in the field and lack specialized knowledge. Many of opinion leaders of those religious groups have not pursued formal Islamic studies as undergraduates, being dentists, physicians, accountants, etc without having real Islamic orientation. As might be expected, the mess could hardly be worse. Many of them too come originally from countries where the cultural level is low and Islamic teachings have been intermingled with sectarian views, societal habits, and superstitions which are far from real Islam.

What makes it easy for those to communicate their wrong, and sometimes fanatical, ideas is that they have the tool: fluent English. One major disadvantage for many learned scholars from a country like Egypt, educated at Al Azhar, for instance, is that they mostly do not have a good command of English. Hence, their voices are not heard, and their contributions are limited to written works that need to be translated, with all that translation involves in creating further misunderstandings. People who are learned scholars and who have a command of English good enough for them to be able to communicate exactly what they want are mostly lacking.

> An important feature of the reporting that maintains this audacious deception—not consciously but through an internalized sense of what is "just not done"—is to relay our enemies' "claims" of benign motives *as* claims, while reporting our governments' claims without comment, or as obviously true—the message, tirelessly repeated, gets through to the public and an important propaganda function is thereby fulfilled. This is called 'honest, factual reporting'. (Edwards 2002)

But there are timely questions that should immediately be addressed: Can we realize a regional arrangement to secure 'peace and stability'? But then, a related series of questions would start cross firing at this point: For whom and from whose point of view? For the poor masses? For social integrity or for the elite interests? Who will rule in the near future – the secular ideas, or religious ones?

This research analytically reviews the media fabric of the Middle East with its 3Cs – the Content, Context and Contest – to draw an empirical map of the sociopolitical and economic setting that led to the current status of the media.

Theoretical Framework

In this section, the researcher attempts to examine various theoretical frameworks in order to establish the basis for the research. This research involves three interrelated theories: *Just War Theory*, *News Framing* and *Global Opinion Theory*. A few frameworks work alongside one another in the creation of conditions that exist presently within the Arab Media with regard to the *Just War Theory*.

One theory under consideration is the 'Theory of Framing and Opinion Formation in Competitive Elite Environments' (Chong and Druckman 2007). The theory asserts that the issue of public opinion often depends on how elites choose to frame issues. These researchers attempt to also understand how opinion formation works in competitive mass communication (framing) environments. After extensive review of literature on framing and public opinion and studying control groups, they present a theory that identifies the psychological processes and contextual factors that determine which frames will have the greatest impact on public opinion.

Chong and Druckman (2007) have used the term 'frame' in two ways: Firstly, there is a *frame in communication* or a *media frame* which refers to the words, images, phrases and presentation styles that a speaker uses when relaying information about an issue or event to an audience. Secondly, there is a *frame in thought* or an *individual frame* which refers to the understanding of a given situation in an individual's cognitive perception. This refers to what an audience member believes to be the most important aspect of an issue.

The fact that the call for *just war* is dealt with in a one-sided framing is the dominant form used with no competition in the picture. Multiple frames, as suggested in the theory, will not include a debate style framing, but rather, it may be possible that multiple frames are created and projected to accomplish a larger frame within the same context, which may fit more into an agenda setting process.

The majority of the Arab public have agreed on the threat of the western world, especially the US; this notion may work well with the framing of the *just war/holy war* when addressing their dogma and ideology, especially when that mix of religion and politics serves the interests of all parties involved. The context affects the strength of the effectiveness of the frame. So, in which context have the *just war/holy war* image have to be presented to the public in order to form a certain image of them? There are numerous theories of persuasion that Chong and Druckman (2007) have adopted as having an effect on the attitudes by influencing the salience of the underlying evaluative process based on the contextualization of the target audience.

The second theory is the *Just War Theory* that provides moral justification for resorting to armed force. The idea here is not that the war in question is merely politically shrewd, or prudent, or bold and daring, but fully moral and just. It is an ethically appropriate use of mass political violence. Power and national security, realists claim, motivate states during wartime and thus moral appeals are strictly wishful thinking. Talk of the morality of warfare is pure balderdash: ethics has got nothing to do with the rough-and-tumble world of global politics, where only the strong and cunning survive.

There are two views of this theory; the first comprises pacifist, moral concepts that can be applied fruitfully to international affairs. Where *just war theory* is *sometimes* permissive with regard to war, pacifism is *always* prohibitive. The theory is probably the most influential perspective on the ethics of war and peace that has enjoyed a long and distinguished pedigree, including such notables as Augustine, Aquinas, Grotius, Suarez, Vattel and Vitoria. Hugo

Grotius is probably the most comprehensive and formidable classical member of the tradition.

The founders of *just war theory* are probably the triad of Aristotle, Cicero and Augustine. Many values have been codified into contemporary international laws governing armed conflict, which are doubly influential, dominating both moral and legal discourse surrounding war that sets the tone, and the parameters, for the great debate. *Just war theory* can be meaningfully divided into three parts, which in the literature are referred to, for the sake of convenience, in Latin. These parts are: 1) *jus ad bellum*, which concerns the justice of resorting to war in the first place; 2) *jus in bello*, which concerns the justice of conduct within war, after it has begun; and 3) *jus post bellum*, which concerns the justice of peace agreements and the termination phase of war.

The Third Theory is the *Global Opinion Theory*, which argues that the construction of national identity derives, in part, from a negotiation between a nation's *Selbstbild* (or the nation's national consciousness, or the image its citizens have of their country) and a nation's *Fremdbild* (or the nation's perceived or actual international image in world opinion).

A fundamental question regarding expressions of national pride are whether they are directed towards a state, considered as a set of governmental institutions and arrangements, or a nation, considered as an ethnic or religious entity. For the measures of pride analysed here, the results suggest both factors are at work.

The traditional requirements upon the waging of a just war are ostensibly independent, but in actual practice each tenet is subject ultimately to the interpretation of a legitimate authority of global opinions that mix pride and nation, whose declaration becomes the necessary and sufficient condition through the priming of news frames. While just war theory presupposes that some acts are absolutely wrong, it also implies that the killing of innocents can be rendered permissible through human decree.

This conception is related to how nations are conventionally delimited, and leaders are conventionally appointed. Hence, any group of people could band together to form a nation, and any person could justify his/her deeds to protect the pride of the nation. The controversy here is related to the approach itself and could assume absolutism while implying relativism, the stance being paradoxical and hence rationally untenable (Calhoun 2001).

Surprisingly, such a *just war theory* was advocated by adversaries in opposite directions creating a real 'media hostile effect' that promoted news frames of 'egalitarian devils'. This approach serves to convince the public in the two campaigns that the enemy is 'evil' and that they are fighting for a 'just cause'. Both sides of the conflict use communication platforms in shaping the information environment that was fomenting the 'culture of death' that ennobled suicide bombers and the cult of terrorism. But in both situations, they define 'when it is permissible to wage war': *jus ad bellum*.

A new sense of direction in outreach policy is needed to counter the insurgent propaganda in a focused and effective manner that can deal with the current mediation of the *just war* mechanism.

The main strategy of *just war* is how to pacakge a news discourse that can cope with different contexts and cultures, and with different communication systems to take a stance with regard to the respective 'otherness'. Often, each side categorises the respective 'otherness' as one single and stigmatised/ stereotyped cluster (Saleh 2008: 186), amongst others reinforcing orientalism (Said 1978), occidentalism (e.g. Buruma and Margalit 2004), and conspiracy theories, as well as maybe leading to what Lifton (1967) coins 'psychic numbing', a sense of alienation and "an exclusion of feeling and disconnectedness" (Shor 2002; Saleh 2009: 161, 173).

Such approach of *just war media* reflects the pitfalls in international and intercultural media communication. One has to concede a serious lack of thorough knowledge of foreign cultural and linguistic systems and contexts in which media operate. Hence, advanced intercultural media literacy and competence are needed in order to achieve more than well-meaning intercultural understanding. Sometimes, it seems to be more appropriate to search for and accept/respect rather cultural differences (variance) than similarities (universality) in global media communication. This can help to undisclosed 'hidden news' and 'blind spots' in media coverage in order to avoid intercultural misunderstandings.

- It starts with *The Preliminary Stage*, during which the country concerned comes to the news, portrayed as a cause for 'mounting concern' because of poverty/dictatorship/anarchy;
- *The Justification Stage*, during which big news is produced to lend urgency to the case for armed intervention to bring about a rapid restitution of 'normality';
- *The Implementation Stage*, when pooling and censorship provide control of coverage;
- *The Aftermath*, during which normality is portrayed as returning to the region, before it once again drops down the news agenda.

Such media analyses follow Herman and Chomsky's assumption that news discourse reflects the dominant ideological and regime interests of the nation of origin. While the media's national origin does not determine its discourse, it does provide clues to how certain issues are discussed and certain terminology framed.

Past studies have shown how use of this phrase varies with nation, region and historical context, but that one may detect an international consensus forming when the meaning and agenda for world opinion converge across several nations' newspapers:

> Key forms in the political imagination of international order may be globally, transnationally shared and yet may have profoundly different significances and uses in specific, local sociopolitical contexts. On the one hand, internationalism is a transnational cultural form – a mobile set of representations and practices that has globally translatable currency and that is *supra-local* in its significance. On the other hand, internationalism is also an intensely *local* phenomenon and is likely to vary in form and meaning from place to place. (Mallki 1994)
>
> (Mallki, 1994:41–68)

The Cultural Media Context of the Middle East

The media in the Middle East exist in a cultural context that must be understood before they can be accurately evaluated. During the eighteenth and the nineteenth centuries, religion and the state were unified entities. At that time, religion was culture, ethnicity and social identity; hence, it was citizenship. This was the case for Zoroastrians, the Jews, Christians, Muslims and others, as each group tried to enforce a specific vision of its beliefs.

Most of the people deal with the media in isolation of the basic questions related to the nature of the relationship with 'the other'. The public in the Middle East faces an increasing crisis of cultural integrity and religious identity as a result of the ineluctable globalization of the media. Hence, there is a split in the social fabric between the romantic, sentimental attachment to the idealized beauty of the past and the rebellious movements against the rigidity of the classic aesthetic. In this new spirit of cultural revolt, both conservatives and liberals manipulate the media to project solely their own perspectives.

Territorial expansion was always associated with religious proselytizing and each religion was the 'religion of the sword'. In fact, 'holy war' did not originate from Islam, but through the Crusaders who gave a purported theological legitimacy to what was in reality a battle for land and trade routes. Hence, the public in the Middle East were torn between the internal subjection to dictatorial governments as well as the external cut off from the world due to the stereotypical negative images accusing them of savageness and barbarism.

Extremists interpret some religious concepts wrongly to reach certain desires in the name of god and Islam. Such interpretation uses the slogan of

'Just War' to kill and sacrifice others from different religions with the pretext that they complying with the Islamic religious doctrine (Saleh 2006)!

Some of these major extremist groups include Takfir wal-Hijra (Egypt/ Sudan/Algeria), Jemaah Islamiyah (Southeast Asia), Al-Gama'a al-Islamiyya (Late 1970s–present; Islamists; Egypt), Armed Islamic Group (Algeria), Al-Aqsa Martyrs' Brigades, Ansar al-Islam (present; Islamists; Iraq), Al-Qaeda (Afghanistan, Pakistan and worldwide). Others comprise Jama'at al-Tawhid wa'al-Jihad/Al-Qaeda in Iraq, Abu Musab al-Zarqawi's Sunni network, Egyptian Islamic Jihad in Egypt (active since the late 1970s) (Saleh 2006).

Demonization serves geopolitical and economic objectives. The terms 'Islamic-fascism' and 'Manifest Destiny' serve to degrade the policies, institutions, values and social fabric. The enemy in both cases is characterized as evil, with a view to justifying military action including the mass killing of civilians. It is not limited to assassinating or executing rulers, journalists and politicians, but rather extends to the entire populations. It purports to break national consciousness and the ability to resist the invader. It denigrates the peaceful Islam, or the respect and tolerance to others, manifested in religious or non-religious societies.

Undoubtedly, the inspiration is Iran as a full-fledged militant Islamic theocracy, and thus embodies a model as well as indispensable spiritual hope and fuel. Iran is also a leading supporter of Hamas, Islamic Jihad and Hezbollah. As a secondary priority, a *just war* ends state sponsorship of terrorism by Arab states out of political expediency. In this context, supporting *Islamic Totalitarianism* gains power through the advocacy of antiwestern media discourse.

The majority of people in the Middle East adhere to Islam and the religion has official status in most countries. Shariah law exists partially in the legal system in some countries, especially in the Arabian peninsula as in the Kingdom of Saudi Arabia, while others are secular like in Egypt. Besides, the majority of the masses adhere to Sunni Islam. Iraq is an exception because Shiaats are a majority in the country (60 per cent), while Lebanon, Yemen, Kuwait and Bahrain have large Shiaat minorities. In Saudi Arabia, the eastern province Al-Hasa region and the western provinces of Jizan, Najran, Asir, Al-Bahah and Abha have a Shiaat majority.

The average literacy rate is 66 per cent, one of the lowest rates in the world. In Mauritania, Morocco and Yemen, the rate is even lower than the average, being barely over 50 per cent. But in Kuwait and the Palestinian Autonomous Territories, the rate is over 90 per cent. Yet the absolute number of adult illiterates fell from 64 million to around 58 million between 1990 and 2000–04.

Gender disparity is high in the region, and among the illiterate, women account for two-thirds. Also, the gender disparity can be observed in Egypt, Morocco and Yemen. Besides, the literacy rate is higher among the youth than adults. It is 89.9 per cent for males and 80.1 per cent for females.

However, more than one third of the youth remain illiterate in Djibouti, Mauritania, Somalia, the Sudan and Yemen.

Media in the Middle East cater to and compete for their audiences' hearts and minds. Accordingly, regional history and its absence of democracy accounts for the pan-Arab media's content and their success among Arab populations. Audiences watch the news through a prism of individual and collective humiliation and resentment. As a result, the media portray the distorted reality created by this prism; and to compete with each other, they exaggerate the distortion. Despite emergent signs that regime reform may indeed be gaining ground in the region, regnant regimes have much to lose in terms of power and wealth, threat of bloody insurgencies by jihadists, or retribution from those who replace them.

There are a number of causes for the current media fatigue: weak economic base, high costs of production and printing; heavy political patronage; cultural fragmentation; geographic concentration; and low credibility and prestige. In addition, media laws and regulations are unclear, which has contributed to the media's subjugation to dictatorial government as well as their low standing outside the region (Rugh 2003).

Such mediation of *just war* facilitates the outright appropriation of the countries' resources, urges potential backlashes, and leads the way to inter-ethnic solidarity, bringing people together in confronting the invaders. This is exceptionally true due to the domination of religious players such as the Muslim Brotherhood, which has inordinate influence over Qatari-subsidized Al-Jazeera that served the media market needs of the so-called pan-Arab market.

This situation raises the question about the news media coverage of terrorist proclamations and acts. Such images fulfill terrorist agendas to frighten and intimidate the Western public and most importantly validate the *just war* as proposed by such movements through media in a sort of 'Muslim Jihad'. For example, Al-Qaeda is a militant, religious, ideological movement best designated as 'Islamic Totalitarianism', which enjoys the widespread and growing support throughout the Arab-Islamic world. Such movement uses continuous media messages through satellite and on-line to spread their perception of *holy war* to encompass the aggregate view that the world must live in total subjugation to the dogmas of Islam and that *jihad* must be waged against those who refuse to do so.

In reference to what was mentioned, the researcher quotes what Mundir Badr Haloum, a lecturer at a Syrian university stated in the Lebanese daily al-Safir (September 13, 2004):

The Islamic press searches for something that will absolve "Islam" of the crimes of the Shahada [martyrdom]... It is Islam that adorns television screens with body parts... Islam—whether those who praise its mercies like it or not—is the foul odor of the putrefaction of Islamic history and its stench... Indeed, we as Muslims produce terrorism, succor it, and praise it. We condemn it only when forced to. Motivated by considerations of power, interests, and diplomacy, we wear a pained expression on our faces but in our hearts we rejoice at the brilliant success—a large number of casualties.

The target audience for this insurgent propaganda is 'young, technically savvy, educated, and often middle-class and above', (Kimmiage and Ridolfo 2007). The dominant language of insurgent media is Arabic, and the leading delivery channels are Arabic-language websites and discussion forums. Most of the audiovisual material requires a high-speed Internet connection to download files running up to several hundred megabytes.

There are two groups of 'typical consumers' – sympathizers who seek out insurgent materials on the Internet in order to obtain more details than they can find in the mainstream Arab media, and the media professionals who create the content for the mainstream Arabic media. For the insurgent groups, the sympathizers are important as a potential source of financial support, while making materials available to media professionals ensures that their message reaches a larger audience (Kimmiage and Ridolfo 2007).

Islamists intertwined media discourse and jihad to justify every step, preparing the Arab audiences to accept it as natural, reasonable, & urge to direct and manipulate the Pan-Arab spirit against the US imperialist intentions in the region. The Islamic terrorists incinerated thousands of innocent individuals with an internationally labeled cause, the holy war, or the *just war* Besides, Al-Qaeda bombs civilians even inside the Arab states and threaten of fueling a global war, then releases video messages to announce its alleged justified causes.

Today, however, it is the truly pan-Arabic satellite channels that compete for, speak to, and shape the attitudes of the 'Arab street' away from discussing the main complicated and unpleasant civil liberties reality to maximize their market share (Alistair Campbell, 2004). For example, media scandals at Abu Ghraib and Guantanamo have strengthened the 'Just War' ideas of the Islamic movements as a result of the contradiction between U.S. policies and values (Haass 2005).

The Middle Eastern political arena is the preoccupation with Israel; which in turn, has lead to exaggerating the importance of one Arab actor, the Palestinian Authorities. The masses in the Middle East has also felt alienated and even felt stereotyped by the other non-Arabs/non-Muslims. For example, Anwar as-Sadat became a media star in the 1970s because he took the step to end the state of war with Israel; Housni Mubarak remains obscure to the west because he has taken no major initiative vis-à-vis Israel (Pipes 1984).

The publics in the Middle East felt betrayed by the global public opinion during the Lebanese civil war that began in April 1975 and continued over a decade later; it never a news item became in the global media till 1978 when Israel launched an operation into southern Lebanon. Then attention lapsed again, to be resumed only with the second Israeli incursion in the summer of 1982. It is worth mentioning the grapes of wrath in the Middle East as a result of the spiral of silence that continued through out the years of civil war, though some of them experienced thousands of victims such as at Tel az-Zataar and Damur (Pipes 1984).

One of the preliminary findings that gave way to the emergence of *just wars* as the name of the game is the realization by the masses in the Middle East that it is never the number of lives taken, or the brutality of the killers on their own is not newsworthy; Israel's presence turns the occurrence into a media spectacular. It is the bold reality that the majority of the journalists analyzing the Middle East neither have the language or knowledge, nor understand its culture and demographics, thus, media effaces the Arab presence, and thus removes today's the Middle East situation from all considerations of time and place.

Similarly, the current wars in the Middle East are often judged without regard to the actions of its enemies. During there is a mixture between using the news framing to promote a politicized religioius discourse that adheres to just wars, which makes the idea of Islamic nation coincides with the Arab/muslim pride. Such combination serve the goal of extremists to kill innocent civilians had been exposed to danger in the first place by their governments and external threats looking for oil. The real test comes down to the discrepancy between fundamentalists' actions and politicians' ideals.

This particular situation has initiated directly and indirectly alternative media channels to favor the 'Just War' and make the underground voices of dissent to be channeled into and through radical Islamist movements. When the regimes jail, torture, and oppress dissenters, they and their supporters often become radicalized. Al-Zawaheri, the second-ranking man in al Qaeda, for instance, became radicalized while jailed in Egypt (Lawrence Wright 2006).

Research and Methodology

This paper studies the interrelation between *Global Opinion Theory, News Framing* within the *Just War Theory*. Then, the research methodology is divided into three complimenting parts; the first includes the analysis of the news discourse of Nile TV International, government controlled Free to Air channel, prime time newscasts at 6 p.m. over a period of 90 days from Jan 1–April 2, making the sample include 450 news items. The second task is a case study of the cartoon controversy of Muslims' Mohamed in two Egyptian dailies over a time span of three months From January 15–March 15, 2006.

This study considered the two most circulated daily newspapers in an attempt to reflect different political and religious colors in Egypt. Such discourse analysis dealt with the whole publications during the designated time: the first is *Rosa l-Youssef*, a government owned and managed newspaper that projects the official mainstream media, and the second is *Al-Wafid*, a partisan opposition that is secular and neo-liberal.

Third, the research take show cases of *Just Wars* in the Middle East, through a qualitative approach, the nature of the news coverage of wars in different Middle East countries as in the case of Iraq, Lebanon and Sudan.

Discourse Analysis of Nile TV International

Diverting the attention of Egyptian publics is one of the astonishing facts that can be deduced out of this study is the conflicting interests in coverage between the media agenda and public agenda. The Egyptian channel has double standards because 39.65 per cent of the topics are related to broken news of either protocol news or soft news that are not related to the main public agenda in the region. However, the other less important priming of news is related to the conflict issues and utilizing the security aspect to mobilize the public. The Arab Israeli conflict comes second in position (33% per cent), which should have been prioritized due to the many socio-political issues involved. And the image of Palestinians is completely damaged in contrast to the official political stance of the Egyptian government, as the

Figure 14.1. Main Topics Included the Discourse of the Channel.

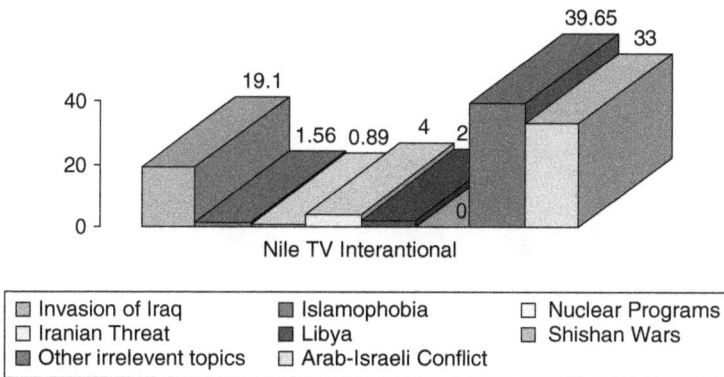

suicide bombers become the most commonly used term to refer to the Palestinians. Within this context, all facts are used to serve the purpose of *Just War* so we never have priority given to invasion of Iraq (19.1 per cent), while other things are neglected like Islamophobia (1.56 per cent), and nuclear threats (0.89 per cent).).

The Egyptian channel presented (33 per cent news items) about the conflict. Only (20.95 per cent) as a first news item, while second (26.7 per cent) and third is (25 per cent), however such statistical indication is misleading because it refers to only (33 per cent) of the total news items of the whole sample of (450 items).

The researcher divided it into five because there are many cases, where you find a news frame positive to one side without being negative to the other side. In reference to the study, there is a clear trend of using a negative perspective of each contender towards the other so one finds the Egyptian channel uses (43 per cent), while it offered only (9 per cent) as negative frames to Arabs. However, this

Figure 14.2. News Items' Order of the Arab-Israeli Conflict in the First Five Items.

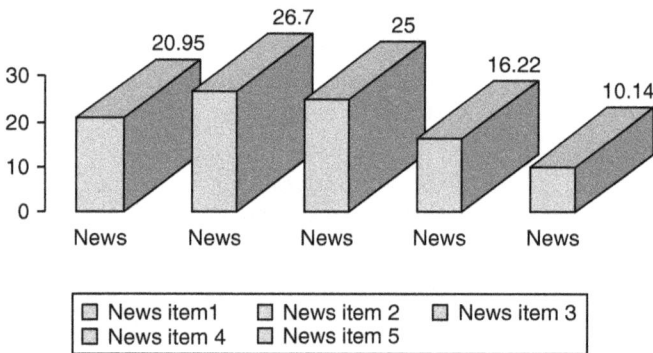

Figure 14.3. Relation between News Frames and News Items.

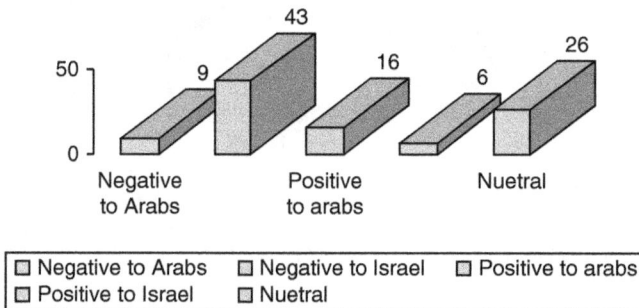

Figure 14.4. Main Topics Related to the Arab Israeli Conflict.

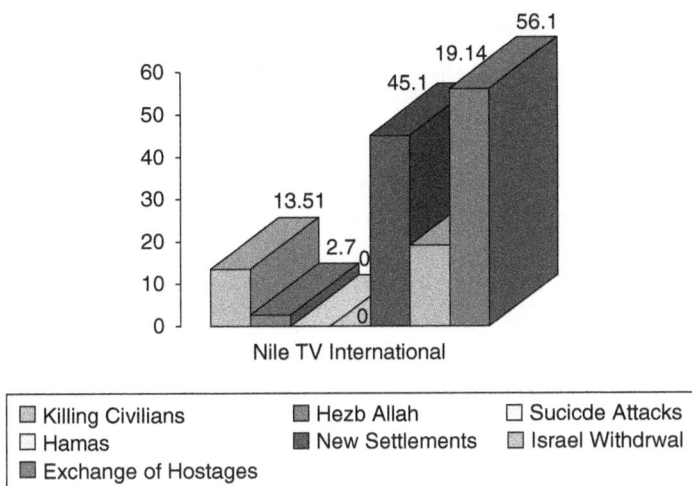

coverage was not accompanied by finding explanations to certain events, but rather just focusing on the negative side clustering all Israelis in one basket that contradicts with the nature of colors co-existing in one society. The channel never interviewed either Israelis or Palestinians and stopped at the level of using official statements. This situation did not help the Arabs to put things in context, and never defended rationally the Arab cause in the conflict.

The media agenda emphasizes a real dilemma of how news media serve political interests. For example, one finds that the news of killing Palestinian civilians in Nile TV international (13.51 per cent), while Hezbollah (45.1 per cent) and the utmost coverage was given to hostage exchange (56.1 per cent). Nile TV International gave emphasis on Hamas as a Muslim political entity and dealt with this issue with a superficial neutral way without giving a real sense of news, but rather a very diplomatic approach. Language used in the news items was rather a reflection of the current futile environment.

The Egyptian channel was entrapped with its static bureaucratic formal terms. Besides, there is an absence of differentiation between the use of Jews and Israelis, suicide bombers and martyrs etc. Such mobilizing weak discourse has certainly stipulated unintentionally the *Just War* approach, though the Egyptian State has clearly followed a very balanced political and diplomatic stance.

To sum up, the split between the public agenda and the media agenda has certainly contributed to the meditation of Just War in the hands of the fundamentalists. An extraordinary prominence given to things Israeli conveys the impression that Israel is the key factor in all aspects of Middle East politics.

Not only does this downplay other important factors, such as Islam and Pan-Arabism, but it also narrows the complexity of Middle East politics to a single dimension.

The truth is that Israel does not account for the volatility of Arab politics, the anti-Western policies of OPEC, the Iraq-Iran war or the civil war in Lebanon. Within the current media hostile effect in the region, news media has lost its direction in informing the public. In contrast, it has further widened the gap between governments and public on one hand, and the further disintegrated the Middle Eastern socities. Such perplexing situation has given rise to an extreme narrowness of vision, which in turn accounts for the great number of distortions and mistakes of journalism with regard to the Middle East.

Discourse Analysis of Two Egyptian Daily Newspapers

It is important to note that *Thematic News Frame* focuses on the specific incident or event understudy such as the cartoons of the prophet without referring to other related events such as the *Just War*, or Islamophobia that are considered to be Episodic News Frame. In addition, Mobilizing Language aims to influence the reader directly or indirectly to take a (positive or negative) stance with regard to a specific issue, while Rational Language is a logical approach to things through explaining a point of view or arguing against a point of view without advocating a certain opinion, or without urging the readers to take any stand. The opposition paper, Al-Wafid, had less coverage of the cartoon issue than the government-leaning Rosa-Al-Youssef (see Table 14.1). This situation is completely reversed from the coverage of local issues such as constitutional change, criticizing the president, or evaluating government performance. The ratio between reports and opinions is proportionate, although they differ in number. Surprisingly, the balanced frames of both opinions and

***Table 14.1.* Number of News Items: Episodic/ Thematic and Mobilizing/Rational Language**

		Al-Wafid	Rosa-Al-Youssef
Total		57	77
Items	Episodic	37	46
	Thematic	20	31
Language	Mobilizing	10	6
	Rational	47	71

Figure 14.5. Episodic and Thematic Items, Negative, Positive or Balanced.

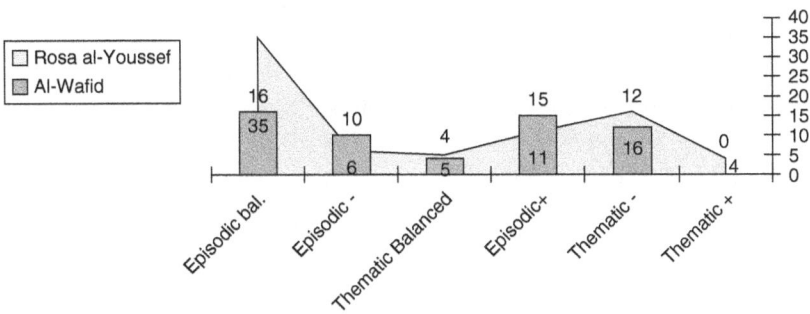

reports seem considerably higher in the government-controlled newspaper. Not surprisingly, the proportion of mobilizing language is somewhat lower in the government-leaning paper than in the opposition paper, while the larger part of items in both papers belongs to the rational language category.

The positive frame seems to be absent in the items with mobilizing language in both papers (see Figure 14.1). A few negative items with mobilizing language can be found in the opposition paper. Both papers published a considerable number of articles that were negatively framed with rational language as well as those from balanced frames with rational language.

The difference between thematic frames and episodic frames is a major element in the discourse analysis. The difference reflects the nature, scope and degree of clarity in tackling the issue. Both newspapers used episodic frames more than the thematic ones, in part due to the nature of the controversy. al-Wafid tended to use more balanced than negative frames, while Rosa Al-Youssef tended to use more negative frames. Episodic stories were more balanced than negative in both papers. Both only minimally used positive frames for reporting on this controversy (Gilliam and Bales 2001).

Surveying Middle Eastern Wars

Darfur Conflict

Overemphasizing the drastic nature of the conflict would have required more action be taken on the parts of the regional and international actors, but meddling in other states affairs is a troublesome activity and without clear international mandate, this can create problems.

Media coverage of the conflict in Darfur used words such as 'killings', and talk shows often referred to potential (or real) acts of genocide. It is clear that satellite coverage viewed the government as failing to conduct *jus in bello*, while the portrayal of the rebels supported a notion of *jus ad bellum*.

Invasion of Israeli to Lebanon Al-Manar featured many propaganda videos showing destruction of the country and the capturing of the two Israeli soldiers. However, LBC & Future criticized Nesrallah.

Abu-Dhabi TV could not compete with Al-Jazeera coverage of 'Wall to Wall'. It was very successful to reflect the Arab street that is hostile to the West and Israel (PBS 2006).

Al-Arabiya focused on the victimization of the Lebanese citizens (Kalb & Saivetz 2006).

Iraq War:

Al-Jazeera channel was the first to anticipate the war to land slide the failure in Afghanistan and control of the oil. While, the news frame used was 'A Mad cowboy playing with a rifle'. Al-Arabiya focused on the hypocrisy of the congressmen for supporting the war. However, Abu Dhabi had a discourse warning from the future repercussions in the region.

The three channels accused the Arab governments of submission, though they did so differently. Al-Arabiya did it subtly through screening documentaries reflecting the weak role, while Al-Jazeera used talk shows for clear stances pressuring the governments, while Abu Dhabi used scope enlargement by involving international players in this crisis management.

To assess this qualitative part, one can rationally state that terrorism is always evil, though terrorists also claim that the atrocities they commit are sometimes necessary. Nevertheless, the response of horror by Western audiences at incidents of suicide terrorism is often genuine, though it might be feigned sometimes. In that regard, using news frames mixed with *just wars* have usually added more stereotypes to the Middle East, and filled the majority public of disparities from the future awaiting for them (Haass 2005).

> The idea behind mass mediated *just wars* is not only scope enlarge the act of terrorism all over the world, but also emphasizing the intrusion of fear into everyday life, the deliberate violation of private purposes, the insecurity of public spaces, and the endless coerciveness of precaution. Nevertheless, many civilians across the region encourage the terrorists, by worshipping them as heroes. Accordingly, politicizing religion has been magnified with the clerics promise to terrorists with a glorious afterlife.
>
> 'Extreme Religious networks' indoctrinate the publics with Islamic Totalitarianism. Even civilians, who do not entirely support the methods

of the 'terrorists' are often sympathetic to and encouraging of their goal of Islamic world domination.

The smart way to keep people passive and obedient is to strictly limit the spectrum of acceptable opinion, but allow very lively debate within that spectrum—even encourage the more critical and dissident views. That gives people the sense that there's free thinking going on, while all the time the presuppositions of the system are being reinforced by the limits put on the range of the debate. (Chomsky 1998)

As a final note in this section, one has to admit that the Just War Media in the Middle East is overwhelmed with their military and technological victory from being an international bully, terrorizing the rest of the world. The problem is that nothing can stop the fundamentalists after tasting the bliss of technological perfection from inducing other wars when domestic issues become too pressing and diversion becomes necessary, except dialogue and understanding.

Conclusions

Since September 11, many people have remarked on the oddity of the phrase 'the war on terror' that quickly dominated public discourse. Many critics argue that at the time there is a legal definition of war, there should also be a moral distinction between warfare (a state function), and terrorism (the disruptive activity of ruthless individuals), which could underlie a tradition of thinking about *just war*.

One of the main conclusions of this study that it is often claimed that particular wars may be unjustly declared, use immoral means and concluded in a vindictive way, though these wars are sometimes necessary. In contrast, terrorism is always evil, though terrorists also claim that the atrocities they commit are sometimes necessary.

Many terrorists abide by what the liberal political thought presumes in the modern sovereign state having an absolute right to defend itself, which could use a suicidal war with incalculable global consequences as a legitimate form of self-defense. This complexity has urged different conflicting sides' campaigns to 'soften up' the public opinion through the media in preparation for an armed intervention as a just war approach. Hence, there will always be a dead baby story that comes at the key point of the Justification Stage in the form of a story whose apparent urgency brooks no delay, specifically, no time for cool deliberation or negotiating on peace proposals. As the news frames (Episodic frame) that include human-interest stories are ideal for engendering this atmosphere.

This conclusion negates the hypothesis that there is a general frame of reference within the country that would affect the national news media systems in the frequency, and the manner in which news frames construct the concept of world opinion from these components, especially when it comes to deeply entrenched conflicts regarding the influence of world opinion. For example, different mass media in Egypt have a tremendous impact on the prediction and assessment of the *Just War* in the Middle East, especially Sudan, Lebanon and Iraq in addition to the Arab-Israeli conflict; however it is well known that the news coverage is uneven with regard to how systematic it might affect early warning and monitoring.

There is an obvious 'media fatigue' in the Middle East and how the number and type of events reported in public sources change as a conflict evolves. This result reflects very high levels of aggregation distinguished only by conflict and cooperation. Such findings have two implications. First, the limitations of media fatigue in both broadcasting and in print news; this is particularly important in long-term monitoring. Second, much of the variance provided by media reports is found in the existence of the reports in the detailed content of those reports. The situation in Egypt is witnessing a dichotomy between media agenda and public agenda, as the Nile TV International has an unclear that is colored with passivity. This feature is not only related to Egypt but rather to the whole Middle East, where passivity enables regimes to commit atrocities against innocents at home and abroad.

The *Just War Theory*, in both its classical and contemporary versions, upholds war as a 'humanitarian operation'. This situation has stipulated the 'just' war, a cosmic struggle between 'good' and 'evil' making the real magnitude of enemy casualties and the 'collateral damage' to enemy civilians were covered, with a picture of war that is justified and holy. Fundamentalists mediate just wars on ethical and moral grounds against the enemy, whether this evil is 'rogue states', 'Islamic terrorists', or even the US 'neo-liberal colonization' in the region.

Such dilemma of *Just War Theory* has been embodied into the current foggy middle east, where media drives for a 'just war on terrorism' and the right to 'self defense against the evil on the other hand'. But neither sides really cares to define 'when it is permissible to wage war': *jus ad bellum*, nor stop the *Jus ad bellum* of building a consensus within the Armed Forces command structures to fight and eliminate the US dominance or succeed on the war of terrorists against the Totalitarianism Islamists.

An equally deep horror remains at the prospect of what is likely to happen in the months and years ahead with regard to the notion of 'just war'.

What will the extremists do with their alleged *Just War*? However, the fact is that these fundamentalists are now delirious in their military and technological victory, from being an international bully, terrorizing the rest of the world, now that its media power seems challenged by no countervailing power? What will prevent these networks from demanding more of such weapons at the expense of basic human needs, or from inducing other wars when domestic issues become too pressing and diversion becomes necessary?

Indeed, the current media in the foggy Middle East has followed despairing, sobering thoughts, where autocratic governments push for extreme media messages to ensure their control over their public, however such setback in civil liberties and absence of diversity and freedom has magnified the impact of the 'Islamic terror network'. And the antiwar movements against the illegal invasions were isolated, while the civil society organizations had swallowed the media lies and government media propaganda.

As Robin Wright explored this argument in the *Washington Post* 'Outlook' article,

> It's hard to imagine political evolution in the next twenty years that does not include the Islamists. They have established legitimacy and a following and you won't make them disappear overnight by supporting the activities of a small elite of secular modernists…you have to image a political space that has both. (Wright 2004)

Blowing the whistle of the *Just War Theory* is not a luxury, but mandatory as a commitment to justice and peace to be chastened, compelled to shed their complacency and wishful thinking. The researcher believes that this war for Islam is one for Muslims to fight. It is for them to recover their faith from the purveyors of terror. This won't happen until the public in the Middle East recognizes itself as an institution and a change agent by claiming their rights and obligations.

It is not plausible that widespread suspicion and hatred associated with the emerging fundamentalism have gained an increasing market share, especially among the mostly illiterate, poor, unemployed youth who comprise at least one-third of the region's population. Consequently, changes in the region are becoming bloodier and even more confusing. Bloody because so much is at stake for the regional actors, confusing because no one is quite sure who the actors are and what they represent.

References

Alterman, J. 1998. *New Media, New Politics? From Satellite Television to the Internet in the Arab World.* Washington, DC: Washington Institute for Near East Policy.

Azar, E. E. 1980. "The Conflict and Peace Data Bank (COPDAB) Project." Journal of Conflict Resolution 24, (1):143–52.

Azar, E. E. and Ben-Dak, J. 1975. *Theory and Practice of Events Research.* New York: Gordon and Breach.

Brooks, D. 2004. 'War of Ideology', *New York Times*, July 24, 2004.

Bull, H. 1977. *The Anarchical Society: A Study of Order in World Politics*. New York: Columbia University Press.

Buruma, Ian and Margalit, Avishai 2004. *Occidentalism. A Short History of Anti-Westernism*. London: Atlantic Books. New York: Penguin Press.

Campbell, A. 2004. 'I was wrong about al-Jazeera', *Guardian Unlimited*, September 15, 2004.guardian.co.uk, Online:http://www.guardian.co.uk/media/2004/sep/15/broadcasting.politicsandiraq

Cady, D. 1989. *From Warism to Pacifism: A Moral Continuum*. Philadelphia, PA: Temple University Press.

Cahill, L. S. 1994., *Love Your Enemies: Discipleship, Pacifism and Just War Theory*. Minneapolis: Fortress.

Campbell, D. and Dillon, M. 1993. *The Political Subject of Violence*. Manchester: Manchester University Press.

Ceadel, M. 1987.*Thinking about Peace and War*. Oxford: Oxford University Press.

Childress, J. 1978. 'Just-War Theories', *Theological Studies* (39).

Chomsky N. 1998. *The Common Good*. Interview by D. Barsamian. Tucson, Ariz.: Odonian Press. Dewey, J. 1916. Democracy and Education. New York: MacmillanPress.

Chossoudovsky, M. 2007. *America's War on Terror*. Montreal: Global Research.

Cochran, D. R. 1998. *Force Protection Doctrine: An Operational Necessity*. Newport, RI: Joint Military Operations Dept., Naval War College.

Eleven, N. (2009). Al-Qaida's Committee in the Islamic Maghreb (AQIM):"Claim of Responsibility for the Killing of the American Christopher Leggett, " Finding Answers (NEFA) Foundation, June 24, 2009 www.nefafoundation.org – info@nefafoundation.org Retrieved August 8, 2009.

Edwards, D. 2002. Burying Big Business – The Guardian, National Missile Defence and Climate Change, MEDIALENS MEDIA ALERT, May 22nd 2002. Online: http://209.85.135.132/searchq=cache:BtcDTfx37XIJ:www.medialens.org/alerts/02/02052 2_de_Big_Business.html+Burying+Big+Business&cd=1&hl=ar&ct=clnk&gl=eg

Elshtain, J. B. 2003. *Just War Against Terror* New York: Basic Books.

Fallows, J. 2005., 'Success Without Victory', *The Atlantic*, January/February 2005.

Gilliam, F. D. & Bales, S. N. (2001). Strategic Framing Analysis: Reframing America's Youth. Center for Communications and Community. Available (26 May 2005) online at <http://repositories.cdlib.org/ccc/children/005>.

Haass, R. 2005. 'Freedom is not a Doctrine', *Washington Post*, January 24, 2005.

Hill, C. J., Rusciano, F. L. and Fiske-Rusciano, R. 2004. *International Media Perspectives on World Opinion during the War with Iraq*. Paper presented at the annual meeting of the International Studies Association, Le Centre Sheraton Hotel, Montreal, Quebec, Canada. Online: http://www.allacademic.com/meta/p72750_index.html (Accessed 2006–10–05).

Kalb, M. & Saivetz, C. (2006). The Israeli—Hezbollah War of 2006: The Media as a Weapon in Asymmetrical Conflict, The Harvard International Journal of Press/Politics, Vol. 12, No. 3, 43–66 (2007).

Khawaja, Irfan 2006. Victory: Means and End, Symposium: Angelo Codevilla's No Victory, No Peace, Reason Papers 28 (Spring 2006): 7–18, 2006, John Jay College of Criminal Justice, City University of New York, US. Online: http://www.reasonpapers.com/pdf/28/rp_28_1.pdf

Lifton, Robert Jay 1967. *Death In Life. Survivors Of Hiroshima*. New York: Random House.

Malkki, Liisa (1994). Citizens of Humanity: Internationalism and the Imagined Community of Nations. Diaspora 3(1):41–68.

Mundir Badr Haloum, al-Safir (September 13, 2004): "Facing up to unholy terror," USNews.com. September 20, 2004. Online: http://www.jihadwatch.org/archives/2004_09.php
Pipes, D. 1984., 'The Media and the Middle East,Commentary, June 1984, Online: http://www.danielpipes.org/article/166
Rand, A. and Mayhew, R. (ed.). 2005. *Ayn Rand Answers*, New York: Penguin Group.
Said, Edward W. 1978. *Orientalism. Western Conceptions of the Orient.* New York: Pantheon.
Sabry, D. and Saleh, I. 2007. 'The Role Played By Qur'an Translations In Steering Public Opinion Against Islam In Non-Muslim Communities', Quranic Studies. Online: http://www.quranicstudies.com/articles/language-of-the-quran/the-role-played-by-quran-translations-in-steering-public-opinion-against-islam-in-non-muslim-communities.html
Saleh, I. 2006. *Prior to the Eruption of the grapes of Wrath in the Middle East: The Necessity of Communication Instead of Clashing.* Cairo: Taiba.
_____.2007. 'A Cat on a Hot Tin Roof: Arab Civil Society', *The International Journal of Not-for-Profit Law* (9)3.
_____.2007. 'Sitting in the Shadows of Subsidization in Egypt: Revisiting the Notion of Street Politics', *World Association For Public Opinion Research* (WAPOR).
_____.2007. 'The Cartoon Controversy in Egypt: Professional Disparities & Religious Disruptions' An International Analysis on Free Speech & Political Spin, Center for Advanced Study', *International Journalism* (1).
_____.2007. 'The Arab Search for a Global Identity: Breaking Out from the Mainstream Media Cocoon,' in *NEW MEDIA AND THE NEW MIDDLE EAST*, edited by Philip Seib, New York: Palgrave MacMillan.
_____.2008. The Bubble World of Polarization. Failing to Realize the Blind Spots in the Cartoon Controversy. In: Eide, Elisabeth, Kunelius, Risto and Phillips, Angela (eds): *Transnational Media Events. The Mohammed Cartoons and the Imagined Clash of Civilizations.* Göteborg: Nordicom, pp. 173–190.
_____.La alfabetización mediática en Medio Oriente y Norte de África. Más allá del círculo vicioso del oxímoron. Media Literacy in MENA. Moving beyond the Vicious Cycle of Oxymora. In: Frau-Meigs, Divina and Torrent, Jordi (eds): Políticas de educación en medios. Aportaciones y desafíos mundiales. Mapping Media Education Policies in the World. Visions, Programmes and Challenges. *Comunicar* – Revista Científica Iberoamericana de Comunicación y Educación. Latin American Scientific Journal of Communication and (Media) Education (special issue), 16(32), pp. 119–129. New York, Huelva: The United Nations-Alliance of Civilizations (UN-AoC), Grupo Comunicar, (UNESCO, European Commission), pp. 155–174.
Sanger, D. E. 2002. 'Beating Them to the Prewar', *New York Times*, September 28, 2002.
_____.2004. 'Pakistan Found to Aid Iran Nuclear Efforts', *New York Times*, September 2, 2004.
Schechter, D. 2006. 'The Media War In the Middle East Targets the Truth', MediaChannel.org.
Shaprio, S. M. 2005., 'The War Inside the Arab Newsroom', *New York Times Magazine*, January 2, 2005.
Shor, Fran 2002. Psychic and Political Numbing in Preparations for War. *CounterPunch* (bi-weekly newsletter ed. Cockburn, Alexander and St. Clair, Jeffrey), 12 August, http://www.counterpunch.org/shor0812.html 24 May 2009.
Uhlmann, M. M. 2003., 'The Use and Abuse of Just War Theory', *Claremont Review of Book*, Summer 2003.

Vlahos, M. 2002., *Terror's Mask: Insurgency Within Islam*. New York: Johns Hopkins.
Walzer, M. (1977), *Just and Unjust Wars, 3rd ed*. New York: Basic Books.
Wright, L. 2004. 'The Kingdom of Silence', *The New Yorker*, January 5, 2004.
———.2006. *The Looming Tower: Al-Qeda's Road to 9/11*. New York: Penguin Books.
Wright, R. 2004. 'After Grief, the Fear We Won't Admit', *Washington Post*, 'Outlook', September 12, 2004.

Chapter 15

EVALUATION CAPACITY DEVELOPMENT IN THE ARAB REGION: HOW MONITORING AND EVALUATION IS PERCEIVED AND APPLIED?[1]

Doha Abdelhamid

Introduction

Globalization cannot be merited on its right unless it realizes development by the people, and for them. Anti-globalizers are keen mostly on portraying many of its discontents; while pro-globalizers tend to emphasize the contrary (Stiglitz 2002). The ongoing debate on the global front bids for a pause and reflection about the 'winners' and 'losers' of the collapsing walls and borders leading to fast-track mobility of goods, services, benefits, costs and, notably, risks.

Development is all about 'people'. Countries which were able to infiltrate macro-gains to the micro-local citizens are said to realize this undertaking. Some others retain a classical view pertaining to the measurement of 'growth indicators' that lacked focus on the 'impact of development' policy, program and project interventions. Democratic participation, governance and public accountability are important elements that can catalyze development impact on the grass root citizen.

Juxtaposed to an open world vulnerable to contagious hazards, a constant rise of development 'monitoring and evaluation' (M&E) came into being more vehemently since the early 1980s. The Arab region continues to be at the dawn of development impact measurement despite its many riches. Many aspects of governance continue to lag behind, let alone the numerous attempts to globalize, modernize its state structures and reverse gear towards extroversion (Abdelhamid 2005). Genuine interest in the cause of development monitoring and evaluation is yet to come. This global public good component has to be considered and enforced as part and parcel of the desired multi-tiered global governance framework.

The Development Evaluation Gap in the Arab Region

Development thinking in the recent past has been strongly influenced by the importance of adopting a 'people-centered' approach. This adds to the growing consensus that development is all about enhancing individual freedoms, expanding human capabilities, widening choices, and assuring citizens their basic human right, while recognizing the intimate interconnection between the fulfillment of social, economic, political and civil rights (Segone and Ocampo 2008).

In the Arab region, development is reduced and measured in official announcements mainly in terms of economic growth and wealth accumulations with disregard to genuine development challenges, such as growing poverty, mal-distribution of income, new public sector management, a consensus on measurable reform roadmap, etc.

This can be proven by rewinding one's memory to a regional conference that was held last March 2008 in *Bibliotheca Alexandrina*, Alexandria. The conference represented the Annual Assembly of the Arab Reform Forum that came as a result of calls by the civil society and governments in the region at the then 2004-assault called the Broader/Greater Middle East Project, announced during the G-8 Meeting in Sea Island in 2003.

The reason for using the term 'assault' is that people of the Arab region 'perceived' this project as a dissipation of the Arab identity and language, despite cultural richness and diversity. It was, and is still, thought that this project meant that Arab nations would be engrossed in a terrorist-war zone upon the 9/11 aftermath. This led Arab leaders and the civil society to launch the Arab Reform Forum and to initiate reforms from 'within' the region.

The above background is laid to pave the way to the last March 2008 conference event in which the first tracking report of the 'perception' of the Arab intelligentsia (a sample of 494 exhaustively surveyed) on economic, political, social and cultural reforms in the Arab region generated a composite index on those fields for the first time (Bibliotheca Alexandrina 2008.). The following was reported – the overall Arab Reform Index achieved 52.2 per cent of the aspired reforms, broken down as follows: Cultural reforms assumed prime position at 57.3 per cent progress rate; political reforms at 51.2 per cent; economic reforms at 47.2 per cent; and finally social reforms (relating to income distribution, poverty and social safety nets) at 46.9 per cent.

A deeper look classifies Arab countries into 3 categories, no different from the acclaimed Arab Human Development Reports (AHDRs, which will be reverted to in the following lines): first, there was the group of oil-rich countries which achieved an above-average progress, comprising the United Arab Emirates (UAE), Bahrain, Kingdom of Saudi Arabia (KSA), Oman, Qatar and Kuwait; second were mid-rating countries which represented the majority of Arab nations including Egypt, Lebanon, Iraq, Jordan, Palestine, Syria, Morocco, Algeria, Tunisia and Libya; and finally, there were the below average human development countries in the Arab world, namely Somalia, Sudan, Mauritania, Djibouti and Yemen.

Not only did the Alexandria 2008 Arab Reform Report show development deficiencies in the region, but the AHDRs issued since 1999 and the Millennium Development Goals Reports (MDGRs) to date showed repeated shortfalls in the region in human development, on the one hand, democratic governance, accountability and transparency, on the other hand, and attached to them a feeble capacity of development monitoring and evaluation.

Of course, the AHDRs and MDGRs affirmed knowledge, technology and digital divides, gender, future generations and youth, climate change and water issues all leading to possibilities of the non-attainment of the MDGs by 2015. This comes in stark contrast to the resource abundance the region is endowed with, namely, youth/labor force, oil, agricultural crops and tourist attractions. The reports' series Check harped on the lost development opportunities faced by the Arabs and the need for more accountable governments (AHDRs 2002–2009; and AMDGR 2005).

Parallel to the conclusions drawn in the Middle East Arab region comes the global scene: the Paris Declaration in 2005 (Segone 2008) ratified by 116 developed and developing nations, 26 donors, and 14 civil society organizations. Of the signatories, nine countries were Arab (8 per cent approximately, and they are Jordan, Kuwait, Morocco, Tunisia, Egypt, KSA, Sudan, Syria and Yemen); there was a single Arab donor (4 per cent approximately, the Arab Bank for Economic Development); and there was not a single Arab civil society organization (0 per cent).

Despite the gloomy outlook above, a positive conclusion can still be drawn – the mere fact that Arab countries represented 8 per cent of total signatory countries contrasts with the fact that those nine countries represent 41 per cent of the total 22 Arab countries. And, because countries that signed the Paris Declaration agreed voluntarily to be subjected to 12 indicators of progress on aid effectiveness to be achieved by the year 2010, they were grouped into 5 major categories, viz. ownership of country development strategies; alignment of donors to partner country public financial and procurement systems; harmonizing aid disbursement plans on development program-bases; managing results through the institution of Results-Based Management (RBM) systems and tracking performance measures transparently; and both parties mutually accountable by performing joint evaluation missions to assess development progress and aid effectiveness (OECD 2005).

Therefore, it can be assumed that the nine Arab signatory countries do already have M&E systems in place, or 'thought/perceived' they had them.

Then came 2006, when 34 signatory countries around the globe subjected themselves voluntarily to the first baseline study of the Paris Declaration; of them only 2 Arab countries came forward to engage in the survey (6 per cent approximately). They were Egypt and Yemen. Both scored 'Ds', the lowest rating of all on 'performance assessment frameworks'; while many other African countries received better positions (e.g. Kenya, Ghana, Ethiopia, etc. were rated at a 'C;' and Tanzania and Uganda got the highest rating among the surveyed, i.e. 'Bs').

The M&E Network Architecture

The overall picture of the evaluation associations and networks architecture is as follows:

Figure 15.1. Evaluation Associations and Networks.

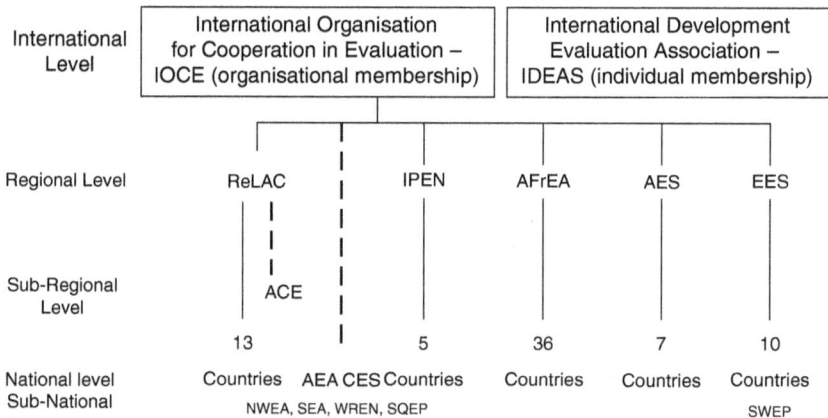

Source: Quesnet 2006.

Over the last few years the number of national, regional and international evaluation associations evolved from half a dozen in 1997 to more than 50 in 2007. Most of these new organizations are located outside Western Europe and North America, that is to say, mainly in developing nations.

Two global organizations, the International Organization for Cooperation in Evaluation (IOCE) and the International Development Evaluation

Association (IDEAS), were launched in 2003, with organizational members in the former and individual-practitioner evaluation members in the latter.

The following tier includes regional evaluation organizations such as Red de evaluacion de America Latina y el Caribe (ReLAC), 13 countries; International Program Evaluation Network (IPEN) [Russia and newly independent states – evalnet] – 5 countries); African Evaluation Association (AfrEA), (26 countries; Australasian Evaluation Society (AES), 7 Australian–Asian countries; and European Evaluation Association (EES), 10 countries; then follows the national and local tiers, respectively.

The observation drawn from this analysis is: *No* Arab society was included in the IOCE roster; an Israeli Association for Program Evaluation (IAPE) from the Middle East and North Africa (MENA) region is listed; the same goes for an organization named the Egyptian Evaluation Society that had a contact that is inoperative, that does not possess an internet website or a known mailing address.

One can easily draw the following conclusion for the aforementioned evidence: The Arab people are not only deprived of democratic governance, accountability, transparency, human development and lost opportunities; Arabs are also deprived from tracking their countries' development progress and, even worse, from what is commonly known on the global front as ECD (Evaluation Capacity Development) to a large extent.

A pressing question that comes to mind immediately is: How would citizens know that they have gained the fruits for which they elected their political party candidates, unless the latter provides them positive indications about the route treaded and the grip they would have on the direction that the future would take?

Who are the ECD Target Groups?

In order to do proper ECD targeting in the Arab region, which is currently very deficient in many respects, an ECD strategy has to be developed and target groups have to be identified clearly.

Literature surveys encountered tend to emphasize that the only stakeholder reported at length seemed to be 'governments' (AfDB 1998; DBSA 2000). A questionable finding, indeed.

An ECD strategy should define the ways and means to strengthen M&E skills of each of the following groups:

1) Agencies that commission and fund evaluations: These include development partners, foundations, government budget and funding agencies and national and international non-governmental organization (NGOs).
2) Evaluation practitioners who design, implement, analyse and disseminate evaluations. These include evaluation units of line ministries, planning and

finance ministries, national and international NGOs, foundations and development partners, evaluation consultants and university research groups.

3) Evaluation users. These include government, development partners and civil society organizations that use the results of evaluation to help formulate policies, allocate resources and design and implement programs and projects.

4) Groups affected by the programs being evaluated. These include community service organizations, farmers' and trade associations, business groups, trade and workers' unions and many other groups affected directly or indirectly by the programs and policies being evaluated.

5) Public opinion. This includes broad categories such as the general public, the academic community and civil society (Seegone and Ocampo 2006).

Further report on the specific M&E skills required by each group can be elaborated, yet the point that has to be made is the need to 'look at' and 'perceive' stakeholders differently from the way the literature normally does. Even more, 'evaluator–practitioners' themselves have to denounce the attitude of being self-conscious of their very being to consider any other group out of their circle as 'their stakeholders'. This should be replaced by a perspective whereby the 'evaluator–practitioners' stay as they are while their effective stakeholder has in-built M&E or ECD capacity as well. If this is managed well, Arabs, in the general sense of the word, will speak and practise the evaluation language of the world around.

Even Development Partners Err

Despite scarcity, a meticulous M&E literature reviewer would come across two donor reports, specifically produced by the United Nations Development Programme (UNDP), in the form of workshop proceedings held in Syria in 2005 and in Jordan in 2007. The findings from the review show that the reports comprised the views of the United Nations (UN) staffers in the Regional Bureau of Arab States (RBAS) in New York and those in the Arab region who voiced loudly the deficiencies existing in the UN evaluation system. Points were made on the limited capacity of in-country office staff relating to the M&E science, practice, terminology and methodologies required for outcome and impact assessments. They also found, in many instances, that program designs are defragmented due to the lack of robust logical frameworks linking policies to programs and projects in the way known as the 'policy evaluation cycle' (Abdelhamid 2006) around the globe, insufficient knowledge of appropriate outcome and impact indicators; same for lack of accountability of senior program country officers in headquarters' management.

Surprisingly, in the back of the minds of many Arabs, as well as the rest of the world, UNDP was 'thought' and 'perceived' to be the leading organization in the institution and in the 'application' of M&E systems; and how can this be negated while global, regional and national human and millennium development reports continue to be generated punctually and are, in fact, used as yardstick reference in the Arab region, and others, for periodic development metrics. Even this measure has cast skepticisms to the effect that once evaluated, those national, regional and global reports were considered 'output' measures of development, except perhaps some recent reports starting from 2002 that came to generate more 'evaluative knowledge'.

The courage shown by the UNDP in identifying its M&E weaknesses and in acting to develop its first evaluation strategy in 2007 has to be encouraged and acknowledged. Self-criticism and assessment stand to be useful tools as long as they are taken constructively to return en route.

Thus, the faint evidence of the presence of coordinated and integrated ECD effort and M&E practice in the Arab region (except, sparingly, some cases that came to the author's personal attention such as in Morocco, Bahrain, Kuwait, Jordan and Egypt) can be attributed to the mere recognition, again, that accountability and governance mechanisms remain a taboo in many Arab societies with some recent progress; and that sustained M&E cultures do not sufficiently exist except in a patchy manner through the vehicle of donor-funded projects mainly, rather than through well-designed and coordinated programs, with genuine stakeholder participation and mapping.

What Do Arabs have to Do?

A synthesis of recommendations elicited from a series of workshop/conference reports generated by the donor community and especially the World Bank (WB), which voiced the needs of government officials, civil society, research institutes and local universities in African and Arab nations in developing M&E capacities, seem worthy of careful scrutiny by Arabs and others interested in this region, that is to say, the donor community, the German Development Institute (DIE) research community or any other. They are as follows:

1) The main precondition for the development of a national evaluation system is country 'demand' – an evaluation system cannot be effectively forced on an unwilling government (the instance of Egypt[2] is a case in point). There are particular risks if the impetus for an evaluation system is donor-driven; this is not to say that donors cannot take the lead in 'selling' or 'promoting' the merits of evaluation systems to countries, but that until

and unless countries accept the strength of such arguments, or reach their own conclusion that that evaluation has much to offer, an evaluation system is unlikely to be sustainable.

2) Two building blocks for effective demand are the sensitization of key stakeholders to the need for and benefits from evaluation, and the building of awareness of suitable techniques and approaches.

3) Experience informs that the main barriers to developing evaluation systems in developing countries have been: lack of genuine demand and ownership in countries; lack of a culture of accountability, often related to issues of ethics and corruption; lack of evaluation, accounting, or sufficient auditing skills – there is a need to develop the supply of these governance-enhancing skills and systems to match demand as and when it grows; poor quality of financial and other performance information, and of accounting/auditing standards and systems; lack of evaluation feedback mechanisms in decision-making processes; and the need for the efforts to develop evaluation systems to have some minimum critical mass to be sustainable.

4) Another lesson of experience is that the development of an evaluation system should NOT be viewed as a stand-alone activity if the institutional framework and incentives do not support it. If the framework and incentives (carrots and sticks) (Bemelmans et al. 2003) are insufficient then this is a strong argument for ensuring that the development of the evaluation system is part of a broader initiative to develop governance; this approach recognizes synergies between performance measurement/evaluation and performance management.

Catalytic Factors for ECD Success

Experience has also revealed that there exist a number of success factors for the development of an evaluation system (Outcome Mapping (OM) or others), and that this should be pursued only if a number of them (catalytic factors) already exist or if there are reasonable prospects for developing or creating them:

1) One factor is the powerful role which a 'champion' ministry or agency can have in supporting, encouraging and pushing the development of an evaluation system. This requires a lead agency with power and influence, such as the Cabinet of Ministers machinery, a Finance or Planning ministry (as in Morocco, Kuwait, Bahrain and Egypt), a national audit office or a civil society organization, etc. Added to this is the development of a core group supporting ministries to walk the talk. The existence of an explicit and high profile country evaluation strategy can also be effective in selling the message, as can

the support of individual ministers or the cabinet as a whole – particularly through a sustained legislation, ministerial or presidential decree.

2) Sustained government (or simply 'champion's') commitment is also important (The case of Egypt is evidential of this – when commitment vanished, the system collapsed) (Abdelhamid 2004). An evaluation system cannot be developed overnight; indeed experience indicates that it can take at least a decade at the whole-of-government level to embed such a system in a sustainable manner – to gain an understanding and belief of merits, to develop necessary skills, and to set up civil service structures and systems that would put evaluation findings into utility. The counterpart of the need for sustained government support is the need for sustained support from development partners.

3) A whole-of-government approach (as the ones applied in Indonesia, Chile, Canada and Australia) has an advantage in achieving momentum and helping to ensure that laggard ministries endeavour to keep up with leading ministries. A whole-of-government approach might be especially feasible if a major series of reforms is being contemplated, such as major changes to public expenditure management (i.e. budgetary processes and decision making) in response to budgetary imperatives (Kuwait and Bahrain applied a whole-of-government approach within a Medium-Term Expenditure Framework (MTEF)/Public-Expenditure Tracking System (PETS) and after piloting) (Abdelhamid and El Tohamy 2004; Abdelhamid 2008). But a whole-of-government approach might be unrealistic in a number of developing countries – it can be difficult in achieving due to resource, local capacity constraints or both. In many countries a more achievable and modest approach might be to start with an initial focus on ongoing performance monitoring, possibly in particular sectors or ministries (Kuwait started by education in 2006, health in 2007, then moved to whole-of-government in 2008) in order to create a demonstration effect (Egypt adopted a pilot approach) (Abdelhamid 2004), and then seek to spread the approach to other sectors/ministries and to other performance measurement tools (such as evaluation) as opportunities present themselves to be created. This type of sequencing implicitly depends on perception of satisfactory benefits vis-à-vis costs across time sufficient enough to generate demand for answers about program outcomes and causality and these are the types of question which only summative/impact program evaluations can fully answer.

4) Next, there is a need to tailor the approach for developing evaluation capacity to the circumstances and opportunities available to and in each country or contextualization, so no one-size-fits-all.

5) The final lesson is that incentives are crucial to ensuring both that an evaluation system is developed and that evaluation findings are actually

utilized. While working with national government and/or else, it is important for those it is important for those providing technical assistance to understand the incentive frameworks in the country. This would typically involve conducting an institutional diagnosis as a precursor to provision of advice, and to ensuring that this work includes a close dialogue with the beneficiary. Zimbabwe followed a similar approach and it worked well. This approach should also examine the extent of evaluation capacity in a government or organization – it is often the case that governments, specifically (unlike private sector firms who are always under cut-throat competition), over-estimate the extent and quality of their evaluation capacity.

6) An assessment of who would lose if information were disseminated and became accountable has to gain the observant eye of the evaluator. He/she will have to postulate the effect on accountability and 'behavioral changes', the latter being a key area in OM.

7) This leads to the issue of who should be responsible for measuring performance – impartial outsiders, or expert insiders. The former approach stresses objectivity and independence, while the latter stresses expert knowledge and ownership of the evaluation results, and this in turn is likely to encourage learning by managers and their staff; therefore always emphasize the importance of learning from improved performance and emphasize as well accountability leading to better governance and transparency (Mackay 1998).

As an Arab, the author puts herself in the place of all Arab people and lists a set of points on what she thinks is needed from the global and donor community to enhance appreciation of the intrinsic value, perception and practice of M&E:

1) Arabs need development partner agencies to view the provision ECD training and technical assistance as part of a sustained, ongoing partnership and dialogue with Arab governments, private sector, civil society and citizens. The role of development partners cannot be neglected – they can build a conducive environment or hinder the development of evaluation capacity by this.

2) Arabs need development partners around the globe to work in partnership with national governments, consultants, civil societies and citizens in enhancing accountability through developing and implementing democratic governance programs with support components to parliaments, political parties, media; and open a dialogue with governments on passing data dissemination legislations and M&E action plans with funding support from program budgets.

3) Arabs need development agencies to offer technical assistance – through their advice and sharing of lessons and good practice, as much as the provision of funds for methodological development, dissemination and training in centers of excellence, distance or CD learning tools. This will help in capturing credibility for the trained and perhaps encourage the development of regional and national professional networking organizations. Donors can also help to build national and regional evaluation systems and literature in Arabic for ease of use and access. Their support will offer governments assurances and confidence on the robustness of reforms adopted.

4) Conversely, donors can hinder by excessive, conflicting or multiple donor requirements for evaluation. There is a particular danger that scarce country evaluation capacity will be diverted to satisfy donor requirements for the evaluation of development assistance activities, while neglecting the main reform area undertaken. Build a grand evaluation-capacity base to sustain and suffice M&E skill shortages in the Arab region.

5) Arabs need their development partners to develop new lending instruments, which provide multi-year soft funding for TA activities, and are likely to be better tailored to meeting country needs for long-term commitment and support in this area.

6) Arabs need development partners to coordinate funding pools by themselves (donors) for joint evaluations by governments and donors can be helpful in reducing costs and conflicting multiplicities of evaluations.

7) Sharing collective knowledge repositories in the field of developing ECD for closer donor collaboration and partnership in this area is important, as the Arab region lacks in documented track record of evaluation cases. This could take place via: the sharing of existing case studies, which are invaluable learning tools on country contexts; identification and analysis of existing good practice or promising practice countries; development of approaches undertaking country diagnoses and identifying their potential to put evaluation systems in place; and sponsorship or other support for regional collaboration including the sharing of experience via virtual discussion group networks, conferences, and/or workshops as the one we are in right now.

Finally, M&E is all about building a *performance culture* in the mindset which takes care of the *'perception-part'* of it, and in the daily *'practice'* that will infiltrate sooner or later to the qualities for and by all the people in the Arab region if persevering and collaborative work is put in place for the development future of the region in the light of the hegemonic power shifts in the globe and the new political economy for managing global governance prospects worldwide. Development M&E is indeed a public good of value no less important than managing global governance itself.

References

Abdelhamid, D. 2004. 'Painful Yet Rewarding: Paving the Road to Results-Oriented Budgeting in Egypt', Conference Paper, Parliamentarian– Government Policy Dialogue on Reform and Fiscal Issues, World Bank, Rabat.

———. 2005. 'Regulatory Competition in An Open Market World: Experiences and Lessons Learnt from the Developed and Developing Financial World'.

———. 2006. 'Use of Evaluation in the Policy Cycle', in depth workshop training materials, World Bank, International Finance Corporation, and Carleton University, Ottawa.

———. 2008. 'From Policies to Development Impact: A Modern Perspective to Economic and Fiscal Policies in Egypt', keynote conference paper, Center for Political Research and Studies, Public Policies Conference: Between Development Necessity and Effectuation of Citizenship, Cairo University, 16–17 March 2008.

———. 2008. 'How M&E is Perceived and Applied in the MENA Region?', keynote address to the 'Outcome Mapping Users in MENA Workshop', the International Development Research Center and the American University in Beirut, Environment & Sustainable Development Unit, Cairo, 9–11 April 2008.

Abdelhamid, D. El Tohamy, S. 2004. 'Fiscal Autonomy and Public Accountability', Egypt Human Development Report, the UN Development Program and the Institute of National Planning of the Ministry of Planning.

AfDB and WB/OED. 1998. *ECD in Africa: Selected Proceedings from a Seminar in Abidjan*, Washington D. C.

Bemelmans-Videc, M., Rist, R. and Vedung, E. (eds). 2003. *Carrots, Sticks and Sermons*. USA: Transaction Publishers.

Bibliotheca Alexandrina. 2008. *The Arab Reform Forum Monitor, Part I, the Report*, Bibliotheca Alexandrina, Alexandria.

DBSA, AfDB and WB/OED. 2000. 'M&E Capacity Development in Africa', Johannesberg, 25–29 September 2000.

Mackay, K. 1998. 'ECD: Lessons from National Experience', ECD Working Paper Series No. 1, World Bank, Operations and Evaluation Department, Washington D. C.

OECD. Paris Declaration, Online: (Accessed).

Segone, M. and Ocampo, A. (eds). 2006. 'Creating and Developing Evaluation Organizations', IOCE, UNICEF & CDEPD.

Segone, Marco, ed, Bridging the Gap , UNICEF, IDEAS, WB, DevInfo, MICS, Geneva, January 2008.

Stiglitz, J. 2002. *Globalization and Its Discontents*. New York: W. W. Norton and Company.

Chapter 16

UNEP INSTITUTIONAL REFORM WITH ITS IMPACT ON DEVELOPING COUNTRIES

Chengxin Chen[1]

Introduction

This paper begins with two main assumptions. The first assumption is that the United Nations Environmental Programme (UNEP) is the key institution of global environmental governance. Developing countries and their individual concerns play a crucial role within the discussion surrounding the reform of the global environmental governance system. UNEP's current ability to perform its functions properly needs to be developed. The second assumption is that developing countries have to promote the process of development as well as environmental protection. Therefore, they need to participate better in global environmental governance.

Following from the main assumptions, several guiding questions are of crucial importance. First, is institutional reform of UNEP necessary and what are the main challenges? Second, what is the impact of UNEP institutional reform on developing countries? What are developing countries' political positions on UNEP and its possible reform? Third, what will UNEP look like in the future and how can developing countries better utilize and strengthen the institutional frameworks that currently exist?

To answer the research questions, a multiple methodology design was adopted. The first method involved documentary research such as: collecting, analyzing, and summarizing related documents and achievements. Three sets of interviews were conducted with scholars and organizations relating to UNEP reform including IISD (International Institute for Sustainable Development), IGSD (Institute for Governance & Sustainable Development), Department of Geography and Environment at King's College and others.

Interviews with permanent missions of both developing countries and developed countries to the United Nations in Geneva and New York were also undertaken. In addition, interviews with the UNEP regional offices both in Geneva and Paris were conducted and a study of institutional reform models was made.

In Section 2, after a concise introduction of the analytical framework on which this paper is based, I will first discuss the necessity and importance of global environmental governance and the need to promote UN institutional reforms; then review the background and debates of UNEP institutional reform. Section 3 illustrates the current challenges from two perspectives. Lack of resources, lack of capacities, lack of co-ordination and the North-South gap have become severe obstacles for developing countries in their attempts to promote environmental governance and contribute to UNEP institutional reform. There are also challenges from the increase in the number of decision-making bodies for global environmental governance. Meanwhile, assessment of existing UNEP institutions which is based on three elements of analysis provides another profile of the difficulties associated with UNEP reform. Section 4 tries to to find out how to improve UNEP's mandate, its governance structure and its capacity to address developing countries' needs,by drawing on the experience of past models of institutional reforms for reference. Finally Section 5 will discuss related policy recommendations both to UNEP and developing countries for current reform debates and possible future arrangements for global environmental governance in a harmonious world order.

Background and Summary of UNEP Institutional Reform

Global Environmental Governance

Global governance institutional reforms are indispensable to developing countries' future position in a globalized world. A major priority for developing countries in facilitating their contribution to global governance is to enhance their capacity to construct the norms, rules and laws of global governance. As the sum of organizations, policy instruments, financing mechanisms, rules, procedures and norms that regulate the processes of global environmental protection,[2] global environmental governance is taking shape in a complex structural system with multinational corporations interacting in trans-national standard setting networks.

Existing environmental institutions like UNEP have achieved a great deal in reducing the speed with which environmental degradation is proceeding, but there is still a number of pressing environmental problems prevailing throughout the world. These include air and water pollution, the loss of biological diversity, desertification and climate change. Furthermore, accelerated globalization has caused an increase in the number of cross-border environmental problems. The challenges of environmental governance are vast in extent and still growing. It is ironic that as the evidence for environmental degradation becomes more convincing, the political will for action becomes weaker. The key reason for this is the fragmented system of global environmental governance that lacks wide-spread structural stability.

What is more, developing countries continue to face the challenges of development and environmental protection. Environmental threats severely affect developing countries. Therefore, it is essential to clarify who the key players are in present global environmental governance and which governance functions they perform best in terms of particular environmental threats.

The Need of Promoting UN Institutional Reforms

Considering the change of geopolitics and economics in developing countries, a stronger, streamlined, accountable and effective UN system is required to respond effectively to the needs of the south. Developing countries have not been able to participate effectively in a coordinated manner in the UN due to a lack of technical and financial resources. Reform would need to include updated policies, modern systems, streamlined means of delivery and prioritizations while simultaneously emphasizing and reviewing outputs. Change is needed within the UN's agencies internal systems and intergovernmental bodies. Surely the precondition for reform includes the restoration of the UN as the central institution for global governance and the democratization of UN's decision-making process.

Historical Review and Current Situation of UNEP Institutional Reform

It has generally been recognized that the proliferation of environmental agreements, institutions, mechanisms and processes has exacerbated the fragmentation of global environmental governance. This can be readily observed from a historical review.

In 1972, UNEP was created and meant to be 'a central coordinating mechanism in the United Nations to provide political and conceptual leadership, to assess the state of the global environment and to contemplate methods of avoiding or reducing global environmental risk and of working out joint norms'. In 1998, the Environmental Management Group (EMG) was set up within UNEP largely for the purpose of reporting to the World Summit on Sustainable Development. Since then, EMG has been providing services related to environmental site assessments, soil and groundwater assessments, environmental compliance, indoor environmental quality, indoor air quality, mould and water intrusion, asbestos, lead-based paint, and environmental training. In reality, this process has not yet brought about the required cohesion to the international governance of environmental issues.

In 2003, a French proposal was presented to the 58th Session of the UN General Assembly that detailed the creation of a United Nations Environment Organization (UNEO). An informal working group was subsequently set up in New York to facilitate dialogue between governments on UNEP reform. In 2004, the 8th Special Session of the Governing Council/Global Ministerial Environment Forum addressed the issue of global environmental governance as a follow-up to the 22nd regular session of the Governing Council. In 2006, the High-level Panel on UN System-wide Coherence in the Areas of Development, Humanitarian Assistance, and the Environment, made a number of recommendations for strengthening international environmental governance and for making it more logical and effective. In 2007, the UNEP Governing Council/Global Ministerial Forum agreed on an enhanced programme to reduce health and environmental threats from toxic mercury pollution, supported by 140 governments. UNEP also revised its institutional functions by working in alliance with other international organizations including the International Olympic Committee and nation-states. One interesting example of this refers to Beijing. After a review of studies and technical assessments by the Olympic organizers, as well as field visits to China by UNEP and communications with relevant NGOs, UNEP concluded in a report, that 'considerable effort has gone into fulfilling the letter and spirit of the promise by the Beijing Olympic Games Organizing Committee (BOCOG) to deliver a 'Green Olympics'.[3]

Current Challenges

Challenges for Developing Countries

Lack of Resources and Capacities

Developing countries require continued assistance from developed countries in terms of technology support and capacity building initiatives to respond effectively to environmental challenges. However, worldwide financial resources allocated to environmental issues are scarce. To add to this problem, a significant portion of the available resources come from voluntary contributions and are therefore unpredictable.

Another impediment for developing countries is the lack of capacities to build and maintain strong environmental institutions, lack of capacities to set up effective environment monitoring and implementation schemes, lack of capacities to create a strong scientific knowledge base for environmental policy, and lack of capacities to fully integrate environmental concerns into Poverty Reduction Strategies and other related documents.

Some developing countries perceive the current system of international environmental governance as unbalanced in the sense that the agenda is mainly driven by northern countries and does not sufficiently address the specific needs of developing countries.

Lack of Coordination

The current international system is comprised of a wide variety of institutions and activities that are sometimes uncoordinated and it does not adequately take advantage of synergies. While different key players have their own mandates, implementation of these mandates often disregards optimum use of scarce resources. The rapid increase of multilateral environmental agreements (MEAs) may result in the danger of some contradictory frameworks, particularly in regards to interconnected issues.

UNEP is responsible for providing general policy guidance for the direction and coordination of environmental policies within the UN system. However, its resources and authority are generally regarded as insufficient to adequately fulfil this mandate. The Commission on Sustainable Development has also not been able to overcome the co-ordination deficits.

Challenges from the Increase of Decision Making Bodies for Global Environmental Governance

The increase of decision-making bodies for global environmental governance could also add insult to injury and make the current situation in developing countries more difficult with regard to the following aspects: to undertake and monitor the implementation of all agreements and conventions on the national level; to ensure coherence among strategies derived from different agreements and approaches; to negotiate and participate actively in the decision making processes; to respond to the growing demand of monitoring and reporting.

Assessment of Exisiting UNEP Activities

UNEP is entrusted by member states with responsibilities for policy co-ordination as well as capacity building and providing technical support to developing countries. UNEP also supports international negotiations on environmental issues and provides reliable scientific information. With its modest resources, UNEP has operated a remarkably varied and important set of programmes. A point of interest is the fact that UNEP has never been systematically reviewed externally.

At present, UNEP lacks the resources to perform all its governance functions effectively and to pressure states to pursue environmentally sustainable policies. It seems to be widely recognized that UNEP cannot perform all its assigned tasks, and some argue that it should concentrate on its scientific function and coordinate science-related activities throughout the UN system (Hass et al 2004).[4] They propose that UNEP should oversee environmental monitoring, and provide the accumulated data to the international community through various channels. If monitoring activities were spread across environmental issues, it would be possible to improve economic efficiency and accelerate the flow of early warning information.[5]

Debates on Upgrading UNEP

In the beginning, UNEP was primarily coordinating national governments in negotiations on international conventions regarding issues such as: climate change, chemical products, etc. So for a while, UNEP functioned as a mechanism for consolidating common understanding and raising people's awareness of environmental protection through analysis and forecasts. Going beyond this institutional purpose, quite a few proposals have called for a full-fledged environmental organization (EO) within or outside the UN.[6] The EO would have its own legal identity, and would contain a general assembly, executive structure and secretariat. It would incorporate UNEP and GMEF and take up UNEP's mandate with respect to its normative function. There would still exist counter-productive aspects of these proposals such as:[7]

1) A large number of existing organizations are already performing environmental activities. Therefore, the new specialized agency would be one among many and would create counterproductive competition. Moreover, existing organizations would have traditions and well-established relations with constituencies within national and international bureaucracies. A new specialized body would therefore not be well-placed to exercise leadership or coordinating functions.

2) A widespread dissatisfaction among many developed countries with UN agencies has taken hold since the 1970s, especially in the United States. They are viewed as unnecessarily hierarchical, bureaucratic, and cumbersome, impeding initiative, flexibility, and expertise that are deemed necessary in the emerging environmental field. The unwieldy administrative and governing arrangements within a new UN agency could not be deployed quickly enough to respond to emerging issues. In addition, the rigid staffing practices

are counterproductive for the recruitment of a secretariat with the necessary skills and qualifications.

3) Environment is an integral issue that should not be relegated to one single agency responsible for just this one sector. In fact, the establishment of a specialized agency for environment was deemed unbeneficial because its focus on the environment as another "sector" would marginalize it. The core functions could "only be performed at the international level by a body which is not tied to any individual sectoral or operational responsibilities and is able to take an objective overall view of the technical and policy implications arising from a variety of multidisciplinary factors."[8]

As a programme, UNEP has the least amount of independence and authority in the UN hierarchy as it is a subsidiary organ of the General Assembly. Programmes are small and membership is not universal.[9] Programme budgets rely on voluntary financial contributions. Though the regular UN budget was originally expected to cover the costs of staff and fundamental operations, these contributions have only been a few per cent of UNEP's budget. Additionally, the proposal for establishing UNEP is unpractical since it disregards the current overlap within the UN system, and therefore neglects the root cause of fragmentation.

Institutional Functions and UNEP Orientation

UNEP was designed to be a leading co-ordinator with other environmental organizations. UNEP has long-standing experience with coordinating fluid and widespread networks around the world. Thus it may be capable of serving an organizational role to ensure that the multiple elements of MEAs are coordinated, to anticipate any gaps, and to keep members of international policy networks in communication with one another. It could serve as an 'air-traffic controller' for issues on the international environmental agenda, as well as for the multitude of associated ongoing studies and negotiations. The Secretary-General's High-level Panel on UN System-wide Coherence in the Areas of Development, Humanitarian Assistance, and the Environment recommended that 'efficiencies and substantive coordination should be pursued by diverse treaty bodies to support effective implementation of major multilateral environmental agreements'.[10] Rather than serving as a coordinating body of MEAs, a reformed UNEP could more effectively serve as a control centre for enhancing synergies and reducing disruption.[11]

UNEP performs three core functions: the first being knowledge acquisition and assessment – including monitoring of environmental quality, evaluation of collected data, and forecasting of trends; scientific research; and information exchange with governments and other international organizations. The second function concerns environmental quality management – including setting goals and standards through a consultative, multilateral process; crafting of international agreements; and devising guidelines and policies for their implementation. UNEP's third and final function is to facilitate international supporting actions – or what we now term capacity building and development – including technical assistance, education and training, and public information.[12]

However, from the very beginning, UNEP had to contend with larger political powerhouse organizations that had significant environmental impact, but no interest and no incentive to be "coordinated" by UNEP which is one of the youngest of all international organizations. To make matters worse, the member states have never honestly attempted to give UNEP the political capital to meet the mandate of coordination they so generously lavished upon it. Some have argued that the member states, particularly the more powerful ones, have actually wanted UNEP to fail in this particular task.[13]

The rapid growth in the number of players that now have an impact on global environmental governance has made coordination both more important and difficult. The creation of the Global Environment Facility (GEF) as a main financing mechanism, the various MEA secretariats and the Commission on Sustainable Development (CSD) have further undermined UNEP's authority and led to fractious territory wars and complex inter-agency politics.[14]

UNEP itself is fragmented and it can therefore be difficult to coordinate its 8 divisions; 6 regional offices; 7 liaison offices; 7 out-posted offices; 6 collaborating centres; a number of convention secretariats; and 5 scientific advisory groups.[15] During the Stockholm negotiations of 1972, there was general agreement that environmental action needed a framework, but countries were deeply divided over the appropriate institutional approach. The only politically acceptable solution was an organization that would "have minimal administration and not compete legally or financially with existing organizations."[16] UNEP was created to 'promote international cooperation in the field of the environment and to recommend, as appropriate, policies to this end, and to provide general policy guidance for the direction and coordination of environmental programs within the UN system'[17] and designed in a way that prevented it from fulfilling this mandate. It was, what Konrad von Moltke called, 'the organization of the impossible'.[18]

The failure of the policy coordination mandate has been evident since the creation of UNEP: well-established UN agencies working in the field of environment[19] refuse to be coordinated by a new, weak agency lacking authority. Later, new bodies were established that did not feel the need or want to recognize UNEP's authority (for instance,GEF and CSD) and this further weakened UNEP's role in global environmental policy. Although

UNEP has been very successful in catalyzing negotiations on new MEAs, it has been relatively unsuccessful at coordinating the policies and activities arising from the conventions once they are launched, as conventions become autonomous.

Institutional Strucutre and Member States' Support

Several structural features have inhibited UNEP's ability to actualize this impossible mandate:[20] Although it is more realistic to strengthen UNEP rather than to establish a new environmental organization, UNEP's status as a programme rather than a "specialized agency" limits its influence within the UN hierarchy. Programmes are subsidiaries of the General Assembly, whereas specialized agencies are separate, autonomous intergovernmental organizations with governing bodies independent of the UN Secretariat and the General Assembly. Its governance structure allows for the possibility that the needs and demands of member states may take precedence over its general mission. UNEP's financial structure which is considered to be insufficient, unstable and unpredictable, is overly dependent on voluntary contributions and, therefore, unreliable and subject to donor whims; UNEP's location in Nairobi—the only UN agency to be headquartered in the South—endeared it to the developing countries in its early years and has, in fact, made it far more South-friendly than most international organizations. It has also, however, bred a certain resistance and hostility from the North and kept it distant from any avenues of influence.

At its inception in 1972, UNEP was provided with two sources of funding: an allocation from the UN regular budget and the Environment Fund consisting of unrestricted voluntary contributions. Both of these financial sources have proved inadequate – an oft-cited reason for lack of action in global environmental governance. The financing mechanisms for the environmental institutions, however, were not intentionally designed to be ineffective and inadequate.[21] For many analysts, UNEP's limited financial resources is a key factor to consider when explaining its difficulties.[22]

The majority of donor countries (about 90 per cent of resources come from the top 30 donors), increased their contributions, mostly by small amounts, or maintained the same level of contributions. A few countries increased their payments two and even more than threefold in order to meet or exceed their voluntary quota of contributions and that of the UN scale of assessment. Unfortunately, at the same time there were a few cases where major donors decreased their voluntary annual payments, including one major donor country which did not make any contribution to the Environment Fund in 2006. As a result, and in spite of increased payments by more than 60 countries, the total

Table 16.1. **Contributions To UNEP's Environment Fund, 2000–2006**[24]

	2000	2001	2002	2003	2004 *	2005 *	2006 **
Contributions and pledges USD	41 mio.	44.1 mio.	48.3 mio.	52.6 mio.	59.5 mio.	59.6 mio	59.2 io.

* Includes pledges. ** Includes pledges and estimates, without estimate for Italy.

income of the Environment Fund is expected to be nearly $12 million below the target of $72 million for 2006.[23]

Regarding supplementary funds which include trust funds, trust fund support and earmarked contributions, UNEP has continued its work within existing partnership agreements with Belgium, Ireland, Norway and Sweden. UNEP has also concluded a new long-term partnership with the Government of Spain by signing a framework agreement in November 2006. This cooperation will focus mainly, but not exclusively, on support for the achievement of the Millennium Development Goals, especially Goals one and seven. Another long-term partnership agreement with the Netherlands ended in mid-2006 and is currently being evaluated.

UNEP, in particular, has been saddled with a huge and expanding mandate without the necessary financial and human resources. The first step in improving UNEP's management performance is for member states to provide it with a stable and continuous source of funding.

Model Study of Institutional Reforms

Learning from models of institutional reform is important for promoting UNEP reform. Over the years, many reform proposals have been circulated.[25] UNEP pursued internal efforts at streamlining its activities and achieving synergies amongst its various projects in its 1990 System Wide Medium Term Environmental Programme (SWMTEP).

The 1997 Task Force on Environment and Human Settlements, established by UN Secretary-General Kofi Annan, suggested strengthening UNEP by elevating it to a Specialized Agency[26] and improving its ability to coordinate activities with other specialized agencies. No clear guidelines were given, however, on how such coordination was to be achieved in the absence of strong political will by member states or the heads of the agencies. This prompted the Task Force to make the recommendation that an "issue management" approach be set up within the UN to address issues that cut across the mandates of specific institutions concerned with environment and sustainable development, such as

UNEP and UNDP (United Nations Development Programme), and to some extent MEAs.

Subsequently, the High-level Advisory Board on Sustainable Development was discontinued and replaced by the establishment of the Environment Management Group (EMG),[27] chaired by the Executive Director of UNEP.[28] The EMG was formed to assist in the coordination of activities between UNEP, UNDP and other UN agencies, Funds and Programmes and MEA secretariats, and to "adopt a problem-solving, results-oriented approach that would enable United Nations bodies and their partners to share information, consult on proposed new initiatives and contribute to a planning framework and develop agreed priorities and their respective roles in the implementation of those priorities in order to achieve a more rational and cost-effective use of their resources."[29] However, to date, its coordinating functions are not very effective.[30] A revitalized UNEP has also been supported by UNEP's 1997 Nairobi Declaration on the Role and Mandate of the United Nations Environment Programme.[31]

More extensive proposals have called for the creation of a new World Environmental Organization (WEO) which would possibly replace UNEP, and be given stronger and more centralized resources and influence. The campaigners calling for the creation of a centralized WEO assign it many of the responsibilities currently distributed throughout the UN system.[32] Upgrading UNEP requires less financial and diplomatic investment than creating a completely new organization. While UNEP has a record of institutional success and progress, its potential to perform when given improved legal status, more funds and more staff is promising.[33]

Policy Suggestions

UNEP reform could provide certain opportunities and risks from a developing country's perspective. Rationalization could lead to more effective management and co-ordination at the international level in view of the proliferation of MEAs. However, in the process of possible rationalization, attention should be given to ensure that budgetary provisions aimed at fostering capacity building, skills and technological transfer to LDCs and developing countries are not ignored. This is of particular importance given the relatively high cost of appropriate technologies at present and the fact that developed countries would be the main benefactors. An additional risk exists with the possibility of an increase in well-known environmental terms, which could place an even higher burden on developing country exporters and pave the way for a new form of protectionism under the guise of environmental concerns.

Policy Recommendations for UNEP

UNEP is the right kind of organization to set global standards and to coordinate system-wide environmental activities. It should be strengthened with a renewed mandate, improved funding and a general awareness for international environmental governance. However, while taken for granted today, UNEP's creation was less than certain in the 1970s.[34]

The salient point is that a more ideal system of global environmental governance will not be able to prevent environmental degradation unless UN member states fully commit themselves to making the system work. A comprehensive assessment of the financial resources that member states are ready to invest could be a proactive step in the UNEP institutional reform process.

Improve UNEP Institutional Form by Eliminating Competition in UN and Redefining Orientation

Do not involve UNEP in 'one UN' pilot countries. UNEP has neither the budget nor the capability to make a difference through activities on a national level, even if some of its member states demand such results and the Bali Plan opens a space for UNEP to get involved in this direction. They are pointless and damaging to UNEP's relations within the UN family. A possible exception involves capacity strengthening, but even this should be reoriented, as suggested below. That said, if UNEP is to withdraw, others – and in particular UNDP – will have to pick up the slack, and UNEP will have a role in ensuring that they do so.[35]

UNEP must not appear to be in competition with the very organizations it is supposed to be coordinating. Other agencies in the international system are better equipped to manage development projects and to consider the budgetary and political implications of environmental degradation when they are carrying out activities in their respective fields. UNEP should only exist in an advisory capacity in regards to these issues.

To become indispensable, UNEP should be catalyzing the most cutting-edge scientific work on global environmental issues (as it has done in the past). Technical competence and scientific prominence should be UNEP's key focal points. UNEP collaboration centres, the role of which would be to use UNEP's convening power and platform to galvanize leading scientists and scholars (including within academia, NGOs, the private sector) into undertaking relevant research and then to coordinate and synthesize the results of such research for policy-makers, could play an important role in this process.

As the principal environmental advisor to the UN Secretary-General, the UNEP executive director should be able to provide the UN system and the world with authoritative scientific assessments. Such an assessment should detail the state of the global environment, of ongoing policy initiatives and of unforeseen environmental challenges.

The scientific agenda and UNEP's resulting focus on global issues are important to all UNEP member countries, but they are especially valued by developed countries. Developing countries are more concerned with the link between poverty and environment and immediate assistance on a national level.[36] There is a need for change when considering that UNEP does not have and likely never will have adequate resources to make a definitive impact through direct, national-level activities. There are better ways to serve its constituency of developing countries such as overseeing a change in narrative. This could involve moving away from the "poverty" agenda with its negative connotations to a "prosperity and equity" agenda.[37] This new approach would focus both on the environmental underpinnings of prosperity and the search for it, and on the patterns of consumption and production that underlie prosperity. It would help focus the world community on the root causes of environmental stress, on the extraordinary, equity-denying affluence in some parts of the world. This fresh perspective would also draw attention to the consumption patterns on which that affluence depends and which make sustainability hard to reach. Second, knowledge production from UNEP should be made more inclusive by ensuring fair representation of developing country experts within global processes, and also by building developing country capacity for meaningful participation in such processes.[38]

However, if UNEP should mobilize the key developing countries behind the new directions it wishes to progress in, it must do so in a way that avoids this agenda becoming an "OECD plus BRICs"[39] agenda, serving the emerging elite and leaving the less fortunate developing countries behind.

Improve UNEP Institutional Functions by Selective Focus

This title means strengthening UNEP in key areas and strengthening key support functions. Improving institutional functions is related to improving institutional form that can be considered as the prerequisite of the former. UNEP should clearly remain the central hub for all matters related to the environment.[40] Advancing environmental mainstreaming is essential, which means that UNEP should be given the resources and the ability to "coordinate" the system where it is supposedly placed at the centre (especially in terms of coordinating other environmental organizations). UNEP's coordination mandate and functions should be realistically reassessed and clarified. In order to do so, UNEP will need to revert to its original focus on technical competence and move away from more operational projects that will be better implemented by other agencies.

The selected focus for UNEP should be broad policy issues, capacity building, and knowledge generation.

Turning UNEP into a leading authority within the UN system for scientific assessment and monitoring the state of the global environment would include the management of scientific assessment, monitoring and early warning work of UNEP; provision of policy makers or governments with authoritative scientific knowledge on the state of the environment and early warning; interaction with scientific work of MEAs and submission of integrated reports to political decision making organs; identification of emerging threats and information to the respective UNEP policy bodies, including information relevant for early warning purposes.

Concerning knowledge production, UNEP should move towards the advanced science of environment and supply professional data-based policy advice by setting the standard for the experts all over the world. There should be serious consideration for a system that supports research and the creation of knowledge, as well as its use and dissemination, and that takes into account the special needs of underprivileged countries. The facilitation of independent and authoritative knowledge assessments[41] is also required. In addition, UNEP needs to do a more substantive job on providing capacity building to developing countries especially LDCs and SIDS (small island developing states), rather than focusing all attention on training. The focus in its capacity building should be on issues of relevance to low-income countries. It should make it easy for these countries to undertake their own environmental research and assist the people in gaining the appropriate knowledge.

Broad policy issues for UNEP relate to periodic reporting on the performance of the global environmental governance system, and development and maintenance of a financial tracking system for the environment. Developing countries should be provided with additional resources for investment and policy implementation that will aid in ensuring sustainable growth. Providing sustainable development policy space for developing countries, setting up a structure to promote developing countries' participation and South-South cooperation on environmental issues need to be further assessed. Any solution has to be equitable and based on the principle of common but differentiated responsibilities and the respective capabilities.[42]

Improve UNEP Institutional Structure by Networking

Transforming the global environmental architecture into a more comprehensive and coordinated structure is an ambitious task that requires the involvement of not only UNEP, but other UN agencies, permanent missions, intergovernmental and non-governmental organizations and other interested parties. In other words, UNEP should cooperate closely with appropriate regional organizations, civil society and the private sector, which should be provided the opportunity to contribute to global knowledge formation, knowledge sharing and monitoring. NGOs as well as the private sector often have access to information and insights not available to states and have the potential to make innovative contributions for complex environmental problems. Networks must be actively and continuously sustained in order to be effective. Scientific as well as financial monitoring networks can be efficiently and effectively established by civil society. They should embrace the best practices in reporting and auditing procedures, such as social audits or efforts to monitor compliance, and combine them with voluntary initiatives such as codes of conduct.

It has often been suggested that UNEP should be given the ability to assess its own budget. This may be useful, but not to any great extent. A consortium of key donors, led by countries in support of meaningful global environmental governance reform, should commit to providing stability and predictability for the UNEP budget, at least for a period of around five years. Such a conglomerate of donors should take the lead in committing to (and encouraging other countries to commit to) separate caches of long-term institutional funding and shorter-term issue funding. While the latter tends to be tied to the immediate political priorities of individual donors, the former is necessary if organizations are to plan a coherent budget based on strategic global policy priorities. Last year, UNEP played a crucial role in the Bali Consensus which paved the way for the emergence of financial capabilities and a concrete governance structure. Eighty per cent of the funding came from the private sector – one more reason to demand higher involvement from business and civil society in the consultations.[43]

To the extent possible, UNEP should be encouraged to explore innovative sources of financing. While inadequate financing is one source of management inefficiencies, it is not the only problem. The financial basis of UNEP could be strengthened through a better balance between earmarked and non-earmarked resources and by the continued application of the indicative scale of assessment.

Policy Recommendations for Developing Countries

The strong concerns of the South in the early 1970s, that environmental protection should not be achieved at the expense of needed development, underlies the North-South divide then as it does now. Referring to this, Chinese President Hu Jintao enunciated China's propositions on climate change at the outreach session of the G-8 Summit[44]: 'How we cope with climate change is related to the country's economic development and people's practical benefits. It's in line with the country's basic interests'.

The developing countries must work together to place action on global environmental governance in the context of sustainable development, and to ensure that a well-articulated development agenda is incorporated as a central component in global environmental governance regime.

Integrate UNEP into National Strategies

On the one hand, in the context of UNEP institutional reform, institutional arrangements may fulfil similar functions in different countries, but their form varies from country to country, as well as within the same country over time. Likewise, the diversity of culture and historical experiences means that, while general principles can be identified, there is no refined model for improved, growth-enhancing governance and institutions. On the other hand, many countries have recognized that the linkage between environment and development needs to be established. Environmental issues have to be brought to the forefront of any economic model or development path; progress in this area should be accompanied by similar advancement on issues of development and social equity.

Developing countries need to integrate the systematic ideas of UNEP and effective measures of environmental issues which are from UNEP, into their own national strategies, especially long-term objectives, according to their characteristics. Developing countries should reinforce their efforts in establishing national institutions, legal frameworks and technical capacity to address environmental concepts, global standards of environmental protection and environmental data from UNEP.

Participate More Actively in UNEP

Developing countries should not be afraid that this system will result in unattainable financial demands, as countries will still be able to negotiate these contributions. The Bali Strategic Plan for Technology Support and Capacity-building could serve as the overarching guiding framework for operational activities of MEAs, UN agencies and the international financial institutions at country level. With universal membership and a reliable financial position, UNEP would be better prepared to serve as the platform for analytical work, norm setting, policy learning and coordination. Developing countries could therefore have a positive view on UNEP's future and put more enthusiasm into their participation. Developing countries should make full use of this platform to advocate their needs on an international level, to bring their own interests and consideration into dialogue and negotiations, and to get support at the operational level, which should be left to the responsibility of existing funds and programs. Meanwhile the Resident Coordinator and the UN Country Team should make full use of UNEP, to respond to the needs of developing countries and countries with economies in transition with regard to the strengthening of government capacities in order to achieve the objectives of the Bali Strategic Plan.

Strengthen Experience Sharing and Cooperation Via UNEP

Last but not the least, there is a need for developing countries to intensify efforts directed towards institutional capacity building, including through the exchange of expertise, experiences, information and documentation between the institutions of the South in order to develop human resources and strengthen the institutions of the South. Experience sharing and learning from more sophisticated models can create new opportunities for more development paths. In spite of different domestic situations, countries can learn form the mistakes and successes of others, especially in an international setting that creates a global pool of existing experiences. Regional arrangements or South-South cooperation may help countries to deal with some issues, forge consensus and establish a common bargaining position. In order to strengthen such experience sharing and cooperation, encouraging UNEP to establish a partnership forum to enhance and promote cooperation could be a sensible choice for developing countries.

References

An Update on International Environmental Governance. 2008. Report Paper, 25. February 2008.

Biermann, F. 2000. 'The Case for a World Environment Organization', *Environment* (42)9.

_____.2001. 'The Emerging Debate on the Need for a World Environment Organization, A Commentary', *Global Environmental Politics* February 2001.

_____.2007. 'Reforming Global Environmental Governance: From UNEP Towards A World Environment Organization', in L. Swart and E. Perry (eds) *Global Environmental Governance: Perspectives On The Current Debate*, Center for UN Reform Education.

Biermann, F. and Bauer, S. (eds). 2005. *A World Environment Organization: Solution or Threat for Effective International Environmental Governance?* Aldershot, UK: Ashgate.

Chambers, W. B. 2005. 'From Environmental to Sustainable Development Governance: Thirty Years of Coordination within the United Nations', in W. B. Chamber and J. F. Green (eds) *Reforming International Environmental Governance: From Institutional Limits to Innovative Reforms*, Tokyo: United Nations University Press.

Charnovitz, S. 2002. 'A World Environment Organization', *Columbia Journal of Environmental Law* (27)2.

Dodds, F. 2000. 'Reforming the International Institutions', in F. Doods (ed.) *Earth Summit 2002*, London: Earthscan.

Esty, D. C. 1994. 'The Case for a Global Environmental Organization,' in P. B. Kenen (ed.) *Managing the World Economy: Fifty Years After Bretton Woods*, Washington, D.C.: Institute for International Economics.

German Advisory Council on Global Change (WBGU). 2001. *World in Transition 2*. London: Earthscan.

Haas, P. M., Kanie, N. and Murphy, C. N. 2004. 'Conclusion: Institutional Design and Institutional Reform for Sustainable Development', in N. Kanie and P. M. Haas (eds) *Emerging Forces in Environmental Governance*, Tokyo: United Nations University Press.

Halle, M. 2007. 'The UNEP That We Want – reflections on UNEP's Future Challenges', www.iisd.org

Informal Consultative Process on the Institutional Framework for the United Nations' Environmental Activities. 2007. Co-Chairs' Options Paper, New York, 14 June 2007.

Ivanova, M. 2005. 'Can the Anchor Hold? Rethinking the United Nations Environment Programme for the 21st Century'. New Haven: Yale School of Forestry and Environmental Studies. Online: http://www.yale.edu/gegdialogue (Accessed March 2006).

————.2007. 'Moving Forward By Looking Back: Laerning From UNEP's History', L. Swart and E. Perry (eds) *Global Environmental Governance: Perspectives On The Current Debate*, Center for UN Reform Education.

Kanie, N. 2007. 'Governance With Multilateral Environmental Agreements: A Healthy Or Ill-equipped Fragmentation?', in L. Swart and E. Perry (eds) *Global Environmental Governance: Perspectives On The Current Debate*, ed. Lydia Swart and Estelle Perry, Center for UN Reform Education.

Meyer-Ohlendorf, N. and Markus, K. 2007. 'A United Nations Environment Organization', in L. Swart and E. Perry (eds) *Global Environmental Governance: Perspectives On The Current Debate*, ed. Lydia Swart and Estelle Perry, Center for UN Reform Education.

Najam, A. 2003. 'The Case Against a New International Environmental Organization', *Global Governance*, (9)3.

Najam, A., Papa, M. and Taiyab, N. 2006. *Global Environmental Governance: A Reform Agenda*, IISD.

Rechkemmer, A. (ed.). 2005. 'UNEO—Towards an International Environment Organization, Approaches to a sustainable reform of global environmental governance'. Nomos Baden-Baden.

UN General Assembly. 1972. *Resolution 2997 (XXVII): Institutional and Financial Arrangements for International Environmental Cooperation*.

UNEP. 1981. 'Development and Environment: The Founex Report: In Defence of the Earth', *The Basic Texts on Environment*. UNEP Executive Series 1, Nairobi.

————.1997b. Nairobi Declaration on the Role and Mandate of UNEP (UNEP/GC19/1/1997). Adopted during the Nineteenth Session of the Governing Council.

————.2001. Proposals of the President of the United Nations Environment Programme Governing Council for Consideration by the Open-Ended Intergovernmental Group of Ministers or Their Representatives on International Environmental Governance (presented at the fourth meeting of this group, Montreal, 30 November—1 December 2001), UN Doc. UNEP/IGM/UNEP/IGM/4/2 of 12 November, 2001.

————.2001a. Implementing the Clustering Strategy for Multilateral Environmental Agreements—A Framework. Background Paper for the Fourth Meeting of the Open-Ended Intergovernmental Group of Ministers or Their Representatives on

International Environmental Governance, Montreal, 30 November—1 December 2001, UN Doc. UNEP/IGM/4/4 of 16 November, 2001a.

————.2001b. International Environmental Governance: Report by the Executive Director. Prepared for the Fourth Meeting of the Open-Ended Intergovernmental Group of Ministers or Their Representatives on International Environmental Governance, Montreal, 30 November—1 December 2001, UN Doc. UNEP/IGM/4/3 of 16 November, 2001b.

————.2004c. Resource Mobilization, Environment Fund, 2004c. Online: http://www.unep.org/rmu/en/Financing_environmentfund.htm

UN Secretary General. 1998. 'Environment and Human Settlements'. A/53/463, 1998. Online: http://www.un.org/documents/ga/docs/53/plenary/a53-463.htm (Accessed in March 2006). UN General Assembly Document A/53/463.

Von Moltke, K. 1996. 'Why UNEP Matters', in *Green Globe Yearbook 1996*. Oxford: Oxford University Press.

————.2001. 'The Organization of the Impossible', *Global Environmental Politics*, (1)1.

————.2005. 'Clustering Multilateral Environment Agreements as an Alternative to a World Environment Organization', in F. Biermann and S. Bauer (eds), *A World Environment Organization: Solution or Threat for Effective Environmental Governance?*, Aldershot: Ashgate.

Annex

Acronyms

AOSIS (SIDS)—Alliance Of Small Island States (Small Island Developing States)
BRIC (s)—Brazil, Russia, India and China
CDM—The Clean Development Mechanism
CSD—Commission on Sustainable Development
GEF—Global Environment Facility
GMEF—Global Ministerial Environment Forum
IADGs—the Internationally Agreed Development Goals
IISD—International Institute for Sustainable Development
IGSD—Institute for Governance & Sustainable Development
IPCC—The United Nations Intergovernmental Panel on Climate Change
KP—The Kyoto Protocol
LDCs—The Least Developed Countries
MEA—Multilateral Environment Agreement
NAPA—A National Adaptation Programme of Action to Climate Change (A National Action Plan on Adaptation)
ODA—Official Development Assistance
OECD—Organization for Economic Cooperation and Development
R&D—Research and Development
SWMTEP—System Wide Medium Term Environmental Programme
The Principle of CDR—The Principle of Common but Differentiated Responsibilities
UNCBD—United Nations Convention on Biological Diversity
UNCCC—United Nations Climate Change Conference
UNCCD—United Nations Convention to Combat Desertification
UNFCCC—United Nations Framework Convention on Climate Change
UNEP—United Nations Environment Programme
WTO—World Trade Organization

Environmental Management Groups

Basel Convention Secretariat
Convention on Biodiversity Secretariat
Convention to Combat Desertification Secretariat
Convention on International Trade in Endangered Species Secretariat
Convention on Migratory Species Secretariat
Economic and Social Commission for Africa
Economic Commission for Europe
Economic and Social Commission for Latin America and the Caribbean
Economic and Social Commission for Asia and the Pacific
Economic and Social Commission for West Asia
Food and Agriculture Organization
Global Environment Facility
International Atomic Energy Agency
International Civil Aviation Organization
International Fund for Agricultural Development
International Labour Organization
International Maritime Organization
International Strategy for Disaster Reduction Secretariat
International Trade Center
International Telecommunication Union
Office for the Coordination of Humanitarian Affairs
Office of the High Commissioner for Human Rights
Ramsar Convention on Wetlands
UN Conference on Trade and Development
UN Department of Economic and Social Affairs/Div. for Sustainable Development
United Nations Development Programme
United Nations Environment Programme
United Nations Educational, Scientific and Cultural Organization
United Nations Framework Convention on Climate Change Secretariat
United Nations Population Fund
United Nations Human Settlements Programme
United Nations High Commissioner for Refugees
United Nations Children's Fund
United Nations Industrial Development Organization
United Nations Institute for Training and Research
United Nations University
Universal Postal Union
World Food Program
World Health Organization
World Intellectual Property Organization

Chapter 17

THE HEILIGENDAMM PROCESS AND EMERGING POWERS: MORE OF THE SAME OR A GENUINE GLOBAL GOVERNANCE INNOVATION?[1]

Garth le Pere, Julia Leininger, Mario Riestra and Thomas Fues

Introduction

In recent years, the exclusive club of leading industrialized countries, the Group of 8 (G-8), has suffered from a growing legitimacy crisis due to its lack of representativeness and effectiveness (Cooper and Kelly 2007; Lesage 2007). Propelled by the economic and political rise of new powers from the global South, such as the 'Asian drivers of global change' (Kaplinsky and Messner 2008), the controversy over the G-8 summit architecture has gained new momentum. Present and past leaders of the West such as Britain's Tony Blair and Gordon Brown, French President Nikolas Sarkozy and Canada's former Prime Minister, Paul Martin, have called for the formal enlargement of the G-8. In her attempt to strike a balance between those in favour of inclusion and those defending the status quo, German Chancellor Angela Merkel, as host of the 2007 summit, decided to launch an innovative outreach effort towards five emerging powers. The so-called Heiligendamm process (HP) has a two-year life span and will engage Brazil, China, India, Mexico and South Africa (the G-5) in an institutionalized dialogue on four critical issue areas.

This paper examines the implications of the HP for the system of global governance and asks some critical questions: Will the 'structured dialogue' lead to a more inclusive summit arrangement and strengthen the position of emerging countries in the international order? Will the G-5 be able to coordinate their positions and extract concessions from industrialized countries that not only benefit themselves but also the developing world in general? Or will the HP, on the contrary and in the end exacerbate North-South antagonism since it could prove incapable of delivering tangible outcomes? The paper proceeds as follows: We will first outline the background and structure of the Heiligendamm process. The second part will pay special attention to the role of emerging/middle powers in the global system. Since the G-5 is a "newcomer" in the summit architecture, the third section will examine the underlying interest structures of the G-5 countries and analyze their potential for consensus building. We will conclude with the possible contributions that the HP could make in promoting a more cooperative world order and one that better serves the interests of the developing world.

To sum up our conclusions: We see the Heiligendamm process as a legitimate attempt to broaden the institutional basis for informal policy dialogue among traditional and emerging powers in the context of the highly contested terrain of global governance. However, the process carries certain risks for all parties involved. The intentions of the G-8 seem, at this stage, highly ambiguous, contradictory and vague. We cannot ascertain yet whether industrialized countries are genuinely interested in an inclusive summit architecture or more cynically perhaps, if they rather see the HP as a window-dressing exercise, meant to subtly preserve their global eminence. The G-5 appears similarly undecided what to make of the process, particularly if it fails to deliver tangible progress for the developing world. Continued G-5 interaction with the G-8 will only make sense if this leads to substantive policy shifts by industrialized countries in key global issue areas.

Key Features of the Heiligendamm Process[2]

Before we turn to the Heiligendamm process, a brief contextual survey about the G-8 and its historical background would be useful in order to capture the logic of its actions. The G-6 (the precursor to the G-8) was formed in 1975, following a French initiative, with the purpose of coordinating responses of major economies to the global recession that was touched off by the oil crisis and the breakdown of the Bretton Woods system. Canada joined the group one year later. A point of special interest is the inclusion of the then European Economic Community, now the European Union (EU), represented by the president of the European Commission since 1977. Finally, Russia became a formal member in 1998 after several years of close collaboration. The presidency of the group, which rotates annually among member countries, sets the annual agenda and hosts the midyear summit attended by heads of state and government.

Each presidency is free to invite guests for brief encounters on the sidelines of the summit. Beginning in the year 2001 at Genoa, Italy outreach efforts were addressed mostly to African nations, but included concerns of developing countries relating to trade, aid and debt relief. The involvement of five emerging powers, Brazil, China, India, Mexico and South Africa, began in 2005 at Gleneagles, where the British presidency initiated the 'Gleneagles Dialogue on Climate Change, Clean Energy and Sustainable Development'. International organizations have also been invited to the summits. This process began in 1996 with the presence of the executive heads of the United Nations (UN), the International Monetary Fund (IMF), the World Bank (WB) and the World Trade Organization (WTO) as a post-summit with the then G-7. Institutions like the African Union, the International Energy Agency (IEA), the World Health Organization (WHO) and the Organization for Economic Co-operation and Development (OECD), amongst others, have also participated on some occasions.

Following a proposal from the German presidency in 2007, G-8 and G-5 leaders agreed to launch the Heiligendamm process, as a 'structured dialogue' for a period of two years.[3] The circumstances of the meeting between both groupings as well as the genesis of a joint statement are objects of considerable controversy. The G-8 communiqué announcing the HP was made public one day before the five leaders from the South had joined their counterparts.[4] A former leading U.S. development official voiced scathing criticism of this approach: 'At the 2007 G8 summit in Heiligendamm, Germany repeated the gestures of recent summits by inviting heads of state of China, India, Brazil, South Africa and Mexico ("the outreach five") to a session on energy and climate change after the G8 had completed its own discussion, decisions and communiqué on the issue. This is an outrageous practice' (Bradford 2008). Similarly, the Indian Prime Minister, Manmohan Singh, complained to journalists after the summit that G-5 leaders were not treated as equals. He insisted that consultations and agenda-setting for future meetings would need to be more inclusive if they were to be acceptable to the G-5 (Williamson 2007).

After some negotiations and discussion at Heiligendamm, it was decided that HP would concentrate, on the basis of parallel working groups ('pillars'), on four issues of critical importance to participants:

- cross-border investment;
- research and innovation;
- energy efficiency; and
- development, particularly in Africa.

Overall responsibility for the process rests with the HP steering committee, which is composed of all 14 sherpas (G-8 + G-5 + European Commission). All HP bodies (except the support office) will have two co-chairs, one from each of the country groupings, to foster joint ownership of the process. Germany will hold the chair of the steering committee beyond its G-8 presidency until the end of June 2008. Then, the Japanese side will take over for the rest of the year to be followed by Italy in 2009. This formula seeks to ensure a strong and continuing commitment to a process that is generally seen as more of a German concept. The manner in which Japan and Italy assume responsibility will significantly influence its outcomes. Formally, the HP was not directly linked to the next summit in Hokkaido, but G-5 countries insisted on a leaders' dialogue that, in format and content, reflects their status as equals. Justifiable doubts that the Japanese presidency could fail to include such a dialogue on their summit agenda were groundless. But only a limited time frame was granted to exclusive G-5 and G-8 dialogue during breakfast of the third summit day. Topics high on the G-5's priority list, such as the Doha development trade round, aid, debt, migration and reform of international institutions, were not officially included on the agenda.

HP participants decided to have two high-level meetings of sherpas per year and at least two meetings of each of the four working groups at director general level. On 21 February 2008, the first meeting of the development group took place. All delegations (with the exception of Brazil) came from their capitals and consisted of high-ranking officials. France and South Africa were appointed as co-chairs of the group. The following G-8 and G-5 members will be in charge of chairing the other groups: United States and Mexico – investment; United Kingdom and India – innovation; and Canada and India – energy (see Figure 17.1).

Figure 17.1. Organizational Chart of the Heiligendamm Process.

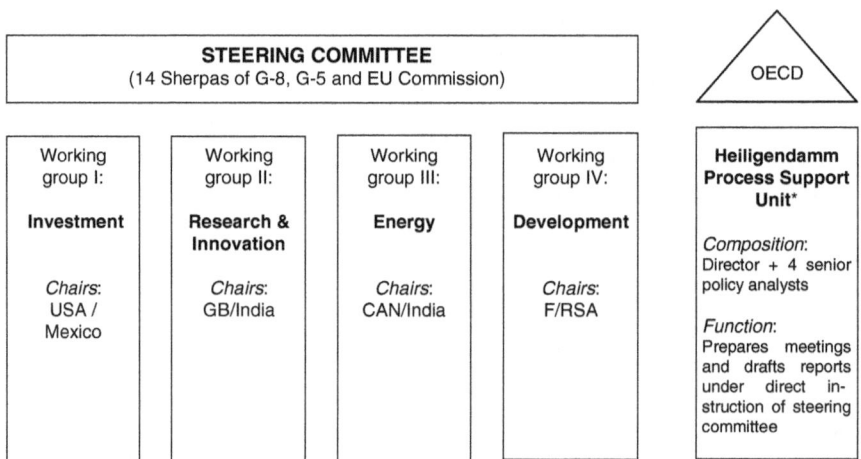

STEERING COMMITTEE (14 Sherpas of G-8, G-5 and EU Commission)				OECD
Working group I: **Investment** *Chairs:* USA / Mexico	Working group II: **Research & Innovation** *Chairs:* GB/India	Working group III: **Energy** *Chairs:* CAN/India	Working group IV: **Development** *Chairs:* F/RSA	**Heiligendamm Process Support Unit*** *Composition:* Director + 4 senior policy analysts *Function:* Prepares meetings and drafts reports under direct instruction of steering committee

* Independent unit at the office of the OECD Secretary-General.

Germany has provided the bulk of the financial resources needed for a small support unit that is attached to the Secretary-General's office at the OECD; Italy and France have only made symbolic contributions.[5] The office is not part of regular OECD structures and is not linked to its outreach efforts towards emerging powers.[6] It is headed by a director (namely, the former director of the German sherpa office), and consists of four senior policy analysts plus technical staff. Its function is limited to logistical and organizational support under the guidance of the steering committee. This is the first time, remarkably, that the G-8 has established a joint administrative entity, since secretarial functions are routinely handled by the respective presidencies.

At the first session of the steering committee on 17 October 2007 in Berlin, participants agreed on key issues regarding structure, procedures and time frame for the process. Sherpas also began discussions on a "concept paper" which was meant to define the agenda of the working groups. By the end of 2007, no consensus had been reached on this document. While Germany and Mexico, as representatives of their respective country grouping, were able to arrive at a comprehensive agreement, some members of the G-5 apparently objected to certain types of phrasing, reportedly concerning corporate social responsiblity and the Paris Declaration on aid effectiveness. Nevertheless, nearly all sections of the draft have been accepted by all parties and has served as a pragmatic starting point for the working groups. Meanwhile the concept paper has lost practical significance because each working group met and defined its agenda since the beginning of HP.

There is a general consensus among participating countries that the HP is an informal, open-ended political dialogue, and not a negotiating forum that would generate binding decisions among the parties. Since there is no pre-defined substantive outcome, trust-building and mutual understanding can be characterized as the main objectives, at least from the perspective of the industrialized countries. The G-5 countries may be more interested in tangible results to justify their involvement vis-a-vis the developing world. All participants understand the HP as an approach that is complementary to existing multilateral and regional fora.

However, there are opportunities and risks associated with the HP. It may provide a stimulus to break the stalemate in global negotiations, for example, on trade and environmental issues. The constructive role of emerging powers played in the Bali climate negotiations (December 2007) could be interpreted as an early harvest for deepened interaction with the G-8. The G-8 could benefit from increased legitimacy and effectiveness while the G-5 may enjoy enhanced international status. The weaknesses of the process, however, are also evident. The extension of informal club governance may undermine the universal structures of the United Nations and provide mementum for trends towards a new constellation of great powers (Drezner 2007). If the HP fails to produce tangible results, not just for the main protagonists but for developing countries in general, emerging powers may withdraw and North-South distrust could deepen.

The Role of Emerging/Middle Powers in Global Politics

The emergence of the G-5 and their interface with the G-8 invites a reflection on their role as middle or emerging powers in international relations.[7] Middle powers have become significant role players since new systemic and power realities bind countries together, as never before, as overlapping 'communities of fate' in a world paradoxically characterised by persistent conflict as well as centrifugal effects associated with inequality, endemic poverty and growing insecurity. The dialectic between globalisation and interdependence has created cross-border and global problems that require greater cooperation and joint problem-solving on the basis of new forms of global governance that are beyond the capacities of a single nation state. In a normative sense, crises and turbulence in a mercurial global system now demand a common vision based on values of solidarity, social justice, and responsibility such that an appropriate milieu is established in which states can cooperate more intensively. The G-5 thus represents a species of countries which have contributed to the passing of the 'Westphalian moment' where the transcendant interests of global order and stability, and the welfare and fate of mankind pose new imperatives for ethical conduct by states and new challenges for their sovereignty (Brown 2001).

Thus middle powers and their emergence test some of the realist core assumptions about the nature of world politics, namely, that international relations are necessarily conflictual and that norms, rules and principles are meaningless (Melakopides 1990). By promoting internationalism, middle powers such as the G-5 show that the realist logic that underpins the contemporary state system might be dominant but it is not immutable. As has been argued, middle powers function '...within a relational dynamic that is essentially derived from a materialist account of states and power set within the framework of the international system as a whole. From this perspective middle powers are understood to be committed multilateralists as a means of overcoming their material deficiencies in terms of structural power' (Alden and Vieira 2005).

The conduct and behaviour of middle powers derive their *raison d'etre* from the ethical underpinnings of interdependence and by virtue of this, they are subtly changing the basic patterns of world politics, but most importantly the practice of statecraft that has defined relations between developed and developing countries over the last five decades or so. The G-5 represent a newly emerging constellation of power that is shaped by, among others, their rise in the global economy, the rapid and sustained growth of their economies and populations and the dominant roles they have come to play in their respective geographic neighbourhoods.[8] What they do have in common is that middle powers have come to be seen as drivers of global change in the sense that they have become 'catalysts' for promoting global concerns, 'facilitators' in building coalitions, 'managers' within their regions for adhering to norms and rules, 'good international citizens' for upholding the legitimacy of multilateral institutions and improving cooperation, and 'niche diplomats' in advancing certain global and regional causes (Cooper 1997). While it is argued that '[m]iddle powers by themselves are unlikely to have overwhelming influence on the international stage' (Flemes 2005), it is these attributes that add to their collective weight in international settings and which contribute to a shared belief '…in their entitlement to a more influential role in world affairs' (Hurrell 2006).

Together they evince hope for a de facto multipolarity and a renewed systemic order, mindful of course that the US will remain a dominant player in the institutional and multilateral matrices constructed since the end of the Second World War (Ikenberry 2004). The cause for hope and renewal is based on the tectonic shifts in the global governance complex and the dramatic changes that have taken place in the nature and character of world politics. To name but a few, new international institutions and regimes have emerged; the scope, range and substance of international rules and norms have been broadened considerably; new approaches to global governance invite wider participation and pluralism; and almost a decade of UN summitry has introduced compacts, conventions and agreements that involve a greater number of countries in shaping the future of the global commons. All these developments have been consequential in contributing to a denser network of actors, institutions, transnational relations, exchanges and communication, and formal and informal regimes which all intersect in one way or another in addressing major threats to world order, which are essentially humanitarian, environmental and economic. This systemic logic has exerted a powerful gravitational pull that does not even exempt rich and powerful countries; if anything, they have become more enmeshed in the interdependent fabric of international relations (Rosenau 2000). In other words, 'a new *raison de systeme* is developing that will alter and ultimately displace old-fashioned notions of *raison d'etat*' (Hurrell 2006). This conjures a Kantian image where there is a progressive diffusion of liberal values as interests converge, rules are observed, and countries become more integrated in a common global agenda as is the case with climate change, trade liberalisation and nuclear proliferation (Held 1999). This is the conceptual context then that will determine the success or otherwise of the G-5's engagement with the G-8 but importantly, we must be mindful that the central claims of realism will continue to hold powerful sway, especially as far as the continuities of conflict and tension as well as power-political competition are concerned.

Middle Powers and Soft Power

These considerations now bring us the questions of power. In doing so, we have to start with the question of ontology and contest the realist notion that relies on an anarchic system consisting of territorial states in which they must be self-reliant in generating and maintaining the conditions for their survival and well-being. The uncertainties and insecurities that result from this Hobbesian framing is that world politics is a natural setting for conflict and that competition is a characteristic mode if interaction (Bull 1977). The touchstone of realist thinking is that power is 'the final arbiter of things political' (Gilpin 1984, 290) and this helps to explain the perpetual quest for power by states in a zero-sum contest. In realist thinking, the preoccupation with wealth and power is above all a rational response to the cold realities of international relations.

By contrast, the shifting nature of contemporary global politics suggests a different ontology that is based on defining new political spaces in which states and societies are locked into interdependent processes of integration and fragmentation but are also subject to localisation and fission with respect to political forms, identities, economics, war, technology, the environment, climate change, poverty, collective norms and so on (Ferguson and Mansbach 2002). There is also greater mutual vulnerability that stems from intractable inequalities in global wealth. In GDP terms, some 54 countries were poorer in 2003 than in 1990 (and 20 of these were in sub-Sahara Africa). Other illuminating figures include: between 1988 and 2000, the world's poorest 5 per cent lost almost a quarter of their real income and, for the same period, the top 5 per cent gained 12 per cent of theirs; for every US$100 in world exports, $97 goes to high- and middle-income countries and only $3 to low income countries; if Africa, East Asia and Latin America were to increase their exports by just 1 per cent, it could lift 130 million people out of poverty; and a 1 per cent increase of Africa's share of world trade would generate US$70 billion or five times what the continent has received in aid and debt relief over the last five years (World Bank 2004).

Financial crises have also highlighted the extent to which volatility associated with global capital markets can compound the problem of inequality among developing countries. For example, high inflows of capital generate inflationary pressures and damage labour-intensive agriculture and manufactured exports, especially but not only under fixed exchange rates. In Asia and Latin America and large parts of sub-Sahara Africa, Gini coefficients of inequality increased during the good years of high capital inflows in the 1990s. In these regions, the poor gained less and were often the first-line victims when things went badly with cyclical downturns. In Asia especially, this is when capital fled, and high interest rates were imposed as countries sought to protect their currencies, thereby hurting small businesses and reducing employment in general (Soederberg 2002).

The new security doctrines of the US after September 11 and the rush to war in Iraq in 2003 gave priority to a narrow security agenda, defined by unilateralism and pre-emptive war. This agenda contradicts and in many ways is hostile to the core tenets, norms, and institutions that have been developed in international relations since 1945. It casts aside respect for open political negotiations and heralds an intensification rather than an amelioration of adversarial conflicts and tensions (Cox 2007). As a consequence the systemic machinery of the multilateral order has become weaker, with serious deficits. In particular, the value of the UN system has been called into question and there has been a clamour for reform of the Security Council. The future of the EU is also highly uncertain and, in the midst of its expansion in membership, there is a deep sense of unease in Brussels about what will happen over the next decade, especially in view of an ageing population, changing demography and indeed, whether the European social model can survive in its present form. The WTO faces its own existential crisis because of the de facto collapse of the Doha Development Round, while the G-8 seems less capable of delivering on its pledges with regard to trade, aid, and debt relief to African countries. And in trying to craft a new financial architecture, the roles of the World Bank and IMF are increasingly coming under scrutiny, amid pressures for their reform and restructuring. There are calls, mostly from developing countries in the Bretton Woods Institutions, for more participatory and prudential management of global imbalances, capital flows, development finance, and poverty reduction (Kaplinsky 2005).

It is at this juncture of globalization that the G-5 countries are having a marked effect on global markets and traditional balances of power. The US remains the preponderant and unrivalled superpower, with a military reach and resource base that is unprecedented in history (Brooks and Wohlforth 2002). As a consequence, there is no country or alignment of countries that has the capability to provide an axis of 'hard balancing' to check the power of the US; but what has emerged is a countervailing power dynamic in the form of 'soft balancing' (Paul 2004). Soft balancing in turn depends on the ability of countries to deploy 'soft power' whose logic is based on their ability to attract others to their particular points of view, which are perceived as being legitimate and credible. The power of attraction and values are important characteristics of the soft power spectrum and arises from the attractiveness of a country or group of countries' culture, political ideals and policies. Essential hallmarks of soft power and soft balancing are agenda setting, compromise and consensus, especially as far as codifying international norms and institutions of governance is concerned (Nye 2004). To be effective, soft power and soft balancing must recognise that the strategic environment is influenced by globalization and as such a multidimensional approach is needed in the distribution and application of power. Such an approach becomes very relevant in the pursuit of common interests, especially as these relate to economic matters, domestic incentives, security, prosperity and global governance. Since developing countries singly or collectively lack the hard power resources, resort to soft balancing on the basis of building multipolar alliances and 'like-minded' coalitions becomes an important strategic intervention in subtly changing power dynamics (Pape 2005).

All countries in the G-5 maintain strong linkages with the United States and depend on its public goods. None have the wherewithal to challenge US power with military means; indeed, 'soft balancing does not directly challenge US military preponderance' (Flemes 2007). Yet with 42 per cent of the world's population and 26 per cent of global GDP, and with China adding greater buoyancy, the group is well placed to significantly expand its capacity to influence the contours of world politics through soft balancing. This will enable the G-5 as emerging powers, to challenge the current international hierarchy, to provide global public goods in their own right, to improve the modalities and outcomes of global governance as well as to significantly expand their own foreign policy options.

The Interests and Objective of HP Participating Countries

This theoretical and contextual exegesis provides a useful register to consider some of the normative dimensions relating to how the parties, especially within G-5, define and understand their interests and objectives; and the extent to which these may be complementary or in conflict with each other.

Convergence and Divergence Within the G-5

At the invitation of Mexico, G-5 countries met the evening before the Heiligendamm summit in Berlin to formulate a joint position paper vis-à-vis the G-8.[9] In this, they laid out their agenda for desired change in global governance structures (such as strengthening voice and participation of developing countries in international financial institutions) and addressed specific policy areas such as trade, technology transfer, development cooperation and migration. While the G-5 paper demonstrates some convergence with G-8 positions on issues such as a commitment to joint global problem-solving, the overall orientation of emerging powers strongly diverges from the policy framework of industrialized countries.

The G-5 countries have expressed the need for new modalities in policy coordination so as to be better prepared for dialogue with the G-8. They have managed to present a common front even though they do not always share the same interests. Mexico has been charged with acting as a coordinator and spokesman for the group in their interactions with the G-8. Rather than simply being reactive, the G-5 seeks to become a pro-active player in the international arena (Varadarajan 2007). While there are some indications of this, like the meeting of foreign ministers on the sidelines of the opening of the UN General Assembly in September 2007, the proposal by Brazil to constitute the G-5 as a formal body has not yet materialized (Bidwai 2007; Myatt et al. 2007, 9). The Indian Prime Minister, among other G-5 leaders, seems to be highly sceptical since the country does not want to appear disloyal to its traditional Southern alliances such as the G20 in the WTO context (Bagchi 2007). However, formalized G-5 interaction is progressing; for example, there was the sherpa meeting in April 2008 in China.

The G-5 can be said to be pursuing the advancement of stronger norms of cooperation on the basis of good international citizenship and through the impulses provided by the use of 'soft' negotiating power and authority. There are several parameters that help to define good international citizenship: firstly, the expanding agenda of global problems is such that no country can provide solutions on its own, be it in the areas of terrorism, disease, organised crime, climate change, environmental degradation or nuclear proliferation; secondly, the magnitude of these challenges demand international cooperation, legitimised through multilateral organisations and international regimes; thirdly, rules are important for enhancing cooperation and encouraging moderation where unmitigated struggles for power might otherwise be the order of the day; fourthly, good international citizenship is not about doing good per se, but is 'an exercise in enlightened self-interest; an expression of idealistic pragmatism' (Wheeler and Dunne 1998 854), which ultimately serves the national interest; fifthly, promoting the general welfare of mankind and stability in global order are seen as inherent virtues of being a good global citizen and where there is also a national interest symbiosis. Thus, 'good international citizens should endeavour to uphold universal standards of acceptable behaviour' (Geldenhuys 2006, 96), in a manner that they become 'entrepreneurs' in upholding, advocating and formulating certain norms. In essence, good international citizenship entails openly confronting the vagaries of international relations and its Darwinian character and often staking out a high moral ground that could be tantamount to advancing agendas and charters that are counter hegemonic.

The G-5 and the HP thus emerge at a time when power fluidities and the waning verities of a realist order in the international system make possible a wider political and strategic space to act as international citizens. This provides a useful context to examine the anatomy of the G-5 in terms of the countries that constitute it. Most importantly, India, Brazil and South Africa make up the India-Brazil-South Africa (IBSA) Trilateral group, which in itself makes for an interesting dynamic in how the G-5 will harmonise its positions *vis-á-vis* the G-8. The IBSA Dialogue Forum (also referred to as the Trilateral Forum) was launched on 6 June 2003 at a meeting of the Foreign Ministers of the three countries in Brasilia, the capital of Brazil. The primary motivation of the meeting was to put in place an institutional mechanism and diplomatic vehicle for triangular cooperation that would not only improve relations among the partners across a range of dimensions but also serve as a platform for advancing South-South cooperation and solidarity (Alden and Vieira 2005). A Joint Trilateral Commission was set up to drive an ambitious agenda based on carefully defined principles of cooperation that covered technical, social and economic elements, including a focus on poverty alleviation, sustainable human development, service delivery and employment creation. But there would also be a strong focus on strategic areas of international relations, where the countries acting in concert, could become fulcrum points for a targeted reform agenda. Key themes include promoting the letter and spirit of international law, advancing trade equity in the WTO and reform of the UN Security Council and Bretton Woods Institutions.

In addition to the annual forums of foreign ministers, several trilateral sectoral ministerial meetings have taken place involving ministers concerned with defence and security, science and technology, health, energy, and transport. This has led to the establishment of trilateral working groups with an expanded sectoral focus on agriculture, culture, defence, education, energy, health, information society, trade and investment, social issues, science and technology, tourism and transportation. One of the most significant developments in the life of IBSA was the first summit of heads of state in Brasilia in September 2006 attended by Presidents Lula and Mbeki and Prime Minister Manmohan Singh. This was followed by another high-level summit of heads of state in Pretoria in October 2007.

Together the three countries have a total population of 1.2 billion people and a combined GDP of about US$1.1 trillion. Moreover, they are democracies, middle powers and emerging markets. India is regarded as an established democracy and Brazil and South Africa as consolidating democracies. However, they suffer from high levels of inequality and poverty. Although poverty is much more endemic in India, South Africa and Brazil have some of the highest levels of inequality, with Gini coefficients of close to 60, compared to 33 for India. They are subject to great social pressures such as rapid urbanisation, the HIV/AIDS pandemic, informal settlements and high levels of crime and violence (Dupas 2006). IBSA's current and limited membership represents the economic and political dominance of the three countries in their respective regions. This leadership position gives the three countries an anchoring and pivotal role in providing a new centre of gravity for a different type of South-South engagement devoted to a more progressive global agenda, deepened trilateral relations, and improved inter-regional cooperation. The aim is to multiply three-way trade from its current US$4.6 billion to US$15 billion by 2010.

In the case of South Africa, since 1994 there has been an avowed commitment to locating the country's interests and foreign policy thrust squarely in Africa and the global South. The promotion of North-South dialogue is also an important goal. In the broad spectrum of issues that animate South-South relations, South Africa has recognised the Asian region for its growing geo-strategic and economic importance and has sought to develop and strengthen political and economic relations with Latin America and the Caribbean. In terms of its own pragmatic-idealist outlook, South Africa has been mindful of the need to advance an activist agenda that would address growing asymmetries and changing post-Cold War dynamics in international relations but there was also the challenge to address the conceptual limitations of an ineffective and desultory south axis. Indeed, when he was still deputy president, Thabo Mbeki already articulated the idea of a 'G-8 of the South' that would craft a more coordinated approach to the imperatives of globalization but that would critically extract abiding commitments from the G-8 on key issues of concern to developing countries, including trade reform, debt relief, and improved aid and development support (Alden and le Pere 2003).

The formation of IBSA flows from strong bilateral relations that South Africa established with India and Brazil since its own democratic transition in 1994. The formal Bi-National Commissions (BNCs) are the anvils on which the establishment of IBSA have been forged and in the triangular relationship, South Africa has emerged as playing a pivotal role. The South Africa-Brazil BNC was established in 2000 and the South Africa-India BNC in 1995. In turn, India and Brazil have reached a strategic bi-national agreement in mid-2006. Not surprisingly, the agendas of IBSA have been influenced by the thematic issues of the BNCs and agreements but have been broadened to address a matrix of international concerns. IBSA has thus expressed itself on 'new threats to security' and this includes terrorism, transnational organized crime, the HIV/AIDS pandemic, natural disasters, nuclear proliferation, the transit of toxic chemicals and radioactive waste. There is a commitment to vigorously combat poverty and disease in the three countries by promoting sustainable development. The countries are seeking to promote scientific and technological research, and development in biotechnology, information technology and renewable energy. They encourage adherence to the Kyoto Protocol as an instrument for dealing with atmospheric warming and greenhouse emissions;

and they are committed to cooperation in trade diplomacy, especially as this affects the goals of the Doha programme.

IBSA is thus indicative of a new post-Cold War order that is trying to come to terms with a changing and more complex global environment and where multi-polarity holds out new promise for a restructured world order. While still open and contingent as far as changing real balances of power are concerned, we must also factor in China's rise which has been accompanied by that of India and Russia, together with a host of other consequential developing countries that are anchored in regional and sub-regional economic communities. These countries also pursue an active multilateralism through inter-regional and transnational South-based frameworks such as the G77+China, the G-20 in the WTO and the Non-aligned Movement whose declaratory diplomacy has elevated the voice of heretofore marginalised countries in global forums. There is also the expanding China-Russia led Shanghai Cooperation Organization which now includes India, Iran, Mongolia and Pakistan.

India, Brazil and South Africa realize the challenge of ensuring that there are concrete results that flow from their cooperative endeavour. This rationale is again based on a less than encouraging track record of South-South initiatives. The impetus behind IBSA is to work towards demonstrable results. This is grounded by the significant political affinities, strong commitment to the process and mutual confidence that have been developed and which exists among the countries' leadership (Alden and Vieira 2005). Delivery, structure and strategic direction become important organizational principles. The mode of operation is defined by close coordination, sharing of experiences and expertise, joint piloting and evaluation of projects, and developing a dedicated cadre of professionals to administer the process.[10]

The current dynamics in IBSA are relevant insofar as how these might refract and impact on the G-5. The IBSA relationship draws from a large reservoir of political will to make it succeed, but there are challenges that relate to the respective roles and interests of the countries. India brings the most multilateral experience and has placed great emphasis on IBSA's functional coherence and ability to deliver tangible results. Indeed, it was India that suggested the involvement of business that has resulted in the formation of an IBSA Business Forum (Alden and Vieira 2005). Brazil emphasizes the potential for IBSA to become an incubator for a rejuvenated South and its President Lula has travelled extensively among developing countries to make the case for a new approach to South-South cooperation (De Lima and Hirst 2006). South Africa, the smallest of the three, provides the political linkages among strategic countries of the South and North. Its role as anchor will be critical to the future of the IBSA alliance, especially in acting as a bridge between current and future members and facilitating dialogue with external partners (Dupas 2006). For example, both

Russia and China have expressed an interest in joining IBSA. This poses a problem because of the different bilateral chemistry that exists between IBSA countries and these states. While China might be keen, India might be less inclined because of its growing competitive rivalry with China, several unresolved bilateral issues and historical boundary tensions, compounded by the fact that China is not a democracy and has a questionable human rights record. Brazil and South Africa both enjoy close ties with China, and South Africa is the only country in the whole of Africa that has a BNC with China. Both Presidents Lula and Mbeki have made state visits to China in May 2004 and November 2006, respectively. For them China would add strategic weight, would be a tactical asset and would raise the profile and amplify the impact of the alliance, especially as far as IBSA's global agenda and emphasis on South-South cooperation is concerned. While India would welcome the inclusion of Russia based on its close historical ties and the strategic partnership signed in 2000, South Africa and Brazil might not share this enthusiasm since their relations with Russia are at an embryonic stage and there might be legitimate concerns about Russia's pedigree and credentials as a partner of the South.[11]

In the G-5 and at first blush, it would seem that the presence of Mexico could be a dilemma in terms of a broader strategic calculus. Mexico has historically been locked into the American sphere of influence and as such, has had a somewhat schizoid and ambivalent relationship with its neighbours and generally, with developing countries depending, of course, on the regime in power. Under President Vicente Fox, however, it would appear that Mexico's foreign policy leanings have become distinctly more internationalist, witness his participation at the Gleneagles meeting of the G-8 in July 2005, where Mexico joined Brazil, China, India, and South Africa as part of a developing country axis. Mexico has also come to play an important role in trade matters both in its near abroad as well as in the WTO. It has helped to strengthen Latin American forums for political consultation and cooperation, such as the Rio group and has provided momentum in sub-regional initiatives such as the Tuxtla Mechanism and the Puebla-Panama Plan that, with Mexico, incorporates countries of Central America and the Caribbean. Its international credentials and credibility have been further enhanced by a Partnership Treaty with the EU, its participation in APEC and a growing trade engagement with the economic powers of the Asia-Pacific. Of all countries in Africa, Mexico has close relations with South Africa. In 2001, the countries put into operation the Mechanism for Consultations on Issues of Mutual Interest as a means of promoting greater collaboration in social development, education, science and technology, air and maritime transportation, agriculture and tourism. In addition Mexico is also a member of the OECD club of industrialized countries, while South Africa enjoys 'enhanced engagement' as a precursor to full membership.

There is more that binds the G-5 in this common HP enterprise than divides them. Fundamentally, they share the normative constructs that constitute the bedrock of multilateralism and global governance. This embedded DNA makes for a genetic code of shared values, ideas and principles.[12] The institutionalized IBSA platform certainly provides useful synergies but the two year experience as members of the G-5 should positively assist mutual learning and the building of trust and confidence that will be salutary for cooperation at other levels and global forums. The big challenge though is to ensure that the societies of the G-5 become part of the discourse and that tangible results flow in the four areas that define the G-5 and G-8 interface. Societal acceptance and building norms of social citizenship across these countries with very diverse political cultures will be a test. Mechanisms must be created for developing what Habermas (1998) called 'elective affinity' that encourage the emergence of groups outside the circles of government and elites so far involved in the HP. Thus professional bodies, social policy experts, voices from civil society and so on must become an alternate epistemic community in order to enrich the dialogue but also to act as a critical sounding board. The legitimacy of the HP could be significantly enhanced by making it more accessible and open.

These reflections should not detract from the problem of who it is that the G-5 actually represent other than themselves. Any skepticism in this regard would, indeed, be wholly justified since there are a large number of countries in the developing world that are mostly poor and underdeveloped, who look to the Non-Aligned Movement, the G-77+China and regional bodies as the essential platforms for advancing their concerns and positions in multilateral institutions. Groupings such as IBSA, the G-5 and other ad hoc formations that have especially emerged in the WTO, have provoked considerable debate about their motivations, interests, and legimacy. The declaratory commitment to representing developing country interests is often seen as arrogant and presumptuous in view of an absence of mandate and their issue-based concerns. The G-5 must, therefore, guard against any presumption that they have the support of developing countries simply by virtue of what could be seen as a charade and pretence of representation. Quite critically, as has been mentioned, without demonstrable outcomes that might flow from the interface with the G-8, doubt and skepticism could become self-fulfilling prophecies that conspire to make the HP end up as a monumental failure.

The Interests and Objectives of the G-8

While all members have agreed to the HP, the G-8 is divided on the medium-term prospects for the summit architecture. Leaders from Britain and France advocate formal enlargement to a G-13. Although Russia has not taken a clear position in the current debate, it has promoted formal G8 enlargement before. The former president Putin has called for India's formal inclusion into the summit architecture and also supported official membership for China and Brazil after the Russian summit of 2006. The US and Japan clearly prefer the status quo. Accordingly, attitudes towards the HP among G-8 countries vary. The reformist camp hopes to translate progress through institutionalized dialogue into formal membership, whereas the status quo group wants to prevent this dynamic. The division within the G-8 could create serious problems for the HP. To balance the exclusive focus on the five Heiligendamm countries, Japan has decided to also invite Australia, Indonesia and South Korea. This may be interpreted as a less than friendly act by the G-5 that undermines the strategic potential of the HP. As such, it could negatively affect their commitment to the HP. No matter where they stand on matters of formal enlargement, G-8 leaders do not seem prepared, at this juncture, to entertain the idea of a genuine overhaul of the global governance architecture. Instead, they apparently wish to integrate emerging powers into the existing framework of multilateral institutions that reflects Western dominance on their own terms and in a manner that reflects and advances their own narrow interests.

Conclusion: The Outlook

The HP is obviously a highly ambivalent exercise for all participants. While there are areas of converging interests, contradictions between the G-8 and G-5 are clearly evident. By comparing the G-5 position paper with the joint declaration of the German G-8 presidency and the G-5, Mario Riestra (2007) has provided an in-depth analysis of the compromise reached by the two country groupings. The G-5 paper emphasizes technology transfer and pays less attention to the protection of innovation and intellectual property rights, while issues of development ranks high in both documents. Investment and energy issues are strongly emphasized in the G-8/G-5 declaration of June 2007 but assume a rather modest role in the G-5 paper. Three major issues of importance to the G-5 are excluded altogether from the HP agenda, namely, reform of global governance institutions, international trade, and migration. While compromise will obviously be an important principle in advancing the letter and spirit of the HP, differing expectations and emphases could undermine the overall thrust of cooperation.

It would be an egregious error for the G-8 to take G-5 interests for granted in their ongoing interaction without taking into account their specific perspectives and expectations. The Heiligendamm Process can only bring about progress if it functions as a dialogue of equals where both sides stand ready to search for new modalities and new substantive ground in promoting a cooperative multilateralism. It is not clear yet if G-8 diplomacy has fully understood the challenges which this normative imperative represents.

The HP has emerged at a critical juncture of global politics. Emerging powers are challenging the traditional positions of Western countries in the international order. Deepening political interaction with industrialized countries is only one of several options that they can pursue. South-South cooperation, as in IBSA, and regional integration, such as through the East Asia Summit or Mercosur, are gaining increasing attention. There may be only a small window of opportunity for reform of the summit architecture before emerging powers from the South seize alternative strategic opportunities. The Heiligendamm Process must deliver tangible benefits for the developing world if the G-8 is to remain an attractive counterpart for dialogue and policy coordination in the eyes of the G-5. What are the prospects for success until the summit of 2009? A fundamental divergence between G-8 and G-5 exists in different notions of legitimacy that each side brings to the HP. While industrialized countries stress input legitimacy in keeping the process fluid and open-ended, the G-5 are mainly interested in output legitimacy, that is concrete results which would require significant policy shifts by the G-8 in areas such as trade, financing for development, international labour mobility and voting rights in international financial institutions. While this may seem highly unlikely in the immediate future, it is still too early to predict the final outcome of the HP.

The HP has great potential for fostering political dialogue between the G8 and G5 through trust-and confidence-building in an atmosphere of informality. This is especially important since the international debate is increasingly being defined by stereotypes that incite popular anxieties and aggravate rivalry between traditional and emerging powers. Hence, one of HP's major virtues could be to reduce destructive tensions in the global system and open up avenues of cooperative multilateralism with a clear focus on pressing global problems. The issue of summit reform will, however, need a new concerted effort after the HP comes to an end in 2009. Any modification of the summit architecture must recognize the paramount importance of the United Nations as universal cornerstone for a fair and effective multilateralism. Europe is faced with a special challenge in the quest for equitable global governance. It must relinquish out-dated positions of power in the international system and accept the need to reduce the quantum of its formal representation in multilateral bodies in order to open more space for the voices of emerging and developing countries to be heard. If member states of the EU could agree on reduced voting rights and a rationalised collective representation of its interests, as in the excecutive boards of the IMF and the World Bank, the influence of its member states could still be maintained. A gesture in this regard towards the G-5 would be of significant symbolic value, especially concerning the leadership of IMF and World Bank. The G-8 could symbolically demonstrate their readiness for new forms of power sharing by accepting suitable candidates from the global South for IMF and World Bank.

In short the HP could be a harbinger of a new type of engagement for promoting a more substantive multilateralism and a different systemic order. The key challenges will be to ensure that several criteria are met: the process must have clarity of purpose and there must be consensus in terms of objectives and outcomes; there must be consistency, equality and commitment with regard to norms and techniques of engagement; the participants must agree to continuity of the engagement and introduce a long term perspective that is not hostage to debates about G-8 enlargement; and finally, the process has to be flexible enough to adapt to the exigencies of a fast changing global landscape. If these basic imperatives are not met, the HP will be remembered more for what it did not achieve.

References

Alden, C. and le Pere, G. 2003. 'South Africa's post-Apartheid Foreign Policy—from Reconciliation to Revival?' Adelphi Paper 362. London: International Institute for Strategic Studies.

Alden, C. and Vieira, M. A. 2005. 'The New Diplomacy of the South: South Africa, Brazil, India and trilateralism', *Third World Quarterly* (26)7.

Bagchi, I. 2007. 'PM fears G-5 may become yet another forum', in: *The Times of India*, 12 June Online:<http://timesofindia.indiatimes.com/PM_fears_G-5_may_become_yet_another_forum/articleshow/2116262.cms>

Bidwai, P. 2007. 'G8, G5 Or G4? A Tough Choice for India', *Inter Press Service News Agency*, 23 June Online: <http://ipsnews.net/news.asp?idnews=38289>

Bradford, C. 2008. *Foundational Transformation in America's Role in the World*, unpublished manuscript. Washington, D.C.: Brookings Institution.

Brooks, S. G. and Wohlforth, W. C. 2002. 'American Primacy in Perspective', *Foreign Affairs* (81)4.

Brown, C. 2001. 'Ethics, interests and foreign policy', in: K. E. Smith and M. Light (eds), *Ethics and Foreign Policy*, Cambridge: Cambridge University Press.

Bull, H. 1977. *The Anarchical Society: A study of Order in World Politics*. London: Macmillan Publishers.

Cooper, A. (ed.). 1997. *Niche Diplomacy: Middle Powers After the Cold War*. Basingstoke: MacMillan.

Cooper, A. F. and Jackson, K. 2007. 'Regaining Legitimacy: The G8 and the "Heiligendamm Process"', *International Insights* (4)10.

Cox, M. 2007. 'Is the United States in decline—again? An essay', *International Affairs* (83)4.

De Lima, M. R. S. and Hirst, M. 2006. 'Brazil as an intermediate stated and regional power: action, choice and responsibilities', *International Affairs* (82)1.

Drezner, D. 2007. 'The New New World Order', *Foreign Affairs* (86)2.

Dupas, G. 2006. 'South Africa, Brazil and India: divergences, convergences and alliance perspectives', in: F. Villares (ed.), *India, Brazil and South Africa: Perspectives and Alliances*, Sao Paulo, Brazil: Institute for the Study of International Economics.

Ferguson, Y. H. and Mansbach, R. W. 2002. 'Remapping Political Space: Issues and Nonissues in analyzing Global Politics in the Twenty-First Century', in: Y. H. Ferguson, R. Jones and J. Barry (eds), *Political Space: New Frontiers of Change and Governance in a Globalizing World*, Albany, New York: State University of New York Press.

Flemes, D. 2007. *Emerging Middle Powers' Soft Balancing Strategy: State and Perspectives of the IBSA Dialogue Forum*, GIGA Working Papers, No 57, August, Hamburg: GIGA.

Fues, T. and Leininger, J. 2008. 'Germany and the Heiligendamm Process', in A. F. Cooper (ed.), *Reaching out to BRICSAM. The Heiligendamm Process and Beyond*, Waterloo: The Centre for International Governance Innovation, forthcoming.

Geldenhuys, D. 2006. 'South Africa's role as international norm entrepreneur', in W. Carlsnaes and N. Philp (eds), *In Full Flight: South African Foreign Policy After Apartheid*, Midrand, SA: Institute for Global Dialogue.

Gilpin, R. 1984. 'The Richness of the Tradition of Political Realism', *International Organization* (38)2.

Habermas, J. 1998. *Communicative Ethics*. Cambridge, MA: MIT Press.

Held, D. et al. 1999. *Global Transformations: Politics, Economics and Culture*. Cambridge, UK: Polity Press.

Hurrell, A. 2006. 'Hegemony, liberalism and global order: what space for would-be great powers?', *International Affairs* (82)1.

Ikenberry, J. 2004. 'Liberalism and empire: Logics of order in the American unipolar age', *Review of International Studies* (30)4.

Kaplinsky, R. 2005. *Globalization, Poverty and Inequality*. Cambridge, UK: Polity Press.

Kaplinsky, R. and Messner, D. 2008. 'The Impact of Asian Drivers on the Developing World', *World Development* (36)2.

Lesage, D. 2007. 'Is the World Imaginable without the G8?', *Internationale Politik und Gesellschaft* 4/2007.

Martens, J. 2007. 'Controversy over "Heiligendamm Process": The wrong forum', *Development + Cooperation* 2007/07–08.

Melakopides, C. 1990. 'Ethics and International Relations: A critique of cynical realism', D. G. Haglund and M. K. Hawes (eds), *World Politics: Power, Interdependence and Dependence*, Toronto: Harcourt Brace Javanovich.

Myatt, T., Sayao, C., Torney, D. and Zommers, Z. 2007. ''Outreach 5' Country Assessment Report', 2007 Heiligendamm Summit, G8 Research Group – Oxford.

Nye, J. 2004. *Soft Power: The Means to Success in World Politics*. New York: Perseus Books Group.

Pape, R. A. 2005. 'Soft Balancing against the United States', *International Security* (30)1.

Paul, T.V. 2004. 'The Enduring Axioms of Balance of Power Theory', in T. V. Paul, J. W. Wirtz and M. Fortmann (eds), *Balance of Power Revisited: Theory and Practice in the Twenty-first Century*, Stanford, California: Stanford University Press.

Riestra, M. 2007. *The Heiligendamm Process. A Breath of Fresh Air for the Discussion of Global Challenges*, unpublished manuscript, Bonn: German Development Institute.

Rosenau, James N. 2000. 'Beyond postinternationalism', in H. H. Hobbs (ed.), *Pondering Postinternationalism*, Albany, New York: State University of New York Press.

Soederberg, S. 2002. 'On the Contradictions of the New International Financial Architecture: Another Procrustean Bed for Emerging Markets', *Third World Quarterly* (23)4.

Varadarajan, S. 2007. 'Brazil proposes G5 summit', in *The Hindu*, 11 June Online: <http://www.hindu.com/2007/06/11/stories/2007061115070100.htm>

Wheeler, N. J. and Dunne, T. 1998. 'Good international citizenship: A third way for British foreign policy?', *International Affairs* (724)4.

Williamson, H. 2008. 'Emerging powers flex muscles to push for more influence on G8', in *Financial Times*, 4 April 2007.

World Bank. 2004. *World Development Report 2005: A Better Investment Climate for Everyone*, Oxford: World Bank and Oxford University Press.

NOTES

4. Institutional and Policy Implications of International Public Goods: The Case of Global Commons

1　This chapter draws some material and ideas from a previous article written by the authors (see Pinto and Puppim de Oliveira, 2008).

2　Globalization is here understood as the increasing flow of capital, goods, information and people across national boundaries.

3　As defined by the Paris High Level Forum on Aid Effectiveness of March, 2000 (OECD-DAC, UNDP, AfDB, AsDB, EBRD, World Bank and IDB) and in the "Strategic Framework for the World Bank's Global Programs and Partnerships". In this chapter, national endowments, such as the ozone layer are treated as a global common, not a public good such as a VGP.

4　It is estimated that one third of Official Development Assistance (ODA) at the country level is being channeled through VGPs. The World Bank estimates that contributions to VGPs represent 3 per cent of Overseas Development Assistance (ODA).

5　A national policy is a type of public good known as 'government good'.

6　For the purposes of this discussion a distinction is made between a natural asset or endowment and a public good as a product of collective human action.

7　*Sub-tractability or rivalry* implies the degree to which one person's use of a resource diminishes the availability for use by others. *Excludability* is the property of excluding potential users from consuming a good.

8　A more dramatic example of migratory patterns with cross-border implications is refugee flows due to international conflict, civil war or natural disasters, creating huge and sudden demands for peacekeeping, refugee and relief work. In some cases, such flows are among countries with very weak or effectively collapsed states with limited capacity to produce the NPGs that such refugees require, hence the need for IPGs, the business of the UN High Commission on Refugees and the UN Peacekeeping corps.

9　While few countries explicitly encourage emigration, there are economic advantages in the form of remittances which, in some cases are an important source of foreign hard currency.

10　US President's Program for Aids Reduction (PEPFAR and the US Government Millennium Account would fit this characterization.

11　Some observers argue that most common pool goods are neither excludable nor rivalrous.

12　In September 2000, the Development Committee of the World Bank endorsed five critical IPGs intended to: Preserve the environment, control communicable diseases, strengthen the international financial architecture, enhance developing countries' participation in the global trading system and create and share knowledge for development.

13 Despite the overwhelming evidence of the causes and consequences of global warming, there are still dissenting segments of the scientific community – albeit in minority – that argue that the weather phenomena being experienced on a global scale is not man made, but dictated by millennial climate cycles.

14 For example, one type of HFC, HFC-23, generates 12,000 times more greenhouse gases than carbon dioxide.

15 However, the expansion of crops that generate bio-fuels can expand the agricultural frontier and encroach on the Amazon forest (which can generate losses in biodiversity and global warming), if not managed properly.

16 Sponsors of this forum are: OECD, UNDP, AFDB, ASDB, EBRD, IDB and World Bank.

17 The remaining 0.5 per cent of GGEs comes from the burning of non-renewable fossil fuels (Diewald and Pinto op. cit).

18 The $338.5 million that Brazil receives from GEF is the largest source of funding for its VGPs, on par with the funds for the PPG-7.

19 The Montreal Protocol on protection of the ozone has its own funding mechanism, the Montreal Protocol Fund (MPF).

20 IBAMA is an executive agency of MMA, with police powers.

21 See www.mct.gov.br/clima

22 GEF funding currently supports only 1 WB-executed project for US $7 million to combat desertification in Brazil.

23 Adapted from Folha de Sao Paulo, November 12, 2000.

24 See PPG-7 evaluation draft report, manuscript, MMA, 2007.

25 Examples are of communities growing organic coffee in Chiapas, and organic honey in the Yucatan peninsula in Mexico (see Damiani, 2001). Another example is the use of sugarcane ethanol as fuel and the creation of protected areas in Brazil (Puppim de Oliveira, 2002a, 2002b) In Costa Rica the emblematic case is represented by the numerous eco-tourism projects that rely substantially on local communities.

26 The World Bank through International Development Agency (IDA) is gearing up to provide funding for 'Climate Action Work' see, World Bank, "IDA and Climate Change: Making Climate Action Work for Development", IDA 15, October 2007.

27 For example, MIGA (Multilateral Investment Multilateral Investment Guarantee Agency) or the CRIID (Center for the Resolution of International Investment Disputes), both of the World Bank Group.

28 For this reason, strengthening the international financial architectures was singled out as one the five IPGs endorsed by the World Bank Development Committee.

29 This evidence was brought forth and widely disseminated by a report published in October of 2006, known as the "Stern Review of the Economics of Climate Change", directed by Sir Richard Stern, and by Nobel laureate Albert Gore's widely acclaimed documentary "An Inconvenient Truth" done under the auspices of the Intergovernmental Panel on Climate change also awarded the Nobel prize jointly with Albert Gore.

30 A recent report of the World Bank indicates that commitments of the International Development Agency (IDA) a concessional funding window of the World Bank Group has increased significantly from US$ 155 million during 1995–200 to US$ 993 million during 2001–2006. See IDA 15 background paper "The Role of IDA in the Global Aid Architecture: Supporting the Country-based development model", IDA, Resource Mobilization Department (FRM), June, 2007.

31 The World Bank, for example carries out for each of its client countries a regular collection of studies such as Country Assistance Strategy; Public Expenditure Review;

Country Economic Memorandum, Institutional and Governance Review, in addition to the very credible Global Economic Prospects Report, among others which constitute a source of up-dated knowledge on clients, valuable for the substantiation of VGPs.

32 The recently issued report of the World Bank on 'Global Public Goods: A Framework for the Role of the World Bank', while covering a broad range of topics relevant for VGPs, is silent on the institutional aspects of the engagement of these programs with national institutions. However, a 2006 report also issued by the World Bank on 'Integrating Partnerships Programs with Country-led National Programs' does cover this institutional requirement. Both reports carried out by the World Bank's Global Programs and Partnerships Group (GPP).

33 International financial assistance to developing countries is tied to state reform programs in very significant ways. The emergence of internationally funded projects to reform national public administration, legislative and judicial systems of these countries attest to that.

34 In the case of VGPs, this exchange was launched as part of the preparation of a 2006 seminar of the Paris High Level Forum on Aid Effectiveness.

35 The Multilateral Investment Guarantee Agency (MIGA) and the International Center for Investment Disputes (ICID) of the World Bank Group provide good examples of producers of IGGs that are becoming essential to ensure an enabling international environment for cross border or regional activity. International courts to resolve disputes and administer justice in commerce, human rights, patents etc. complement national judicial systems. While they will remain necessary and grow with the increase in volume of international transactions, their importance as replacements for national judicial inadequacies should decrease as national reform processes restore the international credibility of national conflict resolution mechanisms and judicial systems.

36 Exception to this is increasing international collaboration to deter and prosecute money laundering.

37 Notwithstanding these constraints, international organizations have stepped up their assistance programs to fight corruption at the country level, and have set absence of corruption as a condition for financial assistance.

5. Economic Challenges for Global Governance

1 Import substitution is a strategy for economic development that replaces imports with domestic production. It may be motivated by the infant industry argument, and it contrasts with export promotion.

2 The *Washington Consensus* was described by Williamson (1990) as a list of policy proposals including ten points: fiscal policy discipline; redirection of public spending from subsidies toward broad-based provision of key pro-growth, pro-poor services like primary education, primary health care and infrastructure investment; tax reform – broadening the tax base and adopting moderate marginal tax rates; interest rates that are market determined and moderately positive in real terms; competitive exchange rates; trade liberalization – liberalization of imports, with particular emphasis on elimination of quantitative restrictions (licensing, etc.); any trade protection to be provided by low and relatively uniform tariffs; liberalization of inward foreign direct investment; privatization of state enterprises; deregulation – abolition of regulations that impede market entry or restrict competition, except for those justified on safety, environmental

and consumer protection grounds, and prudent oversight of financial institutions; and, legal security for property rights.

3 Data concerning FDI are taken from UNCTAD (1999), unless otherwise specified.

4 Maximizing the world growth rate can maximize knowledge and resources for all economic objectives, including equity and ecological well-being.

5 Today, at the beginning of the twenty-first century, transnational corporations are truly gigantic. According to Anderson, Cavanagh and Lee (2000), transnational corporations have expanded their activities throughout the globe. Here are some examples. The Swiss electrical engineering giant, ABB, has facilities in over 100 countries. Royal Dutch/Shell has offices in 64 nations and refineries in 34. Cargill, the US's largest grain company, operates in 59 countries with 105,000 employees. ICI, Great Britain's front line chemical company, employs 36,000 people in 200 plants in 55 countries.

6 For a summary of this topic and references, see Williamson (2004, 2005); Dobado-González, Gómez-Galvarriato and Williamson (2006).

7 <http://www.krysstal.com/inventions.html>.

8 For an analysis of the historical development of trade and modern economic growth, see Mayer Foulkes (2006a).

9 By 1899, large corporations like the United Fruit Company controlled 90 per cent of banana imports in the United States. In 1914, Royal Dutch/Shell produced 20 per cent of Russia's oil. Corporations like Standard Oil of New Jersey, Singer, International Harvester, Western Electric and (around 1914) Ford Motor Company, owned important production facilities outside the US (Beaudreau 2004).

10 All data concerning FDI are taken from UNCTAD (1999), unless otherwise specified.

11 Data taken from the US Bureau of Economic Analysis, based on historical costs.

12 The proportions of flow of FDI out of Western Europe, the United States and Japan are 68.3 per cent, 22.3 per cent and 4.0 per cent, respectively (UNCTAD 1999).

13 Author's estimate based on the World Bank database.

14 The term *endogenous* means that economics theory explains quantitative and qualitative decisions taken by agents, as the result of the incentives they face. Thus, the endogenous theory of technological change puts forth a set of assumptions based on which a rate of equilibrium for technological change can be established.

15 Constant returns to scale means production can be replicated as often as desired, encountering neither decreasing returns nor advantages to large scale production.

16 See Wan (2004) for a comparative study of East Asian development that explains how technological transfer was achieved. A summary, and a discussion of India and China, is presented in Mayer-Foulkes (2007b). FDI only played an important role in Singapore.

17 According to the World Bank classification of countries according to income, high-income countries have a log relative per-capita income of -1.4 or higher (relative to the US), while log relative per-capita income of upper middle income countries lies between -2.5 and -1.4 (about 8–25 per cent of US income).

18 Developed countries applied quite different policies to attain development. The same is true when they fall into trouble, as in the current credit crisis, cf. Stiglitz' comments on financial hypocrisy (Economist's View 20 November 2007).

19 Extraordinary profits from globalization, unmatched by equally high investments in less developed countries, may be the funding source for the sequence of bubbles we have witnessed in investment markets.

6. The Rule of Law in Multilateral Institutions and International Aid for Development: Judicial Reform in the Global Order

1 Of course, these appeared principally in Europe.

2 The process of democratization in Latin America, the fall of the Soviet regime and the like are some examples. Now independent, the globalization of justice has extended and internationalized judicial cooperation, namely mutual assistance provided by States in order to go beyond the requesting State's territory and take the various steps needed to carry out a process or investigation.

3 This is understood as management and the neutral resolution of inter-subjective conflicts.

4 In the legal field, it is now commonplace to say that an inefficient and costly judicial system increases and exacerbates social inequalities. Mexico is a good example of this. For Ruben Goldberg, president of the International Financial Intermediaries Association, "foreign banks will significantly affect the absence of recoverability and performance of credit or investment contracts that take place in Mexico, which makes the country unable to take a quantum leap to underpin its economic expansion." Rubén Goldberg, "La banca extranjera en México" [Foreign Banks in Mexico], *El Financiero*, April 11, 2002, p. 5.

5 The basic legal way to achieve equality among citizens is through a derivation of equality itself, that, for instance, corresponds to different social relationships as in the case of economic sanctions.

6 Of course, there is no formula or applicable standard in universal terms, nor can we speak of success over a short period of time.

7 These are the steps that pave the way to achieving the political goals of the United Nations Millennium Declaration to halve extreme poverty by 2015. United Nations Millennium Declaration, [online] September 13, 2002, <http://daccessdds.un.org/doc/UNDOC/GEN/N00/559/54/PDF/N0055954.pdf?OpenElement>. [Available: August 8, 2007].

8 The impetus for the ratification of international human rights conventions is an important part of promoting democracy and global governance.

9 There is a significant difference between European (aimed broadly in a social market economy) and American aid (which favors only a market economy).

10 Specifically from the Fourth World Conference on Women [online], Beijing, September 1995. <http://europa.eu/scadplus/leg/es/cha/c11903.htm>. [Available: August 8, 2007]. Germany's financial contribution to international cooperation alone increased by $ 40 million for projects for specific legal issues on gender. *'Empowerment' von Frauen in der entwicklungspolitischen praxis. Die 40 Mio-Dollar-Zusage von Peking für projekt der Rechts- und sozialpolitischen Beratung*, Germany, the Federal Ministry of Economic Cooperation and Development of Germany: BMZ-Special 012, May, 2000, p.8, [online]. <http://www2.gtz.de/gender_project/downloads/BMZEmpowerment.pdf>. [Available: August 8, 2007.]

11 In general, this power works as a real 'family court' operating in patronage networks, movement of patronage, corruption, influence in handling appointments, transfers and budget allocation. For example, this is one of the endemic justice problems in Latin America.

12 Especially after the creation of a judicial career and its checks and balances, Mexico is a good example of the resistance these changes can pose to the judiciary. When the

Federal Institute of Justice was created in 1994, the Supreme Court ruled that one of its functions was to administrate the Judiciary of the Federation's budget. However, the Supreme Court of Justice claimed it had this function and refused to relinquish it. Then, the Institute's powers were further reduced in its other role (apart from creating a Jury to oversee Judiciary magistrates) that gave it the power to prosecute members of the judiciary. Subsequently, the Supreme Court decided that any Judiciary Council decision was to be reviewed by the Supreme Court, which would ultimately return a final decision, again reserving the right to penalize the judiciary, i.e. to handle the weight of influence. Thus, the judiciary regains its former attributes and the Institute is reduced to a school for forming judicial officials that feed the system. Carpizo, J., 'Otra', 2000, p. 211.

13 German cooperation in Latin America prompted the adoption of the figure of the Ombudsman despite the fact that this figure does not exist in German law.

14 A good example of this situation is found in those countries in which there is an Islamic legal order (Sharia). In these countries, it is necessary to work with strategies and tools that modify the country's representation value regarding customs, and where, at the same time, legal customs increase the prospects of realizing the right State (political rights, association, etc.).

15 In terms of gender, the use of the Swedish term *ombudsman* is absolutely neutral.

16 Often the same structure provided that cooperation was uncoordinated and external resources were used in contradictory ways. Carothers, *Agenda*, 1999, p. 15.

17 This refers to judicial reform in Bolivia that was backed by USAID and the EU.

18 In this same sense, this aspect presents the different trends of international cooperation without any assessment. In Latin America, for example, (despite -or because of- the reforms set in motion by this cooperation), a decline of 8 per cent in public confidence in the administration of justice, placing it almost within the lowest ratings of public institutions, is recorded from the middle of the last decade to the present day. Galindo, *Estudios*, 2003, p. 26.

19 Mexico is a good example of the latter as prosecutors bear the burden of both investigation and prosecution at the same time.

20 The best-known example of this type of process is the reform of the criminal system in Bolivia (since 1998). The aim is for the new criminal procedure to be done quickly and effectively and it extends to all courts in the country. In support of this reform, international cooperation is working on: creating a monitoring system and disseminating the reform nationwide, as well as implementing organizational adaptations in the pertinent institutions (for example, officials in criminal courts, prosecutors' offices, public defenders, etc...), training and specialization of judicial officials in the new criminal procedure, while supporting civil society organizations that advocate for rapid acceptance of the reform (this is one of the few points in which European aid coincides almost entirely with the objectives of American aid).

21 This item in particular is upheld by American aid.

22 One example of this is the reconstruction of institutions of law in Rwanda and Burundi to deal with the consequences of genocide.

23 The meeting between the Chinese government and European Union representatives in June 2000 resulted in talks on legal issues. It also provided the framework for international cooperation activities on issues of global governance and justice reforms. Since then, European cooperation at a State level has centered on economic, labor law and drafting laws and rules of administrative law and procedure. This work was supplemented by civil society organizations operating within the context of individual rights protection and in the highly sensitive area of human rights.

7. Global Power Shifts and South Africa's Southern Agenda: Caught Between African Solidarity and Regional Leadership

1 Elizabeth Sidiropoulos is the national director of the South African Institute of International Affairs. She would like to thank Leaza Kolkenbeck-Ruh for her assistance.
2 The initiative examined the management of the UN secretariat and the way that it could be reformed and strengthened from a member state and governance perspective.
3 The voting group comprises Poland, Serbia and the ex-Soviet republics of Azerbaijan, Tajikistan, Turkmenistan, Uzbekistan and Kyrgyzstan, and Switzerland.
4 This is largely drawn from a SAIIA paper on South Africa's North-South engagement produced for the Presidency's 15-year review in 2008.
5 The Director General of the National Treasury remarked at a symposium organised by the Institute for Global Dialogue in November 2007 that 'it doesn't matter what formula you use Africa's voting share will decline owing to its relative decline in the global economy'.
6 Unpublished SAIIA paper on South Africa's North-South engagement produced for the Presidency's 15-year review.
7 I am grateful to Peter Draper for these observations.

8. Mexico as an Emerging Power in the Present World Scenario: Global Economy Without National Development Strategy?

1 In May 2007, the Hertie School of Governance and the German Institute of Development (DIE), organized in Berlin, Germany, an international conference titled 'Democratizing Global Governance: Perspectives of Emerging Powers'. In the context of the previous days of the summit of the Group of Eight leading industrialised countries (G8), held in Heiligendamm, Germany, different representatives from China, India, South Africa, Brazil and Mexico (Group of Five), made presentations and discussed with some representatives from G8 countries. To continue that debate, the present document is our contribution on the importance and weakness of the Mexican economy as an emerging power in the global arena. We would like to thank Professor Thomas Fues (DIE) for his kind invitation to take part in that international conference and to write this paper.

10. South America and US Relations: Implications for Regional Security

1 One exception seem to be the research of L. Axworthy, on 'Human Security and Global Governance' (2001).
2 In many works such as: *People, States & Fear: An Agenda for International Security Studies in the Post-Cold War Era* (Buzan 1991), *Security: A New Framework for Analysis* (Buzan, Waever & Wilde 1998) e *Regions and Powers: The Structure of International Security* (Buzan & Waever 2003).
3 This law is also known as Nunn Amendment because it was the Democrat Senator Sam Nunn who proposed it to Congress.

4 INC is considered to be the more versatile institution of American government to combat illicit drugs. It aims at funding interdiction and eradication operations, as well as promoting economic and social assistance, which include alternative development programs in areas of drug production, judicial reform programs and humanitarian assistance to victims of conflicts related to drug traffic (Freeman, et al, 2005).

5 In both summits, the countries identified as sources did not integrate into a uniform coalition. In Cartagena Summit, for instance, Bolivia's President was more worried with economic development and substituting coca leaf crops by other products. Colombia's President, Virgilio Barco, affirmed that combating drug traffic depended on efforts on the reduction of the demand. Peruvian representatives, although disagreeing on the American conduct on the subject towards Latin America, believed that militarization was the more apporpriate solution in the short run (PASSETTI 1991, 70–71).

6 White House, Washington, 02/1996 (see <http://www.fas.org/spp/military/docops/national/1996stra.htm#III>. Accessed April 2007).

7 IEEPA was approved in 1977 and allowed the President of the United States to announce the existence of a threat to national security. It also gave to the American President the power to block and freeze any transaction suspected to cooperate financially with the propagation of this threat. In this sense, the IEEPA turned into na instrument of the American government to order embargo to countries, international organizations and individuals that have any involvement with the threat. See: <http://www.treas.gov/offices/enforcementofac/legal/statutes/ieepa.pdf> Accessed November 2007.

8 The INCSR are formulated anually by the INC of the Department of State, according to the Foreign Aid Act (FAA). These INCSR contain information about the development of programs and policies related to the drug combat, the American government assistance as well as a outlook as regards the situation of the countries in this theme (see http://www.state.gov/p/inl/rls/nrcrpt/, accessed November 2007).

11. The Future Developments in Global Governance – Multilateralism & Regionalization Process: India's Role

1 Jawaharlal Nehru's speech as reported by *The Hindu* in the issue of August 15, 1947.

2 ITEC Division, Ministry of External Affairs, Government of India www.itec.nic.in

3 Focus: Africa A Programme for Enhancing India's Trade with the African Region, Ministry of Commerce, Government of India.

4 *Annual Report, 2003–04*, Ministry of External Affairs, Government of India, P. 70.

5 Exim Bank of India http://www.eximbankindia.com/

6 Economic Times, 20 June 2006.

7 Detail of these projects can be obtained from their websites respectively http://www.rites.com/ and http://www.ircon.org/

8 Business Line 29 July 2006.

9 Ruchita Beri, 'India's Africa Policy in the Post Cold War Era: An Assessment', *Strategic Analysis*, Vol. 27 No. 2, April–June 2003, P. 227.

10 www.nepad.org

11 Interview of Mr. Rao Indrajit Singh, Minister of State, Ministry of External Affairs, Government of India, Date 25 Jan. 2006. www.mea.gov.in

12. Managing Social Issues for Sustainable Development: The Indian Experiences

1 Director, Jaypee Business School, Noida (India) ravi.shanker@jiit.ac.in

13. Unity in Diversity: South Coalitions as Governance Adaption Vehicles in Global Trade Governance

1 For the purposes of this paper, the phrase "developed countries" refers to States that are Member States of the Organization for Economic Cooperation and Development (OECD) or the European Union (EU). "Developing countries" refers to those States which are members of the Group of 77, and may be used interchangeably with the term "South." States which do not fall in either category would be the "economies in transition", composed mostly of the non-EU Member States of Eastern Europe and the successor States of the former USSR.

2 UNCTAD 2007 para. 8. South-South trade in goods is estimated to have increased from US$577 billion in 1995 to US$1.7 trilling in 2005, resulting in a rise of the South-South share of global trade in goods from 11 percent in 1995 to 15 percent in 2005. Overall, the share of developing countries in global trade has increased from 29 percent in 1996 to 34 percent in 2006. See id., paras. 15–16.

3 Developing country exports 'nearly tripled between 1996 and 2006, whereas those from the G-7 only rose by some 75 percent. In this area, Asia clearly dominated the picture, with transition economies and Latin America coming in second, and Africa showing exactly the same increase as the G-7.' Asia's imports rose by 170 percent in the same time, while those of transition economies rose by 150 per cent. Ibid., para. 15.

4 WESS 2006, at 2.

5 UNCTAD 2007, para. 15. See also GEP 2007, at 42, where the World Bank projects that '[t]here would be a further falling behind in Sub-Saharan Africa with its modest per capita growth below the high-income average, and Latin America would see little if any convergence on average.'

6 The pattern of income convergence as a result of growth, according to the UN, seems to be that convergence occurs at the extremes of the income spectrum, where incomes among richer countries tend to converge upwards while incomes among poor countries tend to converge downwards, resulting in greater income disparities between the two groups. See WESS 2006, at 15.

7 See e.g. G-77 Doha Declaration of the Second South Summit (G77/SS/2005/1, 15 June 2005), para. 10. Available at http://www.g77.org/southsummit2/doc/Doha%20 Declaration(English).pdf

8 See e.g. G-24 Communique (April 2007), paras. 3–9. Online: http://www. imf.org/external/np/cm/2007/041307.htm; G-77 Final Communique of the 41st Meeting of the Chairmen/Coordinators of the G-77 Chapters (February 2007), para. 12. Online: http://www.g77.org/chmeeting/0702/communique.php; G-77 Special Ministerial Statement (May 2006), para. 14. Online: http://www.g77.org/ doc/putrajaya.htm; G-77 Ministerial Statement (September 2006), para. 6. Online: http://www.g77.org/ammfa/30/conclusion.html

9 See e.g. G-77 Special Ministerial Statement (May 2006), para. 14. Online: http://www. g77.org/doc/putrajaya.htm; G-77 Doha Declaration of the Second South Summit

(G77/SS/2005/1, 15 June 2005), para. 15(xv). Online: http://www.g77.org/southsummit2/doc/Doha%20Declaration(English).pdf

10 See e.g. G-77 Final Communique of the 41st Meeting of the Chairmen/Coordinators of the G-77 Chapters (February 2007), para. 8. Online: http://www.g77.org/chmeeting/0702/communique.php; G-77 Doha Declaration of the Second South Summit (G77/SS/2005/1, 15 June 2005), para. 22. Online: http://www.g77.org/southsummit2/doc/Doha%20Declaration(English).pdf

11 See e.g. G-77 Doha Declaration of the Second South Summit (G77/SS/2005/1, 15 June 2005), para. 15 (ix). Available at http://www.g77.org/southsummit2/doc/Doha%20Declaration(English).pdf

12 As the authors have pointed out: '[l]ong-standing institutions represent frozen configurations of privilege and bias that can continue to shape the future choices of actors' within that institution. In this article, the authors defined 'power' as 'the production, in and through social relations, of effects that shape the capacities of actors to determine their circumstances and fate.

13 See pg. 58, stating that 'the institutional rules that establish a particular focal point also serve to generate unequal leverage or influence in determining collective outcomes ... the institutions that are established to help actors achieve pareto-superior outcomes also create 'winners' and 'losers,' to the extent that the ability to use the institution and, accordingly, collective rewards are unevenly distributed. This institutional context, moreover, lingers into the future, thus constraining action in ways that might not have been intended but nevertheless limit choice and shape action." They went on to state that "great powers" have the ability "to establish international institutions and arrangements to further or preserve their interests and positions of advantage into the future, even as they do not directly or fully control those future arrangements'.

14 See, e.g. WTO, Singapore Ministerial Declaration (WT/MIN(96)/DEC, 18 December 1996), para. 6; WTO, Geneva Ministerial Declaration (WT/MIN(98)/DEC, 20 May 1998), para. 4; Doha Ministerial Declaration, para. 10.

15 See e.g. Amrita Narlikar, WTO Decision-Making and Developing Countries, TRADE Working Paper No. 11 (South Centre 2001); Richard H. Steinberg, In the Shadow of Law or Power? Consensus-Based Bargaining and Outcomes in the GATT/WTO, 56:2 INTERNATIONAL ORGANIZATION (Spring 2002); South Centre, Institutional Governance and Decision-Making Processes in the WTO (SC/TADP/AN/IG/7 December 2003). For an in-depth account of power politics in the WTO, see e.g. Fatoumata Jawara and Aileen Kwa, Behind the Scenes at the WTO: The Real World of International Trade Negotiations(2003).

16 The UN has pointed that '[i]n practice ... developing countries find it difficult to follow negotiations or invest in studies that evaluate the implications of the trade reforms for their economies, or they simply have no resources even for sending delegates to the negotiations. ... the role played by developing countries is limited and changing the rules of the game in their favour is hard, making asymmetries difficult to redress'. WESS 2006, at 26.

17 This is reflected in, for example, references to 'less than full reciprocity' in the Non-Agricultural Market Access (NAMA) negotiations championed by the NAMA-11, 'paragraph 6 flexibilities' championed by the Paragraph 6 countries, 'special products' and the 'special safeguard mechanism' in the agriculture negotiations being promoted by the G-33, the more than 35 references to 'development' in the Doha Ministerial Declaration itself, LDC positions relating to the provision of special and differential treatment, as well as proposals by the Core Group on Trade Facilitation together with the African Group, ACP and LDC Groups to link new disciplines on trade facilitation

to binding commitments on technical assistance, capacity-building and special and differential treatment.

18 See e.g. G-33 Ministerial/Senior Officials Coordination Meeting Statement, 15 November 2007, stating the group's commitment to 'secure a more balanced outcome that addresses the development dimensions of the Doha Development Agenda as well as the genuine concerns of small, poor and vulnerable farmers worldwide", at http://www.tradeobservatory.org/library.cfm?refID=100807, see also the G-33 statement on 17 December 2007, at http://www.tradeobservatory.org/library.cfm?refID=101176; G-20 Communique, 15 November 2007, stating that the WTO negotiations' outcome must be one that delivers on the development dimension of the Round within the shortest period of time possible", see http://www.brazil.org.uk/newsandmedia/pressreleases_files/20071116.html; Small Vulnerable Economies (SVEs) Statement, 18 December 2007, at http://www.tradeobservatory.org/library.cfm?refID=101175; the Joint Statement of the G-20, the G-33, the NAMA-11, the ACP Group, the LDCs, the African Group, the Small, Vulnerable Economies (SVEs), and the Cotton-4, 15 November 2007, stating that 'the full integration of developing countries into the multilateral trading system will only be achieved if the WTO reflects their development needs and concerns', at http://www.tradeobservatory.org/library.cfm?refID=100810

19 See e.g. India Trade Minister Kamal Nath's response to a question about the role of the developing country negotiating blocs. He explained that 'India's responsibilities as a leader of the G-20 bloc of countries did not constrain it in negotiations. Rather, representing the G-20 has guaranteed that India pursues a balanced deal because the G-20 itself groups together a broad range of offensive and defensive interests across different sectors. The positions taken by the G20 already represent a compromise between the interests of many developing countries'. See http://www.carnegieendowment.org/events/index.cfm?fa=eventDetail&id=1016&&prog=zgp&proj=zted

20 For example, in the trade facilitation negotiations, while the over-all African Group coordinator for 2007 is Uganda, the African Group focal point on trade facilitation is Morocco. For the LDCs group, the overall coordinator is Bangladesh, while the trade facilitation focal point is Nepal.

21 The South Centre is the only intergovernmental organization composed solely of developing countries which provides policy research and analysis and technical negotiating support to developing countries in, inter alia, the WTO. It also supports developing country groups and coalitions in other international forums such as the World Intellectual Property Organization (WIPO) and UNCTAD. In the WTO negotiations, the South Centre has provided direct negotiating assistance and technical policy research and support to the African Group, ACP Group, LDC Group, SVEs, Paragraph 6 NAMA Group, NAMA-11, G-33 and the Core Group on Trade Facilitation.

22 For example, the use of technical policy input provided by the South Centre to various developing country groups such as the African Group, LDC Group, ACP Group, G-33, NAMA-11, and the Core Group of Developing Countries on Trade Facilitation, is completely at the discretion of the group concerned. The recipient may choose to accept, amend, revise, or disregard the input provided. For organizations providing such support, an iterative and consultative process with the intended group partner is therefore necessary.

23 Joint Statement of the G-20, the G-33, the NAMA-11, the ACP Group, the LDCs, the African Group, the Small, Vulnerable Economies (SVEs), and the Cotton-4, 15 November 2007, at http://www.tradeobservatory.org/library.cfm?refID=100810

24 The ITO, under the 1947 Havana Charter, was to be an institution with a wide mandate covering virtually all issues in the area of trade, employment and development. The trade rules and disciplines embodied in the GATT were to form the core of the ITO's trade regime once the Havana Charter entered into force. Since the Havana Charter never came into force as a result of its non-ratification by the United States and other developed countries (who had objected to the inclusion of "non-trade" issues such as commodities, employment, and restrictive business practices, in the Charter), the GATT's provisions continued to be applied provisionally by its contracting parties until the establishment of the WTO and the subsequent incorporation of the GATT into the WTO's legal framework. To a large extent, the establishment of international principles, norms and rules in the other areas covered by the Havana Charter – e.g. investment, restrictive business practices, commodities, and development – were pursued within the UN system, especially by UNCTAD.

25 See http://www.g77.org/doc/members.html for the list of G-77 members.

26 The Group designations come from the lists of States contained in the Annex to UN General Assembly Resolution 1995 (XIX) which created UNCTAD. The G-77 and China includes those States which fall under Group A (Africa, Asia and the Pacific) and Group C (Latin America and Caribbean). The latest membership lists for each Group can be found in UNCTAD, Membership in UNCTAD and membership of the Trade and Development Board, TD/B/INF.209, 19 October 2007, at http://www.unctad.org/en/docs/tdbinf209_en.pdf

27 See http://www.g77.org/doc/Joint%20Declaration.html

28 See http://www.g77.org/doc/index.html

29 While it focused on UNCTAD for from the mid-1960s to the mid-1970s, by the late 1970s and early 1980s, the G-77 had become very active in New York as it started tackling more and more issues there. From the mid-1970s, the G-77's 'center of activity ... shifted from Geneva to New York'(Iida 1988).

30 In this regard, while the South Centre, while being an intergovernmental thinktank for developing countries, is mandated by its treaty to "respond to requests for policy advice, and for technical and other support from collective entities of the South such as the Group of 77 and the Non-Aligned Movement", it does not serve as the secretariat for the G-77 nor the Non-Aligned Movement (NAM). For more information on the South Centre, please see http://www.southcentre.org

31 For a discussion of the cause-and-effect dynamics with respect to the creation of group negotiating positions by the G-77 and Group B in UNCTAD during its early years, see e.g. Walters 1971. International Organization and Political Communications: The Use of UNCTAD by Less Developed Countries, 25:4 International Organization (1971), at 825, stating that 'the cohesion between the LDCs forced the advanced Western states to aggregate their interests, largely through the, in responding to the aggregated demands facing them in UNCTAD'; and Gosovic 1972. UNCTAD Conflict and Compromise: The Third World's Quest for an Equitable World Economic Order through the United Nations, at 269, stating that '[t]he behavior of the 77 at the Geneva Conference brought about counter-measures by the western countries, which also began to take up joint negotiating positions in an attempt to shield themselves from the assault by the developing countries'; and Boutros-Ghali 2006. Reinventing UNCTAD, South Centre Research Paper 7, 2006, at 2 (hereafter Boutros-Ghali), stating that 'the aggregation of the demands of developing countries through the mechanism of the Group of 77, triggered aggregation of responses by developed countries through the OECD'.

32 These lists can be found at http://www.unctad.org/en/docs/tdbinf209_en.pdf

33 See e.g. General Principle Fifteen, UNCTAD I, Final Act, para. 54, in South Centre, RECALLING UNCTAD I AT UNCTAD XI (2004), at at 11, available at http://www.southcentre.org/publications/pubindex.htm#books, which states as follows: The adoption of international policies and measures for the economic development of the developing countries shall take into account the individual characteristics and different stages of development of the developing countries, special attention being paid to the less developed among them, as an effective means of ensuring sustained growth with equitable opportunity for each developing country.

34 'The Group was also deprived of important support given to it by UNCTAD in the past, which had served as a major source of ideas, analysis and synthesis, and offered the logistical support that was required. The resulting dearth of intellectual ammunition and data to reinforce G77 policy views and aspirations on a continuing basis affected its unity and negotiating stance, made it less effective vis-a-vis the developed countries' negotiators and in defending common interests, and was not conducive to its assuming initiatives and playing a proactive role in the world arena, as it did in earlier times'. See South Centre 2004, at 6.

35 See e.g. Lavelle 2001, at 42, stating that 'in taking on the role of coach in the multilateral trade negotiations, the UNCTAD secretariat could not challenge the game itself, or advance the group interests of the G77. While the G77 as a whole supported technical assistance initiatives in UNCTAD, the UNCTAD programmes which resulted aggregated the needs of a region, or a state, and not the needs of the G77 as a whole. Hence, the G77 never functioned in the Uruguay Round'.

36 Instead, developing countries formed ad-hoc developing country-only groupings such as the Like-Minded Group (LMG), or else joined ad-hoc North-South groups such as the Cairns Group, in order to press for their interests during the Uruguay Round.

37 See e.g. South Centre 2004, at 8.

38 Since the late 1990s, in UNCTAD, as European integration became more solid, the group dynamics in Group B have also evolved. While developed countries generally tend to have similar views and negotiating positions and consult frequently with each other, Group B no longer acts as a solid group. Rather, the Member States of the European Union (represented by its rotating presidency) negotiate as a bloc, while the rest of the developed countries generally speak on their own behalf.

14. In the Foggy Middle East: Just Wars Remain the Name of the Game

1 The Fog of War: Eleven Lessons from the Life of Robert S. McNamara is a *documentary film* about the life and times of *Robert S. McNamara*. It was directed by *Errol Morris* and released in December, 2003. The film includes an original score by *Philip Glass*. It won the *Academy Award for Documentary Feature* for 2003.

15. Evaluation Capacity Development in the Arab Region: How Monitoring and Evaluation is Perceived and Applied?

1 This paper is a revised version of a keynote speech delivered by the author in 'Outcome-Mapping in MENA Workshop', organized by the International Development Research

Center and the American University in Beirut (AUB) – Environment and Sustainable Development Unit (ESDU), Cairo, 9–11 April 2008.

2 In her earlier capacity as fiscal reform programs manager, the author acknowledges the program of performance-based budgeting monitoring and evaluation capacity development in partnership with UNDP, WB and local expertise (January 2001 – July 2004).

16. UNEP Institutional Reform with its Impact on Developing Countries

1 Institute of Political Science, Chinese Academy of Social Sciences. This study has been prepared as part of the Managing Global Governance Programme, an initiative of the German Ministry for Economic Cooperation and Development (BMZ), implemented jointly by the German Development Institute (DIE) and Capacity Building International Germany (InWent) in 2007.

2 Adil Najam, Mihaela Papa, Nadaa Taiyab, Global Environmental Governance A Reform Agenda (IISD, 2006).

3 The Chinese government has implemented an increasing number of initiatives and legislation to incorporate environmental sustainability with its rapid economic growth and invested in 20 key projects to improve Beijing's environment.

4 See also UNEP Science Initiative http://science.unep.org

5 Norichika, K. 2007. 'Governance With Multilateral Environmental Agreements: A Healthy Or Ill-equipped Fragmentation?', Global Environmental Governance, Perspectives On The Current Debate, ed. Lydia Swart and Estelle Perry. (Center for UN Reform Education.

6 For example, Biermann Frank, "Reforming Global Environmental Governance: From UNEP Towards A World Environment Organization", Global Environmental Governance, Perspectives On The Current Debate, ed. Lydia Swart and Estelle Perry (Center for UN Reform Education, 2007); Meyer-Ohlendorf Nils and Knigge Markus, "A United Nations Environment Organization", Global Environmental Governance, Perspectives On The Current Debate, ed. Lydia Swart and Estelle Perry (Center for UN Reform Education, 2007).

7 Based on own interviews and Ivanova Maria 2007.

8 Maurice Strong advanced this point, see United Nations Press Release 1971.

9 For example, thirty-six countries are members of the Executive Board of the UN Development Programme (UNDP), thirty-six countries are members of the Executive Board of the World Food Programme (WFP), and fifty-eight are members of the Governing Council of UNEP. As an integral part of the United Nations, however, they are subject to oversight by the General Assembly and therefore all UN members have a say in their governance.

10 It further recommends that "stronger efforts should be made to reduce costs and reporting burdens and to streamline implementation." See Annex 8.3.

11 Kanie Norichika 2007.

12 Ivanova Maria, 2007.

13 Najam, A., 2003. "The Case Against a New International Environmental Organization." Global Governance, 9(3): 367–384. Von Moltke, K., 2001. "The Organization of the Impossible." Global Environmental Politics, 1 (1): 23–28.

14 Ivanova, M., 2005. *Can the Anchor Hold? Rethinking the United Nations Environment Programme for the 21st Century.* New Haven: Yale School of Forestry and Environmental Studies. Accessed at http://www.yale.edu/gegdialogue in March 2006.: 32.

15 UNEP offices at www.unep.org

16 Chambers, W. B., 2005. "From Environmental to Sustainable Development Governance: Thirty Years of Coordination within the United Nations." In *Reforming International Environmental Governance: From Institutional Limits to Innovative Reforms.* Edited by Chambers, W. B. and Green, J. F., 13–39. Tokyo: United Nations University Press.

17 United Nations Conference on the Human Environment, held in Stockholm in June 1972, the General Assembly, in resolution 2997 (XXVII) of 15 December 1972.

18 Von Moltke, K., 2005. "Clustering Multilateral Environment Agreements as an Alternative to a World Environment Organization." In *A World Environment Organization: Solution or Threat for Effective Environmental Governance?* Edited by Biermann, F. and Bauer, S., 173–202, Aldershot: Ashgate.

19 WHO, FAO, IAEA, WMO, World Bank, GATT/WTO.

20 Najam, 2003; Ivanova, 2005.

21 Ivanova Maria, 2007.

22 Konrad von Moltke, "Why UNEP Matters," in Green Globe Yearbook 1996, (Oxford: Oxford University Press, 1996a); Adil Najam, "The Case Against a New International Environmental Organization," Global Governance 9 (3) (2003): 367–384.

23 As of December 2006, UNEP received contributions from 108 countries and payments continue to arrive. UNEP is expected to receive approximately $59,200,000, with a zero estimated contribution from one of the top ten donors. This is about $400,000 less than 2005.

24 Data from UNEP funding of 2006, http://www.unep.org

25 See Felix Dodds, "Reforming the International Institutions," in Earth Summit 2002 ed. Felix Dodds (London: Earthscan, 2000); Steve Charnovitz, "A World Environment Organization," Columbia Journal of Environmental Law, vol. 27 No 2, (2002): 323–362; and Frank Biermann and Steffen Bauer, A World Environment Organization: Solution or Threat for Effective International Environmental Governance? (Aldershot, UK: Ashgate, 2005).

26 Thus UNEP could at least be entitled to a fixed and regular budget.

27 See Annex 8.2.

28 http://www.unemg.org/

29 UN General Assembly Document A/53/463, Par. 11.

30 Adil Najam pointed out that the reasons of ineffectiveness are: 1) there has been little high-level engagement in its work, 2) the negative perception of EMG as UNEP's tool to assert control over the work of other agencies, and 3) lack of a clear sense of outcomes. See Adil Najam, Mihaela Papa and Nadaa Taiyab, Global Environmental Governance: A Reform Agenda, (IISD, 2006).

31 Dodds 2000; Charnovitz 2002.

32 Daniel Esty, "The Case for a Global Environmental Organization," in Managing the World Economy ed. Peter B. Kenen, 287–310, (Washington DC: Institute for International Economics, 1994); Frank Biermann, "The Emerging Debate on the Need for a World Environment Organization," Global Environmental Politics February (2001): 45–55; and Frank Biermann, "The Case for a World Environment Organization," Environment 42 (9) (2000): 22–31; German Advisory Council on Global Change (WBGU), World in Transition 2 (London: Earthscan, 2001).

33 Based on own interviews and Adil Najam et al., 2006.
34 Ivanova Maria, "Moving Forward By Looking Back: Learning From UNEP's History", Global Environmental Governance, Perspectives On The Current Debate, ed. Lydia Swart and Estelle Perry (Center for UN Reform Education, 2007).
35 Based on own interviews and Adil Najam et al., 2006.
36 The Bali Strategic Plan articulates the latter orientation and gives UNEP its marching orders in this respect. Moving forward in a way perceived by many as contrary to this plan will inevitably look like a betrayal of the developing member states.
37 But whatever solution is chosen, UNEP must reinforce its regional presence and strengthen its regional offices.
38 Adil Najam et al., 2006.
39 OECD is an acronym of Organization for Economic Cooperation and Development, which is an international organization of 30 countries that accept the principles of representative democracy and free-market economy. Most OECD members are high-income economies with a high HDI and are regarded as developed countries. In economics, BRIC or BRICs is an acronym that refers to the fast-growing developing economies of Brazil, Russia, India and China. "OECD plus BRICS" refers to a combo of main developed countries and the fast-growing developing economies.
40 Some researchers even pointed out that UNEP should not be involved in managing projects. See Adil Najam et al., 2006.
41 IPCC, Biodiversity Assessment, Millennium Ecosystem Assessment, etc.
42 Based on own interviews. Delegations in the Informal Consultative Process on the Institutional Framework for the United Nations' Environmental Activities which was held in New York, 14 June 2007, called for maintaining the principle of shared but differentiated responsibility in a strengthened international environmental governance system.
43 An Update on International Environmental Governance (Report Paper), 25th. February 2008.
44 G8 Summit 2008 was held on July 7–9, 2008 in Hokkaido, Japan.

17. The Heiligendamm Process and Emerging Powers: More of the Same or a Genuine Global Governance Innovation?

1 This chapter was concluded before the Hokkaido G-8 summit of July 2008.
2 This section is partly based on Fues/Leininger (2008).
3 See 'Joint Statement by the German G8 Presidency and the Heads of State and/or Government of Brazil, China, India, Mexico and South Africa on the occasion of the G8 Summit in Heiligendamm, Germany, 8 June 2007' <http://www.indianembassy.de/news/pmvisit3.htm>
4 The summit declaration 'Growth and responsibility in the world economy' was issued on 7 June 2008. The meeting with G-5 leaders took place on 8 June 2007: 'At the Heiligendamm Summit we discussed with the leaders of Brazil, China, India, Mexico and South Africa the major challenges that have arisen in the world economy... Building on our discussions, we decided to launch a new form of specific cooperation with major emerging economies in order to discuss substantive topics in a comprehensive follow-up process with the aim of reaching tangible results in two years'. (summit declaration, p. 36; http://www.g-8.de/Content/EN/Artikel/__g8-summitanlagen/2007-06-07-

gipfeldokument-wirtschaft-eng,templateId=raw,property=publicationFile.pdf/2007-06-07-gipfeldokument-wirtschaft-eng)

5 Normally, the positions created within the OECD are reserved for nationals of the thirty members but in the case of the support unit, the recruitment is open to professionals from all G-5 countries.

6 Mexico is the only country within the G-5 that is a member of the OECD. The current Secretary-General of the organization, José Ángel Gurría, is a Mexican national and former Minister of Foreign Affairs and Finances of that country.

7 There are some differences in terminology but they all converge around the same meaning. Thus countries such as the G-5 are often referred to as 'regional powers'; others have used the categories of 'intermediate states', 'emerging economies', and 'would-be great powers' (Flemes 2007).

8 China and India could be distinguished as 'middle powers-plus' because of their nuclear and military capability with a regional and, potentially, global reach.

9 'Joint Position Paper of Brazil, China, India, Mexico and South Africa participating in the G8 Heiligendamm Summit, 7 June 2007' <http://www.indianembassy.de/news/pmvisit4.htm>

10 Tswane IBSA Summit Declaration, 17 October 2007.

11 The following are relevant and appear in the same issue of *International Affairs*, 82:1, January 2006: S Neil Macfarlane, "The 'R' in BRICS: is Russia and emerging power" 41–57; Amrita Narlikar, "Peculiar chauvinism or strategic calculation? Explaining the negotiating strategy of a rising India" 59–76; and Rosemary Foot, "Chinese strategies in a US-hegemonic global order: accommodating and hedging," 77–94.

12 G-5's common normative constructs refer in particular to their positions and alignments in global politics. In contrast, they have differing visions and interpretations about democracy, which, for instance, is an important underlying principle in the way that IBSA defines itself.

www.ingramcontent.com/pod-product-compliance
Lightning Source LLC
Chambersburg PA
CBHW022346280326
41935CB00007B/95